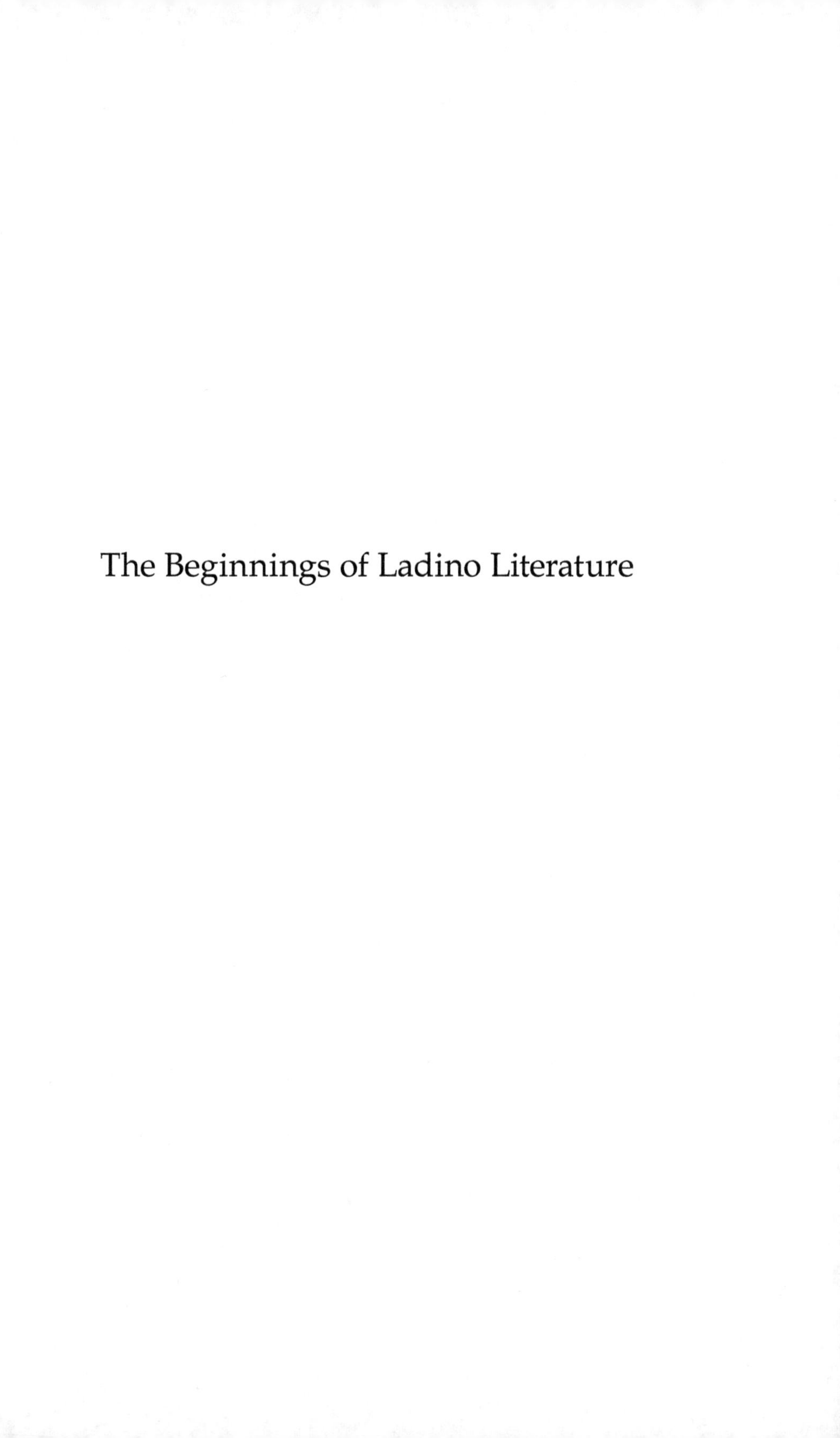

The Beginnings of Ladino Literature

INDIANA SERIES IN SEPHARDI AND MIZRAHI STUDIES

Harvey E. Goldberg and Matthias Lehmann, editors

The Beginnings of Ladino Literature

MOSES ALMOSNINO AND HIS READERS

Olga Borovaya

INDIANA UNIVERSITY PRESS
Bloomington and Indianapolis

This book is a publication of

INDIANA UNIVERSITY PRESS
Office of Scholarly Publishing
Herman B Wells Library 350
1320 East 10th Street
Bloomington, Indiana 47405 USA

iupress.indiana.edu

The paper used in this publication meets the minimum requirements of the American National Standard for Information Sciences—Permanence of Paper for Printed Library Materials, ANSI Z39.48–1992.

Manufactured in the United States of America

Library of Congress Cataloging-in-Publication Data

Names: Borovaya, O. V. (Ol'ga Vol'fovna), author.
Title: The beginnings of Ladino literature : Moses Almosnino and his readers / Olga Borovaya.
Description: Bloomington and Indianapolis : Indiana University Press, [2016] | Series: Indiana series in Sephardi and Mizrahi studies | Includes bibliographical references and index.
Identifiers: LCCN 2016024515 (print) | LCCN 2016026872 (ebook) | ISBN 9780253025524 (cl : alk. paper) | ISBN 9780253025845 (eb)
Subjects: LCSH: Ladino literature—History and criticism. | Almosnino, Moses ben Baruch, approximately 1515-approximately 1580. | Sephardim—Turkey—Intellectual life.
Classification: LCC PC4813.5 .B67 2017 (print) | LCC PC4813.5 (ebook) | DDC 860.9—dc23
LC record available at https://lccn.loc.gov/2016024515

1 2 3 4 5 22 21 20 19 18 17

To the memory of my mother,
Irina Borovaya

CONTENTS

ACKNOWLEDGMENTS

Thirteen years ago, Julia Phillips Cohen gave me an exciting birthday present, Moses Almosnino's *Crónica de los reyes otomanos.* I decided that one day I would write about it and perhaps translate it into English. The present book does both. During my work on it, Julia was always very enthusiastic about the project and, until the final version was sent to the press, faithfully looked out for anything I might find useful (including something as unlikely as an ad on a French radio show about Almosnino!). In addition, I am extremely grateful to Julia for her astute comments on the final version of my manuscript.

Still, I might not have finished this project without Aron Rodrigue's unwavering friendship and unconditional support, which kept me going. Furthermore, while constantly reminding me that the sixteenth century is "not his period," as he read each chapter he always offered helpful comments and pointed to mistakes. I also thank Aron for making me stop at some point, or this book would have been a lot longer.

I am also indebted to Vincent Barletta, Sarah Abrevaya Stein, David Wasserstein, and John Zemke, who read different chapters of this book and provided insightful suggestions, which often prompted me to go in new directions. I am grateful to Peter Mann for editing my translation of *Extremes* and Vladimir Hamed-Troyansky for being a most reliable and efficient research assistant. I thank Paula Daccarett for her help with chapter 5.

I want to thank my friend Becky Bob-Waksberg who, during her visit to Istanbul in February 2016, made a special trip to take a picture of the Büyükçekmece Bridge, which I needed for chapter 3.

Working on this book with Indiana University Press turned out to be an exceptionally smooth and pleasant experience. This was possible thanks to Dee Mortensen, Editorial Director, Paige Rasmussen, Assistant Acquisitions Editor, and Nancy Lightfoot, Project Manager, who were extremely friendly, accommodating, and responsive. In addition, all of them were unusually prompt correspondents. Finally, Nancy amazed me by her outstanding attention to the smallest details in my book, for which I am greatly indebted to her.

My friend Daniela Blei proved to be the most considerate and thoughtful copyeditor I have ever had. In addition to improving my writing and spotting typos even in Ladino words, she showed that working on copyedits does not have to be torture for the author but, instead can be a true pleasure. I am also grateful to her for assembling the index.

Finally, I am profoundly grateful to my father, Volf Borovoy, for preparing the illustrations for this book, which, needless to say, is an infinitesimal part of what he has done for me throughout my life.

Chapter 2 is derived in part from my article published in *Journal of Medieval Iberian Studies* on 29 Nov 2013, available online: http://www.tandfonline.com/doi/full/10.1080/17546559.2013.857424

Chapter 4 is derived in part from my article published in *Journal of Medieval Iberian Studies* on 15 July 2016, available online: http://dx.doi.org/10.1080/17546559.2016.1204555. I thank the journal's editors and anonymous readers for their help.

NOTE ON TRANSLATIONS, TRANSCRIPTIONS, TITLES, AND PROPER NAMES

In this book, the term "Ladino" refers to the Ibero-Romance language used by Sephardim in the Balkans and the eastern Mediterranean from the sixteenth century to the mid-twentieth century. In rare cases, I call it "Judeo-Spanish." Other names of this language appear only in quotations.

All translations, unless otherwise indicated, are mine.

The Bible is quoted either from the King James Version or the New Revised Standard Version, depending on which style better fits the context.

For the sake of consistency, in transcribing original Ladino texts and quoting those already transcribed into Latin characters, I use a single system. Regardless of how they appear in published sources, I follow the system adopted by the periodical *Aki Yerushalayim* with one difference: the letter Yod representing the consonantal element in diphthongs is rendered here by "y" (e.g., *tyempo*, not *tiempo*). This also applies to titles of Ladino works, with the exception of quotations and references. (Hence, *Rejimyento* in my text and *Regimiento* in references and citations.) (It must be remembered, however, that "Crónica de los reyes otomanos" is the Spanish title given to Almosnino's untitled work by Pilar Romeu, who published it in Latin script.)

In the titles of Ladino books and periodicals, I capitalize only the first meaningful word, as is done in other Romance languages. (For instance, *La Güerta de oro*.)

Biblical names commonly used in English appear in their Anglicized form. (Thus, "Moses," not "Moshe.") Turkish words and proper names, unless they are widely used in English, follow modern Turkish spelling. (Hence, "pasha" but Mahmut Paşa, a neighborhood in Istanbul.)

While transliterating Hebrew, I follow the Library of Congress rules with two exceptions: the letter Het is represented by "ch," and Ayin is not indicated.

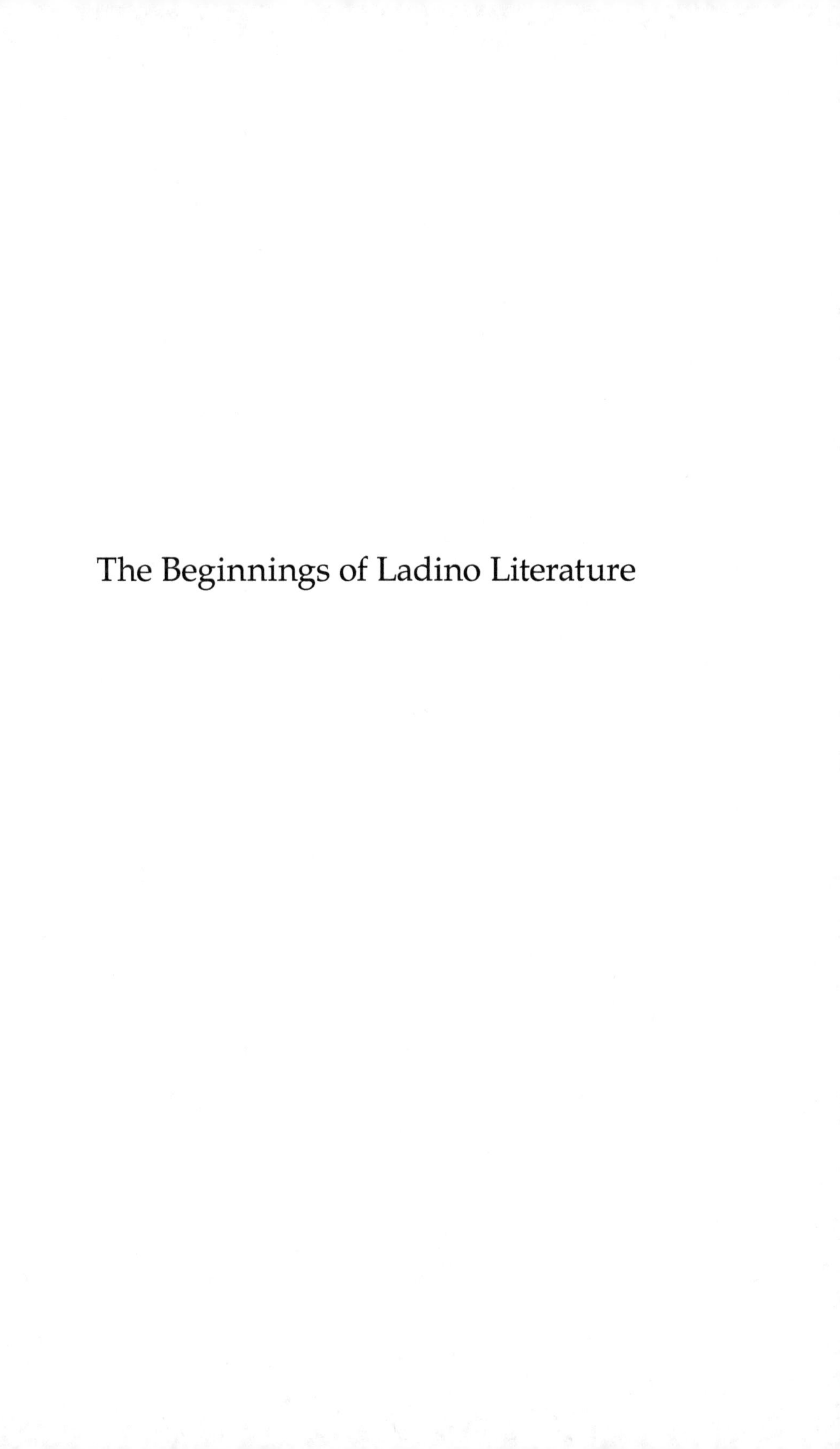

The Beginnings of Ladino Literature

Introduction

I.

Moses Almosnino (1518–1580) was arguably the most famous Ottoman Sephardi writer and the only one known in Europe both to Jews and Christians. The author of a few important Hebrew works appreciated by his colleagues, he became renowned for his vernacular books that were venerated by many rabbis and lay intellectuals in various periods.[1]

His name first became known in Europe in 1638, when Jacob Cansino published *Extremos y grandezas de Constantinopla* (The extremes and great things of Constantinople) in Madrid.[2] It is an abridged adaptation in Latin script of Almosnino's work, which was published by Pilar Romeu as *Crónica de los reyes otomanos* (The chronicle of Ottoman kings).[3] Jacob Cansino, a Jew from Oran, like several generations of Cansinos before him, served as an interpreter for Spanish kings whenever there was a need to translate a text from a Semitic language. Yet it was his own idea to "translate" *Crónica* "from Hebrew letters in which it was written into the Spanish language."[4] Apparently, this volume, dedicated to the Count-Duke of Olivares, had a large print run (some copies bearing his portrait). In the early twentieth century it was still available in Spain, where some Sephardi visitors bought it.

About two hundred years after its publication, the Cansino volume was used as a source on Ottoman history by the Austrian Orientalist Joseph von Hammer, who cites it a few times in his ten-volume *Geschichte des Osmanischen Reiches* (A History of the Ottoman Empire)

(Pest, 1827–1835).[5] Hammer notes "the only European historian" to have noticed that Suleyman had been the tenth sultan was "the scholar Rabbi Moses Almosnino of Salonica, in his work *Extremos y grandezas de Constantinopla*, little known due to its rarity."[6] This book was also cited in 1849 by Eliakim Carmoly, a French Jewish historian and Almosnino's first biographer, in his essay on the Almosnino family.[7]

As far as I can tell, the two earliest references to *Extremos y grandezas* by Ottoman Jews appeared in 1897. David Fresco, editor of the newspaper *El Tyempo* of Constantinople (Istanbul), refers to Almosnino as "the author of a picturesque description of Constantinople later translated by Jacob Kozino [*sic*]."[8] While Fresco obviously had not seen the book, Moïse Franco, author of the first comprehensive history of Ottoman Jews and educated in Paris, might have seen it himself (unless he borrowed its full title from Carmoly) and cited it in his *Essai sur l'histoire des Israélites de l'Empire Ottoman depuis les origines jusqu'à nos jours* (Essay on the history of Ottoman Jews from the beginning until the present day).[9] Other Sephardi historians of the same generation and the next, such as Abraham Danon, Joseph Nehama, and Isaac Emmanuel, used the Cansino edition as a historical source, although Danon seems to have owned a full manuscript. It is remarkable that they viewed it *only* as a historical source, though, as we will see, it is an entertaining read.

Almosnino's other vernacular book, *Rejimyento de la vida* (The regimen of living), which is by far less interesting for the modern reader, was always more famous and highly respected.[10] Printed in Hebrew characters in Salonica (Thessaloniki) in 1564, together with a shorter work, *Tratado de los suenyos* (A treatise on dreams), it appeared in Latin script, and with minor changes, in Amsterdam in 1729. (The other treatise was published by the same press in 1734.) This edition of *Rejimyento* was dedicated to Aaron de David de Pinto, a member of one of the most prominent Sephardi families of Portuguese origin, on the occasion of his *bar mitzvah*. The Commendatory HASKAMAH (APPROBATION), in this case in Portuguese, says that the merit of Almosnino's book, "a work of great importance worthy of its wisest author," as well as his great repute make it commendable reading.[11] (See cover image.)

As it turns out, the 1564 edition reached not only Amsterdam, with its significant Sephardi community, but also Salamanca. Tomás Antonio Sánchez de Uribe, a Spanish cleric known for publishing a multi-volume anthology of basic medieval Spanish texts, *Colección de poesías castellanas anteriores al siglo XV* (Collection of Castilian poetry from before the fifteenth century) (Madrid, 1779–1790), discovered Almosnino's work while compiling a catalogue of rabbinic writings at the library of the Colegio Trilingue of Salamanca. Though Sánchez's largely positive characterization of Almosnino's work was cited, among others, by Franco, Emmanuel, Michael Molho, and the *Jewish Encyclopedia*, it has never been quoted in full, for obvious reasons.[12] Here is what he said: "The teaching of this book is based on Aristotle whom the author frequently cites, as well as on many other ancient philosophers whom he mentions. His Castilian is pure, his style is natural and simple, and his teaching is good, except for some rabbinic nonsense (*patrañas rabínicas*) which one finds in a few places in the book, mainly where it talks about dreams."[13]

In the 1730s the prestige of Almosnino's work among Ottoman rabbis must have been very high, because, as I will show later, Jacob Huli, author of the popular Bible commentary *Meam Loez*, a classic of Ladino literature, goes to great lengths in his introduction to prove the obvious, namely, that *Rejimyento* could not be used for the education of the "foolish masses." In 1871, a Salonican publisher and journalist, Saadi Halevy, announced his intention to publish an adaptation of "the famous book by the rabbi and philosopher Moses Almosnino called *Rules of Living*."[14]

In addition, every history of Jewish Salonica covering the sixteenth century has discussed Almosnino's role in returning old tax privileges to his community. And every Jewish encyclopedia includes an entry either on him or the whole family. In other words, Moses Almosnino, famous in his own time, was not forgotten by later generations of Ottoman Jews or historians. Hence, one expects to find a whole library of books, articles, and dissertations about him and his vernacular works that earned him such fame.

About thirteen years ago, I read *Crónica* for the first time and was enchanted by it, but there was a great deal I did not understand. I hoped to find answers to my questions in the scholarship on Almosnino. That is when I discovered, to my dismay, that there was almost nothing to read about his vernacular works. Only Meir Bnaya's *Moshe Almosnino of Saloniki* (Tel Aviv, 1996) exists, but this biography says next to nothing about this subject. Spanish linguists published a few articles about the language of *Crónica*, and Pilar Romeu discusses it in the introduction to her edition.[15] Michael Molho wrote a very short piece on *Rejimyento* and *Crónica*, yet it includes nothing but facts and dates.[16] There is only one article that discusses Almosnino's work as a literary text, namely, John Zemke's introduction to his transliterated edition of *Rejimyento*. Thus, my own article on Almosnino's epistles was just a second literary study of his work.[17]

How do we explain literary scholars' lack of interest in Almosnino's two famous books? The answer is both simple and shocking: most scholars who read them (mainly linguists) decided that *Rejimyento* and *Crónica* were written in Castilian and, therefore, were not part of Ladino literature. Others accepted this verdict without looking at these works. Of course, as Zemke's introductory essay to *Rejimyento* shows, one does not have to consider Almosnino's work part of Ladino literature to be interested in it. Nevertheless, Zemke's essay remains an exception, emphasizing Almosnino's marginality in Sephardic Studies, which is a consequence of a more fundamental misconception.

II.

Most histories and overviews of Ladino literature start in the eighteenth century, even though Ottoman Sephardim began to publish vernacular works in the early sixteenth century.[18] This is primarily because many scholars consider the fact that the Sephardi vernacular reached its final shape only by the eighteenth century sufficient reason not to regard earlier texts created by the same speech community in the same territory and in a language that its members believe to be the same as part of this literature. As a result, sixteenth-century Ladino literature has not been treated or even conceptualized as such, and some of its texts are seen as an extension of Spanish (Castilian) literature, while others are not even studied by literary scholars. In the absence of any vernacular works from the seventeenth century, it is generally assumed that, aside from a number of random texts in various Ibero-Romance varieties written in the sixteenth century, during their first two hundred years in the Ottoman Empire, Sephardim did not produce a vernacular literature of their own.

Scholars of other literatures, as we know, do not use language standardization (whether formal or *de facto*) as a criterion of inclusion, which is why, for example, the study of Spanish literature begins with *El cantar del mío Cid*, written circa 1200 in an early Ibero-Romance variety. The history of Yiddish literature, according to its students, starts in the thirteenth century, despite the fact that this language underwent an enormous evolution, and texts were produced in different parts of Europe.[19] Although from a sociological standpoint it is obvious that Sephardi vernacular literature emerged in the sixteenth century, literary scholars, following linguists, believe that this happened two centuries later.

Elena Romero, author of the most comprehensive and authoritative work on Sephardi vernacular literature, *Creación literaria en lengua sefardí* (Madrid, 1992), dedicates only a few lines in the "Introduction" to Almosnino's and other sixteenth-century works produced by Sephardim in the Ottoman lands, stating that they were written "in pure *aljamiado* [i.e., in Hebrew characters] but in a language which barely displays any features distinguishing it from the Spanish of its time and which can be described, at the most, as 'pre-Judeo-Spanish.'"[20]

Iacob Hassán, who mentions some sixteenth-century works in passing, starts his overview of Sephardi literature with the first volume of *Meam Loez* (1730), because, as he puts it, the language of "the few Sephardi works that have survived from the sixteenth century (Almosnino, compilations of religious precepts, and translations)" had not yet become "independent from contemporaneous Spanish."[21] This rather vague statement apparently means that in terms of language, those sixteenth-century works (compilations of religious precepts included) are closer to literary texts produced in Spain than to *Meam Loez*. Even if one agrees with this notion (obviously not true for religious texts), are we to conclude that they should be considered part of Castilian literature and studied by the scholars of Antonio de Guevara? Not surprisingly, with the exception of Sánchez, whose peculiar conclusion was quoted above, they have not claimed as Castilian these works written in a Hebrew script.

Scholars who categorize "the literary language of the educated class of Salonican Jews in the mid-sixteenth century" as "Spanish" often cite Almosnino, who once referred to the language of his writings as *romanse kastelyano*.[22] We have no evidence, however, showing that he distinguished between the written and oral forms (let alone between different varieties), since he referred to both as *romanse* and *lengua ajena* (foreign language, i.e., not Hebrew). Moreover, in one case, he calls it *franko* (i.e., European) as opposed to Turkish.[23] But if we are to accept the terms used by sixteenth-century speakers, we can also call the language of Ottoman Jews "Ladino," because one of Almosnino's colleagues says that Ladino is "the [language] most commonly used among us."[24] The same was said about "Spanish."[25]

The use of the term "Castilian" (or "Spanish") to refer to the language of a few works, as opposed to the variety used by the rest of Sephardi vernacular texts, is also misleading because it suggests that there is a fundamental cultural difference between the two corpuses. More precisely, it implies that the works of Almosnino and some others are an extension of Castilian literature, and thus are irrelevant for Sephardi culture and its study. It is, therefore, not surprising that based on Hassán's essay quoted above, historian Matthias Lehmann, among many others, came to believe that sixteenth-century Judeo-Spanish books were "isolated cases," and that Almosnino's works were "still written in Castilian Spanish."[26] Viewed as an extension of Spanish literature, they indeed appear to be "isolated cases" that were once produced, but then somehow "disappeared from the life and cultural memory of the Sephardi Jews."[27] As we have already seen, this is not true for Almosnino.

Obviously, the use of "Spanish" (or "Castilian") vs. "Ladino" (or "Judeo-Spanish") is not a purely terminological issue but a reflection of a deeply rooted belief that Ladino, invariably associated with popular culture, did not produce high-culture works, unlike Castilian. Indeed, scholars of Ladino literature consider the eighteenth century its "golden age," despite the fact that during that period, only religious books saw light in the Ottoman Empire. This literature, whose purpose was to provide religious and general education to the unlearned and illiterate in a popular language, is described as "patrimonial." In addition to religious subjects, the topics of these works included "history, law, good manners, and gastronomic folklore . . . that is everything that constitutes the intellectual and lived heritage of many generations of Jews and is gathered in the vast Hebrew (and Aramaic) literature, such as Talmud, midrash, and other classical sources of Judaism."[28]

Yet the discussions of some of these subjects in "the literary language of the educated class" and with quotations from Aristotle and Plato alongside the Bible (to say nothing of accounts of Ottoman history) are not considered Ladino literature. By privileging popular religiously introverted writings to the exclusion of intellectually demanding works for educated readers, one implies that Ladino literature was produced only for the benefit of the ignorant. If we add to this the fact that nineteenth-century fiction and theater are generally considered less "authentic" and inferior to "golden age" Bible commentaries and *koplas* (coplets), we see that European influences on Ladino literature at all times are considered alien to it. Almosnino is the first victim of this belief.

By contrast, I propose to regard as Ladino (Judeo-Spanish) literature the entire corpus of literary texts produced by Sephardi Jews in the Ottoman Empire between the sixteenth and mid-twentieth centuries in the Ibero-Romance vernacular they considered their native language, regardless of what they called it.[29] Furthermore, I find it more productive to approach Ladino from a new perspective, which I formulate in chapter 1, and which is demonstrated by this book as a whole. I argue that like most other languages (including Yiddish), at least at some moments in its history, Ladino had more than one functional style (or register). Therefore, the vernacular works produced by Almosnino and some of his contemporaries that used, in my classification, the high register, are as much a part of Ladino literature as Huli's *Meam Loez* or *koplas* written in a folksy style.

As I see it, the history of this literature begins in the sixteenth century, which calls for a new periodization. Elena Romero identifies three moments in its history that divide it into two periods. During the first one, which started in the eighteenth century and continued until the middle of the nineteenth, the language was "fully mature" and "fit both for free creations and translations." The second period, which lasted through the 1940s, was brought about by profound cultural changes that led to "a rupture from the traditional patterns and openness to the non-Jewish cultural world of the West." World War II, the Holocaust, and subsequent mass migrations effectively put an end to literary creativity in Ladino, which had lasted "as long as historical and social conditions allowed."[30]

One can choose various principles of periodization, for instance, the history of Ladino literature can be presented as three educational projects prompted by real or perceived social needs and didactic goals of self-proclaimed educators (who always abounded among Ottoman Jews). Thus, the sixteenth century witnessed the first adult Jewish education project, which aimed at overcoming the consequences of mass conversions by teaching normative Judaism to males who had vague or no knowledge of it and could not read Hebrew. It generated the smallest corpus of vernacular texts. The second project (coinciding with Romero's first period) was a consequence, albeit an indirect one, of the Sabbatean crisis and the rabbis' conviction that Sephardim of both sexes and all ages illiterate in Hebrew needed a proper Jewish education. Strictly speaking, the rabbis' endeavor lasted through the end of the nineteenth century but was most productive in the eighteenth. This corpus was much larger than the first. The third project overlapped with the second, as its credo—European-style education as a universal remedy—was first formulated in Ladino in 1778 by David Attias, a Sephardi merchant from Sarajevo residing in Livorno. While his work, *La Güerta de oro* (The garden of gold), hardly known to Ottoman Jews, could not have had any impact on them, the same program was proclaimed by the Ladino press in the mid-1840s and indefatigably implemented by Sephardi literati and educators, in two stages, through the first third of the twentieth century. The third project created the largest corpus of texts intended for different readerships in various genres. To be more precise, this was the only time when not all literary works in Ladino were written and printed for educational purposes. It is this period in the history of Ladino literature, when both secular and religious works were published, that deserves to be called its golden age.

After World War II, a number of Sephardi authors in various countries published a few works in Ladino. This cannot, however, be considered the literary production of a Sephardi community but rather should be viewed as single works by individual writers. Ladino literature, which had been in decline even before the war, was completely destroyed together with most Ladino speakers.

III.

My previous book, *Modern Ladino Culture* (Bloomington, 2011) as well as other scholars' works on this subject, dealt with the emergence and flourishing of modern Sephardi print culture starting in the mid-nineteenth century. Eighteenth-century Ladino literature was examined at a conceptual level and in its historical setting only by Matthias Lehmann in his groundbreaking study of rabbinic vernacular writings, *Ladino Rabbinic Literature and Ottoman Sephardic Culture* and his analysis of *La Güerta de oro*, "A Livornese 'Port Jew' and the Sephardim of the Ottoman Empire," also the first and only work on this important text.[31] Therefore, the only chapter in the history of Ladino literature that is still missing is a study of its sixteenth-century corpus, the product of the first educational project.[32] This endeavor has been studied by historians, and a number of texts it generated were analyzed by linguists.[33] Thus, what we still lack is a literary study of the sixteenth-century corpus in the context of the events that led to its production.

The present book is not intended to be this missing chapter, because it examines the works of just one sixteenth-century writer, albeit the most prominent one. On the other hand, trying to understand Almosnino's writings is often the same as dealing with sixteenth-century Ladino literature as a whole, because, as I will show, they can be understood only if read in their specific cultural and historical context.

Hence, I consider my study of Almosnino's works the first attempt to set a framework for a more focused examination of this literature, and to establish its place in the history of Ladino print culture as a whole. This is why my book will not offer an in-depth analysis of all of Almosnino's extant Ladino works, but only of those that help me answer some questions about the emergence of Ladino literature and its first audience.

Despite the fact that each of the five chapters of this book, its prologue, and epilogue deal with a different subject, they are united by one underlying theme that is also present in the title: the theme of audience. I am interested in Almosnino's readers, intended and real ones, contemporaries and those of later generations, Sephardi intellectuals, and modern scholars. This study explains what and why Almosnino wanted to tell his target audience and how he did it, why his message was misunderstood by later readers, and how and why they reinterpreted it.

The history of Ladino literature can also be presented in terms of its readerships, which is a useful analytical tool, because readers' perceived needs shaped the texts produced for their benefit. As I will show, this approach allows me to explain the emergence of Almosnino's vernacular works, their genres and stylistic registers, and the disappearance of high-register literature. Furthermore, it helps us to understand the long hiatus in Ladino book printing in the seventeenth century.

It is self-understood that any analysis of vernacular production in a diglossic community has to start by looking at the audience that would have been interested in it, and at the distribution of labor between the two languages. The emergence of a new vernacular literature in such a community is usually caused by social changes or new circumstances that augment the number of monolingual readers. This is why the prologue goes back to the pre-expulsion period and discusses Jewish vernacular culture in Christian Iberia, whereas chapter 1 examines new sociocultural conditions and their impact on Sephardim's linguistic practices after their relocation to the Ottoman lands.

The new social group whose educational needs stimulated the development of vernacular literature were ex-*conversos* who were usually not monolingual but did not know Hebrew, because they had lived in Europe as Christians. After immigrating to the Ottoman Empire, they embraced Judaism and had to be educated as Jews even before they learned Hebrew. This was the main factor that brought Ladino literature into existence.

Due to his own scholarly interests and his social and professional connections to better-off Portuguese ex-*conversos*, Almosnino was particularly dedicated to the integration and religious instruction of those otherwise educated men. Unlike other rabbis who produced translations and adaptations of Hebrew texts, he chose to write original works in the vernacular to answer the questions of his addressees on science, philosophy, and theology that were previously discussed among Jews in Hebrew. Initially intended for specific individuals, these answers were then turned into didactic treatises meant for all well-read ex-*conversos* and even their children, as well as all educated men willing to read vernacular texts. The best known among these treatises, discussed in chapter 2, is *Rejimyento de la vida*, which I examine only briefly, focusing on its genre features. I show how Almosnino created his own subgenre, the scholarly Ladino epistle, which was a cultural and linguistic compromise for a scholar used to writing in Hebrew.

In chapter 3, I turn to *Crónica de los reyes otomanos* and examine two of its four parts, the Ottoman Chronicles, which raise an entirely different set of questions. Their style and message suggest that they also targeted educated men, mainly ex-*conversos* known for their social mobility, who were encouraged to serve Ottoman authorities, differing from other subjects only in their religious practices. I argue that this was an assignment entrusted to Almosnino by wealthy Jews close to the court who aspired to strengthen their community's relations with their new masters.

Almosnino's chronicles of Ottoman sultans, as I show, fundamentally differ from his contemporaries' Hebrew histories of non-Jewish monarchs represented in biblical terms. What we see is a skillfully constructed political, if not propagandistic, narrative aimed at making Sephardim feel that they were living at the right time in the right place, and that they should be good Ottoman subjects. In terms of their goals and motivation, Almosnino's chronicles are similar to the editorials of the first Ladino periodical and Ottomanist discourse in the Ladino press at the turn of the twentieth century. In fact, *El Tyempo* even published two excerpts from *Crónica* to reinforce its own political claims.[34] Hence, rather than being a reliable source on Ottoman history for which it is commonly taken, Almosnino's *Crónica* should be seen as a window onto the concerns and aspirations of the Jewish community not conveyed by other documents.

Chapter 4 deals with one of the most misinterpreted Ladino texts, the section of *Crónica* that gave the title to the Cansino volume, *Extremos y grandezas de Constantinopla*. My close reading of this text makes it clear that rather than being a conventional ad hoc travelogue in Constantinople, as is usually believed, it is an idiosyncratic treatise on the Ottoman capital described in terms of health regimens and philosophical writings by Hippocrates, Aristotle, Maimonides, Ibn Sinna, and other classical and medieval authors well known to Almosnino's intended audience, but much less familiar to non-specialists today. And, since the main feature of this account is intertextuality, instead of taking it at face value, one has to read it with a commentary.

Chapter 4 turns the subject of audience in a different direction since it demonstrates that by replacing the genre expectations of the intended readership with new ones, Cansino deliberately masked and transformed the meaning and message of Almosnino's work. To make the text under analysis accessible to those who do not know Ladino, I have included my translation in the Appendix, which is the first English version of any vernacular work by Almosnino.[35]

At the turn of the seventeenth century, *converso* immigration virtually came to an end. As a result, there were no longer any educated Jews unable to read Hebrew, and all intellectual matters could be discussed in this language that once again and for a long time, became the only vehicle of high culture. Hence, Ladino's high register used by Almosnino and two other authors whose books were published in Salonica, disappeared together with the respective genres.

A study of the emergence and disappearance of the short-lived ex-*converso* audience sheds new light on the processes of audience formation not explored until now in the Sephardi context.[36] In view of its theoretical importance, in chapter 5, I briefly look at Ladino readerships formed after the demise of the first one. The fact that in the seventeenth century, to our knowledge, no Ladino books were published in Salonica or Constantinople, is commonly explained by the general economic decline of the empire. But how then do we explain that the flourishing Jewish community of Izmir (Smyrna), which had a printing press between 1658 and 1675, did not produce any Ladino books? And why did Ladino literature bloom so spectacularly at the end of the nineteenth century when the empire was rapidly approaching its collapse?

My analysis of the Izmir case explains why its growing Jewish community did not experience a need for new Ladino books in the seventeenth century. The eighteenth century, however, saw the appearance of two new readerships brought into being by completely different factors and needs. With regard to the first, I further develop the argument formulated by Lehmann in his study of Ladino rabbinic literature. This educational project, unlike the sixteenth-century one, was not called for by an actual need to provide proper Jewish education to the Sephardi masses who were illiterate in Hebrew. Rather, it was undertaken by a group of rabbis because of their own beliefs rooted in the Lurianic kabbalah spread by the Sabbatean movement. It is those rabbis who produced several volumes of *Meam Loez* and numerous adaptations of Hebrew texts.

The case of the second eighteenth-century Ladino readership is entirely different. As far as we can tell, in the last quarter of that century (and possibly earlier), there actually existed a new audience consisting of somewhat educated male readers not fluent in Hebrew and not interested in Bible commentaries in any language. We learn this from David Attias's *La Güerta de oro* that was intended mainly for merchants like himself who wanted to gain professional knowledge and participate in international trade. Of course, we do not know the numbers of men who were interested in commercial information and secular knowledge in general, but their needs were certainly real. The existence of this readership is corroborated, albeit later, by the fact that in 1845–1846, similar statements appeared in the pages of the first Ladino newspaper that was also published by a merchant for male readers engaged in commerce.

The early Ladino press, which targeted a male readership, did not adopt the style or didactic means of *Meam Loez* to which it had no affinity in any sense. Yet the press that emerged in the 1870s spoke to the same mass audiences as the rabbis and used some of their methods of instruction. This press and its connections to rabbinic vernacular writings are examined in my previous book (chapter 1).

This overview puts the first educational project, its creators, readers, and texts into a general perspective of Ladino print culture. Among many other things, one realizes that Almosnino was unique in that his work was known to educated readers in various periods. In the epilogue, I show what he meant to Sephardi intellectuals in the twentieth century and their interest and pride in his writings. I demonstrate that Almosnino's language, which led some scholars to exclude his work from the corpus of Ladino literature, in the eyes of those Sephardi literati, was an indisputable argument in favor of considering him the first Ladino author. Together with the language they believed they shared with him, Almosnino was one of their connections to Europe past and the present. This means that his work also served as a link between sixteenth- and twentieth-century Sephardi vernacular cultures.

Notes

1. For a full list of Almosnino's Hebrew works, see Naphtali Ben-Menachem, "Writings by Rabbi Moses Almosnino," *Sinai* 19 (1946–47): 268–285 (Heb.).

2. *Extremos y grandezas de Constantinopla compuesto por Rabí Moysen Almosnino hebreo, traducido por Iacob Cansino* (Madrid, 1638).

3. Moisés Almosnino, *Crónica de los reyes otomanos*, ed. Pilar Romeu Ferré (Barcelona, 1998). In chapter 3, I explain the differences between various versions of Almosnino's work. Although the manuscript is untitled, for the sake of convenience, I will refer to his lost original text and Romeu's edition as *Crónica*.

4. *Extremos y grandezas de Constantinopla*, 3.

On Jacob Cansino and his possible motivation for this translation, see Jean-Frédéric Schaub, *Les juifs du roi d'Espagne. Oran, 1507–1669* (Paris, 1999), 65–81.

5. Isaac Emmanuel indicates the following pages in this edition (some of which appear to be erroneous): vol. IV, 5, 240, 290, 301, 490, 514. For the French translation, the page numbers are correct: *Histoire de l'empire Ottoman*, vol. V (Paris, 1835–1843), 5, 401–402. (Emmanuel, *Histoire des Israélites de Salonique* [Paris, 1936], 181.)

6. Hammer, *Histoire de l'empire Ottoman*, vol. V, 5. (I was unable to locate this statement in the original.) It is curious that Hammer perceives Almosnino as European, probably because his book was printed in Spain.

7. Eliakim Carmoly, *La Famille Almosnino* (Paris, 1850), 11.

8. "[David Fresco], Los judyos de Turkia en el dyes i seyshen siglo," *El Tyempo*, June 28, 1897, 5.

9. Franco, *Essai sur l'histoire des Israélites de l'Empire Ottoman depuis les origines jusqu'à nos jours* (Paris, 1897), 76.

10. See Moshe ben Baruh Almosnino, Regimiento de la vida. Tratado de los suenyos, ed. John M. Zemke (Tempe, 2004).

11. Moses Almosnino, *Regimiento de la Vida*, ed. Samuel Mendes de Sola and associates (Amsterdam, 1729).

12. Franco, *Essai sur l'histoire des Israélites de l'Empire Ottoman*, 78. Emmanuel, *Histoire des Israélites de Salonique*, 179. Molho, "Dos obras maestras en ladino de Moisés Almosnino," in *Estudios y ensayos sobre tópicos judíos* (Buenos Aires, 1958), 95–102. 99. Isidore Singer, ed., *Jewish Encyclopedia* (New York, 1901–1906), "Moses b. Baruch Almosnino."

13. Tomás Antonio Sánchez, *Colección de poesías castellanas*, vol. I, 186, no. 262.

14. Quoted in Romero, *Creación literaria*, 84.

15. The most important among them are: Pascual Pascual Recuero, "Las 'crónicas otomanas' de Moisés Almosnino," *Miscelanea de estudios arabes y hebraicos* 33 (1984): 75–104; Pilar Romeu, "Turquismos en la *Crónica de los reyes otomanos* de Mosé ben Baruh Almosnino," *Miscelanea de estudios arabes y hebraicos* 37–38 (1988–1989): 91–100; Pilar Romeu and Iacob M. Hassán, "Apuntes sobre la lengua de la *Crónica de los reyes otomanos* de Moisés Almosnino según la edición del manuscrito aljamiado del siglo XVI," *Actas del II Congreso Internacional de Historia de la Lengua Española* II (Madrid, 1992): 161–169.

16. Molho, "Dos obras maestras."

17. Olga Borovaya, "Moses Almosnino's Epistles: A Sixteenth-Century Genre of Sephardi Vernacular Literature," *Journal of Medieval Iberian Studies* 6, no. 5 (2014): 251–269. Eleazar Gutwirth has a few pages on Almosnino in his article, "*Acutissima patria:* Locating Texts before and after the Expulsions," *Hispania Judaica* 8 (2011): 19–38, 30–36.

18. The first known Ladino book, *Dinim de shehitah i bedikah* (The rules of ritual slaughter and inspection of animals), was printed in Constantinople, c. 1510. (See Abraham Yaari, *Hebrew Printing at Constantinople* [Jerusalem, 1967], no. 29. [Heb.]).

19. See, for example, Gerald C. Frakes, "Introduction," in *Early Yiddish Texts: 1100–1750*, ed. Gerald C. Frakes (New York, 2004), lviii–lix.

20. Romero, *Creación literaria*, 18. Later, she briefly discusses some sixteenth-century Bible translations referring to their language as "Eastern Judeo-Spanish calque." (39).

21. Iacob M. Hassán, "La literatura sefardí culta: sus principales escritores, obras y géneros," in *Judíos. Sefardíes. Conversos*, ed. Angel Alcalá (Valladolid, 1995), 319–30, 320.

22. Aldina Quintana, "Aportación lingüística de los romances aragonés y portugués a la coiné judeoespañola," in *Languages and Literatures of Sephardic and Oriental Jews: Proceedings of the Sixth International Congress for Research on the Sephardi and Oriental Jews*, ed. David Bunis (Jerusalem, 2009), 221–255. For instance, Romeu and Hassán, "Apuntes sobre la lengua de la Crónica de los reyes otomanos," 161.

23. Almosnino, *Crónica*, 251.

24. This was said by Joseph Formon, the translator of *Obligasyon de los korasones* quoted in Molho, *Literatura sefardita de Oriente* (Madrid, 1960), 229.

25. See Romero, *Creación literaria*, 37–38.

26. Matthias Lehmann, *Ladino Rabbinic Literature and Ottoman Sephardic Culture* (Bloomington, 2005), 34.

27. Quintana, "From Linguistic Segregation Outside the Common Framework of Hispanic Languages to a de facto Standard," in *Studies in Modern Hebrew and Jewish Languages Presented to Ora (Rodrigue) Schwarzwald*, eds. Malka Muchnik and Tsvi Sadan (Jerusalem, 2012), 697–714, 703.

28. Hassan, "La literatura sefardí culta," 323.

29. Ora (Rodrigue) Schwarzwald proposes a much broader definition: "Ladino literature refers to written or oral verbal compositions in the language of Sephardic Jewry." (Judith Baskin, ed., *Cambridge Dictionary of Judaism and Jewish Culture* [Cambridge, 2011], "Ladino Literature"). The obvious problem with this definition is that its meaning depends on what one considers to be the language of Sephardi Jewry, and scholars disagree on this subject. (I will return to this problem in the prologue.) In any case, according to Schwarzwald, Ladino literature existed already before the 1492 expulsion.

30. Romero, *Creación literaria*, 19.

31. *Jewish Social Studies* 11, no. 2 (2005): 51–76.

32. Actually, the first history (or, rather, anthology) of Ladino literature, Molho's *Literatura sefardita de Oriente* (Madrid, 1960) starts in the sixteenth century, but that section of the book is very short.

33. For instance, Yerushalmi, "The Re-education of Marranos in the Seventeenth Century," *The third Annual Rabbi Louis Feinberg Memorial Lecture in Judaic Studies* (Cincinnati, 1980).

The most prolific among the linguists is Ora (Rodrigue) Schwarzwald. The following articles of hers are particularly relevant to the history of Ladino literature: "The Relationship between Ladino Liturgical Texts and Spanish Bibles," in *The Hebrew Bible in Fifteenth-Century Spain: Exegesis, Literature, Philosophy and the Arts,* eds. Jonathan Decter and Arturo Prats (Leiden and Boston, 2012), 223–243; "Linguistic Features of a Sixteenth-Century Women's Ladino Prayer Book: The Language Used for Instructions and Prayers," in *Selected Papers from the Fifteenth Conference on Judeo-Spanish Studies* eds. Hilary Pomeroy, Chris J. Pountain, and Elena Romero (London, 2012), 247–260; "Ladino instructions in *Meza de el alma* and in *Seder Nashin* from Thessaloniki in the sixteenth century," in *Around the Point: Studies in Jewish Literature and Culture,* eds. Hillel Weiss, Roman Katsman, Ber Kotlerman (Cambridge, 2014), 121–134.

34. Abraham Danon, "Abu Suad i rabi Moshe Almosnino," *El Tyempo,* April 17, 1902, 5–6.

35. Zemke translated into English Almosnino's Hebrew introduction to *Rejimyento.* (See Almosnino, *Regimiento de la vida*, "Hakdamah," fols. 1a–8a.)

36. For a brief general introduction to the history of reading in the relevant period, see Roger Chartier, *Order of Books: Readers, Authors, and Libraries in Europe Between the Fourteenth and Eighteenth Centuries*, trans. Lydia G. Cochrane (Stanford, CA, 1994).

Prologue

JEWISH VERNACULAR CULTURE IN FIFTEENTH-CENTURY IBERIA

I.

The question whether Iberian Jews had a language or a dialect of their own has been discussed for so long that any agreement is unlikely.[1] Examinations of extant texts created by Sephardim before and soon after the expulsion have convinced many scholars that Iberian Jews spoke the same dialects as Iberian Christians, and that Judeo-Spanish emerged only after 1492 in the Ottoman Empire, mainly as a result of dialect mixing.[2] Looking at the available material, these linguists did not find any specifically Jewish features aside from the lexicon and phraseology related to Jewish religious practices, law, and commerce. Others, on the contrary, claim that Iberian Jews had a language of their own already on the Peninsula.[3] According to this view, the language or dialect of Iberian Jews differed from that of their Christian compatriots in certain lexical, morphological, and syntactic aspects.

Elaine Miller has suggested that the two perspectives based on the same evidence are not diametrically opposed, and that disagreement is caused by the lack of definitions determining "how much a language variety must differ from the norm to be considered a separate dialect."[4] This approach would be fruitful if the discussion had not become ideologically charged. As Miller's own reasoning demonstrates, in reality, the two theories reflect opposing views on the question of Jewish separation from the majority society, and thus the issue of Jewish identity. Arguing in favor of the second theory, Miller does not use any formal criteria but instead resorts to unprovable psychological arguments, including the "perhaps unconscious" desire of Spanish Jews to alter the norms of the language spoken by non-Jews.[5] She recognizes that it is very difficult to prove the existence of Judeo-Spanish language in Iberia, or even to identify the differences that existed "in the eyes and ears of the community members," yet she *believes* that the Jews must have had such a language.[6]

Following Miller's methodological proposition (albeit not adopted by her), I suggest that since vocabulary is only one of many elements of language (and there is no reliable evidence of any other deviation), the use of some terms and avoidance of others are not sufficient to constitute a separate language or dialect, but only a sociolect. Since sociolects are used mainly for oral communication, a study of long-extinct ones is nearly impossible. Scarce evidence allows us to posit the existence of a number of Jewish sociolects on the Iberian Peninsula that diverged from one another as much as regional dialects did, which differed mainly in terms of vocabulary.[7] However, since I am not concerned with their specific linguistic characteristics here, but rather with their functions in the diglossic situation obtaining in the Sephardi community, I will refer to them in the singular as "the vernacular" or "Ibero-Romance." Vernacular texts written in Hebrew characters will be called *aljamiya.*

Today, diglossia is commonly understood to mean the use of two (or more) languages or varieties within the same speech community for different social functions. These two languages are referred to as H (high) and L (low), where H is "the vehicle of a large and respected body of written literature . . . and is used for most written and formal spoken purposes but is not used by any sector of the community for ordinary conversation."[8] In all Jewish communities, the H language associated with religion, education, and other aspects of high culture was Hebrew, while the L, which served everyday needs and was used at home and at work, was the local vernacular referred to as *laaz,* i.e., "non-Hebrew" (sometimes translated as "foreign" language).

In some periods, however, Jews had more than one high-culture language and combined or replaced Hebrew, depending on the genre and function, with Aramaic or Arabic. Also, they often spoke two or three vernaculars, one Jewish, the other non-Jewish. In fifteenth-century Iberia (except the Kingdom of Granada), Arabic was no longer used, but it was common to speak Aragonese and Catalan, or Portuguese and Castilian. In other words, "Spanish" became a Jewish vernacular only after the expulsion, when it began to function as an ethnic marker of Sephardi Jews.

As Joshua Fishman has shown, though diglossia (a societal arrangement) presupposes and institutionally buttresses bilingualism (individual linguistic behavior), not all members of a diglossic society are bilingual.[9] This happens because the superposed language is learned later and in a formal setting, which often leaves those who have no access to education monolingual. Such was the case in the Jewish world where Hebrew was taught in school and at the synagogue, i.e., exclusively to boys.

However, in many epochs, Jewish primary schools were notorious for their poor teaching of Hebrew based on memorization of the Scriptures, which is why many men did not know it either, even if they were able to recite prayers and recognize a memorized text when they saw or heard it. It is this form of functional illiteracy, as we would call it today, that Jacob Huli complained of in 1730: when reading the Bible, "even those who know the words do not understand what they are saying."[10]

After the destruction of the Jerusalem Temple in 70 CE, Hebrew lost much of its practical significance, but its symbolic role became more prominent, which is when rabbinic literature began to refer to it as *lashon ha-kodesh* (the holy language).[11] The loss of Hebrew competence among Jews and the decline of the "holy tongue" became a common motif in rabbinic literature. The use of vernaculars among Jews was explained by a generally accepted cliché, *b'avonot* (because of our sins).

As is well known, the anti-Jewish pogroms of 1391 were followed by mass conversions. In 1403, in response to these conversions and their willingness to use "Christian languages," Profayt Duran (d. ca. 1414), a prominent Catalan thinker and grammarian who himself had converted under duress, named two causes of Hebrew's "corruption." The first cause, he contended, was "the wickedness of the 'foolish nations' that persecuted Israel in exile" and destroyed its books. The second cause was of an internal nature. Duran blamed the ancient sages for having "abandoned the chosen language and written their treatises in Aramaic."[12] Duran's contemporary, Solomon ben Meshullam De Piera, decried Jewish vernacular poets for betraying Hebrew and compared them to monkeys attempting to play tambourines and flutes.[13] Despite the criticisms and calls to stop using the vernacular in the aftermath of the anti-Jewish violence of 1391 that swept the Spanish realms, Sephardi authors produced literary texts in Ibero-Romance until the expulsion.

In her insightful discussion of "Hebraico-French" literature, Kirsten Fudeman succinctly describes a diglossic situation common, *mutatis mutandis*, to all medieval Jewish communities. For the Jews of medieval France, "French was the unmarked, or usual, choice when it came to speaking." In writing, however, the unmarked choice was Hebrew, and thus most medieval Jewish texts created in France are in Hebrew.[14] Therefore, it is the vernacular literary production that requires explanation.

Iberian Jews, like all other Jews, used the vernacular for everyday needs. But non-literary texts, such as domestic correspondence and oral statements quoted in responsa (answers to legal questions), that might have been written in the vernacular, did not survive the expulsion, while a surprising number of Hebrew manuscripts were preserved, and some of them later published. In fact, the only two extant court testimonies in the vernacular from the pre-expulsion period reached us because they were included in the collection of responsa by Isaac bar Sheshet Prefet (1326–1408) from Barcelona, which was published in 1559 in Constantinople.[15] The existence of vernacular correspondence is also attested in Hebrew sources. For instance, De Piera reprimands a fellow poet for writing to him in the vernacular.[16] However, the chief reason for writing in *laaz*, which was common to most Jewish communities, was low Hebrew proficiency among uneducated people, women in particular. Needless to say, we have no data that would allow us to assess the numbers of such people in Iberia, even approximately. But, in any case, it is reasonable to assume that the mass conversions would have motivated rabbis to try to improve Jewish primary education, since they blamed these apostasies on a poor understanding of the Scriptures. It is well known that there was an oral Sephardi tradition of word-for-word Bible transmission in Ibero-Romance. Certain parts of the liturgy were also translated. Yet no written versions of these texts are extant, and very few paraliturgical texts in the vernacular have survived.

What makes Jewish vernacular culture in Iberia different from those of French and other European communities is that it was produced in two alphabets, since some of the texts written by Sephardi authors were intended for a Christian readership, namely, for monarchs and nobility willing to listen to Jewish scholars, poets, and community leaders. Iberian Jews did not simply dedicate their literary works to their patrons—usually temporal authorities—but in fact corresponded with them, including such influential aristocrats and intellectuals as López de Ayala, Luis de Guzman, and Marqués de Santillana.[17] Moreover, Jewish authors produced literary works for the court milieu. Of course, those writers were not numerous, because, as Eleazar Gutwirth points out, "the court Jews were a minority, as was the court, and as were the Jews themselves." But he also questions the usefulness of the term "minority" as a medieval category, and the notion of elites: "For some medieval Jews, anyone who was not a philosopher was part of the *hamon*, the populace or multitude. For others of that day, court Jews were vulgar ignoramuses who could not read a Hebrew letter."[18] Hence, Jewish authors who produced vernacular texts for a Christian audience, between the mid-fourteenth century and the expulsion, cannot be described as an intellectual elite but rather as individuals (or groups of individuals) particularly interested in and open to Iberian secular culture. All of them used the Latin alphabet that was unknown to most members of their community.

Since the majority of Iberian Jews lived in separate neighborhoods (*aljamas*) with their own schools and courts, and paid taxes directly to the crown, most of them, especially in rural areas, had no opportunities or need to learn the Latin alphabet that was associated with Christianity. Hence, aside from Jewish courtiers and administrators who had to read and write in Latin characters, few Jews (mainly scholars) were familiar with it. An examination of the inventories of some Jewish libraries and Inquisition records demonstrates that even intellectuals usually read Castilian literature in *aljamiya*. Thus, Ms. Pal. 2666 from the Palatine library of Parma contains a miscellaneous collection of philosophical and literary texts in *aljamiya* dating from the mid-fifteenth century.[19] It includes renderings of some important works of medieval Castilian literature among which is *La Visión deleitable de las artes y las ciencias* (The delightful vision of the arts and sciences) by Alfonso de la Torre, a poet of presumably *converso* origin. The manuscript also contains a *Collection of Proverbs of Seneca* and a version of the anonymous Castilian poem *La Danza general de la muerte* (Dance of Death), one of whose characters is a rabbi. There is a Hebrew-Spanish and Spanish-Hebrew glossary of philosophical terms and a glossary of Hebrew terms derived from Maimonides' treatise on logic, *Millot ha-higgayon* originally written in Arabic.[20]

This and other documents bring into sharp relief the deep yet fragile connections between Jewish and Christian intellectuals on the Iberian Peninsula in the fourteenth and fifteenth centuries. They shared a language and many intellectual pursuits but were divided by religion, a division symbolized by the use of different alphabets. Once a Jew converted, he was supposed to abandon the Hebrew alphabet, the use of which by non-Jews became dangerous after the establishment of a national inquisition in Castile (around 1480). It is—literally and figuratively—the knowledge of both alphabets by *conversos*, a new and large liminal group of Spaniards, that made them serve as a link between Iberian Christians and Jews, irrespective of anyone's intentions.

II.

A second wave of conversions took place in the aftermath of the Tortosa Disputation staged by the antipope Benedict XIII (Pedro de Luna) in 1413–1414. It is believed that between 1391 and 1492 about 100,000 Jews converted, most of them under duress or out of fear.[21] Not surprisingly, therefore, a significant number of *conversos* secretly continued to practice Judaism, which often caused them to be persecuted but, until the early 1480s, did not endanger their lives. For obvious reasons, the real numbers of crypto-Jews are unknown, and they were certainly exaggerated by the Inquisition and Zionist historiography. But no less important than the numbers is the fact that conversions continued, even if on a smaller scale, throughout the fifteenth century, and thus there were always first-generation *conversos* who were likely to practice Judaism. And most first-generation *conversos*, whether they were secret Judaizers or "true believers," and even prominent members of the Church hierarchy, maintained contact with those who did not convert. There were at least two reasons for this.

First, despite several attempts to separate *conversos* from Jews by making them move out of the *aljamas*, until at least the mid-fifteenth century, the two groups usually continued to live side by side.[22] This is partly because the poor among "new Christians" (as they were pejoratively called) could not afford to resettle.

Thus, in Soria, the separation legislation of 1412 was not put into effect, and a similar royal order of 1477 was not enforced either. When in 1480, the crown, under pressure from the Castilian Cortes, agreed to issue a general decree constraining Jews to separate walled quarters, they were given two years to move. But even in 1489, some wealthy Jews of Soria were still residing outside the new *aljamas* (the so-called *barrios nuevos*) and close to the cathedral.[23]

Second, since very often only some family members would convert to Christianity while others remained faithful to Judaism, the "new Christians" would join their Jewish relatives for weddings, funerals, and other important occasions, even if they were living in different neighborhoods. This practice, described in anti-*converso* courtly poems and documented in inquisition records, was considered sufficient grounds for persecuting these converts as secret Judaizers. For instance, in 1484, such accusations based on family contacts were brought against Juan Arias Dávila, bishop of Segovia.[24]

In the first half of the fifteenth century, many educated and well-off *conversos* rose to prominent positions at court and in the Church. Their rapid upward mobility and accumulation of wealth and power raised new fears among the "old Christians," boosting their resentment toward converts, which in the middle of the fifteenth century manifested itself as discriminatory legislation and anti-*converso* violence. The *converso* problem was now perceived as a serious social issue that some churchmen and city oligarchs were determined to resolve. Claiming that absorption of *conversos* into Christian society was hindered by their contact with Jews, some authors advocated expulsion of the Jews and the institution of a national inquisition whose purpose would be "to extirpate what was considered by Church and State a heresy and to put a stop to the conversos' relapse and return to the faith and ways of life of their forefathers."[25] Thus the foundation of the Inquisition in Seville around 1480 was inextricably linked both to the violence of 1391 that created the *converso* problem and the expulsion of 1492, which ostensibly aimed at putting an end to it.

Indefatigable research conducted over many years by Eleazar Gutwirth, as well as articles by James Nelson Novoa, Hava Tirosh-Samuelson, and a few other scholars, made unnecessary further polemics with theories of the alleged isolation and cultural decline of Iberian Jews after

1391 put forward by the *Wissenschaft des Judentums* (Science of Judaism) historians.[26] In reality, mass conversions, in many ways, brought Jewish and Christian intellectuals closer together than they had ever been before. Due to the existence of *conversos,* who served as a link between Christians and Jews, the fifteenth century witnessed intense intellectual exchange between these two groups. Of course, Iberian Jews were sometimes persecuted before 1391, and some were forced or chose to convert, which also happened in other European countries. But only in fifteenth-century Spain, which had the largest Jewish community of the day, were converts so numerous and prominent, making a significant impact on the nation's culture.

The presence of "new Christians" and their intellectual interaction with "old Christians" were most visible at the courts. Fifteenth-century *cancioneros* (collections of lyric poetry) reflect both hostility toward *conversos* that was characteristic of that environment, and an impressive familiarity with Jewish customs. The most famous among them is the *cancionero* edited around 1426 by Juan Alfonso de Baena who converted to Christianity in 1391. The Baena collection contains about 600 poems produced by nearly 60 courtiers and poets, including many *conversos.*[27] These texts testify not only to popular antisemitism but also to close social and intellectual relations between Jews, Christians, and *conversos.* For instance, the use of many Hebrew terms by Christian poets to ridicule *conversos,* and by *converso* poets to bicker with one another, suggests that they not only knew them, but also expected their readers to understand such words as *Adonay* (Lord), *shabat* (Sabbath), *shofar* (a ram's horn used on High Holidays), *mila* (circumcision), *hazan* (cantor), *Yom Kipur* (Day of Atonement), and others.[28] The same can be said about references to Jewish cuisine allegedly preferred by insincere *conversos.*

Those who converted as adults had learned Hebrew in childhood, which allowed some to serve as translators in one or both directions. One of the first among them was Moses ben Samuel de Roquemaure, a Hebrew poet and scholar, who, in the second half of the fourteenth century, translated Bernard de Gordon's Latin work *Lilium medicinae* into Hebrew.[29] In the fifteenth century, *The Guide for the Perplexed* and *Kuzari* were available to Castilian Christians in their own language, and some were indeed acquainted with *The Guide* and Maimonides' other works, including his *Treatise on Asthma.*[30] The influence of Maimonides is noticeable in Alfonso de la Torre's *Visión deleitable de las artes y las ciencias*, which he wrote for the Prince of Viana around 1438.[31] Given that it is found in the Parma manuscript, we may assume that it was one of the works that were popular among both Christians and Jews.

On the other hand, Jewish scholars, such as Judah ben Samuel Shalom, Abraham ben Isaac Shalom, Eli ben Joseph Chavilio, Abraham Nachmias ben Joseph, and Baruch ibn Yaish, translated numerous works of Christian scholasticism into Hebrew. These translations influenced Jewish philosophical writings in terms of style and content.[32] Among those Christian authors were Alexander of Hales, Thomas Aquinas, Duns Scot, Johannes Versoris, and a few others. In Tirosh-Samuelson's view, "what distinguishes fifteenth-century Jewish philosophers in Iberia from their predecessors is the grafting of Christian scholasticism onto the Judeo-Arabic philosophic tradition."[33]

Finally, Jewish and Christian scholars shared many interests and read the same texts besides the Bible. Most notably, both venerated Aristotle, whose works were frequently translated and discussed in the Middle Ages by Jewish and Christian scholars alike. Around 1400, Meir Alguadex, the Chief Rabbi of Castille, translated *Nicomachean Ethics* into Hebrew from a Latin paraphrase, justifying his reliance on this text by the fact that "for the Christian writers moral philosophy is a splendid science."[34]

Jewish scholars not only produced numerous commentaries on Aristotle's works, but the very "renewal of halakhic studies in Spain was predicated on the incorporation of Aristotelian logic into the interpretation of the authoritative talmudic text."[35] Among other authors revered by both groups were Seneca and Cicero. Both were "quoted," for instance, in *Dichos de sabios y philósofos* (Sayings of sages and philosophers) translated from Catalan into Castilian by Çadique de Uclés in 1402 for a Castilian patron.[36] As we have seen, a collection of "Seneca's sayings," a popular genre of Jewish literature, is found in the Parma manuscript discussed above.

Even these few examples demonstrate the openness of some Iberian Jewish intellectuals to many Christian and classical influences and their dialogue, even if indirect, with mainstream culture. This is true even for many of those authors who disparaged vernacular writings but borrowed Romance material.[37] Most Jewish vernacular texts, however, were written in Hebrew characters, and thus the responses of their authors, intended for their coreligionists, remained unknown to Iberian Christians. This circumstance is ignored by David Wacks who believes that "even if we focus on Hebrew-language production, we see that Jewish writers in Christian Iberia were full participants in their native vernacular culture."[38] Borrowing themes or devices from a culture—that is not even aware of this, if only because of alphabet differences—is far from participating in it, let alone fully.

Yet, as was previously mentioned, a few Jewish authors indeed chose to participate in the majority culture in its own language and alphabet, or at least contribute to it. The latter is true for the so-called Alba Bible, a Castilian translation produced in 1422–1430 by r. Moses Arragel of Maqueda (ca. 1400–1493), and illuminated by Christian artists. Don Luis de Guzman, Grand Master of Calatrava, who commissioned the translation, explains in a letter to Moses Arragel included in the prologue that the existing versions are written in a "corrupt language" and that some dark passages require glosses, which is why he wants a "glossed and illuminated Romance Bible" (*vna biblia en romance, glosada e ystoriada*). R. Arragel, he believes, is the right person for this job because he is knowledgeable in Jewish law and "his Castilian is very good."[39]

Don Luis also asked Arragel to include rabbinic commentaries, which prompted Fray Arias de Encinas, a Franciscan cleric in charge of the project, to add commentaries of the Church Fathers in those places where Jews and Christians differ.[40] Arragel, for his part, cited many of his predecessors and contemporaries as well as talmudic and kabbalistic sources and classical works.[41] Despite his initial refusal, Arragel was put in charge of the illustrations, which explains why more than fifty out of the 325 miniatures contain Jewish elements presenting scenes of Jewish life and rituals.[42]

Who was the intended audience for the new translation? Given that it was ordered by the Grand Master of Calatrava, it was obviously meant for the courtly milieu, a small group of educated Christians. The order of biblical books and the linguistic differences between this translation and those published by Sephardi Jews for their own use after the expulsion also indicate that the Alba Bible (like the Escorial Bible) was intended for a Christian audience.[43] Arragel explains in the prologue, however, that his work is addressed to Christians who want to learn about Judaism and to the Jews, converted or not, who do not know enough about it.[44] Arragel's choice of illustrations, therefore, might have also served this educational purpose.[45]

Based on the colophon that mentions the Master of Calatrava going to war, Sonia Fellous suggests that by commissioning this translation, Don Luis de Guzman aimed at strengthening relations with the Jewish community at a time when the king needed money for his wars.[46] But all European monarchs waged wars, and they always managed to get Jewish money faster and in less sophisticated ways. Fellous, however, is right to put this project in the context of Pope Martin V's bulla of September 21, 1421, which returned to Spanish Jews the right to exercise the professions banned by the Statutes of Valladolid of 1412. In February 1422, the bulla was followed by the Pope's appeal to the Church to treat Jews humanely.[47] Still, a long-term project involving many scribes and artists would not have been undertaken had there not been a Christian audience, albeit a very small one, interested in a new Bible translation with rabbinic commentaries. No doubt, Don Luis de Guzman himself had genuine interest in this enterprise, which he expressed in his letters to Arragel. Their correspondence is included in the prologue to the Alba Bible and demonstrates Moses Arragel's competence in the art of letter writing.

In fact, in the fourteenth and fifteenth centuries, there existed a Jewish cultural practice of epistolarity in Castilian, Catalan, and Portuguese, which will be discussed in some detail in chapter 2.[48] For now, suffice it to say that the presence in these letters, at various levels, of what Gutwirth describes as currents of vernacular humanism, demonstrates that some Iberian Jews were well versed in contemporaneous humanist writings. Extant samples from the fifteenth century testify to "a wider and deeper intellectual investment in the vernacular letter as a medium for prose composition."[49] The addressees of these mostly legal and business letters belonged to the aristocracy. In the 1470s, Isaac Abrabanel (1437–1508), a renowned Jewish thinker and financier at the Portuguese court, composed a letter in Portuguese to the Count of Faro that was included in a sixteenth-century codex of model letters sent to and received by monarchs and nobility.[50] Abrabanel's epistle demonstrates that he shared with other Iberian intellectuals close to the court, both Jews and Christians, many tastes and interests such as travel, foreign affairs, and literature (for instance, Seneca's tragedies), and thus was part of "a community of interests and authors."[51] Yet, like other Jewish intellectuals, Abrabanel used Hebrew to correspond with his coreligionists, even when they discussed the same subjects.

III.

Undoubtedly, the best known among Jewish authors who wrote in Ibero-Romance languages was r. Shem tob ben Isaac Ardutiel de Carrión (ca. 1290–1369), known in Spain as Santob de Carrión de los Condes, author of the secular didactic poem *Proverbios morales* (after 1351), a celebrated work of medieval Castilian literature.[52] Iñigo de Mendoza, Marqués de Santillana, the first scholar of Castilian literature, famously called Shem tob a "great poet" (*grand trobador*).[53] Little is known about Shem tob's life except for the fact that he held a position at the courts of Alfonso XI and his son Pedro I.[54] In fact, the original title of his poem is *Consejos y documentos al rey don Pedro* (Counsel and Letter to King Don Pedro).

Aside from the author's self-identification as a Jew in the introduction, the text arguably does not reveal direct connections to Judaism. Yet, this first example of gnomic verse in Castilian is closely related to didactic literature produced by Iberian Jews in the vernacular for their coreligionists, including gnomic and wisdom verse, which flourished in Spain starting in the thirteenth century.[55] It is noteworthy that one of the extant manuscript versions of *Proverbios morales* is in *aljamiya*, which testifies both to its popularity among Jews and to the inability of an average person to read Latin script.[56]

Shem tob, who died long before the mass conversions of 1391, obviously found it worthwhile to share words of wisdom with his Christian patron and courtiers in a language and alphabet they understood. A few years earlier, around 1345, he wrote a Hebrew treatise, *Debate Between the Pen and the Scissors*, which discusses the respective virtues of these instruments, both of which can be used for writing, albeit under different circumstances. This allegorical treatise has been interpreted by scholars to represent various polemics.[57] Wacks has suggested that it should be read as a debate between Hebrew and Romance, where the pen likens "the ink with which he writes to divine blessing, claiming that God is on his side." The scissors' writing, which stands for the vernacular, lacks substance and is not meant to be written but only spoken.[58] Wacks concludes that this treatise reveals the ambivalence of Jewish writers regarding "the validity of the vernacular as a literary language" and their guilt for abandoning Hebrew.[59]

However, if this clever interpretation of Shem tob's treatise as a language polemic is indeed legitimate, such a conclusion does not appear to have a basis in the text. The *Debate* contains a simpler and more straightforward message: the pen blessed by God is intended to write on divine subjects, whereas the scissors used by the story's wise old man for trimming hair and cutting fingernails is meant to deal with mundane matters for which ink (the divine blessing) is not needed. If the pen stands for Hebrew and the scissors for Romance, Shem tob's text is a perfect metaphor for diglossia, where the former serves the purposes of high culture and the latter is used for all other needs. Thus, Shem tob does not disparage Romance, as suggested by Wacks, but rather defines its place in the Jewish language hierarchy. Yet, the very fact that he discusses the status of Hebrew and *laaz* suggests that there was no general agreement on this matter.

Indeed, the absence of written rules regulating the use of languages accounts for different practices in different Jewish cultures, and for diachronic redistribution of functions between Hebrew and the vernacular. For instance, "non-sacred writing in Hebrew had a different history in the Ashkenazi community than that in Spain and Italy." In Romance countries, "before and during the thirteenth century learned Jews produced sacred and secular works," while in the Ashkenazi world, Hebrew was used mainly for religious purposes. In Italy, scholarly contact between Jews and Christians made possible in 1279 the translation of an Arthurian romance into Hebrew, which would have been highly improbable in Central Europe.[60] An example of the opposite usage is the practice of including large vernacular fragments in rabbinic responsa common among Ottoman Sephardim, which was not done by Ashkenazim who translated court testimonies into Hebrew.[61] In times of perceived general ignorance, for instance in the eighteenth century, Sephardi rabbis decided that it was advisable to explain the Bible in the vernacular.

In Christian Iberia, Hebrew was used for Bible commentaries, religious instruction, treatises on science, and entertainment while the vernaculars were employed only for the two latter purposes. That is why language-mixing found in some Jewish documents produced in Iberia, such as the *takkanot* (statutes)—instead of testifying to the dual identity of Castilian Jews as both Castilians and Jews—demonstrates that Hebrew was suitable for most social functions.[62] But while it was sometimes used for secular matters and could be interchangeable with *laaz,* Hebrew was the exclusive vehicle of high culture in the Jewish world.

Though Latin continued to play a certain role in Iberian Christian culture, which was still marginally diglossic, Latin's importance had diminished by the mid-fifteenth century. Under the influence of Italian humanism, more classical texts were translated into vernaculars, which made it necessary to assign different styles to different literary genres. For the first time, such a hierarchy was established in 1449 by Marqués de Santillana, in his *Proemio e carta al condestable de Portugal* (Preface and Letter to the Constable of Portugal). He distinguishes three literary styles: high, for translations of Greek and Latin classical writings; middle, for formal works in the vernacular; and low, for ballads and songs. From this standpoint, all vernacular works by Jewish authors belonged to the middle style. But for Jews, as far as we can tell, such categories did not exist: it was either Hebrew or Romance. In the sixteenth century, as we will see, when many more texts are produced in the vernacular, the distinction between style registers, albeit never formulated, will be fully understood and observed by all Jewish writers even within one book.[63]

* * *

Although Iberian Jews did not leave a large corpus of vernacular writings, the extant texts, glossaries, and *aljamiya* renderings of works produced by their Christian compatriots testify to their intellectual engagement with (rather than participation in) mainstream secular culture. Therefore, leaving the Iberian Peninsula in the 1490s, Jews took with them both the vernacular that they shared with Christians, and large cultural baggage associated with it—not only some of the texts they themselves produced, but also those written by Christians, which they read, absorbed, and reacted to, even if negatively or indirectly. As we will see in the following chapters, some works of Castilian literature published after 1492 also found their way to exiles and their children and became important to them.

Notes

1. See Tracy K. Harris, "What Language did the Jews Speak in Pre-Expulsion Spain?" in *Sephardic Identity: Essays on a Vanishing Jewish Culture*, ed. George K. Zucker (Jefferson, NC, 2005), 99–111.

2. Among them are, for instance, Moshe Lazar and Aldina Quintana, "Ladino," in *Encyclopedia Judaica*, 2nd ed., eds. Michael Berenbaum and Fred Skolnik (Detroit, 2007); Ralph Penny, "Dialect Contact and Social Networks in Judeo-Spanish," *Romance Philology* 46, no. 2 (1992): 125–140; Laura Minervini, "The Formation of the Judeo-Spanish Koiné: Dialect Convergence in the Sixteenth Century," in *The Proceedings of the Tenth Conference on Judeo-Spanish Studies*, ed. Annette Benaim (London, 1999), 41–53.

3. For instance, this view is shared by Simon Marcus, "A-t-il existé en Espagne un dialecte judéo-espagnol?" *Sefarad* 22 (1962): 129–49. David M. Bunis is of the same opinion and even believes that this language emerged as early as the 11th century. See his "Judeo-Spanish," in *Encyclopedia of Jews in the Islamic World* (henceforth, EJIW), ed. Norman Stillman (Leiden, 2010).

4. Elaine R. Miller, "The Debate over Pre-Expulsion Judeo-Spanish: Status Quaestionis," in *Languages and Literatures of Sephardic and Oriental Jews: Proceedings of the Sixth International Congress for Research on the Sephardi and Oriental Jewish Heritage*, ed. David M. Bunis (Jerusalem, 2009), 167–187.

5. Ibid., 178.

6. Ibid., 169.

7. Minervini, who also believes that the question of a Jewish language in Spain is an ideological one, rightly points out that Iberian Jews "did not have a common linguistic variety other than Hebrew, used only by some members of the community for some kinds of written texts; rather they used different linguistic varieties diffused in the Iberian Peninsula (Castilian, Leonese, Aragonese, Catalan, Navarran, Galician, Portuguese, etc.)." ("The Formation of the Judeo-Spanish Koiné," 41.)

8. Charles A. Ferguson, "Diglossia," *Word* 15 (1959): 325–340, 336.

9. Joshua Fishman, "Bilingualism and Biculturalism as Individual and as Societal Phenomena," in *Language and Ethnicity in Minority Sociolinguistic Perspective*, ed. Joshua Fishman (Clevedon, 1989), 181–201, 183.

10. David Gonzalo Maeso and Pascual Recuero, eds., *Me'am Lo'ez. El gran comentario bíblico sefard* (Madrid, 1964), vol. 0 (Tomo Preliminar), 146.

11. Seth Schwartz, "Language, Power and Identity in Ancient Palestine," *Past and Present* 148 (1995): 3–47, 18.

12. Irene E. Zwiep, *Mother of Reason and Revelation: A Short History of Medieval Jewish Linguistic Thought* (Amsterdam, 1997), 232.

13. Quoted in David Wacks, "Toward a History of Hispano-Hebrew Literature in its Romance Context," *eHumanista* 14 (2010): 178–209, 184.

14. Kirsten Fudeman, *Vernacular Voices: Language and Identity in Medieval French Jewish Communities* (Philadelphia, 2010), 85.

15. Annette Benaim, *Sixteenth-Century Judeo-Spanish Testimonies: An Edition of Eighty-Four Testimonies from the Sephardic Responsa in the Ottoman Empire* (Leiden, 2012), 66.

16. Wacks, "Vernacular anxiety and the Semitic imaginary: Shem Tov Isaac ibn Ardutiel de Carrion and his critics," *Journal of Medieval Iberian Studies* 4, no. 2 (2012): 167–184, 174.

17. On the correspondence with Guzman and Santillana, see Gutwirth, "Medieval Romance Epistolarity: The Case of the Iberian Jews," *Neophilologus* 84, no. 2 (2000): 207–224.

18. Gutwirth, "Jews and Courts: An Introduction," *Jewish History* 21, no. 1 (2007): 3, 11–13.

19. James Nelson Novoa, "Ms. Parma Pal. 2666 as a Document of Sephardi Literary and Philosophical Expression in Fifteenth-Century Spain," *European Judaism* 43, no. 2 (2010): 20–36.

20. It has been suggested that these glossaries might indicate that the Parma manuscript was put together by a Jew or a *converso* who was studying Maimonides but had insufficient knowledge of Hebrew, especially of philosophical terms. (Ibid., 28.)

21. Haim Beinart, "The *Conversos* and Their Fate," in *Spain and the Jews*, ed. Elie Kedourie (London, 1992), 92–122, 92. Although this figure seems to be exaggerated, there is no way to establish the real numbers.

22. See Henry Kamen, "The Expulsion: Purpose and Consequence," in *Spain and the Jews*, 74–91, 76.

23. Ibid., 77.

24. On this case, see Gutwirth, "Elementos étnicos e históricos en las relaciones judeo-conversas en Segovia," in *Jews and Converso*, ed. Yosef Kaplan (Jerusalem, 1985), 83–102.

25. Beinart, "The *Conversos* and Their Fate," 106.

26. For instance, Elke Klein discusses the Jewish-Christian relations in the sphere of law. See her article, "The Widow's Portion: Law, Custom, and Marital Property Among Medieval Catalan Jews," *Viator* 31 (2000): 147–163.

27. See Francisco Cantero Burgos, "El Cancionero de Baena: judíos y conversos en él," *Sefarad* 26 (1967): 71–101.

28. Cristina Arbós, "Los cancioneros castellanos del siglo XV como fuente para la historia de los judíos españoles," in *Jews and Converso*, 74–82, 79.

29. Gutwirth, "Dialogue and the City, circa 1400: Pero Ferruz and the Rabbis of Alcala," *Jewish History* 21 (2007): 43–67, 56–57. Later, he composed *Sevillana medicina*, considered a pioneering work of medicine in a vernacular.

30. Gutwirth, "Towards Expulsion: 1391–1492," in *Spain and the Jews*, 51–73, 60.

31. Ibid.

32. Hava Tirosh-Samuelson, "Jewish Philosophy on the Eve of Modernity," in *History of Jewish Philosophers*, eds. D. H. Frank and D. Leaman (London, 1997), 499–563, 505.

33. Ibid., 504.

34. Gutwirth, "Towards Expulsion," 60.

35. Tirosh-Samuelson, "Jewish Philosophy on the Eve of Modernity," 503.

36. See Maxim Kerkhof, ed., "Un fragmento desconocido del compendio de dichos de sabios y philósofos, traducido del catalán al castellano por Jacob Çadique de Uclés en 1402": http://parnaseo.uv.es/Lemir/textos/Kerkhof/Dichos.htm (accessed April 13, 2013).

37. For such authors, see Wacks, "Toward a History of Hispano-Hebrew Literature," 200.

38. Ibid., 183. There is no reason to go from the extreme of the isolation theory to the extreme of claiming Jews' full participation in Spanish culture.

39. Sonia Fellous, "Moise Arragel un traducteur juif au service des Chrétiens," in *Transmission et Passages en monde juif*, ed. Esther Benbassa (Paris, 1997), 119–136.

40. Ibid., 122.

41. Ibid., 125.

42. Ibid., 131.

43. See Ora (Rodrigue) Schwartzwald, "The Relationship between Ladino Liturgical Texts and Spanish Bibles," in *The Hebrew Bible in Fifteenth-Century Spain: Exegesis, Literature, Philosophy, and the Arts*, eds. Jonathan Decter and Arturo Prats (Leiden and Boston, 2012), 223–244.

44. Fellous, "Moise Arragel," 133.

45. For a discussion of Arragel's intended audience, see Schwartzwald, "The Relationship between Ladino Liturgical Texts," 320, esp. n. 27.

46. Fellous, "Moise Arragel," 122–123.

47. Ibid., 123.

48. See Gutwirth, "Medieval Romance Epistolarity: The Case of the Iberian Jews," *Neophilologus* 84, no. 2 (2000): 207–224, 207.

49. Ibid., 212.

50. Ibid., 220.

51. Gutwirth, "*Hercules furens* and war: on Abrabanel's courtly context," *Jewish History* 23 (2009): 293–312, 299.

52. See John M. Zemke, *Critical Approaches to the "Proverbios morales" of Shem Tov de Carrión: An Annotated Bibliography* (Newark, 1997).

53. Iñigo López de Mendoza, Marqués de Santillana, *Proemio e carta al condestable de Portugal,* ed. Ángel Gómez-Moreno (Barcelona, 1990), 61–62.

54. "Sem Tob de Carrión, *Proverbios morales,*" in *Diccionario filológico de literatura medieval española*, eds. C. Alvar and J. M. Lucía (Madrid, 2009), 941–944.

55. See Gutwirth, "A medieval manuscript of gnomic verse in Judeo-Spanish *aljamía,*" in *Circa 1492*, ed. Isaac Benabu (Jerusalem, 1992), 98–108.

56. A fragment of this manuscript can be seen at "Textos clasicos españoles ladinizados": http://btjerusalem.com/aspamiac.htm (accessed May 18, 2013).

57. For a discussion of various interpretations, see Susan L. Einbinder, "Pen and Scissors: A Medieval Debate," *Hebrew Union College Annual* 65 (1994–1995): 261–276.

58. Wacks, "Vernacular anxiety," 178.

59. Ibid., 181.

60. Curt Leviant, "General Introduction," in *King Artus. A Hebrew Arthurian Novel of 1279*, ed. and trans. C. Leviant (New York, 1969), 55.

61. This subject will be discussed in chapter 1.

62. Elaine R. Miller, "Hebrew Verb Forms in the Valladolid Taqqanot of 1432," in *Proceedings of the Twelfth British Conference on Judeo-Spanish Studies*, eds. Hilary Pomeroy and Michael Alpert (Leiden and Boston, 2004), 57–68, 67.

63. For instance, in the Ladino prayer book for women discussed in chapter 1.

ONE

Ladino in the Sixteenth Century

THE EMERGENCE OF A NEW VERNACULAR LITERATURE

During the sixteenth century, as a consequence of the 1490s expulsions and continuous mass immigration of Iberian Jews to the Ottoman lands, a new speech community emerged there. It consisted of tens of thousands of speakers whose linguistic interaction led to the formation of a new Ibero-Romance interdialect that later stabilized as the Ladino koiné. Forced conversions in Portugal and the adoption of Judaism by converts and their children upon immigration to the Ottoman Empire brought a new readership into existence: Jews with limited or no Hebrew proficiency in need of a Jewish education. This necessity led to the emergence of a vernacular literature for Sephardi Jews that had not existed in Christian Iberia where Jewish authors wrote in Ibero-Romance only for Christians, using the Latin alphabet for this purpose.[1] The new vernacular audience, albeit numerically small, was more heterogeneous than ever, because it included a large spectrum of readers from barely literate Jews who had never abandoned Judaism to educated ex-*conversos* who were fluent in European languages. This historically unique sociocultural situation lasted only until the turn of the seventeenth century. This chapter looks at the sociopolitical processes that led to the emergence of a Sephardi community in the Ottoman lands; it discusses its linguistic makeup and examines the birth and decline of the vernacular literature that served its needs.

The Formation of the Sephardi Community in Salonica and Constantinople

On March 31, 1492, Catholic monarchs Ferdinand and Isabella signed the Edict of Expulsion of the Jews from Spain and its possessions. Proclaimed a month later, the Edict gave Jews three months to leave or convert. As a result, there were no more Jews in the kingdoms of Castile and Aragon after July 31, 1492.

A similar decree was issued in December 1496 in Portugal, where a large number of Spanish Jews found refuge. Under these circumstances, most Sephardim, including victims of forced mass baptisms, left the country in 1497. After that, the borders closed for mass emigration. Those who preferred to convert and remain in Portugal were given twenty years to embrace their new faith without the fear of being prosecuted for religious transgressions. However, in 1536, under pressure from Spain, the tribunal of the Inquisition was instituted in Portugal, which caused a new wave of *converso* emigration. Unable to integrate into a hostile Christian society and fearing for their lives, great numbers of converts chose to join the first refugees in Italy, North Africa, the Low Countries, and the Ottoman Empire.

In the absence of reliable statistics, scholars estimated the total number of Iberian exiles to be between 100,000 and 150,000.[2] While it was dangerous to return to Judaism in European states (none of which offered Iberian refugees permanent residency), Ottoman authorities, who accepted the largest number of Sephardi immigrants without imposing any restrictions, allowed them to practice their religion freely, and offered the Jewish community as a whole a great deal of autonomy.[3]

The flow of Sephardi exiles coming directly or indirectly from the Iberian Peninsula continued through the first decades of the eighteenth century, but the majority settled in the Ottoman lands in the sixteenth century and the early seventeenth. Scholars disagree about the number of Iberian Jews who arrived in the Ottoman Empire after 1492, but the most realistic estimate, based on Ottoman tax registers, puts it at around 60,000.[4] The two largest centers of Jewish immigration in the empire were Constantinople and Salonica. In the sixteenth century, the Sephardi community of Constantinople did not exceed 1,045 households, i.e., approximately 5,225 people, forming around one third of the city's Jewish population, the rest being mainly Romaniots (local Greek-speaking Jews) and some Ashkenazim.[5]

In the city of Salonica, there were no Jews in 1478, because local Romaniots had been deported to Constantinople as part of Mehmed II's plan for repopulating the Ottoman capital.[6] A new community was established in Salonica in 1492 by Jewish immigrants fleeing persecution in Europe. Already by 1519, 53.23 percent of households in the city were Jewish.[7] By 1530–1531, 59.23 percent of the city's permanent inhabitants were European Jewish immigrants and their descendants who formed a community that consisted of twenty Sephardi congregations "comprising 2,548 households and one Ashkenazi congregation made up of 97 households."[8]

In 1530–1531, about 127 families, i.e., 4.98 percent of "Sephardic" immigrants, were Italian Jews, some of whom had come from Sicily in 1493, and from Calabria and Apulia in 1497.[9] Calabrian Jews continued to immigrate through 1551 when they were joined by refugees from Naples and, after the accession of Pope Paul IV (1555–1559), by Jews from the Papal States and other Italian cities. After the Inquisition was established in Portugal in 1536, followed by the institution of discriminatory laws similar to "purity of blood" statutes adopted in Spain, a significant number of *conversos* arrived from Portugal.[10] Between 1530 and 1567, Salonica's Jewish population increased from 2,645 households to 2,883 households and 2,271 unmarried adult males.[11] In 1613, these numbers were 2,933 and 2,270 respectively, which corresponded to 63.98 percent of the city's inhabitants.[12]

These statistics show that the overwhelming majority of Salonican Jews were Sephardim who continued to arrive through the early seventeenth century, and who spoke mutually understandable Ibero-Romance languages and dialects. In the sixteenth century, Castilian and Portuguese differed less than they do now. More important, in Portugal, where Castilian had higher cultural prestige and functioned as a literary language starting in the late fifteenth century, educated people knew both languages. Besides, it should be remembered that a significant number of Spanish exiles had spent at least a few years in Portugal. As a result, many Sephardim in Europe and the Ottoman lands were bilingual.[13] Because of this, Almosnino, whose family came from Aragon, was able to serve as a rabbi at the congregation founded in Salonica in December 1559 for the purposes of accommodating a new wave of Portuguese refugees.[14] Livyat Hen (Chaplet of Grace), named after its foundress, was established by Gracia Nasi, one of the most prominent Portuguese ex-*conversos* who had come to Constantinople via Italy and the Low Countries in 1553.[15]

She was particularly dedicated to Jewish education and the welfare of Portuguese exiles. In 1554, Gracia Nasi was joined by her nephew and son-in-law, Joseph Nasi, a prosperous merchant and influential courtier whom, in 1566, Sultan Selim II (r. 1566–1574) made Duke of Naxos.[16] Almosnino, undoubtedly, owed his new appointment to his acquaintance, or even friendship, with Joseph Nasi.

Initially, Sephardi congregations were established according to the immigrants' places of origin, and named after Castile, Aragon, Majorca, Portugal, Lisbon, Córdoba, or Sicily, uniting refugees who spoke the same language or dialect and shared the same customs. In the 1570s, a renowned Salonican rabbi, Joseph ibn Lev, noted that "every language group in Salonika had its own congregation," whereas in Constantinople people moved from one congregation to another.[17]

Over time the congregations grew too big for one synagogue, which, together with tax assessment-related discord, often led to a proliferation of new ones that were organized along different principles. For instance, Almosnino's grandparents on both sides, who fled Aragon in 1492, were among the founders of the Catalan congregation.[18] After a series of bitter conflicts, it split into Catalan Yashan and Catalan Hadash (Old Catalan and New Catalan), and then the former split once again.[19]

The numerical predominance of Iberian Jews and the reinforcement of their vernacular, thanks to the continuous flow of new immigrants, led to the cultural and linguistic assimilation of Italian Jews. Sephardim who came from Italy in the 1550s were also fluent in Spanish, which would have accelerated this process.[20] There is evidence showing that by the 1580s, Apulians were no longer able to read or write in their language.[21] The weakening of linguistic and cultural barriers already in the 1550s is illustrated by the fact that Almosnino, who started his career as a rabbi at his own Catalan synagogue, was hired by the Calabria Yashan (Neveh Shalom), after the Calabrian congregation had split into three smaller ones in 1553.[22]

What Languages Did Ottoman Sephardim Speak in the Sixteenth Century?

In the nineteenth century, Sephardi intellectuals erroneously believed that Iberian exiles had initially spoken "pure" Castilian, and that their own language was a product of its "corruption." First of all, in the Ottoman Empire Castilian was spoken only by immigrants from Castile. Second, Ladino is not a form of Castilian, but a koiné, that is a new language formed as a result of contact between two or more mutually intelligible varieties of the same language.[23] So, while refugees from Castile spoke Castilian, those from other parts of Iberia and Italy used Aragonese, Catalan, Calabrian, and other languages or dialects. Furthermore, the varieties spoken by their descendants born in the Ottoman Empire differed from those of the immigrants, which is reflected in private letters and court statements included in rabbinic responsa.

Until recently, the corpus of generally available non-literary texts from the sixteenth century consisted only of some communal ordinances, a few letters found in the Cairo Geniza, and a few testimonies included in responsa.[24] The vernacular fragments from eighty-four rabbinic responsa published by Annette Benaim in 2012 significantly expanded this corpus.[25] Benaim's material is as close to the speech of Ottoman Jews as one can expect given the fact that responsa were usually published after the rabbis' deaths, and were edited and corrected by various scribes and scholars.

These eighty-four vernacular fragments, whose length varies from three lines to a few pages, were inserted into the Hebrew frame of rabbinic responsa, arguably for the sake of preserving the authenticity of testimonies. Among the respondents are such celebrated scholars as Samuel de Medina, Isaac Adarbi, Moses Trani, Joseph ibn Lev, and a few others. As for the witnesses whose vernacular testimonies are discussed by these rabbis, we do not always know in what part of the Ottoman Empire they lived, but it is clear that many were residents of Salonica and Constantinople. Judging by their testimonies, some were well-off merchants while others were less prosperous and less educated men.

Since these 84 texts cover a large variety of topics—such as betrothals, divorces, trade, travel, financial operations, the status of ex-*conversos*, and all other legal matters that Jewish courts in the Ottoman Empire were entitled to adjudicate—they contain lexis from all spheres of Sephardim's lives. The bulk of this vocabulary consists of Romance elements, yet it also includes Hebrew and Turkish loans. Most Hebrew terms, including many abbreviations, are related to religious practices and halakhic (legal) matters, while others are used as euphemisms of various kinds. Since Ottoman Turkish was the official language of the empire, several administrative, judicial, and financial terms of Turkish and Arabic origins entered Ladino, even though few Sephardim actually knew vernacular Turkish, let alone Ottoman (the artificial language of bureaucracy).

In Benaim's corpus, Turkish terms are mainly used in texts dealing with taxes and judicial or administrative issues. Thus, text 47, which discusses a payment receipt, contains six Turkish words in four lines.[26] On the other hand, some testimonies, especially those dealing with marriage and travel, contain no or very few non-Romance loans. Some of these texts would have been fully comprehensible to Spaniards if the Hebrew terms had been replaced with Spanish ones. Yet testimonies treating halakhic matters, such as text 1, on wine importation, could not have been easily adapted because the translation of Hebrew terms would have rendered this testimony meaningless.[27] It is evident, therefore, that Sephardim were able to speak an Ibero-Romance variety comprehensible to all Spanish speakers, but in certain situations their speech, regardless of their intentions, would have been unintelligible to non-Jews.

The linguistic analysis of the eighty-four vernacular texts published by Benaim confirms the conclusions reached in earlier studies of very few non-literary sources available at the time.[28] It is evident that the language spoken by Ottoman Jews in the sixteenth century had numerous phonological, morphological, lexical, and syntactic features that, at the time of the expulsion, were no longer present in Castilian but still found in Aragonese, Leonese, Catalan, Galician, or Portuguese, while others were never attested in Castilian. For instance, the initial /f/ was dropped by Castilian but retained by Catalan, Galician, and Portuguese and was adopted by Ladino (e.g., *(h)allar ~ fallar*). The Ladino adverb *onde* ("where") was borrowed from Aragonese rather than the Castilian *donde*.[29] Some nouns preserved their Latin gender in Aragonese but not in Castilian (e.g., *el fin* in Castilian ~ *la fin* in Aragonese and Ladino).[30] Among other morphological borrowings attested in sixteenth-century Ladino texts is the Portuguese article *a* occasionally used instead of the Castilian *la*. Portuguese influence is also observable on the syntactic level, namely, in the frequent use of *tener* as an auxiliary verb (instead of *haber*). In addition to Ibero-Romance, Hebrew, and Turkish loans, sixteenth-century Ladino had numerous Italian ones, some of which were later dropped. For instance, *eskiraso* (from *schirazzo*, "boat with square sails") is not found in later Ladino texts.[31]

Aside from containing loans and retentions (which led many scholars to describe it as an extremely conservative language), already in the sixteenth century, Ladino produced several innovations on the phonological and lexical levels, though not all of them were successful.[32] In fact, Ralph Penny, who studied phonetic and phonological innovations, emphasizes the openness of Ladino to change, which he explains by certain social processes generated by the resettlement of Iberian Jews.[33] While some innovations (such as *seseo* and *yeísmo* occurring in other Spanish dialects are accounted for by dialect contact, others have no antecedents in any of Ibero-Romance varieties.)[34] Thus, Judeo-Spanish is the only Spanish variety that neutralized the phonological opposition /r/ ~ /r:/ in all positions (cf. *pero* ~ *perro* in Castilian).[35] Another successful innovation is the metathesis *rd* > *dr* (e.g., *tarde* > *tadre*) widely attested both in literary and non-literary documents.[36]

Still, the most salient feature of sixteenth-century Ladino, widespread polymorphism at all levels, often found within one text, was a result of dialect contact and innovations. Among the variations generated by dialect contact is the variation between forms with the diphthong /ue/ and /ie/ and with a simple vowel /o/ and /e/ respectively (as in *ruego* ~ *rogo* or *prieto* ~ *preto*). In both cases "the diphthongal forms were contributed by speakers from the areas of Castile, Leon, and Aragon, while the non-diphthongal forms originated in the speech of those from Galicia, Portugal, and Catalan-speaking regions."[37]

The number and character of innovations and the co-occurrence of competing forms attested in the available sixteenth-century sources indicate that it was a period of active formation of a Judeo-Spanish koiné, resulting from contact between a number of mutually intelligible Ibero-Romance dialects that led to their mixing, followed by leveling and simplification. The widespread heterogeneity of forms, however, shows that the process of leveling through reduction of competing variants was only incipient.[38] In other words, in the sixteenth century, Ladino was still at the stage that Peter Trudgill called "interdialect."[39]

It is believed that the second stage of koineization, namely, focusing (variant reduction) when the new dialect chooses the simplest available variants, can happen as early as in the first generation of native-born speakers and usually no later than the fourth.[40] But in the case of Ladino, it took much longer. Among other factors, this results from the fact that later immigrants, who had significant linguistic influence due to their higher social mobility, brought many non-Castilian innovations.[41] Furthermore, the process of leveling was somewhat delayed, owing to Sephardim's tendency to establish congregations on the geographic principle, which also facilitated penetration into the Judeo-Spanish koiné of a larger number of non-Castilian elements, especially on the lexical level.[42] Finally, unlike the koinés in nineteenth- and twentieth-century immigrant communities studied by Trudgill and others, Ladino emerged when mass media did not exist, and it was not taught in school, which would have accelerated the process of focusing.

Since very few seventeenth-century Ladino texts have survived, it is difficult to establish when exactly the stabilization of the koiné happened. Still, while Ladino was never formally standardized, it can be said that starting in the eighteenth century, competing forms were mainly distributed geographically, corresponding to three distinct koinés that resulted from the convergence of different combinations of Iberian varieties and Italian dialects.[43] In any case, it is obvious that the formation of Ladino began in the sixteenth century (not in the seventeenth, as some scholars claim), when Sephardim first immigrated to the Ottoman lands. Furthermore, this process may have continued for about two hundred years without interruption. Finally, we must bear in mind that during that period there were considerable differences between the written and spoken varieties.[44] Hence, the concept of "pre-Judeo-Spanish" that presents the language used by Ottoman Jews before the appearance of *Meam Loez* (1730) as something that has "not yet" happened, merely a stage on the way to linguistic fullness somehow achieved by the early eighteenth century, is untenable on all counts.

What Languages Did Ottoman Sephardim Read and Write in the Sixteenth Century?

As before the expulsion, the sociolinguistic situation in the Sephardi community in the sixteenth century was marked by diglossia, though of a more complex nature. While the functions of Hebrew remained largely the same, the vernacular acquired new ones. Rabbis continued to produce Hebrew works, but only some were intended for printing as they often addressed a very small group of readers. They circulated among the rabbinic elite in manuscript form. Very few important Ladino works, most notably Moses Almosnino's *Crónica*, also survived as manuscripts, but others (including two of his short treatises) perished as they were not preserved, due to the low status of vernacular literature. In general, as Matthias Lehmann points out, "a Judeo-Spanish book in manuscript effectively did not exist, because it would not generate interest among the limited elite audience that would have access to such a manuscript."[45] For this reason, most extant sixteenth-century vernacular works are printed books.

The leading centers of Jewish printing in the Ottoman Empire were Constantinople and Salonica, where the first printing presses were established in 1493 and around 1510 respectively, by Iberian exiles.[46] In the sixteenth century, these and a few other presses printed around 400 books, only about seven percent of which were written in Ladino.[47] This is not surprising since, at the time, books were intended mainly for the "educated class of students, rabbis, and scholars, and members of the upper levels of the society, who received private education, and not for the lower classes of the general public."[48]

But this does not mean that like in later periods, Ladino books were produced only for uneducated people. On the contrary, as we will see, many extant Ladino texts from the sixteenth century targeted rather sophisticated readers as they were intended primarily for *conversos* embracing normative Judaism, and a significant number of them indeed belonged to the upper social strata and tended to be educated, albeit not knowledgeable in Judaism. While living in Europe, most had secretly continued to practice some form of Judaism, if only by observing a few rituals, and thus were not so much ignorant "as they lacked systematic instruction."[49] It was necessary, therefore, to provide immigrants with a means of quick acquisition of "basic Judaism," such as a vernacular translation of the Bible and the *siddur* (prayer book) in a readable script. But the Latin alphabet was unacceptable.

Instead, upon arrival in the Ottoman lands, male *conversos* were required to learn Hebrew, a fact accounting for a significant number of Hebrew grammars published in the sixteenth century starting in 1505–1506.[50] In addition, a Hebrew-Ladino glossary, *Shaar ha-Yesod*, was published in 1536.[51] Another glossary, *Heshek Shelomo*, was imported from Venice (1588 and 1617).[52] Once immigrants learned the Hebrew alphabet, they were able to read books in Ladino. For instance, the publisher of a vernacular text explained that he printed it in "a Ladino of full [i.e., square Hebrew] letters with vowel-points, so that all can make use of it, even he who knows no more than the letters and the vowels."[53]

Until the end of the nineteenth century, almost all Ladino texts were printed in Hebrew characters, predominantly in the semi-cursive known as Rashi script. Translations and adaptations of sacred and semi-sacred texts were printed in *meruba* (block letters), which were mostly vocalized.[54] Unlike the *meruba* that indicates vowels by means of points, Rashi script uses for this purpose *matres lectionis*, i.e., consonants that can function as vowels (e.g., *heh* is used to indicate [h] and [a]).

Among the first Ladino books we find a translation of the Psalms (Constantinople, 1540) and the famous Constantinople Pentateuch in Hebrew, Greek, and Ladino, published in 1547 by Eliezer ben Gershom Soncino who used square Hebrew letters with vowel signs.[55] An abridged Ladino version of *Shulchan Aruch* entitled *Shulchan hapanim* or *Mesa de el alma* first appeared in Salonica in 1568, only three years after its first Hebrew edition.[56] The following year, one of the most influential works of Jewish philosophical ethics, Bahya ibn Paquda's *Hovot ha-levavot* (The Duties of the Heart), was translated into Ladino and published in Constantinople under the title *Obligasyon de los korasones*.[57] The translator, r. Joseph Formon, echoing many of his colleagues, states in the introduction to this edition (printed in block letters with vowel points) that he wanted to divulge ibn Paquda's teaching among his coreligionists "in Ladino, because this language is the most commonly used among us."[58]

Gedaliah Cordovero, publisher of the anonymous Hebrew-Ladino glossary *Heshek Shelomo* mentioned above found it necessary to produce an affordable glossary of "somewhat difficult" biblical terms, because the bilingual editions of the Bible published in Constantinople and Salonica were too expensive for many people. To keep costs down, the publisher decided not to use vowel points, confident that even without them the book would be accessible to every man able to read a business letter.[59] In other words, this glossary was to serve as a learning tool for small merchants of unspecified origins without a good Jewish education.

The following books, on the other hand, targeted a more affluent and educated, largely ex-*converso* reading public in Salonica. The first, the only extant Ladino *siddur* for women produced in the Ottoman Empire, came out around 1565.[60] In his preface, the editor, r. Meir Ban Benist (who also produced the Ladino *Shulchan Aruch*), stresses that it is the responsibility of fathers and husbands to educate their wives and daughters and teach them to read. One of the purposes of this prayer book is to enable women to celebrate Jewish holidays including Passover, in the absence of men, a common practice in Jewish families. Obviously, only prosperous merchants would travel so far as not to be able to return home for the holidays. The audience for whom Ban Benist intended his *siddur* explicitly included ex-*conversas*, because he indicates that unlike the rest, women who were not born Jewish should not bless God for not creating them gentiles.[61]

The other book meant for an educated audience, *Fuente klara* (The clear spring), first came out in Salonica around 1595.[62] It is a work of Jewish apologetics designed to serve as a tool of re-education for Iberian ex-*conversos*. Its anonymous author, a philosopher and physician, apparently an ex-*converso* himself, who spent many years in Italy and Northern Europe (hence his thorough knowledge of Protestantism), explains to his readers the superiority of Judaism over Christianity. Resorting to the traditional Jewish argument and using the works of Aristotle, Ptolomy, and Galen, the author refutes Christianity for being irrational and contradicting common sense. In 1601, the same Salonican press published *Dialogo del kolorado* (A treatise on scarlet fever) written by another ex-*converso* physician, Daniel de Ávila Gallego, for educational purposes.[63]

The fact that the latter two books, as well as *Libro entitulado Yehus Zadikim* (A book on the burials of *tzadiks* in the Holy Land) (c. 1592), were published at the turn of the seventeenth century means that descendants of *conversos* raised in the Christian world continued to immigrate to the Ottoman Empire, albeit in smaller numbers, and that there were still enough educated men unable to read in Hebrew to justify these publications.[64]

Thus, in the sixteenth century, Ladino served as a language of instruction for Jews of various backgrounds and social classes—for the unlearned who had never converted to Christianity but whose reading was limited to a few biblical passages and prayers, and for educated ex-*conversos* interested in various Jewish subjects, but not yet fluent in Hebrew. The success of the Sephardim's educational project based on translating religious texts into Ladino was admiringly summarized by a contemporary, a rabbi from an Arabic-speaking community:

> [Their] teachers teach them Torah word for word as it is written in their Ladino tongue. . . . They have only a few unlearned amongst them, except for the Converses who have only recently returned to Judaism, and they too have produced a number of wise and educated scholars . . . because they were familiar with the language in which Torah was studied.[65]

Aside from educational purposes, Ladino was used for practical instructions and rules. In fact, the first known Ladino book was *Dinim de shehitah i bedikah* (The rules of ritual slaughter and inspection of animals) (Constantinople, c. 1510), meant to insure that in exile, ritual slaughterers illiterate in Hebrew would have clear instructions for observing the laws of *kashrut.*[66] Almosnino produced at least two "user's manuals" (discussed in the following chapter) explaining how to operate an astrolabe and the sundial he made himself. Perhaps there were more texts in the vernacular containing practical instructions for various activities that did not survive because they were written by obscure authors.

Like in Iberia, the vernacular was considered appropriate for scientific treatises. Thus, the famous work on astronomy, *Ha-Hibbur ha-Gadol* (commonly known by its Latin name, *Almanac perpetuum*), written by the outstanding Spanish scholar Abraham Zacuto in the 1470s, which was immediately translated into Castilian and Latin, appeared in Salonica in 1568 in *aljamiya* under the Hebrew title *Be-ur Luhot Kevod Rav Avraham Zakkut* (The explanation of the tables of the Honorable

Rav Abraham Zacuto).[67] As previously mentioned, a medical treatise, *Dialogo del kolorado*, was also printed in Salonica in 1601.

There is intriguing albeit unreliable evidence of the existence of a vernacular book on medicine used in Constantinople in the sixteenth century. It is mentioned in the anonymous Spanish travelogue *Viaje de Turquía* (Travels in Turkey, 1557?), which is based on a few eyewitness accounts and contains useful information on the lives of Ottoman Jews in the capital. The narrator, a Spaniard captured by Turks, trying to save his life and return home, pretends to be a physician and is successful in treating the governor of Constantinople. This arouses the jealousy of his master's Jewish doctor who wants to discredit the newcomer in the Pasha's eyes. One day, the Jew decides to test his competitor's knowledge of medicine in public and brings out a big book that, according to the narrator, looks like a "church book" and is written in Hebrew letters. The Spaniard asks the Jew about the language of the book and hears in response that it is "pure Castilian ([*lengua*] *fina castellana*), a language common to the two" of them.[68] It is impossible to identify this book (which presumably contained directions for the use of leeches) as one of a few of those circulated among Iberian Jews, for instance *Thesaurum pauperum*, or *Summa experimentorum medicinalis*, an influential medical treatise (also present in the Parma manuscript discussed in the prologue) by Portuguese scholar Petrus Hispanus, later Pope John XXI.[69] Another famous medical work that circulated in the sixteenth century in an *aljamiya* version (found in the Cairo Geniza) belongs to Luis Llobera de Ávila, a physician at the court of Charles V.[70] Usually, scientific texts originally written in Castilian were simply transliterated into Hebrew characters, which is why, from a linguistic standpoint, they do not present much interest for this study.

Some linguists believe that certain sixteenth-century texts were written in Judeo-Spanish while others used Spanish (i.e., Castilian).[71] One of the most consistent proponents of this approach, Aldina Quintana, postulates the existence of a diglossic relationship within the Ottoman Sephardi community between two Romance varieties, where Peninsular Spanish functions as the high variety and Judeo-Spanish as the low one.[72] Obviously, this Fergussonian diglossia would have existed within a broader relationship between two genealogically unrelated languages, namely, Hebrew and the vernacular. This means that Hebrew was the language of law, religion, and rabbinic literature, whereas "Spanish" served as the language of high secular and semi-religious production, leaving all other functions to Judeo-Spanish.

According to this view, there were only three authors whose works, all of them written or published in Salonica, used "Spanish," namely, Moses Almosnino, Daniel de Ávila Gallego, and the anonymous author of *Fuente klara*. Most other extant vernacular books published in Constantinople and Salonica in the sixteenth century are commonly considered to be written in Judeo-Spanish. They are mainly adaptations of Hebrew texts meant to serve as educational tools for those who were not fluent in Hebrew.

A third corpus consists of texts that are neither "Spanish" nor Judeo-Spanish. They are translations of the Bible, prayer books, and other liturgical texts. The mode of these translations is usually called "Ladino-calque" or simply "Ladino."[73] According to Ora Schwartzwald's hypothesis, it was formed during centuries of oral transmission of sacred texts that were recorded in print only after the expulsion, in Latin script in Europe, and in Hebrew characters in the Ottoman Empire.[74] Due to the fundamental structural differences between Semitic and Romance languages, these word-for-word translations were hard to understand for those who were not already familiar with the text and did not know Hebrew. Not only did the word order and morphological and syntactic structures calque the Hebrew original, but even the choice of words was often dictated by their phonetic similarity rather than meaning. Isaac Jerusalmi suggests that these translations were meant to enable the reader unfamiliar with Hebrew to follow Talmudic discussions.[75]

I believe that calling the language of the three above-mentioned works "Spanish" without any qualifications is both incorrect and misleading, and not only because of the great number of interferences from other languages and varieties but, more important, because it is written in a non-Latin script incomprehensible to Spaniards, and thus explicitly intended for a different audience. While the use of two alphabets for one language does not have any effect on it, the same text written in different scripts is likely to have different messages for each target audience. Of course, scripts were also associated with respective religions.[76] All of this explains why when Christian minorities began to write in their own scripts the languages of Muslim majorities, they gave them new names. Thus, Turkish written in Greek characters was called "Karamanli" and Arabic written in Syriac characters "Garshuni." Moreover, Armeno-Turkish literature, that is, Turkish-language works written in Armenian characters, is considered a branch of Armenian literature, because it was designed to meet the needs of Turkish-speaking Armenians in the Ottoman Empire and eastern Europe.[77] Of course, at all times many Ottoman Jews, including those who knew that their language differed from Castilian Spanish, called their language *espanyol* (later, also *muestro espanyol* [our Spanish]). Yet no other Spanish was used in the empire, so there was no need to make a distinction.

Contradictions and misconceptions caused by the use of "Spanish" in reference to some sixteenth-century texts can be resolved if we adopt a somewhat different approach to Sephardim's linguistic practices, and change the terminology correspondingly. If we describe the range of options available to sixteenth-century Sephardi speakers in terms of their functions, the two-level diglossic situation postulated by Quintana becomes a one-level relationship. Since the Ladino koiné was still far from being stabilized, and Castilian enjoyed the highest social prestige among Ibero-Romance varieties, the literary language used by the three Salonican authors, where Castilian elements were dominant, may be seen as a high register (or functional style) of Ladino.[78] As for the other two registers, they are effectively treated as such by Schwartzwald in her analysis of the women's *siddur*. She describes the "Ladino" of prayers and the "Judeo-Spanish" of the translator's instructions as a "written formal style" and one "reminiscent of speech," respectively.[79] Iacob Hassán and Pilar Romeu, speaking about "Ladino-calque" define it as a "stylistic variety."[80]

Thus, all sixteenth-century vernacular texts produced in the Ottoman Empire can be divided into three groups in terms of register. The first includes most translations and explanations of religious precepts, such as *La Mesa de el alma* or instructions for prayers in the women's *siddur*. While their language contains a great number of Hebrew calques and loans, it is much closer to the spoken variety (known to us from responsa) than the translations of the Bible and liturgical texts that form the second group. The third and smallest group is comprised only of original works, namely, *Fuente klara, Dialogo del kolorado,* and the five extant vernacular works written by Almosnino.

As we can see, the sixteenth-century linguistic situation in the Sephardi community was more complex than in earlier periods, chiefly as a result of mass conversions followed by the return of many converts to Judaism, which necessitated their re-education in a language they understood. This led, for the first time, to the production of books in the vernacular. Since sixteenth-century Ladino texts had different cultural statuses and targeted different audiences, they required different functional styles. In the following chapters, I will show how, as a result of particular sociocultural dynamics, some of these registers acquired new functions or disappeared and were replaced by others.

The Role of the Latin Alphabet in Sixteenth-Century Sephardi Culture

In terms of personal and cultural connections, the sixteenth century was the most "European" era in the history of Ottoman Jews, even more so than the period of westernization in the last third of the nineteenth century. Nonetheless, not a single text in Latin script from that time has reached us. Given that all printing presses were brought from Italy and Portugal one would expect that some would have produced books in European languages. Indeed, Pierre Belon who traveled in the Ottoman lands in 1546–1549, writes that the Jews who had been expelled from Spain and Portugal and settled in Turkey, printed Hebrew books in Constantinople without any restrictions. Besides, "[t]hey print in Spanish, Italian, Latin, Greek, and German, but they do not print anything in Turkish or Arabic because they are not allowed to."[81]

Belon's compatriot, Nicolas de Nicolay, who visited the empire in 1551, seems to confirm this evidence by saying that the Jews "banished and driven out of Spain and Portugal . . . set up printing, not before seen in those countries [Ottoman lands]" and print books "in diverse languages, [such] as Greek, Latin, Italian, Spanish, and the Hebrew tongue, being to them natural, but are not permitted to print the Turkish or Arabian tongue."[82] This author, however, is known for frequently using second-hand information.[83] It is obvious, in fact, that de Nicolay's account, first published thirteen years after Belon's travelogue, is partly borrowed from it (a common practice at the time) and, therefore, does not have much historical value.[84]

Although in general, Belon is a rather reliable eyewitness, he says on the same page that many Ottoman Jews knew ten or twelve languages, which is an obvious exaggeration. His statement about Jewish book printing appears somewhat questionable for two reasons. To begin with, while it is known that Jewish presses were authorized by Ottoman authorities to print books in Hebrew and Latin characters, none of the books in Latin script allegedly published in the Ottoman Empire in the sixteenth century has survived or has been mentioned by title or author.[85] Second, as we will see in the following chapter, Sephardi scholars who came to the Ottoman Empire from Europe and continued to produce works in Latin script, sent them to Italy to be printed by Christians. In light of all this, I suggest that in reality no more than a few books in Latin or Greek scripts could have been published, and, not preserved in genizas, they must have perished.

Latin characters do not appear in extant Hebrew or Ladino books printed in the sixteenth century. It is noteworthy that Gershom Soncino, who had Latin fonts in Italy, either did not bring them to the Ottoman Empire or never used them there.[86] All of this suggests that the presses approved by Ottoman rabbis (rather than the state) had only Hebrew fonts. The rabbis' negative attitude toward the use of the Latin alphabet was expressed by r. Isaac Gershon, publisher of the reprint of the Ladino adaptation of *Shulchan Aruch.* Justifying the use of the vernacular by referring to Maimonides who wrote in Arabic, he warns against any attempts to transcribe this Ladino text into Latin characters, which would make it accessible to gentiles who got ahold of all Jewish books printed in Italy.[87] However, this admonition to the Jews of Venice would not have made much sense in the Ottoman Empire, where the use of the Latin alphabet, if not explicitly banned, was probably disapproved of by rabbis concerned about protecting the masses from Christian influence. Reading Christian texts was considered safe for scholars, including Moses Almosnino and Joseph Taitazak, but harmful to those who were not sufficiently educated, for the same reason that works on philosophy were believed to be unsuitable for the general public.[88]

In Salonica, the rabbis' efforts to regulate publishing led to the establishment of rabbinic censorship twenty-five years earlier than in Europe.[89] On August 15, 1529, six rabbis (r. Taitazak among them) signed a document that introduced preliminary censorship of all books to be published in the city. Under the threat of excommunication, it was forbidden to print or buy books that had not been unanimously approved by the council consisting of six rabbis.[90] Though this document claims that "things that were not worthy of being printed were printed" in Salonica, it is unclear what kinds of works were considered inappropriate, and whether this regulation was ever enforced.[91] Nevertheless, Joseph Hacker suggests that it might explain why the well-known Italian printer, Gershom Soncino, who came to Salonica around 1526, moved to Constantinople five years later.[92] There is no direct evidence substantiating this assumption, but Hacker's idea that the purpose of rabbinic censorship was to prevent the publication of popular literature, such as plays and chivalric romances, presumably printed by Gershom Soncino, is plausible.[93] We know for certain, however, that in 1533 in Constantinople he printed *Las Koplas de Yosef*, a well-known medieval poem that served both educational and entertainment purposes.[94]

We may assume that few Iberian Jews among those who came directly to the Ottoman lands knew the Latin alphabet, yet Latin-script literacy would have been common among ex-*conversos*. It is unlikely, however, that they would have taught their children to read in European languages. Nonetheless, some works of secular European literature reached even those Ottoman Jews who knew only the Hebrew alphabet, and not just Sephardim. Thus, in 1540, Gershom Soncino's son, Eliezer Soncino, published a Hebrew rewriting of *Amadís de Gaula* made by the Sephardi physician Yacob ben Moshe Algaba who hoped to instruct his readers "in matters of the world."[95] This edition must have been intended not just for local Sephardim, but also for Romaniots who did not yet have a press of their own, as well as for export to Italy. In fact, it appears to have been popular among Italian Jews for a long time. In 1652, in Venice, a rabbi censured those who read Ariosto's *Orlando Furioso*, *Amadís de Gaula*, and "similar profane books, which are not allowed to be read on sabbatt."[96]

Ottoman Jews, in turn, would have received from Italy Joseph Tsarfati's Hebrew translation of *Celestina* produced in 1507, though this famous tragicomedy written almost entirely by Fernando de Rojas, a Castilian *converso*, in 1499, would have reached Iberian exiles in the original.[97] Unfortunately, we do not know for certain which Castilian books were available to Ottoman Sephardim in the sixteenth century.

It is clear, however, that some were familiar with a few poems by Jorge Manrique (1440–1479), a major Castilian poet whose works began to appear in 1492, and thus would have been brought to the Ottoman Empire by later immigrants or travelers.

Jorge Manrique, a great nephew of Marqués de Santillana, was therefore distantly related to Pablo de Santa Maria, the most infamous *converso* on the Peninsula. The *converso* connection may account for the publication of Manrique's most celebrated poem, *Coplas por la muerte de su padre* (1492; *Stanzas for the Death of His Father*) in 1554 in Ferrara, by the Portuguese Jew Abraham Usque, publisher of the famous *Ferrara Bible* (1553) dedicated to Gracia Nasi.[98] Twenty-three of Manrique's stanzas appeared as an addendum to Alfonso de la Torre's *Visión deleitable*. Since de la Torre was believed to be of *converso* origin, and his work, as will be remembered, was popular among Iberian Jews, this publication probably suggests that Manrique was also claimed by Sephardim as their own.[99] This would explain why the *Coplas* were at least partly transliterated into Hebrew characters by an anonymous admirer in the Ottoman lands.[100]

Of course this text in its entirety (480 lines) with its allusions to Jesus and the war against Muslims would not have been acceptable for a Sephardi audience, but the solemn biblical tone of the poem and its Ecclesiastes-like view of life as a temporary stage on the way to eternity were consonant with Jewish thought. Thus, Manrique's image of human lives as rivers going to the sea is reminiscent of a biblical one: "All the rivers run into the sea . . . unto the place from whence the rivers come, thither they return again" (Eccl 1:7).

Almosnino evidently appreciated the poetry of this *famoso trovador* (famous poet), as he referred to Manrique. In *Rejimyento* (fol. 30a), we find a direct quotation from his poem "O, mundo! Pues que nos matas," a poignant rumination about life and death, which speaks to all humans regardless of religion. Furthermore, I believe that the dedication of *Rejimyento* contains an allusion to Manrique's *Coplas*. Almosnino dedicated to his nephew this book *en el kual se kontyene kuanto konbyene para poder byen andar toda la jornada de la vida umana sin erar* (fol. 1a) (that contains everything needed to make the journey of human life without mistakes). These words bring to mind the famous lines from the *Coplas*: *cumple tener buen tino / para andar esta jornada / sin errar* (one needs good understanding to make this journey without mistakes).

Another Castilian author known to many Sephardim was Antonio de Guevara (1480–1545). His book *Reloj de príncipes o libro aureo del emperador Marco Aurelio* (The Dial of Princes, or The Golden Book of Marcus Aurelius) (1529) was translated into many languages and remained immensely popular for most of the sixteenth century. One of the most powerful chapters of this work—"De lo que dixo un villano del Danubio . . . a todo el senado de Roma" (Book Two, XXXI) understood by contemporaries as an attack on the injustices of the Inquisition—reached Ottoman Sephardim in a Hebrew translation as part of *Shevet Yehuda* (Judah's Staff), a celebrated work on Jewish history. Its principal author, Solomon ibn Verga, was born in Spain, but spent many years in Portugal and Italy as a *converso* before settling in the Ottoman Empire.[101] *Shevet Yehuda* was edited and expanded by his son, Joseph (d. c. 1559), a rabbi in Edirne (Adrianople), where the book was first published in 1550.

Twentieth-century scholars, starting with Fritz Baer, revealed its connections to Spanish literature, namely the works of Alfonso de la Torre and Antonio de Guevara. Eliezer Gutwirth's analysis of its stylistic strategies further uncovered its literary genealogy and demonstrated that many of its motifs were "prominent in late medieval and/or early sixteenth-century Hispanic sources (Jewish and Christian), and particularly those that appear in the thoughts and writings of the *conversos*."[102] Baer described the speech of the Jewish ambassador to the Roman Senate in ibn Verga's book, which is based on the chapter from the *Libro aureo* mentioned above, as the first "translation into Hebrew of a belletristic prose work from a modern European language."[103]

Despite the fact that the majority of Ottoman Jews did not know the Latin alphabet, European Renaissance culture reached many of them

> through contacts with exiled Italian Jewish scholars in the Ottoman Empire, social and business ties between branches of extended Sephardic families, joint ventures with Italian publishing houses, and contacts with former converses who brought the masterpieces of Spanish and Italian letters.[104]

Obviously, knowledge of foreign languages was indispensable for merchants engaged in international trade that was conducted not only in Spanish, but also in Portuguese and Italian.[105] Furthermore, in 1555, the papal bull *Cum nimis absurdum* forbade Jews to keep their account books in Hebrew if they wanted to use them as proof in Christian courts.[106] Since Ottoman Jews had many partners in Italian cities where they spent a lot of time, this ordinance was relevant to them, forcing them to read and write in Latin characters. In addition, since Muslims were not allowed to learn foreign languages for fear that they would imitate their speakers in other ways, European consuls and factors often hired local Jews as translators (*dragomans*) and agents (although in later periods Christian merchants tended to prefer their Ottoman coreligionists). Thus, at least in port cities, there were always small groups of Sephardim who were fluent, at least in Italian, but only in the sixteenth century was Latin-script literacy found among rabbis and community leaders, which is why it was only during that period that European high culture was available to those Ottoman Jews who knew just the Hebrew script.[107]

The End of the First Period of Ladino Literature

Ladino literature emerged at a moment when the Empire's economy was thriving, which ensured the prosperity of its new Jewish communities. The Jews of Constantinople and Salonica were able to afford multiple printing presses that produced books for an audience able to buy them. A few Hebrew books were also published in Edirne, Cairo (by Eliezer Soncino's grandson), and Safed (Tzfat).

This first publishing boom was followed by a decline in book production in Constantinople and a hiatus everywhere else (the shortest one in Salonica), which is usually explained by a general economic downturn in the Ottoman Empire. Yet economic decline per se does not explain why, to the best of our knowledge, no Ladino books appeared between 1601 (Gallego's *Dialogo del kolorado* in Salonica) and 1728 (a Ladino version of Joseph Sambari's *Divre Yosef* in Constantinople).

By the end of the sixteenth century, Salonica's economy began to experience a crisis caused primarily by the decline of the city's textile industry, which employed the majority of local Jews of both sexes. As Salonican manufacturers proved unable to compete with higher quality English and Dutch broadcloth aggressively imported by Europeans, demand for their fabrics sharply dropped. Another blow was the rising price of local raw wool that was now exported to Europe.[108] Furthermore, in the early seventeenth century, the Ottoman Empire entered a monetary crisis caused both by internal and external factors.

These economic developments, together with numerous plagues and fires in the first half of the seventeenth century, led to the mass emigration of Salonican Jews to more prosperous Ottoman cities, causing the community's further impoverishment. Among those who left were not only the most socially mobile artisans but also some prominent rabbis. It is not surprising, therefore, that few books (in Hebrew) appeared in Salonica in the seventeenth century. "In times of economic downturn, scholars suffered from the uncertainty of philanthropic backing, and had to cope with the erosion of the support network that had made much of their production possible."[109] Moreover, in Salonica, in the early seventeenth century, the community leadership, in search of additional sources of revenue, decided to tax Torah scholars, despite the long-standing custom of exempting them from taxation.[110]

If we go back to the statistics, we will notice that during the thirty-six years between 1567 and 1613, the flow of immigrants to Salonica significantly dwindled: during that period, the Jewish population increased by only fifty families, whereas over the previous thirty-six years, 138 new families had settled in the city.[111] This phenomenon was related to the changing nature of immigration. The majority of Iberian refugees, who had left the Peninsula in the 1490s to continue a Jewish life, came to the Ottoman lands mostly before 1510.[112] As for those who converted under duress, many of them tried to survive as Christians in Iberia or Western Europe, often leading a double life, but eventually ended up in the Ottoman Empire, fleeing the Inquisition. Most were merchants (such as Joseph Nasi), though some served as physicians (like Amatus Lusitanus). Those immigrants arrived in Constantinople, Salonica, and other Ottoman cities in the second half of the sixteenth century.

Other *conversos* (or their descendants, also referred to as such) successful in business, managed to survive in Europe by moving from one state to another, until they found safe haven in Venice, Amsterdam, or Livorno where they could both lead a Jewish life and prosper in trade. That is why they were not attracted to communities in crisis with slow commerce. European Christians, for their part, needed *conversos* who had family or business connections in all parts of the world and were thus useful for international trade. This factor eventually shaped the policies of many European states regarding Jews and "new Christians." Jonathan Israel sees this period as the turning point for Jewish existence in most of Europe: "The tentative readmission of Jewry into western and central Europe from the 1570s onwards signaled a reversal of trends which had previously prevailed everywhere west of Poland."[113] As a result, immigration to the Ottoman Empire virtually ended.

The decline of *converso* immigration to the economically weakened Ottoman Empire undermined the position of local Sephardim even more by limiting their connections and hence, their role in international commerce, which was eventually taken over by Greeks and Armenians. Meanwhile, Jews continued to cultivate ties with the Porte, as in the days of Joseph Nasi. Hence, as the Ottoman administration began to lose its position, so did Jews who were engaged in tax farming and internal trade.[114] This was particularly true for the Jewish community of Constantinople which, not engaged in industry, did not experience a deep crisis but entered a long period of stagnation.

Minna Rozen rightly points out that, "[a]s long as immigration from Europe continued, even if on a tiny scale, Jewish society in the empire underwent a process of ferment and change. Once immigration ceased, the catalyst for change disappeared."[115] This was true for all aspects of intellectual life, including rabbinic writings. As new legal questions became less frequent, rabbis turned their attention away from the *Halakhah* and, for various reasons, became much more engaged in mysticism, producing works intended for a small readership and, therefore, circulated in manuscript form.

Once the *converso* immigration came almost to a standstill, there was no longer a need for new vernacular books. Some published in the previous period were still available, and a few others were reprinted in Venice in Hebrew script. For instance, as has been said, the Hebrew-Ladino glossary *Heshek Shelomo* was reproduced in Venice in 1617, and the vernacular version of Joseph Karo's *Shulchan Aruch* appeared there in 1602. Venice provided sufficient numbers of paraliturgical books that were most needed by Sephardim. Thus, *Pirke Avot* (Ethics of the Fathers) first came out in Venice in 1601 and was reprinted multiple times. The same is true for *Seder Haggadah shel Pesach* (order of the Passover

Haggadah) published in 1609 and reproduced a few more times. A Hebrew commentary on the *Song of Songs*, with a Ladino translation, first published in Salonica in 1600, appeared in Venice in 1659.[116]

Thus, general impoverishment and audience decrease ended the first period of Ladino literature. When it re-emerged, however, it turned out that Moses Almosnino, the most important Sephardi vernacular author after Shem Tob de Carrión and the first born in the Ottoman lands, had not been forgotten. The next three chapters focus entirely on Almosnino's vernacular texts and his intended and actual readers.

Notes

1. Nelson Novoa rightly points out that the works of Jewish apologetics produced before the expulsion were often intended both for Christians and Jews who "had embraced the Christian faith and had been estranged from Hebrew." ("The Peninsula Hither and Thither: Philosophical Texts in Vernacular Languages by Sephardic Jews before and after the Expulsion," *Hispania Judaica* 8 [2011]: 149–166, 156.) The same is true for Arrugal's Bible translation. However, none of these works would have been produced if they had not been commissioned by Cristians, or their authors had not aimed at a Christian audience. Besides, those "Jews" were also Christians.

2. See discussion in Esther Benbassa and Aron Rodrigue, *Sephardi Jewry: A History of the Judeo-Spanish Community, 14th–20th Centuries* (Berkeley, 2000), xxxvii.

3. On the legal and actual status of Ottoman Jews, see Minna Rozen, *A History of the Jewish Community in Istanbul: The Formative Years, 1453–1566* (Leiden, 2002), 16–34.

4. See Benbassa and Rodrigue, *Sephardi Jewry*, 9–10, 202–203nn27–40.

5. See chart on p. 51 in Rozen, *Istanbul*.

6. Heath W. Lowry, "When did the Sephardim arrive in Salonica? The Testimony of the Ottoman Tax-Registers, 1478–1613," in *The Jews of the Ottoman Empire*, ed. A. Levi (Princeton NJ, 1994), 203–214, 206.

7. Ibid., 207.

8. Ibid., 209.

9. Ibid., 206.

10. See Fernanda Olival, "Rigor e interesses: os estatutos de limpeza de sangue em Portugal," *Cadernos de Estudos Sefarditas* 4 (2004): 151–182.

11. Lowry, "When did the Sephardim arrive in Salonica?," 208. The number of unmarried males for 1530 is not available. The significant number of unmarried men may indicate that they came from other Balkan cities for work.

12. Ibid., 204.

13. Nevertheless, as Yosef Yerushalmi points out: "the Bible and the liturgy were always printed in Spanish, never in Portuguese, even though from the end of the sixteenth century most of the Marranos were of Portuguese rather than of Spanish extraction." ("The Re-education of Marranos in the Seventeenth Century." The Third Annual Rabbi Louis Feinberg Memorial Lecture in Judaic Studies [Cincinnati, 1980], 8.)

14. Emmanuel, *Histoire des Israélites de Salonique*, 177, 216–218; Cecil Roth, *Doña Gracia of the House of Nasi* (Skokie IL, 2001), 128–131.

15. For her biography, see ibid.

16. For his biography, see Roth, *The House of Nasi: The Duke of Naxos* (Philadelphia, 1947).

17. Rozen, *Istanbul*, 90.

18. Catalan was once the official language of the Kingdom of Aragon and continued to be widely used there. Almosnino's family probably spoke both Aragonese and Catalan.

19. Emmanuel, *Histoire*, 146.

20. See Minervini, "'*Llevaron de acá nuestra lengua . . .*' Gli usi linguistici degli ebrei spagnoli in Italia," *Medioevo romanzo* 19, no. 1–2 (1994): 133–192.

21. Rozen, "Individual and Community in the Jewish Society of the Ottoman Empire: Salonika in the Sixteenth Century," in *The Jews of the Ottoman Empire*, 215–274, 219.

22. Emmanuel, *Histoire*, 147.

23. See "Koinés," in R. Mesthrie, *Concise Encyclopedia of Sociolinguistics* (Amsterdam, 2001), 485–489.

24. For communal ordinances, see Abraham Danon, "La Communauté juive de Salonique au XVIè siècle," *Revue des Études Juives* 41 (1900): 250–265.

On other non-literary sources, see for instance, Gutwirth, "A Judeo-Spanish Letter from the Genizah" in *Judeo-Romance Languages*, eds. I. Benabu and Joseph Sermoneta (Jerusalem, 1985), 127–138; Quintana, "Responsa Testimonies and Letters Written in the 16th Century Spanish Spoken by Sephardim," *Hispania Judaica* 5 (2007): 283–302.

25. Annette Benaim, *Sixteenth-Century Judeo-Spanish Testimonies: Eighty-four Testimonies from the Sephardic Responsa in the Ottoman Empire* (Leiden and Boston, 2012).

26. Ibid., 353–354.

27. Ibid., 191–196.

28. See Minervini, "Formation of the Judeo-Spanish Koiné: Dialect Convergence in the Sixteenth Century," in *The Proceedings of the Tenth Conference on Judeo-Spanish Studies*, ed. Annette Benaim (London, 1999), 41–53.

29. Benaim, *Sixteenth-Century Judeo-Spanish Testimonies*, 153. In sixteenth-century Castilian, *onde* was the equivalent of the modern *de donde* ("from where").

30. Benaim, *Sixteenth-Century Judeo-Spanish Testimonies,* 162.

31. Ibid., 239. See text 14:8.

32. For an excellent summary and classification of sixteenth-century innovations, see Minervini, "Formation of the Judeo-Spanish Koiné."

33. See Ralph Penny, "Dialect Contact and Social Networks in Judeo-Spanish," *Romance Philology* 46, no. 2 (1992): 125–140.

34. *Seseo* is neutralization of the opposition between /s/ (as in *paso*) and /θ/ (as in *mozo*) in favor of /s/. *Yeísmo* is neutralization of the opposition between /ly/ (as in *ella*) and /y/ (as in *yo*) in favor of /y/.

35. Penny, "Dialect Contact and Social Networks," 136–137.

36. Benaim, *Sixteenth-Century Judeo-Spanish Testimonies,* 145.

37. Penny, "Dialect Contact and Social Networks," 129.

38. On the emergence of the Judeo-Spanish koiné, see Minervini, "Formation of the Judeo-Spanish Koiné," 52.

39. On the formation of immigrant koinés and dialect levelling, see Peter Trudgill, "Migration, New Dialect Formation and Sociolinguistic Refunctionalisation: Reallocation as an Outcome of Dialect Contact," *Transactions of the Philological Society* 97, no. 2 (1999): 245–256.

40. Trudgill, *Dialects in Contact* (Oxford, 1986), 95.

41. For other factors, see Quintana Rodríguez, *Geografía lingüística del Judeoespañol: Estudio sincrónico y diacrónico* (Bern, 2006), 302–303.

42. Ibid., 303.

43. On the formation of the koinés of Salonica, Istanbul, and Sarajevo, see ibid., 298–311.

44. Romero, *Creación literaria,* 18.

45. Lehmann, *Ladino Rabbinic Literature,* 40.

46. Joseph Hacker claims that this happened in 1510. ("Authors, Readers, and Printers of Sixteenth-Century Hebrew Books in the Ottoman Empire," in *Perspectives on the Hebraic Book. The Myron M. Weinstein Memorial Lectures at the Library of Congress*, ed. Peggy K. Pearlstein [Washington, DC, 2012], 17–64, 25.) Minna Rosen believes it was 1515. ("Salonica" in EJIW). On the controversial dating of their first book, see Adri K. Offenberg, "The Printing History of the Constantinople Hebrew Incunable of 1493: A Mediterranean Voyage of Discovery," *The British Library Journal* 22 (1997): 221–235.

47. Hacker, "Authors, Readers, and Printers," 19.

48. Ibid., 20.

49. Yerushalmi, "The Re-education of Marranos," 8.

50. The first was David ibn Yahya, *Sefer lashon limodim be'huchmat ha-'dikduk le'hacham ha'shamle* (Constantinople, 1505–1506). (See Yaari, *Hebrew Printing,* no. 4. [Heb.])

51. Ibid., no. 123.

52. Romero, *Creación literaria,* 37.

53. Quoted in Yerushalmi, "The Re-education of Marranos," 9. This comment offers further proof that despite possible difficulties in oral communication, Spanish and Portuguese immigrants were able to read the same texts.

54. David Bunis, *The Historical Development of Judezmo Orthography: A Brief Sketch* (New York, 1974), 20. For more on the scripts used by Sephardim, see idem, *Guide to Reading and Writing Judezmo* (New York, 1975); M. Beit-Arié, "La caligrafía hebrea en España: desarrollo, ramificaciones y vicisitudes," in *Moreshet Sefarad: el legado de Sefarad*, ed. Haim Beinart (Jerusalem, 1992), vol. 1, 289–301.

55. Yaari, *Hebrew Printing*, nos. 130, 144.

56. Yerushalmi, "The Re-education of Marranos," 9.

57. Yaari, *Hebrew Printing*, no. 174.

58. Quoted in Molho, *Literatura sefardita de Oriente* (Madrid, 1960), 229.

59. Quoted in Romero, *Creación literaria*, 37–38.

60. Ora (Rodrigue) Schwarzwald, ed., trans., *Sidur para Mujeres en Ladino: Salonica, Siglo XVI* (Jerusalem, 2012).

61. Quoted in Schwarzwald, "Two Sixteenth-Century Ladino Prayer Books for Women," *European Judaism*, 43, no. 2 (2010): 35–49, 40.

62. Pilar Romeu Ferré, ed. and introduction, *Fuente clara* (Barcelona, 2011).

63. Daniel de Ávila Gallego, *Diálogo del colorado*, ed. and introduction Pilar Romeu Ferré (Barcelona, 2014). Romeu, "Introduction," in *Fuente clara*, 33.

64. Yaari, *Hebrew Printing*, no. 229. It was printed at Belvedere, the Nasi family mansion near Constantinople.

65. Quoted in Hacker, "The Intellectual Activity of the Jews of the Ottoman Empire During the Sixteenth and Seventeenth Centuries," in *Jewish Thought in the Seventeenth Century*, eds. Isadore Twersky and Bernard Septimus (Cambridge MA, 1987), 95–135, 108.

66. Yaari, *Hebrew Printing*, no. 29.

67. See "Abraham Zacuto," *Encyclopedia Judaica*.

68. Marie-Sol Ortola, ed., *Viaje de Turquía* (Madrid, 2000), 317. Of course, the narrator's question seems odd since he could see Hebrew letters.

69. Nelson Novoa, "Ms. Parma Pal. 2666," 29–30.

70. On this and other works on medicine that circulated among Sephardim in the sixteenth century, see Gutwirth, "On the Hispanicity of Sephardic Jewry," *Revue des Études Juives* 145, no. 3–4 (1986): 347–357, 349–350.

71. For instance, Coloma Lleal, *El judezmo. El dialecto sefardí y su historia* (Barcelona, 1992), 18; Quintana, "From Linguistic Segregation Outside the Common Framework of Hispanic Languages to a de facto Standard," in *Studies in Modern Hebrew and Jewish Languages Presented to Ora (Rodrigue) Schwarzwald*, ed. Malka Muchnik and Tsvi Sadan (Jerusalem, 2012), 697–714, 701.

72. Quintana, "Aportación lingüística de los romances aragonés y portugués a la coiné judeoespañola," in *Languages and Literatures of Sephardic and*

Oriental Jews: Proceedings of the Sixth International Congress for Research on the Sephardi and Oriental Jews, ed. David Bunis (Jerusalem, 2009), 221–255, 226.

73. See Haim-Vidal Sephiha, *Le Ladino, judéo-espagnol calque* (Paris, 1973).

74. See Schwarzwald, "The Relationship between Ladino Liturgical Texts and Spanish Bibles," in *The Hebrew Bible in Fifteenth-Century Spain*, ed. J. Decter and A. Prats (Leiden, 2012), 223–244.

75. Isaac Jerusalmi, *From Ottoman Turkish to Ladino. The Case of Mehmet Sadik Rifat Pasha's Risale-i Ahlik to Judge Yehezkel Gabbay's Buen Dotrino* (Cincinnati, OH, 1990), 28–29.

76. One Ladino periodical in the nineteenth century and many in the twentieth moved to the Latin script in areas where it was more familiar to the majority of readers than the Hebrew alphabet. Yet, even though the Latin alphabet was already associated with Europe rather than with Christianity, the editors felt the need to apologize and explain to readers that this was a temporary measure while they were waiting to receive a Hebrew font (that apparently never arrived). Cf. *El Luzero de la pasensia* (November 21, 1885, 1); *El Buletino mensual de la comunidad israelita de Rodes* (November 1928, 2).

77. See "Introduction" in *Eremya Chelebi Komurjian's Armeno-Turkish poem "The Jewish Bride,"* eds. Avedis K. Sanjian and Andreas Tietze (Wiesbaden, 1981), 9.

78. Paloma Díaz-Mas talks about four registers used by various social groups defined by the speakers' gender, age, occupation, education, etc. (*Sephardim: The Jews from Spain* [Chicago, 1992], 91–97.)

79. See Schwarzwald, "Linguistic Features of a Sixteenth-Century Women's Ladino Prayer Book: The Language Used for Instructions and Prayers," in *Selected Papers from the Fifteenth British Conference on Judeo-Spanish Studies*, eds. Hilary Pomeroy, Chris J. Pountain, and Elena Romero (London, 2012), 247–260.

80. Romeu, Hassán, "Apuntes sobre la lengua de la *Crónica de los reyes otomanos*," 168.

81. Pierre Belon du Mans, *Les observations de plusieurs singularités et choses mémorables trouvées en Grèce, Asie, Judée, Egypte, Arabie . . .* (Paris, 1555), part III, ch. 13, 145b.

82. Nicolas de Nicolay, *The Navigations, Peregrinations, and Voyages Made into Turkie* (London, 1585), 131a. (Translator unknown.) Spelling adjusted to the modern standard.

83. Albert Howe Lybyer, *The Government of the Ottoman Empire in the Time of Suleiman the Magnificent* (Cambridge, MA, 1913), 317.

84. Hacker suggests that similar evidence found in the account published by Czech traveler Krystof Harant in 1607 might have been partly borrowed from Belon, but "it is unlikely that he copied the entire description." And, given what we do know about Jewish printing in the seventeenth century, "in sum,

the evidence is credible." (Hacker, "Authors, Readers, and Printers," 18). And yet Harant did copy the whole description from Belon who, a few pages further, says that Jews made their Christian slaves work at their press on holidays. So, regardless of whether we trust Belon, there is no reason to believe that Harant had firsthand information. Hence, since Nicolas de Nicolay also borrowed information from his predecessor, we are down to possibly only one eyewitness account of Jewish printing in the sixteenth century. As for the seventeenth century, I deal with it in chapter 5.

85. Fatma Müge Göçek, *East Encounters West: France and the Ottoman Empire in the Eighteenth Century* (New York and Oxford, 1987), 112.

86. Joseph R. Hacker and Adam Shear, *Jewish Culture and Contexts: Hebrew Book in Early Modern Italy* (Philadelphia, 2011), 73.

87. See Yerushalmi, "The Re-education of Marranos," 9.

88. Taitazak even taught Latin scholastic sources (Hava Tirosh-Samuelson, "The Ultimate End of Human Life in Post-Expulsion Philosophical Literature," in *Crisis and Continuity in the Sephardic World: 1391–1648*, ed. Benjamin R. Gampel [New York, 1997], 223–254, 233). For instance, at the turn of the sixteenth century, in Constantinople, Solomon Almoli produced a philosophic encyclopedia, but out of "fear that philosophy could be harmful to those ill equipped to study it," he printed only the introduction and kept the body of the work in a manuscript, hence, unavailable to the general public. (Ibid., 232).

89. Preliminary rabbinic censorship was first instituted in Europe in 1554 in Ferrara, where a convention of Italian rabbis decided that thereafter no Hebrew book could be printed without written permission of three rabbis and the congregation's president. Purchasing books published without such permission was also forbidden. ("Approbation," *The Jewish Encyclopedia.*)

90. Danon, "La Communauté juive de Salonique," 229. See also Document 23.

91. Quoted in Hacker, "Authors, Readers, and Printers," 59.

92. Ibid., 30.

93. Ibid., 52 n. 44; 59 n. 107.

94. See Minervini, "Les *Coplas de Yosef* de la Genizah du Caire," *Revue des Études Juives* 163, no. 3–4 (2004): 429–444.

95. Yaari, *Hebrew Printing*, no. 128.

96. Minervini, "An *Aljamiado* Version of 'Orlando Furioso': A Judeo-Spanish Transcription of Jeronimo de Urrea's Translation," in *Hispano-Jewish Civilization After 1492: The Fourth International Congress for Research and Study of Sephardi and Oriental Jewish Heritage*, eds. Michel Abitbol, Galit Hasan-Rokem, and Yom-Tov Assis (Jerusalem, 1997), 191–201, 192. This obviously contradicts Wacks's assumption that the Hebrew Amadis was a commercial failure. David Wacks, *Double Diaspora in Sephardic Literature* (Bloomington, 2015), 205; Carmoly, *La Famille Almosnino*, 11.

97. Only Tsarfati's introductory poem is extant. See Dwayne E. Carpenter, "A *Converso* Best-Seller: *Celestina* and Her Foreign Offspring," in *Crisis and Creativity*, 267–281.

98. Helder Macedo, "A Sixteenth Century Portuguese Novel and the Jewish Press in Ferrara," *European Judaism* 33, no. 1 (2000): 53–58, 53.

99. Vincent Barletta, in a private email, suggested that the theme of these 23 stanzas "fits with the broader philosophical and generally religious focus of the *Visión deleitable*. It also seems likely that Manrique's fame was used to sell more copies of the book."

100. A fragment of this text can be found at "Textos clasicos españoles ladinizados": http://btjerusalem.com/aspamiac.htm (accessed May 18, 2013).

101. María José Cano, "Introduction," in Selomoh ibn Verga, *La vara de Yehudah (Sefer sebet Yehudah)* (Barcelona, 1991), 9–12.

102. Gutwirth, "Expulsion from Spain and Jewish Historiography," *Jewish History, Essays in Honour of Chimen Abramsky*, eds. Ada Rapoport-Albert and Steven Zipperstein (London, 1988), 141–161, 144.

103. Ibid., 153. I assume Baer did not consider the Hebrew version of the *Amadís* translation.

104. Tirosh-Samuelson, "The Ultimate End of Human Life," 238.

105. Francesca Trivellato, *The Familiarity of Strangers: The Sephardic Diaspora, Livorno, and Cross Cultural Trade in the Early Modern Period* (New Haven & London, 2008), 178.

106. Ibid.

107. As will be discussed in chapter 5, most rabbis opposed the study of European languages even in the late nineteenth century, although there were exceptions. Documents studied by Matthias Lehmann indicate that in the eighteenth century, Jewish officials in Istanbul "sent letters in Judeo-Spanish (in Latin characters) when they needed to address the Livorno lay leaders directly." (*Emissaries from the Holy Land: The Sephardic Diaspora and the Practice of Pan-Judaism in the Eighteenth Century* [Stanford, CA, 2014], 81.) Yet just one person able to write in Latin characters would have been enough for this.

108. See Benjamin Braude, "International Competition and Domestic Cloth in the Ottoman Empire, 1500–1650," *Review of the Fernand Braudel Center* 2 (1979): 437–451, 445–446.

109. Benbassa and Rodrigue, *Sephardi Jewry*, 56.

110. Rozen, *Facing the Sea: The Jews of Salonika in the Ottoman Era (1430–1912)* (Afula, 2011), 27.

111. Of course, some people were leaving Salonica, but not yet in large numbers. And, more important, most continued to be registered in their home communities.

112. Lowry, "When did the Sephardim arrive in Salonica?" 209.

113. Jonathan I. Israel, *European Jewry in the Age of Mercantilism, 1550–1750*, 2nd ed. (Oxford, 1989), 35.

114. See Daniel Goffman, "Jews in Early Modern Ottoman Commerce," in *Jews, Turks, Ottomans*, ed. Avigdor Levy (Syracuse, 2002), 15–34.

115. Rozen, "The People," in *The Cambridge History of Turkey*, vol. 3: *The Later Ottoman Empire, 1603–1839*, ed. Surayia Faroqhi (Cambridge, 2006), 255–271, 262.

116. Minnervini, "*Llevaron de acá nuestra lengua . . .*," 157.

TWO

Almosnino's Epistles

A NEW GENRE FOR A NEW AUDIENCE

As John Zemke rightly observes, historians do not agree on several essential facts of Almosnino's life, including the years of his birth and death. Yet all scholars coincide "in the portrayal of an extraordinary figure in Salonican communal life," a man who advanced the Jewish community's interests during a critical period in its history.[1] Hava Tirosh-Samuelson who has studied Almosnino's philosophical and ethical works describes him as "the pre-eminent philosopher" of his day.[2] It is far beyond the scope of this study to establish which facts are true, or to discuss Almosnino's scholarship. My chief goal in this chapter is to show how Almosnino created a new literary subgenre that while rooted in Peninsular culture, served the needs of a new audience—educated Iberian exiles. My second purpose is related to the main one. Although it is taken for granted that Ottoman Jews read Castilian literature in the sixteenth century, one finds almost no specific studies that would prove this assumption.[3]

My close reading of Almosnino's Ladino works, as previously mentioned, points to some Castilian authors and texts with which he and other Sephardi intellectuals might have been familiar.

Almosnino and His World

Moses ben Baruch Almosnino (1518–1580), one of the most celebrated Salonicans, was very much part of the new Ottoman Sephardi culture, both by birth and by choice. The Almosnino family was established in the thirteenth century at Jaca in Aragon (Huesca province), where three of its members were prominent Jewish community leaders in the 1270s–1280s.[4] A few members of the Almosnino family are mentioned as book owners in the 1415 inventory of the Jewish libraries of Jaca.[5] In 1465, Abraham Almosnino helped with the readmission of a *converso* to Judaism, for which he was burned at the stake on December 10, 1489. Along with him died Asach Cocumbriel, a maternal ancestor of Moses Almosnino. Afterward, the victims' families fled Aragon for Salonica, where they were among the founders of the Catalan community (without being Catalans themselves). We know that in mid-sixteenth century, Baruch Almosnino (d. 1563), father of Moses, was the head of this congregation and legal proprietor of the synagogue. He had three sons and a daughter; his eldest son took over the family's financial affairs, while his second, Moses, chose to become a scholar.[6] Moses's first wife, Doña Simha, died in 1554, leaving him two sons and a daughter.[7] As we learn from one of his sermons, his daughter moved to Edirne where she gave birth to a boy during her father's long mission in Constantinople.[8] Almosnino's two sons and nephew published some of his works posthumously.[9]

A respected halakhist, celebrated orator, and famous teacher, Moses Almosnino was invited to adjudicate law, preach, teach, and participate in the communal affairs of various Salonican congregations and the Jewish community of the city as a whole. The fact that his twenty-eight extant sermons were delivered at seven different synagogues and the Talmud Torah, testifies to his popularity as a preacher.[10] Judging by his published sermons (Constantinople 1582, Venice 1588), he did not preach every Sabbath, but only on holidays or Sabbaths preceding Purim, Passover, and Yom Kippur, and on special occasions in the life of the community.[11] He also gave eulogies for members of his family (for instance, his mother) and various notables, including Doña Gracia Nasi and her younger nephew, Don Samuel Nasi.[12]

Almosnino's particular commitment to the education of ex-*conversos* is revealed, among other things, by the first condition under which he accepted the appointment at the Portuguese congregation Livyat Hen: in addition to Saturdays, members were required to attend services on Mondays and Thursdays when scriptural readings were included in the ritual.[13] Having served for ten years at Livyat Hen as a *marbiz torah* (congregational rabbi), Almosnino retired in 1570, after a stroke.[14] He died in Constantinople around 1580, but his place of burial is unknown.[15]

Almosnino was a prolific writer. His Hebrew and Ladino writings attest to his wide-ranging interests that included science, philosophy, history, and biblical exegesis. He knew several languages including Latin and Greek and was well versed in Christian scholasticism and European humanism, to which he was introduced by his teacher, Portuguese ex-*converso* Aaron Afia, a celebrated scientist and philosopher.[16] Almosnino also studied with Daniel ben Perahya Hacohen, a well-known physician and scientist.[17]

Aside from his sermons (*Meamez Coah*), Almosnino's Hebrew works include responsa (that survived as quotations in the works of Samuel de Medina and other contemporaries), commentaries on the Five Scrolls (*Yede Mosheh*, 1572), on the Proverbs and Job (lost), a book on some aspects of the Torah and liturgy (*Tefillah le-Mosheh*, 1564), a commentary on the Pentateuch and the prayer book (*Migdal oz*, 1569), a commentary on Avot (*Pirqe Mosheh*, 1563), supercommentaries on the Torah commentaries of Rashi and ibn Ezra (in manuscript), an exposition of Aristotle's *Nicomachean Ethics* (*Pnei Mosheh*), considered the most important philosophical text produced by Ottoman Jews, and a commentary on al-Ghazali's *Intentions of the Philosophers* (both in manuscript).[18] His interest in the sciences is reflected in his commentaries on Aristotle's *Physics* (lost) and on *Sphaera mundi* by Johannes de Sacrobosco (in manuscript). The latter, *Bet Elohim* (House of God), includes a seven-page description of America where Almosnino, for the first time in Jewish literature, mentions Amerigo Vespucci, referring to him as the discoverer of "America."[19]

Finally, Almosnino translated and commented on Georg Peuerbach's *Teorica novae planetarum* (in manuscript) and translated from Latin Aristotle's *Problems* (lost).[20]

Almosnino lived at a moment when many Jewish thinkers, kabbalists in particular, viewed philosophy with suspicion, blaming it for allowing intellectuals to disregard external observance and to believe that one can "worship the true God in his heart in a church as well as in a synagogue."[21] Nonetheless, soon after the expulsion, Sephardi philosophy experienced a revival. It is the "encounter of Sephardi intellectuals with Renaissance culture outside of Iberia which partially explains the efflorescence of Jewish philosophy in the sixteenth century, both in Italy and in the Ottoman Empire."[22]

In fact, persecutions of *conversos* and expulsions of Jews from Italy in the mid-sixteenth century, as well as new legal provisions protecting Ottoman Jews during their travels to Italy, brought Italian and Ottoman Sephardim closer together, effectively creating a common cultural space for intellectual exchange between scholars with a traditional Jewish education and graduates of European universities.[23] The first Spanish edition of Leone Ebreo's *Dialoghi d'amore* is emblematic of this development.

The son of Isaac Abrabanel, Judah Abrabanel (1460–1525?), better known as Leone Ebreo, was educated on the Iberian Peninsula but later spent many years in Italy, as a result of which, as James Nelson Novoa puts it, his work represents "both rupture and continuity with the Iberian tradition."[24] Dialogues between two Jewish courtiers, Filon and Sofia, on the nature of human and divine love borrow from medieval Iberian (Jewish and Christian) philosophy, on the one hand, and Renaissance humanism on the other. Although *The Dialogues* were originally written in Italian (rather than Spanish or Portuguese), Leone Ebreo continues the Jewish-Iberian tradition of producing high-culture literature in the vernacular.

Dialoghi d'amore (*editio princeps* 1535, Rome), a bestseller of its time, was translated into French, Spanish, Hebrew, and Latin.[25] There was also a version in *aljamiya* that may have been made in Salonica.[26] The first Spanish version that appeared in 1568 in Venice, was most likely produced in Salonica by Gedaliah ben Tam ibn Yahya, a well-known physician, translator of Albertus Magnus, and patron of learning. It is clear that a copy of the Italian book was first delivered to Salonica, from where the translation traveled back to Italy, and then some copies of the volume were brought back to the Ottoman Empire. To make it even more symbolic, ibn Yahya, as was customary among Iberian Jews, dedicated his translation to Spanish king Felipe II, expressing the hope that this work of a "Spanish author" would be beneficial for the "Spanish nation."[27]

In the same volume, the work of another Salonican scholar, Aaron Afia's *Opiniones sacadas de los más auténticos y antigos philósofos que sobre la alma escrivieron y sus definiciones* (Opinions of the most veritable and ancient philosophers who wrote about the soul and their definitions) appeared. In other words, this volume included intellectual contributions of three Sephardi Jews, one of whom had immigrated to Italy, another to the Ottoman Empire, and the third, having lived in Europe as a *converso*, embraced Judaism in Salonica.

The latter two, ibn Yahya and Afia, were mentioned by Amatus Lusitanus in the seventh volume of his *Curationum Medicinalium Centuriæ* (1570). Amatus Lusitanus, or Joao Rodrigues de Castelo Branco (1511–1568), a celebrated physician and philosopher, born in Portugal and educated in Spain, lived in Europe for many years, but moved to Salonica in 1558. The seventh part of his famous work is dedicated to Gedaliah ibn Yahya who offered the newcomer his hospitality.[28] One of the interlocutors in a philosophical dialogue included in *Curationum Medicinalium* is Aaron Afia, referred to as a "peripatetic philosopher," either in allusion to his Aristotelian views expressed there, or his life in Europe and immigration to Salonica.[29] Despite his *converso* background, Afia was obviously fluent in Hebrew, since he assisted Almosnino in his translation of Georg Peuerbach's book, but like Leone Ebreo, he chose to write in the vernacular.[30]

Being a member of that "knowledge-seeking circle," as Hacker described it, Almosnino was certainly familiar with the writings of Afia, ibn Yahya, and Leone Ebreo, which he probably read even before they were published.[31] Yet, his interests only partially overlapped with those of his colleagues who specialized in medicine and philosophy, rather than theology. His rationalism had its limits, and, as we will see, he was also influenced by the kabbalah. Tirosh-Samuelson characterizes him as "a moderate rationalist who perpetuated the Maimonidean tradition but modified its intellectualism by highlighting the centrality of the human will in the pursuit of human perfection as well as the dependency of the believer on God's love and grace."[32]

Furthermore, Almosnino was a congregational rabbi, which means that his circle of interlocutors would have included other rabbis, those suspicious of philosophy among them, and that an important aspect of his activity was Jewish education. Hence, while Leone Ebreo, Aaron Afia, and Amatus Lusitanus targeted both Jewish and Christian audiences, Almosnino wrote only for Jews, and thus used only the Hebrew alphabet for his vernacular works. In fact, this was the most natural choice for him, because, unlike these three authors, he was born in the Ottoman Empire.

Almosnino's Ladino works

Almosnino produced at least seven vernacular works, only five of which are extant. They are *El tratado de estorlabyo* (A treatise on the astrolabe) (1560); *El rejimyento de la vida* (The regimen of living) (published in 1564); *El tratado de los suenyos* (A treatise on dreams) (published in 1564); *La crónica de los reyes otomanos* (The Chronicle of Ottoman kings) (1567); and *El Kanon de reloj de plata* (A canon on the silver sundial) (no later than 1570). The first and fourth works are untitled in their original versions. The two missing ones are mentioned by Almosnino in his sermons, and are referred to as *Iggeret techiyat ha-metim* (An epistle on the resurrection of the dead) and *Iggeret ha-nefesh* (An epistle on the soul).[33] I suggest that all of these works, with the exception of *Crónica*, belong to a subgenre created by Almosnino—the scholarly Ladino epistle—that did not exist in Jewish literature before or after him. I will discuss the epistles in this chapter and will turn to *Crónica* in the following two chapters.

It is probably not coincidental that most of Almosnino's vernacular works were written between 1560 and 1570, during his tenure at Livyat Hen when he was specifically concerned with the education of Portuguese ex-*conversos*. Most members of this congregation were rather affluent and, hence, better educated people, but their knowledge of Hebrew, if it existed, would have been limited.[34] In addition, Almosnino made numerous long trips to the capital in the 1560s, where he stayed at Belvedere, the Nasi residence in Ortaköy, and met many educated ex-*conversos* close to his host's family.

One of those people, a person respectfully called by Almosnino "r. Abraham" (but obviously not a rabbi) is the addressee of his earliest extant epistle, *El Tratado de estorlabyo*.[35] All we can glean about Abraham from this text is that he was an educated man of high social standing, probably able to read Hebrew texts (which is why Almosnino refers him to his two books on astronomy), but more comfortable with the vernacular. In addition, while being a resident of Constantinople, he was well informed about business that brought the Salonican rabbi to the capital. Later, Almosnino gratefully mentioned "the clever and influential r. Abraham Salama" who was fluent in Turkish and had access to the Sheyh-ul-islam.[36] Furthermore, the German traveler Stephan Gerlach mentions a "Jew Abraham" among the richest and most important people at Sultan Selim's court in 1573.[37] Whether *Estorlabyo*'s addressee was Abraham Salama (about whom we have no further information) or someone else, this person would have belonged to the circle of prominent Sephardi immigrants close to Joseph Nasi (which is why he was informed about Almosnino's affairs).[38]

During one of Almosnino's visits to the Ottoman capital, Abraham asked him for a brief explanation in "Castilian Romance" (*romanse kastelyano*) that would enable him to perform the operations "described by Ptolemy in his canons" (fol. 1a).[39] Almosnino found this request reasonable, since existing versions of these rules available in the "holy tongue" appeared to be unintelligible. He therefore provided a brief summary of Ptolemy's description of the astrolabe found in *The Almagest*, accompanying it with a few additions of his own. *Estorlabyo* was started on May 1, 1560 and finished on June 13, most likely, at the Belvedere.[40] It will be remembered that only a few months earlier the Salonican rabbi was appointed to Livyat Hen, and thus he might have traveled to the capital to report to his patron, Joseph Nasi, on the affairs of the congregation.

However, according to Almosnino, on Sabbaths the two men discussed other subjects, one of which was the nature and causes of dreams. Nasi's interest in this question prompted Almosnino to write another epistle in the vernacular, *El Tratado de los suenyos*, which was published in Salonica in 1564 together with *Rejimyento*. The author characterizes *Suenyos* as a "book of small quantity but high quality, without prolixity," produced at the request of Don Joseph Nasi who was eager to understand the nature of dreams (fol. 1a).[41] Almosnino explains in the introduction that *Suenyos* was meant to continue the conversation the two men had started at Belvedere on a particular Sabbath.

Dreaming was among other psychophysiological phenomena, such as memory and laughter, that attracted the interest of medieval scholars, Jewish, Christian, and Muslim alike. In fact, the dialogue between Aaron Afia and Amatus Lusitanus in the latter's Seventh *Centuria Curationum* (One Hundred Medical Cases) deals with the source of laughter. A Hebrew book on interpretation of dreams, *Mefasher Halomim* (The interpreter of dreams) by Solomon Almoli, appeared in Salonica in 1515, and evidently had considerable success, since it was reprinted in Constantinople between 1550 and 1570.[42] The interpretation of dreams also has an important place in *Shevet Yehuda* (e.g., "The king's dream and a test of Jewish clairvoyance," ch. 70). Moreover, Nasi himself discusses dreams in his *Ben Porat Yosef* and is quite skeptical about prophetic dreams, seeing them as "pure coincidence" and saying that in the Bible "prophecy . . . was essentially moral warning, rather than precise forecast."[43] (This made Cecil Roth doubt that Nasi would have appreciated Almosnino's "naive treatise" written for his benefit.)[44]

Almosnino's second "user's manual," *El kanon de reloj de plata* (The canon on the silver sundial), is preserved in a manuscript produced in 1570. It has only four folios and deals with the operation of the sundial constructed by the author to calculate the geographic position of Salonica.[45] This work was probably meant for some community members who were not fluent in Hebrew, though here, as in *Estorlabio*, Almosnino refers readers to his Hebrew commentary on Sacrobosco's *Sphera mundi*.[46] (He did the same in *Crónica*.)

All we know about the lost "Epistle on the Resurrection of the Dead" is that it was composed at the request of an ex-*converso* who had settled in Salonica.[47] It must have been somewhat unusual for the time because it dealt with a theological question not normally discussed in the vernacular, but Almosnino obviously found this acceptable in view of the addressee's inability to read Hebrew. The subject of the other missing treatise, "The Epistle on the Soul," was a philosophical one, and thus a Jewish author could treat it in any language depending on the intended audience. Moreover, the description of the human soul written in Arabic, in book five chapter 12 of Judah Halevi's *Kuzari*, is based on Ibn Sinna's *Epistle On the Soul*.[48] And, as was mentioned earlier, Almosnino's mentor, Aaron Afia, discussed this subject in a Spanish treatise, *Opiniones sacadas de los philosophos sobre la alma. . . .*

Regardless of the topic, however, the use of vernacular by a rabbi required an apologetic explanation. Almosnino's justification for writing his five shorter epistles in Ladino was the addressees' limited knowledge of Hebrew, but the case of *Rejimyento*, his most famous vernacular work, is more complicated since it is dedicated to his own nephew.

Rejimyento is by no means a collection of religious precepts, as one may believe based on its Hebrew title, *Hanhagot ha-Haiim*. This genre definition indeed presupposes discussion of small practical details rather than ethical or philosophical principles, since the objective of *hanhagot* literature is to "instruct the individual in the minutest details of daily behavior."[49] As we will see in chapter 4, however, Almosnino's work is an ethical treatise largely based on Aristotle's *Nicomachean Ethics* (an exposition of which is his *Pnei Moshe*). Like classical ethical literature, it aims at teaching the righteous way of living and is divided into parts, explaining how to achieve each moral virtue and thus become perfect. The publishers of *Rejimyento*'s 1729 romanized version summarize its goals as follows: it teaches young men to "be careful in three principal matters. In Ethics, applying themselves to those things that will make them perfect. In Economy, searching out good education. In Politics, understanding good government for the republic."[50] Thus, far from being a collection of precepts, *Rejimyento* discusses the general principles of moral behavior.

As we learn from the *hakdamah* (introduction, in this case, the Hebrew one), Almosnino's nephew, Moses Garson, had asked the author to put into writing the ethical concepts that the latter had explained to him orally. Hence, this book was also written in response to a request, but, unlike Almosnino's other addressees, his sister's son had received a Jewish education and knew Hebrew well enough to read Maimonides (cf. fol. 30a). What, then, made Almosnino write his major ethical treatise in Ladino? His answer is unambiguous and striking.

Almosnino gives his reasons both in the *hakdamah* and the Ladino, "Personal introduction" (*Prologo partikular*), but these explanations, due to genre differences, are somewhat different and mutually complementary. The *hakdamah*, which is full of biblical references and images, is somewhat vague. Yet it contains important information: Almosnino wrote *Rejimyento* when he was proofreading *Pnei Moshe*.[51] We also learn that in spite of being very busy, in view of his nephew's love of learning, the author decided to accede to his request and write a "short book" in the vernacular:

> My words will be in a foreign language . . . And in the eyes of Moshe the deed is bad, but there is no comfort in resting from the work [of] God, [to do so would be] contemptible and despised . . . for as strong as death is the love for my first master the holy language accustomed to pass my lips. (fol. 2a)

It seems that Almosnino's reference to his desire to study Talmud and the proofreading of a Hebrew manuscript (his *long* book) as higher priority than writing a work in Ladino on the same subject, is a way of reaffirming the language hierarchy and his loyalty to Hebrew. In other words, having acknowledged that "as strong as death is the love for [his] first master," Almosnino, in view of his nephew's persistent requests, agreed to write a "short book" in Ladino. Thus, in the *hakdamah*, the author almost apologizes to Hebrew, emphasizing that his "side affair" will be short. Apparently, in his view, writing a *short* vernacular work requested by a person dedicated to learning, such as his nephew or Abraham, was more justifiable.

The Ladino introduction confirms that despite his constantly being busy with "the study of various subjects" from which he cannot excuse himself and a lack of time "for his personal needs," Almosnino decided to accede to the young man's "legitimate request" and produce a book in a "foreign language," because "teaching is more effective when it is received with great enthusiasm and sincere intention to use its fruits" (fol. 13a).

This prologue, while also apologetic, clearly explains Almosnino's rationale for using the vernacular:

> And though it would be easier for me to write for you in our holy and plentiful language, which is more familiar to me, I do not want to excuse myself from writing in the Romance, as you ask me to, because for our sins all our conversations are in a foreign language, and, besides, you will profit from learning some terms the knowledge of which will be most beneficial for you when you speak with some wise men who do not know our holy language. (fol.1 3a)[52]

Thus, Almosnino has two reasons for agreeing to write *Rejimyento* in Ladino rather than Hebrew: a) because Hebrew is not a spoken language, and b) because it is useful for the young man to learn the vernacular. As we have already seen, the first reason, with some variations, was often given by sixteenth-century translators of Hebrew texts. The publisher of *Heshek Shelomo*, the glossary discussed in the previous chapter, justifies the need for using the vernacular by referring to the authority of "our sages" who "once permitted writing in Greek, which was the most perfect and the most used language." And now, he continues, when people do not know the holy tongue and therefore cannot understand the Law, and Spanish is the most commonly used language, "surely the same permission will be granted for [writing in] it."[53]

Obviously, the purpose of this glossary and all other glossaries and translations produced through the twentieth century was to make the Law accessible to those who did not read Hebrew. This is why Almosnino's second reason for choosing Ladino is so astonishing and, in fact, unique in Sephardi rabbinic culture. This sixteenth-century rabbi whom we expect to worry about low Hebrew literacy among young Salonicans tells his nephew about the importance of improving his Romance and using it as a vehicle of secular knowledge brought by new immigrants, educated men not yet fluent in Hebrew. The significance of "secular wisdom" is also mentioned in the *hakdamah*, which says that among "the masses who do not study science" few are wise (fol. 10b).

Furthermore, at the time when Sephardi presses published numerous Hebrew grammars and Hebrew-Ladino glossaries, Almosnino appended to *Rejimyento* a Ladino-Hebrew glossary containing 515 words which, in his view, would have been unknown to his nephew and other second-generation Salonicans. In other words, he wrote in the vernacular not only for the sake of ex-*conversos* but also for the benefit of those who knew Hebrew, to help them refine their "Romance." Symptomatically, however, Almosnino does not encourage his nephew to learn the Latin alphabet. Among other things, Almosnino's glossary suggests that aside from such bookish terms as *klima*, *fantazia*, *mikrokosmo*, and *adversa fortuna*, educated young Salonicans were not expected to know many common Castilian words, including *escrupuloso* (scrupulous), *celebrar* (celebrate), *tranquilidad* (calm), *prohibido* (forbidden), and even *invierno* (winter).[54] While this rich material warrants a separate study, these examples suggest that although it was half a century after the expulsion, Salonican Jews were able to discuss certain subjects in a language comprehensible to Spaniards, in everyday speech they would use non-Castilian words to refer to winter or prohibitions. (In fact, the use of the Hebrew *asur* for "prohibited" is attested in text 1 of Benaim's corpus.[55])

Having agreed to write *Rejimyento* in the vernacular, the author notes in the "Personal Introduction" that it would have been easier for him to do it in Hebrew. Curiously, this statement is absent from the Amsterdam edition, since it probably did not make sense to the publisher. Yet it was by no means a figure of speech. To begin with, Almosnino was not used to writing in the vernacular on philosophical matters, and thus he might have had to borrow some terms from Spanish books. In the *hakdamah*, he indeed states that "his lips" (obviously meaning "pen") are more accustomed to Hebrew. Second, *Rejimyento* is filled with quotations from classical authors, rabbinic literature, and many other sources. In addition to Aristotle, he uses the writings of Ibn Sinna and Hippocrates to explain the principles of healthy living, as well as works by Maimonides, Rashi, al-Ghazali, Plato, Seneca, Cicero, Macrobius, and some Christian authors, such as Boethius, and a few others. Most of these works were not available in Castilian, and thus Almosnino had to translate the passages he needed.

In fact, *Rejimyento* demonstrates his outstanding ability to translate various kinds of texts from Hebrew and Latin into the vernacular. The most frequently quoted source in *Rejimyento* is the Bible, but Zemke's analysis has confirmed that Almosnino did not translate those passages himself (which one would not expect anyway). "The fact that the Spanish of the biblical verses differs from the expository portions in lexicon, syntax, and morphology suggests that the author may have quoted a medieval *romanceamiento* of the Bible."[56] It is possible that at least some quotations from rabbinical sources were also borrowed from earlier translations, but this question requires further research.

Despite Almosnino's love for his nephew, it is unlikely that he would have undertaken this work and published *Rejimyento* if it had been meant only for Moses Garson. Indeed, in the *hakdamah*, the author explains:

> And for the sake of what is good for him and everyone his age, at the end of this book is a table explaining all the foreign words scattered in it so that the reader may understand them.[57] Also, I saw and placed it in my heart to open this study with a key to the interpreters' conversations, and the interpretations I mention, biblical phrases, and sentences of *Razal* [rabbinic literature]). (fol. 2b)

In other words, *Rejimyento* was intended for young men, some of whom had not received any Jewish education, could not read Hebrew, and were not sufficiently familiar with the Bible and rabbinic writings to identify biblical and rabbinical texts quoted and alluded to in the book. For this reason, Almosnino provided a list of those quotations. In addition, *Rejimyento* would have been useful for those who, like Moses Garson, did know Hebrew but had a limited Romance vocabulary. Such young men, Almosnino suggests, would benefit from talking to new immigrants from Europe, while ex-*conversos* would learn from this book about the regimen of life appropriate for Jewish youth.

Almosnino's idea to compose an ethical treatise in the vernacular was in line with the earlier evolution of this genre. Medieval Jewish ethical literature emerged in the Near East and southern Europe in the tenth century, and was initially produced in Arabic. In the twelfth century, Jewish rationalistic philosophy and ethics began to spread "beyond the boundaries of Arabic-speaking countries in the Near East, North Africa, and Spain."[58] However, because Jewish communities outside those areas were unable to read Arabic, some texts were translated into Hebrew. Thus, one of the most important works of Jewish philosophical ethics, ibn Paquda's *Duties of the Heart*, written in Arabic in the eleventh century, was translated by Judah ibn Tibbon into Hebrew in the second half of the twelfth century. It is only in this period that Jewish rationalistic ethics that used to be a part of Judeo-Arabic culture became a genre of Hebrew literature.[59] In the sixteenth-century Ottoman Sephardi community, the situation was the reverse, and *musar* (ethical) literature, became a vernacular genre once again. As was already mentioned, a few years after the appearance of *Rejimyento*, *The Duties of the Heart* was translated from Hebrew into Ladino.

Almosnino's Epistle as a Genre

I suggest that Almosnino's six Ladino works discussed in this chapter belong to one genre category created by him for providing instruction to different educated men who were not fluent in Hebrew. There was no need for this sort of literature before the expulsion, when being an educated Jew implied knowing Hebrew, the language of scholarly discussions. But in the sixteenth century, many ex-*conversos*, educated and competent in various fields of secular knowledge, were initially unable to read Hebrew or, at least, to deal with complicated matters and technical instructions in this language. In search of an adequate literary form to provide answers to their questions, Almosnino developed his own subgenre—the scholarly Ladino epistle. All of his extant epistles and as far as we can tell, the two lost ones, exhibit some of its features, but only *Estorlabyo*, a piece overlooked by most Almosnino scholars, displays all of them. Therefore, I will examine *Estorlabyo* as the ideal example of this subgenre, and indicate which of its features are present in the other epistles. I will also look at its Hebrew version, which highlights the idiosyncratic characteristics of Almosnino's new genre.

The need to discuss scholarly matters in the vernacular prompted Almosnino to resort to the style and rhetorical strategies of Castilian secular literature with which he was sufficiently acquainted. Consequently, his epistles, and *Estorlabyo* in particular, reveal—to borrow Gutwirth's term—his "hispanicity," which means "the attachment to and partaking of non-Jewish Spanish culture of the Sephardi exiles and their descendants."[60] In terms of their literary form and language, Almosnino's epistles are indeed rooted in non-Jewish Spanish culture, and demonstrate a connection to it that until now has not been examined. As will be shown below, while pre-expulsion Spanish editions were hardly accessible to him, Almosnino depended on contemporaneous Castilian literature and the works of fifteenth-century authors, such as Jorge Manrique's poems that were (re)printed in his time. This is undoubtedly true for the epistolary genre.

In Europe, by the twelfth century, letter-writing had become an important cultural practice that was rigorously codified by the *ars dictaminis* (the art of letter-writing).[61] This led to a proliferation of manuals teaching the rules of this discipline, often accompanied by anthologies of sample letters, both real and fictitious.

Among the best-known manuals are Alberico di Monte Casino's *Breviarium de dictamine* (mid-twelfth century), Albertano da Brescia's *Ars loquendi et tacendi* (mid-thirteenth century), Lorenzo di Aquileia's *Practica sive usus dictaminis edita ad utilitatem rudium* (turn of the fourteenth century), and *Livro dos Conselhos de El-Rei D. Duarte* (first third of the fifteenth century). Among the most popular in late medieval Iberia was Brunetto Latini's celebrated encyclopedic work, *Livres du Trésor* (1260s), which contained the theory of letter-writing. There were at least thirteen manuscripts in Castilian, three in Catalan, one in Aragonese, and one in Portuguese.[62] Lorenzo di Aquileia's *Practica*, presenting the *ars dictaminis* in the form of tables, was also diffuse on the Iberian Peninsula.[63]

The influence of vernacular humanism with its rediscovery of the letter as a genre led to the production of a large corpus of epistolography in Ibero-Romance languages.[64]

As was mentioned in the prologue, the epistolary practice of Iberian Jews was also influenced by humanist culture. One of the best examples of vernacular letters composed by Iberian Jews is one written by Moses Arragel to Luis de Guzman on the subject of Bible translation. This long epistle, which combines biblical and Greco-Roman lore, and employs Latin rhetorical devices is, in fact, a "series of Jewish vernacular 'essays' on intellectually and literary demanding topics," such as fame, kings' desire for scholarship, and the question of translation from Hebrew into Romance.[65] Another well-known Jewish letter-writer in Romance was Profayt el Naci who composed an epistle on fiscal reform that exhibits "features that are extremely well rooted in the ancient and medieval Jewish sources alongside a close familiarity with precise textual practices of his courtly milieu and public in fifteenth-century Castile."[66] In other words, in the century before the expulsion, Iberian Jews showed unquestionable interest in the vernacular letter as a literary genre, though authors of extant letters did not strictly adhere to the models prescribed by the *ars dictaminis*.[67]

Personal letters found in the Cairo Geniza make it clear that in the sixteenth century the Iberian tradition of letter-writing in the vernacular was not interrupted.[68] However, these letters differ from the extant vernacular epistolography of the pre-expulsion period in two ways. First, they are addressed to Jews rather than Christians and are, therefore, written in Hebrew characters. Second, since the main purpose of the available letters was to communicate the authors' personal news to friends or relatives, their topics were limited to everyday matters, and they were written in a simple style, in sixteenth-century Sephardi vernacular.

As for Hebrew epistolography, apparently there existed a significant corpus of medieval letter formularies, but very few have survived.[69] One was put together in the fourteenth century in Saragossa.[70] In the late fifteenth century and the early sixteenth, Italian Jews compiled a few manuals and formularies in Hebrew based on the humanist canons of letter-writing. In addition, some included lists of biblical quotations appropriate for various occasions.[71] These formularies, however, mainly included private or business letters. One contained a prayer, but none dealt with scholarly subjects.[72] Iberian exiles published a few manuals on letter-writing in Hebrew, among which are David ibn Yahya's collection (Naples, 1538) and an anonymous compilation that appeared in Constantinople in 1522 or 1523.[73]

On the other hand, the genre of the Hebrew scholarly epistle, which had a long history, was often used by Profayt Duran, Isaac Abrabanel, and other Iberian thinkers to discuss intellectual matters, including history, biblical exegesis, and science. For instance, in the 1370s, Profayt Duran wrote an epistle to Shaltiel Gracian answering his questions on astronomy that involved the use of the quadrant (an instrument for measuring distances from stars).[74] Such letters may be seen as scholarly correspondence similar to responsa, though not dealing with legal issues. Furthermore, as Gutwirth points out, Duran's epistles on Rahab and Ahitophel, as well as his essay on ibn Ezra's *Riddle* are comparable to "the 'humanist letters' . . . that were treated as literary works intended to give evidence of scholarship and win the consideration of those they addressed."[75]

Thus, Sephardim created two epistolary traditions in each language: there were intellectual epistles in Hebrew and in Romance, as well as private and business correspondence in these languages. Needless to say, Almosnino was quite familiar with various kinds of Hebrew epistles written in different epochs, including some by Profayt Duran that were published in the sixteenth century in Constantinople.[76] Yet, while the practice of using the epistle as a means of teaching was old, this was never done in Romance. On the other hand, Almosnino would not have seen Jewish vernacular letters addressed to Iberian Christians, and thus the similarities (albeit not numerous) between them and his epistles are explained only by their belonging to the same culture.

Estorlabyo has forty-four folios and consists of two parts: a short introduction in the form of a letter (fols. 1a–2a) and the actual treatise divided into forty chapters. The introductory letter, remarkable for its eloquence, follows rather closely the five-fold model prescribed by the *ars dictaminis*. Almosnino begins by indicating not only the date when the letter was started (May 1, 5320 [1560]) and the place where it was written ("this most famous city of Constantinople called by Ptolemy 'Bizancis'"), but also the latitude of Constantinople as measured by the astrolabe ("almost forty-two degrees"). These lines serve as a kind of epigraph to the treatise on the astrolabe. The letter starts with a *salutatio* which, consistent with recommendations by all manuals, includes the addressee's name and his attributes introduced by means of a rather sophisticated play on words: "*Magnifiko senyor r. Abraham* [illegible]: *komo sea porpozisyon syerta i manifiesta ke de las linias echadas de punto a punto la mas korta e[s] la mas rekta, vos senyor komo rektisimo i prudente* . . ." (fol. 1a) (Magnificent Sir, r. Abraham [illegible]: as it is certain and evident that the shortest line between two points is the straightest one, you, sir, being most upright [lit. straight] and prudent . . .).

The *exordium* indicates the reason for writing this letter ("you asked me for a very short summary in Castilian Romance"), and moves on to the *captatio benevolentiae*, which discusses the author's circumstances and praises the addressee's qualities. The eulogy was a popular form of *captatio benevolentia*; medieval manuals proposed at least five different ways to introduce and modulate it.[77] Almosnino commends not only Abraham's virtue (indeed commonplace) but also his passion for learning:

> Sir, despite all my present occupations from which, as you well know, I cannot excuse myself, because of your great desire and sincere wish to learn what until now, as you say, nobody has explained to you in a satisfactory way, and because your virtue truly obliges me to accede to your request, I am going to do so in the shortest possible way. (fol.1a)

As will be remembered, Almosnino gave a similar explanation four years later, in the *hakdama* to *Rejimyento*. And in the Ladino prologue, he wrote:

> And since teaching is more effective when it is received with great enthusiasm and sincere intention to use its fruits, I believe it is right to accede to your legitimate request because you have asked me for it with such a good purpose and strong will, although you saw that I am constantly busy with the study of various subjects from none of which I can excuse myself despite not having time even for my personal needs. (fol. 13a)

Almosnino's complaint about being busy is obviously a cliché, an element of *captatio benevolentia*. In his analysis of the non-legal components of Isaac bar Sheshet's responsa, which includes a rich personal correspondence, Gutwirth suggests that the scholar's recurrent references to not having enough leisure for detailed letters should be understood in the context of the "merchant class concern for time, reproduction, and communication."[78] He believes that these letters "convey a sense of organized time, a lack of leisure, and an urgency, which may be compared to what Jacques Le Goff termed 'the merchant's time.'"[79] Yet the sense of urgency can be produced or enhanced intentionally by means of rhetorical devices. This, given the frequency of Bar Sheshet's complaints, seems to be true for his responsa. As was mentioned earlier, they were published in Constantinople in 1559, and Almosnino would have read them. However, he certainly did not borrow this cliché from the Spanish scholar simply because *Rejimyento* was finished a few years earlier. More likely, scholars' references to being busy with more important matters ("the scholar's time") were a social convention that had entered the epistolary genre long before Almosnino, who presents himself as a busy intellectual in all his Ladino works. He leaves his world of "constant study and permanent contemplation" either to serve his community, as in *Crónica*, or to offer instruction to individuals, as in the epistles, when he is asked to do so. In fact, Almosnino complains about not having enough time no matter what he is doing.

In *Suenyos*, he reminds his addressee, Joseph Nasi, that once, while he was enjoying his patron's "divine conversation," the latter expressed a desire to read something good on the nature and causes of dreams. Wishing to satisfy this interest, the scholar produced the epistle. We can infer that the letter on the resurrection requested by an ex-*converso* would have started the same way, with an explanation of why, despite his many occupations, Almosnino had decided to accede to this man's request and write an epistle in the vernacular.

In *Estorlabyo*'s *narratio*, the author explains the principles and organization of his summary of Ptolemy's work. Since this is a response rather than a request, in the *petitio* the scholar does ask Abraham to forgive him but merely for possible errors (as he does not have his books on hand) and for the familiar style he will use for the sake of brevity. Here, once again, he relies on Abraham's "virtue." The letter ends with a short *conclusio* where the author assures the addressee of his unfailing friendship and loyalty. In this epistle, the rhetoric of friendship so important to medieval epistolary practice is limited to a few words, but in *Rejimyento* and *Suenyos* it is artfully elaborated. In *Rejimyento*, Almosnino talks about his love for his nephew, explaining why uncles and nephews resemble one another so closely, but then asks the young man to see him not as his uncle but as "father and teacher" (fols 13ab).

The actual treatise on the astrolabe is preceded by what Almosnino calls a key, and what we would refer to as an expanded table of contents. (The same, though in a less formalized way, is done in *Rejimyento* and *Suenyos.*) In fact, the treatise can be interpreted as the epistle's actual *narratio. Estorlabyo,* indeed, ends like a regular letter (as does *Suenyos*): "At your service, Moses Almosnino" (fol. 44b).[80] In the Middle Ages, doctrinal expositions or precepts were sometimes turned into letters by means of a salutation, and a conclusion was added as needed. This happened, for instance, to the widely known medical treatise written by the Portuguese scholar Petrus Hispanus (mentioned earlier) that for a long time circulated as a fictitious letter sent to various well-known monarchs.[81] In the same way, Almosnino's "Canon on silver sun-dial" could have become a full-fledged epistle (and perhaps, initially, it *was* one).

It is clear from *Estorlabyo's* respectful tone that Abraham was socially superior to Almosnino, but *Suenyos* goes even further in resembling letters written to Iberian nobility. The author indicates that this treatise was composed "at the request of the illustrious lord, lord Don Joseph Nasi, may God protect him and increase his prosperity" (*muy ilustre senyor el senyor don Yosef Nasi ke el Dyo konserve i aumente su prospero estado*) (fol. 1a). Almosnino uses the same formula in *Crónica* (when he speaks about the reigning sultan, and we find it almost verbatim, for example, in Hernando de Pulgar's letter to the Count of Cabra: "May our Lord protect your noble and magnificent person and increase your property." (*Nuestro Señor conserve vuestra muy noble e magnífica persona e acreciente vuestro estado.*)[82]

Closer to the end of *Suenyos*, having discussed the nature of prophetic dreams, Almosnino informs his patron of his own recurring dream. In this presumably prophetic vision, the Nasi brothers, Joseph and Samuel, together with their families, celebrate the Feast of Tabernacles at the luxuriously decorated *midrash* at Belvedere. In the author's interpretation, this dream foretells glory, prosperity, and male offspring for the two brothers. (However, as Cecil Roth put it, "his assurance perhaps outran his judgment, as this last detail at least was not destined to be fulfilled.")[83]

In the concluding part of *Suenyos*, Almosnino resorts to amplification, as was recommended by letter-writing manuals. He confirms the meaning of his dream, because, as he claims, knowing so well the excellence of the Nasi "most blessed house (*beatisima kasa*), even my weak brain cannot help but realize that it is impossible for such a house not to be elevated and raised to the peak of happiness and prosperity bestowed by the divine providence." "And may it be so"—the letter concludes—"and may He confirm it. Amen. At your service, Moses Almosnino" (fol. 162b).

It is doubtful that Almosnino's relationship with Nasi really necessitated such blatant flattery. It seems more likely that his literary strategy was dictated mainly by the conventions of the genre, an epistle to an enlightened nobleman. Iberian Jews were so accustomed to addressing kings and aristocrats that even Gedaliah ibn Yahya, as was mentioned above, dedicated his translation of *Dialoghi d'amore* to the Spanish king in the hope that it would be useful. And, as will be remembered, Cansino dedicated his adaptation of Almosnino's *Crónica* to don Gaspar de Guzman, Count Duke of Olivares. This dedication, also in the form of a letter, full of (perhaps necessary) flattery refers to the addressee as a lover of the sciences and letters.[84] Hence, Almosnino's "prophetic" dream and its interpretation should be understood as a genre feature just like his comparison of Abraham's virtues to a straight line.

* * *

Having finished *Estorlabyo*, Almosnino made a copy of it that he preserved at least until 1570 when he commissioned a professional scribe, Benjamin ben Eliyah Duvan, to produce a manuscript that would include this piece and his other user's manual, *The canon on silver sundial*.[85] As we know, Almosnino composed *Estorlabyo* without access to other works on the astrolabe or even his own books, which is why he warned Abraham that it might contain factual errors and that he would revise it upon his return to Salonica. But he must have decided that this piece was more than *ad hoc* technical instructions and that it would be useful for other people, including fluent Hebrew readers. Since his stay in the capital lasted a few more weeks, he made a Hebrew translation of *Estorlabyo* at once. It is dated Sivan 5320, which means it was produced between June 13, when the Ladino original was finished, and July 5.[86]

The main part of *Estorlabyo*'s Hebrew version differs slightly from the Ladino original in terms of material and organization, and the introductory letter is changed to address a new audience.[87] Yet both versions contain a sentence that might have first appeared in the Hebrew translation or, at least, was added to the Ladino version after the letter was sent (probably with a courier) to Abraham. The following statement from the Ladino version has an almost identical equivalent in Hebrew: "Thus, with God's help, this short treatise will not lack anything a person reading it might need in order to use this famous instrument almost without having to read any other teacher" (fol. 1b). (The word "almost" does not appear in the Hebrew text.)

By translating *Estorlabyo*, Almosnino turned a letter initially intended for one person with limited Hebrew proficiency into a manual that could be used by many Hebrew readers. For this purpose, he removed all references to Abraham and replaced his name with a generic form of address, *ahuvi ve-ratsui* (lit. "my beloved and favored"). As a result, the geometric pun alluding to Abraham's virtues that is part of the *salutatio* of the Ladino letter is also gone. Most important, however, the request for a vernacular explanation was replaced with one for a short summary, which, in turn, required other changes in the *exordium*.

The Hebrew epistle opens with a common formula of rabbinic literature (also found in *Rejimyento*) immediately followed by a revised *exordium*:

> Said the sage and divine philosopher, our teacher r. Moses Almosnino, may God protect and preserve him: Because you, my beloved, asked me for a short summary of what one needs to know in order to be able to use the astrolabe in the ways described by Ptolemy in his chapters. (fol. 1a)

The second part of the *exordium*, the *captatio benevolentiae*, is abridged: it talks only about the addressee's passion for learning, but not his virtues. Here, too, the author mentions being busy, albeit rather briefly. The *narratio*, on the other hand, has become longer, and it juxtaposes the advantages of Almosnino's treatise with the shortcomings of all previous works. This Hebrew epistle with a short *exordium* seamlessly moving to a longer *narratio* perfectly suits its purpose—to serve as an introduction to a generally accessible manual.

While in the Hebrew version all devices of Latin rhetoric are gone, some rabbinical ones, such as set expressions using binary synonyms and amplification, are added. For instance, in the original, the author states matter-of-factly: "at present, I am away from my home and thus deprived of my books and somewhat far from my studies of these treatises." In the Hebrew version, we read, "Since at present I am a wanderer and a vagabond, my lot and consolation and the light of my eyes are only my books, but even they are not with me, and long gone is the time when I studied these subjects."

Almosnino's literary experiment (which he certainly did not see as such) puts in sharp relief his genre innovations. The change of language, which implied a change of target audience and called for some adjustment of rhetoric, transformed a teaching tool intended for educated ex-*conversos* into a regular scholarly epistle similar, for instance, to Profayt Duran's letter on the use of the quadrant.

Neither of *Estorlabyo*'s two versions has a title, but if the Ladino one had been entitled El Tratado de estorlabyo (which is how Almosnino refers to it in the text), he would have translated it into Hebrew as *iggeret* (letter). In medieval Jewish literature, this term was applied both to actual letters and to short ethical treatises, which is why, writing in Hebrew, Almosnino referred to his two lost treatises as *iggeret*.[88] The same term designated treatises on science. *Estorlabyo*'s Hebrew translation reached us in a seventeenth-century manuscript containing works by ibn Ezra and other famous scholars. Among a few other treatises on the astrolabe, the manuscript includes Moses Galino's *Iggeret ketanna* (small epistle).[89] It is a translation of the so-called minor version of al-Zarqāli's treatise, which in its Castilian translation is entitled *Tratado de la azafea*.[90]

To our knowledge, *Estorlabyo* is the only one of Almosnino's epistles intended for two readerships. Yet in the cases of *Rejimyento* and *Suenyos* (and, it seems, the lost letters), Almosnino also starts with an answer to a specific request from someone he knows personally, and then turns his answer into an educational work for a larger audience. As we know, *Rejimyento* was produced while Almosnino was proofreading *Pnei Moshe* (never printed but copied by a scribe). Since *Pnei Moshe* was finished in January 1556, about eight years passed between *Rejimyento*'s composition and publication.[91] During that time Moses Garson had become an adult and the epistle was probably used by his uncle to educate many other young men. Hence, "for the sake of what is good for him *and everyone his age*" could have been added at a later stage. Furthermore, before being published, *Rejimyento* was read, albeit in an abbreviated form, by Joseph Nasi, since Almosnino mentions having sent him, at his request, its revised and abridged version (fol. 139b).

The Language of the Epistles

Almosnino's prose in *Estorlabyo* is highly Latinized at various levels. One of his most favorite devices found in all his writings is the use of binary synonyms, for example, "*intesyon i intento*" (intention and intent), "*la raiz i el orijen*" (root and origin), and "*buen deseo i sinsera veluntad*" (great desire and sincere wish). Another rhetorical figure found in *Estorlabyo* is hyperbaton, for example, "*i kuanto del sere rekerido komo de fidelisimo amigo; por lo kual no nos debemos a elya [memorya] mucho atener*" (which is why we should not very much depend on our memory). Another Latinism is the word order with a finite verb at the end of the sentence, for example, "*me dispongo a haserlo en el mas breve estilo ke posible sera*" (I intend to do it in the shortest possible way) (fols. 1a–1b).

An obvious sign of Latinization is the excessive use of adjectives in the superlative in "*ísimo*": *rektisimo, brevisimo, fidelisimo, famosisimo* (twice). The popularity of the absolute form of superlative (elative) reached its peak in the seventeenth century, but already starting in the second third of the sixteenth century, some influential works of Castilian literature were marked by frequent use of this *cultismo*.[92] Among them are Alfonso de Valdés's *Diálogo de Mercurio y Carón* (*A Dialogue of Mercury and Charon*) and *Diálogo de las cosas ocurridas en Roma* (*A Dialogue of What Happened in Rome*) (c. 1529); Juan Boscán's translation of Castiglione's *Courtier* (1534), an important work of the Spanish Renaissance in its own right; and Pedro Mejía's *Silva de varia lección* (*A Miscellany of Several Lessons*) (1540).[93] The elative is also frequently found in the correspondence of the time, but it was not favored by Juan Valdés or Antonio de Guevara, or by such fifteenth-century authors as Marqués de Santillana and Hernando de Pulgar who were known for their predilection for Latinization.[94]

Thus Almosnino was not only familiar with this stylistic trend, but also made a conscious choice to follow it in all his Ladino works, including *Crónica*. One finds numerous other Latinisms both in *Rejimyento* and *Suenyos*, but mainly on the lexical level and not as often as in *Estorlabyo* (with the exception of adjectives in the elative).[95] Among the rhetorical devices found in *Estorlabyo* is the frequent vocative *senyor* (sir). Discussing an earlier Romance letter, Gutwrith suggests that this device creates "a paratactic effect which accords with its plaintive tone" and, in general, "with the principle, within the *dictamen*, of *benevolentiae petitio*."[96] This device is indeed employed by many Castilian letter writers to the same effect. For instance, Pulgar writes in a letter to the Count of Cabra: "*Yo, señor, soy quien vos bien conocéis, e vos sois un señor que yo pensaba conocer. . . . Yo, señor, no pido que me deis de lo vuestro, mas pido que no me quitéis lo mio.*"[97]

It could also serve other purposes. The repetition of *senyor* (also found in *Suenyos*), together with other devices, creates the effect of oral communication, a study session where a teacher is explaining a difficult subject to a diligent student. In *Rejimyento*, Almosnino directly mentions sessions of this kind that he had with his nephew. For instance, referring to a text they once read together, the uncle says, "I noticed you had some doubts, because you do not know the origin of those thoughts, and it seemed to me you were baffled" (fol. 51a).[98] In *Suenyos* he starts by referring to the conversation on dreams he had with Nasi and returns to it several times. Finally, in *Estorlabyo*, the author warns Abraham that he will use a casual style and speak the way one speaks to his student, "foregoing the terms [of address] and politeness due to you (*vuesa mersed*), and you (*él*), in your goodness (*su virtud*), will forgive me."

Almosnino's use of *vuesa mersed* (the polite "you") patently testifies to his "Hispanicity." Gutwirth and, more recently, Benaim, have refuted Zamora Vicente's claim that the form *vues(tr)a merced* and its contraction, *usted*, were unknown to Ottoman Sephardim until the end of the nineteenth century when some westernized intellectuals began to use it.[99]

In fact, *vuestra merced* was not yet common in Spain in the middle of the sixteenth century, and it is impossible to tell from what sources (books or letters) the Salonican rabbi would have borrowed this form (to my knowledge, not used by any other Sephardi writer). Antonio de Guevara, for instance, did not use *vuestra merced* in his widely read *Epístolas familiars* (*The Golden Letters*) (1539–1542), but it is found in some of Pulgar's thirty-two letters to Spanish nobility and church authorities (*Letras*, 1485). Both Pulgar and Almosnino use it inconsistently, because *vos* with the second-person plural verb was not yet considered impolite. Thus, in *Estorlabyo*'s *salutatio* we see *vos*, but in the rest of the introduction *vuesa mersed* and *él* with the third-person possessive pronoun are used interchangeably:

> *Vos senyor komo rektisimo i prudente me demandaste un kopedyo brevisimo . . . yo senyor, kon todas mis okupasyones de las kuales al presente no me puedo eskusar komo vuesa mersed byen sabe, visto vueso buen deseo i sinsera veluntad de saber lo ke dise hata aki no haber sido en elyo de ninguno alumbrado.*[100] (fol.1a)

The same inconsistency is observed, for instance, in Pulgar's letter to Puertocarrero, lord of Palma del Río:

> *Muy noble y magnífico señor: dice vuestra merced que querra ver mis razones más que mis encomiendas. En verdad, muy noble señor, yo deseo que visedes más mis seruicios que lo uno ni lo otro; pero porque son pocos e flacos, los suplí con aquellas pocas encomiendas que os enbié. Y por tanto, señor, no quiero que resciba vuestra merced este engaño; porque haués de saber que cuando houieire fecho lo último de mi poder por os seruir, certifico a vuestra merced ello valga bien poco.*[101]

Having warned Abraham about treating him as his student, in the actual treatise the author indeed switches to second-person singular pronoun, *tu*, which here is closer in meaning to "one." Yet he closes *Estorlabyo* with "*A servisyo a vuesa mersed.*" In *Suenyos*, however, Almosnino addresses Joseph Nasi only as *vuesa mersed*, which may suggest that it was produced later than *Estorlabyo.*[102] As has been shown above, *Suenyos* was written after *Rejimyento*, which was started at the earliest in 1556, but before 1564 when the two works were printed. Thus, if consistent use of *vuesa mersed* as a polite form of address can be considered dependable evidence, we may conclude that *Suenyos* was composed between 1560 and 1564.

Given the obvious similarities at various levels between *Estorlabyo* and Pulgar's epistles, is it legitimate to suggest that Almosnino read the collection produced by the famous Castilian chronicler? While this proposition cannot be proven, it is certainly plausible. In the early 1480s, Hernando de Pulgar, who came from a *converso* family, took a critical stand against the Inquisition that cost him his position as secretary to Queen Isabel.[103] Later, as the royal chronicler, he described many ills caused by the Holy Office in his *Crónica de los altos y muy esclarecidos reyes católicos* (Chronicle of the great and most distinguished Catholic monarchs) that appeared in Latin in 1545 and 1550, and then in Spanish in 1565.[104] Pulgar was likely to have attracted the interest or even sympathy of Ottoman Jews no less than Manrique did, and his *Letras* reprinted in 1545 were likely to have been available in Salonica from new immigrants to the city.

Estorlabyo shares a similarity with another work of Spanish literature that Almosnino might have known. He indicates that the treatise was written "*en esta famosisima sivdad de Kostantinopla lyamada por el Tolomeo Bizansis ke tyene de latitud casi kuarenta i dos grados, ke tantos parese por el estorlabyo estar alevantado el polo artiko sobre el horizonte*" (fol. 1a).[105] The formula "*la famosísima civdad de . . .*" (a most famous city of . . .) became popular in Spain in the sixteenth century. In fact, chapter 12 of Mejía's *Silva de varia lección* is entitled "*De la muy antigua y famosísima ciudad de Constantinopla*" (on the very ancient and most famous city of Constantinople). Further on in this chapter, we read, "*Está Constantinopla, según Tholomeo, en quarenta y tres grados de latitud (que es dezir, para el que no lo entiende, que tantos grados se aparta de la equinocial y se le alça el polo).*"[106]

Most likely, this is a mere coincidence, though Mejía's book was extraordinarily popular at the time and might have been available in Salonica. *Silva* was printed twice in 1540, when it first appeared, and during the following one hundred years, it went through thirty more Spanish and seventy-five foreign-language editions (thirty in Italian, thirty-one in French, five in English, five in Dutch, and four in German).[107] It is impossible to establish whether Almosnino was familiar with this book, but, more important, it is obvious that in terms of language, *Estorlabyo* closely resembled this text produced by a Peninsular author. At the same time, the differences between them demonstrate the divergence between the high register of Ladino and contemporaneous Castilian.

In addition to the most obvious difference, namely the use of Hebrew script, there are a few minor features distinguishing *Estorlabyo*'s language from Peninsular Spanish, two of them characteristic of the sociolect used by Iberian Jews before the expulsion. First, these texts contain Hebrew words, which are mainly technical terms, such as *minha grande* and *minha chika* (big and small afternoon prayer services) and are not numerous. A second Jewish feature is the use of *el Dyo* (God) instead of the Castilian *Dios*, found in all Ladino texts through the end of the nineteenth century (when some westernizers chose to adopt the standard Spanish term).

In addition, among linguistic innovations specific to Ladino that are attested in *Estorlabyo*, there is a syntactic one that merits special discussion, because it is a Hebrew calque that would persist through the late nineteenth century.[108] Almosnino says that he is going to explain Ptolemy's rules "*alargando en algunos lugares eskuros ke konvyene aklarar su intesyon en elyos*" (dwelling longer on certain difficult places whose meaning has to be elucidated) (fol. 1a). Similar cases are abundant in *Crónica*. For instance, the author promises to describe "*seys konjusyones ke perdimos de konkluirse nuestro negosyo en elyas*"[109] (The six conjunctions in which we failed to conclude our affair). In both cases, we find anaphora in a relative clause (underlined here) common in Hebrew where the relative pronoun is indeclinable.[110] However, in Spanish (and usually in Ladino), in the first case, it would have been *alargando en algunos lugares escuros la inteción de los cuales konviene aclarar.* Obviously, this calque, found only in literary texts, entered Ladino because those who were used to writing in Hebrew began to write in the vernacular. Given its usage in the early Ladino press, this construction seems to have been associated with a higher stylistic register.

Almosnino's spelling makes it clear that he was reading Spanish books. Thus, although the vernacular was in the process of neutralizing the phonological opposition /r/ ñ /r:/, in *Estorlabyo* he sometimes uses two *reshes*, albeit inconsistently (*erado* but *tyerra*). In addition, mute Spanish *h*, in most cases, is represented by the Hebrew letter *heh* (e.g., *hazer, haber, horizonte*).[111] Thus, Almosnino *transliterates* (rather than phonetically transcribes) Spanish into Hebrew letters and tries to preserve the correct Castilian spelling. As a result, his orthography is similar or even better than that of some of his Spanish contemporaries, such as Antonio de Guevara or Juan Valdés, who drop the *h* in *haber* and *hazer.* Almosnino tends to drop the *h* in nouns (e.g., *onra*, *abito*), but these inconsistencies were also typical of sixteenth-century Castilian.

Furthermore, while *Estorlabyo* has many instances of metathesis common to sixteenth-century Peninsula Spanish, the /rd/ > dr/ metathesis, a Sephardi innovation, is not found in this or other texts by Almosnino.[112] Finally, in *Estorlabyo* there is no *yeísmo*: ll ([y]) is represented by *lamed yod.* These features are also found in *Rejimyento* and *Suenyos.*

The fact that Almosnino wrote *Estorlabyo*, a piece of highly Latinized Castilian prose, during his visit to the capital where he was limited not only in time but probably also in the sources he could consult, suggests that he was accustomed not only to reading in Castilian but also to writing similar texts. It is possible that he corresponded with Nasi and other ex-*converso* acquaintances in a similar style, yet, given how closely he follows patterns recommended by the *ars dictaminis*, it is unlikely that he would have learned the art of letter-writing from his correspondents. Rather, he must have read the manuals.

Conclusion

Moses Almosnino is the only author we know who, rather than making vernacular translations for ex-*conversos*, produced original works in Ladino for them. Unlike many other rabbis, he was not only a teacher but also a productive scholar with wide-ranging interests, which may explain why he was particularly attracted to an audience of intellectuals. In addition, even though his epistles were written in Ladino, he endeavored to expand his readership by making them useful for those who were literate in Hebrew, either by enriching their "Romance" or by means of translation, but in both cases going "against the flow."

Since all available genres of Jewish scholarly literature used Hebrew, and all Castilian ones addressed Christian readers, Almosnino had to create a new subgenre, the scholarly Ladino epistle. Unlike the Romance epistolarity of Iberian Jews, Almosnino's epistles were not part of an exchange and did not presuppose a response. On the other hand, they differed from Hebrew scholarly letters produced in Spain because they were didactic. Despite this didactic character, they were not a purely literary form like the Hebrew *iggeret.*

Possessing certain features of these three genres, Almosnino's epistles were written, as can be seen from a close reading, in a literary style similar to that of contemporaneous Castilian fiction and epistolography. Although we can only speculate about his actual sources (with the exception of Jorge Manrique), it is evident that thanks to the constant flow of educated immigrants and other travelers, Almosnino had access to contemporaneous Peninsular literature and, probably, to newly printed earlier works.

Of course, Almosnino may not have read Pulgar's epistles or Mejía's piece on Constantinople and could have found *vuesa merced* and certain rhetorical devices in other sources. What is evident, however, is that he was sufficiently familiar with Peninsular literature and ably adopted its vocabulary and styles. It has been argued that the concern with eloquence and rhetoric patent in ibn Verga's *Shevet Yehudah* should be seen "within a continuum of awareness of form which was present in the Hispano-Jewish communities on the eve of their expulsion in the fifteenth century."[113] The same is true for Almosnino with the difference that his great awareness of form and language was not limited to Hebrew but extended to the vernacular.

Other Sephardi rabbis may have also produced original works in the vernacular, but if so, no such text has survived. *Fuente klara*, a work of Jewish apologetics discussed in the previous chapter, targeted the same audience, but nothing is known about its author or place of composition. In any case, vernacular literature for the learned could not have existed for a long time after Almosnino's death. Once the flow of ex-*conversos* significantly diminished, the audience for scholarly Ladino texts disappeared. Thereafter, all educated Sephardim knew Hebrew.

The virtual end of immigration had yet another effect on Ottoman Sephardi culture. Having lost access to Spanish and Italian books and hence, the ability to read Latin script, Sephardi Jews were cut off from non-Jewish European culture for a long time. Almosnino did not encourage his nephew to learn the Latin alphabet probably because, as a rabbi, he considered this knowledge appropriate only for scholars. But constant travel between Italy and the Ottoman Empire and continuing immigration by ex-*conversos*, whose company Almosnino recommended to the young man, made certain areas of European culture available even to those who did not know the Latin alphabet. No doubt,

Almosnino did not expect this situation to change, because in the sixteenth century the possibility of even a short period of isolation from Europe was inconceivable for Ottoman Jews.

Notes

1. Zemke, "Introduction," in Moshe ben Baruk Almosnino, *Regimiento de la vida*, 3. For a bibliography of works on Almosnino, see ibid., 2.

2. Tirosh-Samuelson, "Jewish Philosophy on the Eve of Modernity," 531.

3. A rare exception is Gutwirth's article on Shevet Yehuda cited in chapter 1, "Expulsion from Spain and Jewish Historiography."

4. All information on the Almosnino family before the expulsion, unless otherwise indicated, is borrowed from Cecil Roth, "Almosnino, Sephardi Family," in *Encyclopedia Judaica*, 2nd ed. (Detroit, 2007).

5. See Eleazar Gutwirth and Miguel Angel Motis Dolader, "Twenty-Six Jewish Libraries from Fifteenth-Century Spain," *Library* 18, no. 1 (1996): 27–53.

6. Meir Zevi Bnaya, *Moshe Almosnino of Saloniki: His Life and Work* (Tel Aviv, 1996), 17 (Heb.).

7. Ibid. Carmoly, who assumes that she was Almosnino's only wife and that she survived him, quotes the epitaph on her tombstone at the Jewish cemetery in Salonica (later destroyed). Carmoly, *La Famille Almosnino*, 11.

8. Marc Saperstein, "Moses Almosnino: Sermon on *Eleh Fequde*," in Jewish Preaching, 1200–1800. An Anthology, ed. M. Saperstein (New Haven and London, 1989), 217–239, 223.

9. Emmanuel, *Histoire des Israélites de Salonique*, 181.

10. Saperstein, "Moses Almosnino: Sermon on *Eleh Fequde*," 218. For a full list of sermons in *Me'ammes Koah* and the occasions on which they were delivered, see Ben-Menachem, "Writings by Rabbi Moshe Almosnino," 273–275.

11. *Meamez Koah* was published by his sons and nephew (Emmanuel, *Histoire des Israélites de Salonique*, 178).On Almosnino's preaching, see Saperstein, "Moses Almosnino: Sermon on *Eleh Fequde*," 218.

12. Bnaya, *Moshe Almosnino*, 85.

13. Roth, *Doña Gracia of the House of Nasi*, 129.

14. Ibid.

15. Bnaya, *Moshe Almosnino*, 26.

16. Carmoly says that Almosnino studied in Constantinople where he learned Arabic and Turkish. (*La Famille Almosnino*, 11). Bnaya believes that his Turkish was very good, since he was able to talk to the Sheyh-ul-islam. (*Moshe Almosnino*, 21.) Yet, as will be discussed in the next chapter, Almosnino could not read Ottoman Turkish, and his oral skills were quite limited. On Afia being Almosnino's mentor, see Tirosh-Samuelson, "Review of Meir Zevi Bnaya, *Moshe Almosnino of Salonika: His Life and Work*," *Jewish Quarterly Review* 89 (1998), 250–252, 251; Emmanuel, *Histoire des Israélites de Salonique*, 176.

17. Emmanuel, *Histoire des Israélites de Salonique*, 176.

18. On Almosnino's responsa, see Morris S. Goodblatt, *Jewish Life in Turkey in the XVIth Century as Reflected in the Legal Writings of Samuel de Medina* (New York, 1952), 66–70. For a discussion of *Pnei Moshe*, see Tirosh-Samuelson, "Jewish Philosophy," 536.

19. Limor Mintz-Manor, "The Jewish Discovery of America," *Jews & Journeys: Travel & the Performance of Jewish Identity.* An Online Exhibition from the Herbert D. Katz Center for Advanced Judaic Studies 2011–2012. Fellows at the University of Pennsylvania. http://www.library.upenn.edu/exhibits/cajs/fellows12/ (accessed June 5, 2012).

20. He mentions this fact in *Rejimyento* (fol. 25a).

21. Joseph Dan, *Jewish Mysticism and Jewish Ethics* (Seattle and London, 1977), 85.

22. Tirosh-Samuelson, "Jewish Philosophy on the Eve of Modernity," 536.

23. On these provisions, see Rozen, *A History of the Jewish Community in Istanbul*, 34–37.

24. James Nelson Novoa, *Los* Diálogos de amor *de León Hebreo en el marco sociocultural Sefardí del Siglo XVI* (Lisbon, 2006), 338.

25. On the original language of Leone Ebreo's work, see idem, "Consideraciones acerca de una versión aljamiada de los *Diálogos de amor* de León Hebreo," *Sefarad* 65 (2005): 103–126.

26. See ibid.

27. For the dedication, see ibid., 112–113.

28. Ibid., 123.

29. Ibid., 114.

30. See "Aaron Afia," *The Jewish Encyclopedia*; Emmanuel, *Histoire des Israélites de Salonique*, 179.

31. Hacker, "The Intellectual Activity," 1987), 95–135, 119.

32. Tirosh-Samuelson, "Review of Bnaya, *Moshe Almosnino*," 252.

33 .Bnaya, *Moshe Almosnino*, 19–20. The first one was finished before January 19, 1556 as it is mentioned in Sermon 27 in *Meamez Koah* (Emmanuel, *Histoire des Israélites de Salonique*, 179).

34. Ibid., 177.

35. This treatise does not have a title, but that is how the author refers to it in the text (Alla Markova, "El Tratado del Astrolabio de Mosé Almosnino en un manuscrito de Leningrado," *Sefarad* 51, no. 2 (1991): 437–446, 440. Nevertheless, Avner Ben Zaken, in his article "Bridging Networks of Trust: Practicing Astronomy in Late Sixteenth-Century Salonika," *Jewish History* 23 (2009), 343–361, claims that it is entitled *Introducción a la astologiá* (sic. o.b.), p. 352. Furthermore, Ben Zaken states that this text "describes how to build a personal horoscope, step by step" and that according to Almosnino, it was produced in "the year 5330 (1552 [sic. o.b.]) which I spent in Constantinople" (ibid). As will soon become clear, the untitled document described and partially published

by Markova has nothing in common with the one allegedly seen by Ben Zaken which, he claims, is housed at the same library in St. Petersburg under the same call number. (Conversely, the text discussed by Ben Zaken has not been seen by any other researcher who worked at that library.)

Not surprisingly, therefore, Ben Zaken believes that the Hebrew version of this text (discussed below) is unrelated to the Ladino one. His quotations from this treatise (p. 354), while recognizable, oddly differ from the text described and published by Carlos del Valle ("El manuscrito hebreo del Tratado de astrolabio de R. Mosé Almosnino," *Sefarad* 51, no 2 [1991]: 455–457). Ben Zaken is obviously unfamiliar with Markova's and Valle's articles.

36. Saperstein, "Moses Almosnino: Sermon on *Eleh Fequde*," 225.

37. Stephan Gerlach, *Aeltern Tage-Buch der von zween . . .* (Frankfurt/M., 1674), 26 ab.

However, Gerlach does not identify him as "Salama," as erroneously indicated by Emmanuel (*Histoire des Israélites de Salonique*, 215).

38. Although Roth mentions Abraham Salama, his information seems to have come from the same source, i.e., Almosnino's sermon. (See Roth, *The Duke of Naxos*, 168.)

39. My transcription and translation of this epistle are made from the text published by Markova, "*El Tratado del astrolabio*," 442–446.

40. The first date is indicated at the beginning of the epistle, and the second appears close to the end of the actual treatise. Almosnino states that *Estorlabyo* was finished "*en esta tyera de Konstantinopla onde agora estamos en el dia de oy ke son* [*sic*] *13 de djunyo*" (In this land of Constantinople, where we are today, which is June 13th). (*Estorlabyo*, fol. 42b.) (Quoted in Markova, "An Unknown Manuscript, on Astronomy by Moshe Almosnino," in *Hispano-Jewish Civilization after 1492*, eds. Michel Abitbol, Yom-Tov Assis, and Galit Hasan-Rokem [Jerusalem, 1997], 41–54, 46.)

41. The Hebrew introduction is quoted in Zemke's translation.

42. Yaari, *Hebrew Printing*, no. 150.

43. Nasi produced a record of the dispute on certain metaphysical matters he had with some Christian scholars at Belvedere in 1575. Don Joseph was hardly fluent in Hebrew because he embraced Judaism only at the age of thirty when he came to the Ottoman Empire where, while patronizing learning and publishing, he did not engage in serious studies himself. He composed Ben Porat Yosef in Portuguese, his native language, but it was published by Joseph Jabez in a Hebrew translation made by r. Isaac Onkeneira (Constantinople, 1577). (Yaari, Hebrew Printing, no. 193.)

44. Roth, *The Duke of Naxos*, 180.

45. On this treatise, see Markova, "An Unknown Manuscript on Astronomy."

46. Quoted in Markova, "El Tratado del astrolabio," 440.

47. Emmanuel, *Histoire des Israélites de Salonique*, 179.

48. Mauro Zonta, "Influence of Arabic and Islamic Philosophy on Judaic Thought," in The Stanford Encyclopedia of Philosophy, Spring 2011, ed. Edward N. Zalta: http://plato.stanford.edu/archives/spr2011/entries/arabic-islamic-judaic (accessed December 1, 2015).

49. See "Ethical Literature," *Encyclopedia Judaica.*

50. Quoted in Zemke, "Introduction," in Moshe ben Baruk Almosnino, *Regimiento de la vida,* 17.

51. *Pnei Moshe*, which, according to Emmanuel, was finished in January 1556 (*Histoire des Israélites de Salonique,* 179) was never published. Perhaps, in 1564, Almosnino had it copied and was proofreading the copy.

52. I do not understand why Nelson Novoa thinks that Almosnino says this "rather disparagingly." W. Nelson Novoa, "The Peninsula Hither and Thither: Philosophical Texts in Vernacular Languages by Sephardic Jews before and after the Expulsion," *Hispania Judaica* 8 (2011): 149–166, 163. My analysis in this chapter shows the opposite.

53. Quoted in Romero, *Creación literaria,* 37.

54. While the rest of the volume is not vocalized, these 515 words are printed with vowel points, so we have what amounts to their phonetic transcription. It is astonishing that Almosnino's glossary, an important source on the vocabulary and phonetics of sixteenth-century Sephardi vernacular, so far has been almost completely ignored by linguists. The only publication that deals with it is a short article, most of which is taken up by the list of Ladino words in Almosnino's glossary: A. W. Wainman, "An Analysis of the Judeo-Spanish Glossary in *El resimiento de la vida* by M. Almosnino (Salonica, 1564)," in *Actes du premier Congrès international des études balkaniques et sud-est européennes*, no. 6 (Sofia, 1972): 175–179. Its title notwithstanding, the article offers no analysis whatsoever.

55. Benaim, *Sixteenth-Century Judeo-Spanish Testimonies,* 191.

56. Zemke, "Introduction" in Moshe ben Baruk Almosnino, *Regimiento de la vida,* 12. However, those *romancimientos*, as Schwartzwald has shown, were recorded as the Constantinople and Ferrara Bibles and thus would be easily identifiable. (See Schwartzwald, "The Relationship between Ladino Liturgical Texts and Spanish Bibles.")

57. Since *Rejimyento* is written in Ladino, it seems that in this case, by "foreign words" Almosnino understood those he borrowed from Castilian. Thus, he was aware that Ottoman Jews did not speak Castilian. Yet, as we have seen, he sometimes refers to the spoken language and that of his works as *romanse kastelyano.*

58. Dan, *Jewish Mysticism,* 16.

59. Ibid.

60. Gutwirth, "On the Hispanicity of Sephardi Jewry," 347.

61. See, for instance, Martin Camargo, *Ars dictaminis, Ars dictandi* (Turnhout, 1991).

62. Rita Costa Gomes, "Letters and Letter-Writing in Fifteenth Century Portugal," in *Reading, Interpreting and Historicizing: Letters as Historical Sources. EUI Working Paper*, no. 2 (2004): 11–38, 28.

63. Ibid.

64. See Carol Anne Copenhagen, "Letters and Letter-Writing in Fifteenth Century Castile. A Study and Catalogue," (PhD diss., University of California, Davis, 1984).

65. Gutwirth, "Medieval Romance Epistolarity," 214.

66. Gutwirth, "Jews and Courts," 5. For a discussion of this letter, see Gutwirth, "Medieval Romance Epistolarity," 212.

67. Ibid., 218.

68. For some of those letters, see Gutwirth, "A Judeo-Spanish letter from the Genizah," in *Judeo-Romance Languages*, eds. I. Benabu and J. Sermoneta (Jerusalem, 1985), 127–138; Quintana, "Responsa Testimonies and Letters Written in the Sixteenth Century Spanish Spoken by Sephardim," *Hispania Judaica* 5 (2007): 283–302; Quintana, "The Merger of the Hispanic Medieval Heritage with the Jewish Tradition in Judeo-Spanish Texts (I): Private Letters," *Hispania Judaica* 7 (2010): 317–333.

69. For samples of Hebrew correspondence in translation, see Franz Kobbler, *A Treasury of Jewish Letters*, vols. 1 and 2 (Philadelphia, 1953).

70. Gutwirth, "Italy or Spain? The Theme of Jewish Eloquence in *Shevet Yehudah*," in *Daniel Carpi Jubilee Volume*, eds. M. Rozen, D. Porat, and A. Shapira (Tel Aviv, 1996), 35–67, 47.

71. See Umberto Cassuto, *Gli ebrei a Firenze nell'età del Rinascimento* (Florence, 1918), 327–340.

72. Ibid., 327.

73. Yaari, *Hebrew Printing*, no. 141.

74. Gutwirth, "Profayt Duran on Ahitofel: The Practice of Jewish History in Late Medieval Spain," *Jewish History* 4, no. 1 (1989): 59–74. 71.

75. Ibid., 60.

76. Duran's famous anti-Christian epistle "*Al Tehi Ka-Aboteka*" (Be not like your fathers) was first published in Constantinople in 1554, with an introduction by Isaac Akrish. Some other works by Duran appeared in the sixteenth century in Italy. ("Profiat Duran," *The Jewish Encyclopedia*.)

77. Costa Gomes, "Letters and Letter-Writing in Fifteenth Century Portugal," 25.

78. Gutwirth, "Hebrew Letters, Hispanic Mail: Communication Among Fourteenth-Century Aragon Jewry," in *Communication in the Jewish Diaspora in the Pre-Modern Period*, ed. S. Menache (Leiden, 1996), 257–282, 274.

79. Ibid.

80. The last page of *Estorlabyo* is transcribed in Markova, "An unknown Manuscript on Astronomy," 43.

81. Costa Gomes, "Letters and Letter-Writing in Fifteenth Century Portugal," 26, esp. n. 39.

82. Fernando del Pulgar, *Letras*. Biblioteca Virtual Miguel Cervantes: http://www.cervantesvirtual.com/obra/letras-o/ (accessed November 29, 2012).

83. Roth, *The Duke of Naxos*, 172.

84. Rabi Moysen Almosnino, *Extremos y grandezas de Constantinopla*, 10–11.

85. Markova, "An unknown Manuscript on Astronomy," 47.

86. Not in spring, as is indicated in Ben Zaken's "quotation" from Almosnino's treatise. ("Bridging networks of trust," 354.)

87. For a description of the Hebrew version and a transcription of its introduction, see Valle, "El manuscrito hebreo del *Tratado del astrolabio*." I am indebted to Alina Polonskaya for her thorough analysis of this text.

88. On this genre, see "Ethical Literature," *Encyclopedia Judaica*.

89. Valle, "El Manuscrito hebreo," 455.

90. An instrument similar to the astrolabe. On this treatise, see "Al-Zarqālī (or Azarquiel), Abū Isḥāqibrāhīm Ibn Yaḥyā Al-Naqqāsh," in *Complete Dictionary of Scientific Biography*: http://www.encyclopedia.com/doc/1G2-2830904769.html (accessed July 25, 2012).

91. For this date, see Emmanuel, *Histoire des Israélites de Salonique*, 176.

92. Margherita Morreale de Castro, "El superlativo en ísimo y la versión castellana del Cortesano," *Revista de Filología Española* 39, no. 1–4 (1955): 46–60, 46.

93. Ibid., 56.

94. For this observation on the works of Juan Valdes and Antonio de Guevara, see ibid., 57.

95. Besides, in *Estorlabyo*, we find the Latin term *e setera* (also used in *Crónica*).

96. Gutwirth, "Medieval Romance Epistolarity," 210.

97. "I am, Sir, [the person] you well know, and you are a person I thought I knew . . . I am, Sir, not asking you to give me what belongs to you, I am asking you not to take away what belongs to me." (Pulgar, *Letras*.)

98. Trans. Zemke.

99. Alonso Zamora Vicente, *Dialectologia española* (Madrid, 1967), 360; Gutwirth, "On the Hispanicity of Sephardi Jewry," 356; Benaim, *Sixteenth-Century Judeo-Spanish Testimonies*, 135.

100. "You, Sir, being most upright and prudent, asked me for a very short summary . . . I, Sir, despite all my occupations from which, as you well know, I cannot excuse myself at present, in view of your great desire and sincere wish to know what until now, as you say, nobody has explained to you."

101. "My noble and magnificent Sir, you say that you prefer to see my reasons rather than my advice. In truth, my noble Sir, I want you to see my services rather than either of the two; but because my services are few and insignificant, I replaced them with the advice I sent you. Nevertheless, Sir, I do not want you

to be disappointed. You have to understand that [even] if I did everything in my power to serve you, I assure you this would be of little value."

102. There might be a connection between Almosnino's adoption of *vuestra merced* with the third-person verb and the usage of the Hebrew term of respect, *maalato*, literally "his highness." It was sometimes used in rabbinical literature and is found in the Hebrew version of *Estorlabyo* (also used inconsistently).

103. Jose Amador de los Ríos, *Historia social, politica, y religiosa de los judíos de España y Portugal* (Madrid, 1960), 685, 817.

104. See, for example, David A. Boruchoff, "Historiography with License: Isabel, the Catholic Monarch and the Kingdom of God," in *Isabel la Católica, Queen of Castile: Critical Essays*, ed. David Boruchoff (New York, 2003), 225–294, 251–254.

105. Here, Almosnino spells *Tolemeo* in the Castilian way, not "Btolomeus" as in the Hebrew version of *Tratado de Estorlabyo*. Another Hebrew spelling was "Tolomeus," which is found, for example, in Saadia Gaon's commentary on the Book of Daniel. I thank Phillip Ackerman-Lieberman for this information.

106. "Constantinople, according to Ptolemy, is situated at forty-three degrees latitude (for those who do not understand, this is how much the [celestial North] Pole departs from the celestial equator and rises above it)." (Pedro Mexía, *Silva de varia lección,* Antonio Castro Diaz, ed. [Madrid, 1989], vol. 1, 263.)

107. Antonio Castro Diaz, Introducción in ibid., 52.

108. In many cases, it was replaced with a Gallicism, a lexical-syntactic French calque: *donde* (where) used for *dont* (of which). Strangely, this syntactic phenomenon does not seem to have attracted the attention of any linguists.

109. Almosnino, *Crónica*, 207.

110. In Hebrew, if the relative conjunction is not the subject or direct object of the clause, it has to be resumed within this clause by an anaphoric element, usually a possessive pronoun bound on a preposition. I thank Sergey Lyozov for this explanation.

111. Even if *Heh* indeed represented a slightly aspirated sound (as suggested by Alberto Várvaro and Laura Minervini, "Orígenes del judeoespañol (II)," *Revista de Historia de la Lengua Española* 3 [2008]: 149–195, 170.), the inconsistency of its usage in Almosnino's works (e.g., *habitasyon* but *abituado*) and the use of *rr* seem to indicate that his spelling was influenced by his reading.

112. With the exception of the word *estorlabyo.* A search in http://www.corpusdelespanol.org/ shows 16 tokens of *astrolabio* in the sixteenth century and not a single one of *estorlabyo* (accessed December 14, 2015).

113. Gutwirth, "Italy or Spain?" 36.

THREE

Almosnino's Chronicles

THE OTTOMAN EMPIRE THROUGH THE EYES OF COURT JEWS

Having discussed Almosnino's epistles, I will now turn to his *Crónica de los reyes otomanos*, the most interesting of his creations and one of the least studied works of Ladino literature. The few scholars who have written about *Crónica* consider it a regular travelogue and describe Almosnino as a "perceptive and impartial observer."[1] However, *Crónica* consists of four books that differ significantly from one another and belong to different genres. In this chapter, I discuss the first two books. In chapter 4 I will turn to the third one and explain why the fourth book is irrelevant to the subject of my study.

The first two books, Almosnino's Ottoman chronicles, like *Crónica* as a whole, were written for the same audience as the epistles, but they were not answers to anyone's questions. Instead, as I will argue, the chronicles were commissioned to Almosnino by a few wealthy Jews close to the Ottoman court and, therefore, express their perspective (obviously shared by the writer). Thus, Almosnino was by no means impartial, and not even so much an observer as a listener, since he had not witnessed most of what he described. This means that the chronicles are not a reliable source on Ottoman history but rather a window on the political concerns and hopes of the Jewish court elite in the 1560s.

Among other things, the first two books of *Crónica* (together with the fourth) are unusual in that they are the first among the very few original narratives in Ladino, that is they were produced by their author independently of any other texts. In addition, *Crónica* as a whole was the first entirely secular work of Ladino literature (except for the scientific treatises mentioned in previous chapters). This is why, in order to construct his chronicles, Almosnino had to borrow elements of some European literary genres. As a result, these two books at first glance appear to belong to various genres at the same time, whereas in reality they do not fit into any formal category and can be adequately defined only in terms of purpose and message. Finally, Almosnino's chronicles of Ottoman sultans, the first vernacular histories written by a Sephardi Jew, beg comparison to the Hebrew histories of non-Jewish monarchs produced by his contemporaries.

In what follows, I will examine the formal characteristics and message of each chronicle and demonstrate that despite outward similarities, these texts are intrinsically different from respective European genres in terms of message and political perspective. In addition, I will briefly compare Almosnino's chronicles with two Hebrew histories to show the profound differences between them at all levels, determined by their methods of interpreting history. In conclusion, I will propose a new genre definition of Almosnino's chronicles based on their content and purpose.

Since a few articles have already focused on its language, I will not analyze *Crónica*'s linguistic aspects, except for briefly commenting on some of the Turkisms, because they are part of the chronicles' message. Because the common perception of *Crónica's* genre has to do with how it reached us, I will begin with its publication history.

The History of *Crónica*

Given what we know about Jewish printing in the sixteenth century, it is not surprising that *Crónica*, Almosnino's seventh Ladino creation, was not published in the Ottoman Empire. In fact, he would not have expected this to happen, since it was a secular work that did not provide instruction in Judaism or the sciences. *Crónica* circulated in manuscript copies, and we have evidence of four of them, though to the best of my knowledge, only one has survived.

The earliest of these copies is mentioned by the poet Saadia Longo (d. 1586) in his book published posthumously in Salonica in 1594. According to Longo, a Salonican rabbi, Aharon Sasson, gave a copy of Almosnino's work to his cousin, Jacob Sasson of Constantinople, during the latter's visit to Salonica.[2] However, Longo refers to it as "A History of Ottoman Kings, Suleyman and his Son Sultan Selim," which may mean that the manuscript included only the first two books of *Crónica.*

As will be remembered, in 1638, Jacob Cansino published an abridged adaptation of Almosnino's work in Madrid, in Latin characters under the title *Extremos y grandezas de Constantinopla*, which is based on a manuscript unknown to us. This edition does not include *Crónica*'s fourth part. The third manuscript, held at the Ambrosian Library in Milan, was purchased by a Venetian merchant from a Salonican scribe in 1666 and later acquired by Moses Lattes after whose death in 1883 it was transferred to its present location.[3] Having compared the manuscript and the Cansino edition, Lattes realized that they significantly differed from each other and made a list of their discrepancies.[4] Pilar Romeu Ferré, who transliterated and published the manuscript in 1998, continued the work of comparison and came to the conclusion that Cansino's text was not based on the extant manuscript.[5]

Finally, the existence in 1902 of a fourth copy of Almosnino's work is indirectly attested to by Abraham Danon's publication in *El Tyempo* (a Ladino periodical of Constantinople) of two excerpts from *Crónica*, slightly adapted for the newspaper's readers.[6] The first excerpt differs in terms of facts from its counterpart in Cansino's edition, and is identical to the one in the Ambrosian Library manuscript, while the second fragment is taken from the part missing from Cansino's version. Moreover, it is clear from Danon's short preface that the organization of material in the manuscript he had used was the same as in the extant one, which was changed by Cansino.[7] Since as far as we know, Danon did not travel to Milan, we may assume that he either saw *Crónica* at another library (which appears unlikely) or that among many other Ladino documents this scholar had in his possession in Edirne, there was a full version of Almosnino's work.

The existence of at least two different versions of *Crónica* and the significant discrepancies between them suggest that in the sixteenth century it had a rather wide circulation that caused these variations and text corruption. These manuscript copies continued to circulate in the seventeenth century; one reached Cansino in Oran, while another version remained in Salonica where it was reproduced, possibly in multiple copies for sale, by a local scribe. These facts suggest that its audience may have been rather large for the time. Moreover, a hundred years after *Crónica*'s creation, the scribe sold the manuscript for two Venetian zecchinos (ducats) and 2.5 feet of purple satin,[8] which was made from silk and was quite expensive at the time. This suggests that in the seventeenth century, it was considered valuable.

Yet, as discussed in the introduction, in later periods, it was not known to Ottoman Sephardim who first learned of its existence at the end of the nineteenth century from Europeans familiar with *Extremos y grandezas de Constantinopla*. By that time, however, Almosnino's message had been largely obscured, and not only because this is the fate of all texts, but also as a result of Cansino's "editing."

Contrary to what he says, Cansino not only transcribed the original text into Latin characters, but also adapted and rearranged it. We can assume that his copy, like at least two others, consisted of three books that were finished on different dates, the third divided into two parts. Book I is an account of Suleyman's death and the accession of Selim II (fall of 1566), Book II is a chronicle of Suleyman's rule (1520–1566), and Book III includes a treatise on Constantinople and a report on the Salonican delegation's negotiations at the court. Since the two parts of the third book present separate works, I will refer to them as Book III and Book IV for the sake of convenience. Preparing his edition for a Christian audience, Cansino had to minimize (though not eliminate) its "Jewishness," which is why he did not include the fourth part, an account of Jewish affairs (which would not have interested his readers in any case). In addition, for political reasons, he had to give less prominence to the Muslim kings. For this reason, he moved the two Ottoman chronicles to the second and third places, and made the third part (a treatise on Constantinople) the opening section of his volume.

In addition to these adjustments, Cansino used a clever marketing device: he gave his book a title that successfully disguised the true nature of Almosnino's work. Wishing to present three parts of Almosnino's work created at different times as one conventional travel account, Cansino entitled his volume *Extremos y grandezas de Constantinopla*, thus placing it in a category of Spanish (and rarely, Portuguese) travelogues that first appeared in the sixteenth century. Among these travelogues, one finds *Libro de grandezas y cosas memorables de España* (A book of great and memorable things of Spain) by Pedro de Medina (Seville, 1548);

Libro de las grandezas y cosas memorables de la . . . famosa Ciudad de Tarragona (A book of great and memorable things from the . . . famous city of Tarragona) by Luis Pons de Ycart (Lerida, 1572); *Grandezas y antiguedades de la isla y Ciudad de Cádiz* (Great and ancient things of the city and island of Cadiz) by Juan Bautista Suárez de Salazar (Cádiz, 1610); *Libro de Ecija i sus grandezas* (Book of Ecija and its great things) by Andrés Florindo (Seville, 1631); and many others.

Although Almosnino does not say anything about the "great things" of Constantinople, the genre expectations prompted by Cansino's title determined, for centuries to come, the perception of *Crónica* as a regular travelogue. Yet it is thanks to Cansino's edition that *Crónica* was not forgotten and became available to Europeans and through them, to Sephardim. Without it, the extant manuscript might not have attracted as much attention from later scholars.

The untitled manuscript held at the Ambrosian Library, on which Romeu based her edition, has 239 pages (on 120 folios) in unvocalized Judeo-Spanish handwriting, almost without punctuation marks.[9] The four books it contains were written between December 1566 and September 1567 in Constantinople.

Crónica is a product of Almosnino's long mission to the Ottoman capital in 1566–1568, when he was a member of the delegation sent by the Jewish community of Salonica to reclaim tax privileges granted to it by Suleyman the Magnificent when he passed through the city in 1537. However, the document stipulating these tax exemptions perished in the great fire of 1545, and was not renewed. The return of heavy taxes and corvées had become a heavy burden for Salonican Jews, which finally compelled community leaders to take action.[10]

After a long and hazardous journey by sea and land, the delegation consisting of three prominent Salonican Jews arrived in the Ottoman capital in late June 1566, but the desired goal was fully achieved only in January 1568, by which time Almosnino's two colleagues had died. The Salonican rabbi returned to his hometown not only with the long-sought charter of privileges, but also with a new manuscript finished in late September 1567, when it became clear that triumph was at hand.

The story of the delegation's travails at the Ottoman court is recounted in *Crónica*'s final part. The delegation first approached authorities during the last weeks of Suleyman's reign, when he was away on a military campaign. Joseph Nasi, who was close to Suleyman's son, Prince Selim, proposed a commission of one thousand ducats to obtain a letter from the prince reinstating tax privileges that would have to be confirmed once Selim became king (237).[11] Almosnino's colleagues declined the offer. Suleyman never returned from his last campaign aimed at capturing Vienna; he died in Hungary on September 6, 1566. Thus the delegation's next six attempts to obtain a "Writ of Freedom" were made at the court of Sultan Selim II (r. 1566–1574).

Hence, Almosnino was in the capital in late November 1566, when Suleyman's body was delivered there. The burial was followed, in early December, by Selim's enthronement, all of which he described in Book I. As dates in the text indicate, Almosnino wrote it in about forty-eight hours, between the evening of December 11 and the evening of December 13, during the coronation festivities. The author summarizes its contents as follows:

> A record of what happened during the last war waged by our great master, Sultan Suleyman, may he dwell in glory, and of his death at the time when his army was besieging Szigetvar, and of how his son, Sultan Selim, may God increase his prosperity, ruled before returning from the campaign and entering Constantinople and his palace, and of everything that happened during his entry. (59)

In addition, it contains a short chronology of the Ottoman sultans who reigned before Suleyman.

Book II was composed in 1567 between April 10 and 24, during the Bayram holiday.

> This book offers, a general summary of the reign of the previous king, may he rest in glory, and of the victories in the wars won through his intercession, and of his noble way of ruling his people with reason and justice, and of his extreme passion for ennobling the empire by means of valuable edifices, and of his courtiers, and of all the benefits they brought worthy of being recorded. (105)

Book III and Book IV belong to different genres. But because, according to Almosnino, they were finished at the same time (September 26, 1567), he describes them together as "an account of some of the extremes without anything in the middle found in the city of Constantinople and of the immense travails that we endured on our journey in the service of

God and our republic" (207). Book III is a treatise on "the extremes" of Constantinople, i.e., a description of the Ottoman capital as seen through its author's idiosyncratic lens, whereas Book IV is a detailed, day-by-day account of the delegation's efforts to obtain the desired charter.

Between the European Travelogue and Jewish History

While unique in Ladino literature in terms of genre and subject, Almosnino's two chronicles are anything but original in the context of sixteenth-century European literature. Descriptions of Constantinople, the "Grand Turk," his court, army, and wealth were among the most popular subjects, especially among Italians. Between 1501 and 1550, over a thousand texts on the Ottoman Empire saw light in Europe, and in the second half of the century, another 2,500 or so appeared.[12] These numbers include not only books but also speeches of Venetian Bailos at their senate and other documents. In addition, many accounts, including those by Giovanni Antonio Menavino, Nicolas de Nicolay, and Benedetto Ramberti, were translated into various languages and reprinted multiple times. A few descriptions of the Ottoman capital and Turkish customs were even used in a work of fiction, the anonymous *Viaje de Turquía* (quoted in chapter 1), which presents Suleyman's rule as a model to be emulated by Spanish kings.[13]

The Republic of Venice, whose relationship with the Sublime Porte was particularly important and which had had its embassy in Constantinople since 1453, was especially interested in Ottoman finances and the army.[14] France also had a special relationship with the Porte, confirmed in 1536 by the capitulations, treaties that allowed both sides (as in the case of Venice) to establish trading communities on each other's territories.[15] The French embassy served not only diplomatic but also cultural purposes and either brought to Constantinople or supported such famous scholars and travelers as the philologist Pierre Gilles and geographer Nicolas de Nicolay, who produced well-known accounts of the Ottoman Empire and its capital.[16]

Almosnino, undoubtedly, read some of the European travelogues, especially those published in Venice that would have been easily available to him through book traders. It is also likely that some ex-*conversos* brought with them a few European travel accounts that they would have read before settling in the empire. Almosnino's familiarity with some of those works is not only evident from certain features of his chronicles, but is directly confirmed by him. In fact, he clearly expected his readers at least to know about the existence of such travelogues. Thus, describing Constantinople, he notes "as everybody writes, the city is eighteen miles in circuit" (80). We find precisely the same sentence in *Libri tre delle cose de Turchi* (Three books on Turkish matters) by Benedetto Ramberti, secretary to the Senate of Venice, who traveled to the Ottoman Empire in 1534. Ramberti indicates "[t]he city is 18 miles in circuit."[17] His book first appeared in Venice in 1539 and four years later, in the same city, it was incorporated into *Viaggi . . . alia tana . . .* (known as "Travels to the Don") and then reprinted multiple times.[18] While it was used by other authors in their travelogues, it is likely that Ramberti himself, at least partly, copied an earlier account, which was common at the time.[19] Hence, the Salonican scholar could have found this phrase in a few different travelogues.

It is also likely that "everybody" included Benjamin of Tudela, a twelfth-century Jewish traveler whose famous account written in Hebrew was for the first time printed in Constantinople by Soncino in 1543 and then reprinted in Ferrara by Abraham Usque in 1559.[20] Benjamin, too, states "the circumference of the city of Constantinople amounts to eighteen miles."[21]

Yet the following vignette is definitely of European origin. Discussing the sultan's couriers (*peyk*), Almosnino notes, "some say, they have their spleens removed at a young age which allows them to walk without getting tired." He admits that he did not believe this until it was confirmed by "someone who knows it very well" (91–92). Once again, he could have found this tale in Ramberti or, in another well-known book also published in Venice, Menavino's *I cinque libri delle legge, religione, et vita de turchi* (The five books of the laws, religion, and life of the Turks) (1548).[22] This belief must have been related to Aristotle's notion of the spleen being a "bastard liver" producing poor-quality blood that continued to be popular in Europe in the first half of the sixteenth century.[23] Apparently, this European myth illustrating both the Turks' barbarity and their efficiency was confirmed by one of Almosnino's friends close to the court.

Almosnino also seems to refer to European authors when, praising the architectural achievements of Suleyman's reign, he appeals to the authority of "more experienced travelers."[24] For instance, claiming that the columns in the Suleymaniye complex built by the chief imperial architect are the thickest, widest, and tallest in the world, Almosnino says "this is confirmed by other people, who are knowledgeable about such things and have seen them [columns] in great numbers in other parts of the world" (181). Admiring the Çekmece Bridge not far from Constantinople, he claims that even those "who have seen more of the world than I did" have never encountered anything like it (200).

Yet, despite all the similarities with European accounts and numerous allusions to them, Almosnino's work drastically differs from all of them in two respects: (a) in the attitude toward the Ottomans, and (b) in the purpose of writing about them. European interest in the empire and its army, in particular, was to a large degree prompted by the fear of a Muslim invasion and the need to understand the enemy. Indeed, Suleyman began his reign by conquering Belgrade (1521) and continued moving the Ottoman borders farther west, hoping to conquer Rome, and attempting to capture Vienna until his last day.[25] In addition, a few accounts written by Christians who had spent some time in the empire as prisoners painted Islam in dark colors, warning Christians of the Ottoman threat. This is true, for instance, of Bartolomeo Giorgievits who, having returned from captivity, published *Turcarum moribus epitome* (The Epitome of Turkish customs) (c. 1544), which, translated into various languages, enjoyed great popularity.

Besides, most travelers and especially scholars, such as Pierre Gilles, felt that the "barbarians," i.e., the Turks, seized what had been part of classical and Christian antiquity and formed the core of European culture. In this spirit, many authors, Ramberti and Nicolay among them, claimed that the Turks had turned the famous Church of Hagia Sophia into the sultan's stables.[26] Therefore, European attitudes toward the Ottomans were a mixture of fear of the potent "barbarous" empire and admiration for its prosperity, splendor, and court ceremonial. Most foreign observers were in awe of the powerful sultan Suleyman I whom they dubbed "the Magnificent."

Among the most insightful and informed European accounts are *The Turkish Letters* of Ogier Ghiselin de Busbecq, ambassador of Ferdinand I of Austria at Constantinople in 1554–1562, who personally met Suleyman more than once. Despite his general openness to new impressions and shrewd criticism of European ways, one finds in Busbecq's

Letters a fundamental rejection and mistrust of Islam. He cannot but feel that what used to be Byzantium is mourning its past: "The land which discovered all the arts and all liberal learning seems to demand back the civilization which she has transmitted to us and to implore our aid, in the name of our common faith, against savage barbarism."[27]

Almosnino's perspective is entirely different if only because he is not a Christian, and as a Jew he has no cultural, religious, or territorial misgivings. In fact, he was certainly aware that in 1561, Suleyman gave the Nasi family special permission to re-establish a self-dependent Jewish settlement in Tiberias.[28] Hence, when talking about Suleyman's capture of Baghdad (1535–1536), Almosnino concludes that it was beneficial for the city and mentions in a matter-of-fact tone that it used to be "abundant in sages expert in our Talmud" (113). On the other hand, his comment about the conquest of Rhodes in 1522, which expanded the Porte's control of the eastern Mediterranean, shows his awareness of what this meant for Europe, and his lack of sympathy for it. He explains that this provoked "great terror and fear in Christendom," which was afraid to lose other lands and fortresses that were weaker than Rhodes. "And," he adds, "they had reason to be afraid" (110).

Most important, however, Almosnino was an Ottoman subject and thus, to a large degree, an insider. His readers are constantly reminded of this by his references to the sultans. Unlike Europeans who call Suleyman "the Grand Turk" or "Grand Seignor," he usually refers to him and his son Selim as "our great master" (*nuestro gran senyor*) followed by an appropriate formula, such as "may he dwell in glory" or "may God increase his prosperity." Most of the time, he adds Hebrew blessings, not commonly used for non-Jews: *nishmato Eden* (may his soul be in Eden) or *yarum hodó* (may He exalt his majesty).

Almosnino was certainly not the first Jew to bless Ottoman sultans and ask God to exalt them. Similar formulas appear in the colophons of a few Hebrew books published in Constantinople in the sixteenth century. The most loquacious of them says:

> The book was completed at the end of the month of Elul in the year 5307 [September 1556] in Istanbul, the fine city, the city of a great king, a faithful shepherd, our master the Sultan Suleyman, may his splendor be exalted, and his honor grow, and in his times and ours may Judea and Israel be redeemed and may the redeemer come to Zion.[29]

Minna Rozen suggests that these wishes reflected the publishers' feelings, and, therefore, should be taken at face value as "an enthusiastic declaration of gratitude to the sultan, expressing the hope that he was the herald of redemption."[30] While it is quite possible that those authors indeed felt gratitude toward Suleyman, colophons were never meant to convey anyone's feelings. At the same time, as Rozen rightly points out, publishers did not expect any Ottoman officials to see these praises. Hence, most likely, they were statements of loyalty whose language is so formulaic and universal that it could refer to any sultan. In fact, a similar formula was used three centuries later by a newspaper publisher in his first editorial.[31]

What is important for us here is that these dedications express the attitude of Jews toward their monarchs in terms of Jewish history, where the function of Ottoman sultans is to protect God's people until the Messiah comes and redeems it.

Almosnino's older contemporaries, Eliyah Kapsali (c. 1483–1555) and Joseph Ha-Kohen (1496–1578), who wrote in Hebrew about Ottoman kings, also remained within this framework because, regardless of what events they related, their subject was Jewish history. Kapsali's *Seder Eliahu Zuta* (The Minor Order of Eliyah), produced in Crete in 1523, is a survey of Ottoman history up to the author's time, which Yosef Yerushalmi considers "a first . . . attempt to write a Jewish history within the framework of general history." Nonetheless, it is "messianic history at its most exuberant."[32] Kapsali presents Mehmed II (r. 1451–1481) as God's instrument called to "attend to His people, the seed of Abraham His servant, the sons of Jacob, His chosen ones, to provide them with a livelihood in the land and to grant them a safe haven."[33]

Ha-Kohen's *Divrei ha-yamim le-malhei Tsarfat u-malhei bet Otoman ha-togur* (The History of the Kings of France and of the Ottoman Turkish Sultans), which appeared in Venice in 1554, displays obvious apocalyptic elements and is "not a mere exercise in French and Turkish history, but an attempt to trace the age-old struggle between Christendom and Islam" seen as the struggle between Gog and Magog.[34] In other words, Ha-Kohen's work has two levels, a historical one and a biblical one.

There is no reason to believe that Almosnino rejected his contemporaries' view of Jewish history, but unlike Kapsali and Ha-Kohen, he produced a straightforward vernacular work without any references or even allusions to Jewish history, the Iberian expulsions, or the future of the Jewish people. *Crónica* is a secular history of an empire where some Jews of unstated origins happened to be living at a particular moment. By "secular history" I mean one that relates historical events without interpreting them from the perspective of any religion.

Not surprisingly, therefore, Almosnino's two chronicles show no continuity with Jewish historiography (that used exclusively Hebrew), which in the sixteenth century continued to interpret the world in terms of Judaism. As far as genre and historical method, *Crónica* is much more similar to contemporaneous European accounts, which, even if they express some Christian idiosyncrasies, are secular in nature and usually motivated by political ideologies. In the following sections, I will show that Almosnino's historical writings, at times akin to propaganda, were also politically motivated, since their production was a pragmatic enterprise.

The First Chronicle

It is commonly assumed that Almosnino produced the first chronicle because someone in Salonica had asked him for an account of the great events he had witnessed in the capital. Yet there is no evidence to support this assumption. Almosnino tells us that he was urged by "some gentlemen" (*algunos senyores*) whom he could not disobey, to write a short summary of what he had seen and of "the information (sic) about the rest which [he] had received from those who were there," because all of this was necessary to understand "the greatness of this great and famous court and exalted state" (78). In the colophon he reiterates "the gentlemen" suggested that he write this book, which includes what was grasped by his "imperfect vision" and what he learned from some "very competent people who are constantly engaged in business at this court" (102–103).

In other words, Almosnino's first chronicle was commissioned by some eyewitnesses connected to the court who provided him with information that would enlighten his readers about the grandeur of the Ottoman Empire. There is no doubt that the key person behind this enterprise was Joseph Nasi, Selim's favorite, at whose mansion the Salonican traveler was staying and who had first-hand knowledge of most of the events described in the first chronicle, as well as access to information about the rest. Other members of the Nasi circle might have also encouraged Almosnino and offered additional information, but, as further analysis will show, it was unquestionably Don Joseph who directed his work and without whom it could not have been written, let alone in forty-eight hours.

Contrary to centuries-old belief, Almosnino witnessed only a very small part of what is related in Book I that covers the circumstances of Suleyman's death and the events that took place before and during Selim's coronation (at which time he stayed home and wrote the first chronicle). In fact, except for one case, he does not even claim to have seen what he describes. All that Almosnino saw during the accession festivities from a shop where he stayed from dawn until noon with some of his "esteemed friends" (*mis senyores i amigos*) (81), was the passage of the new king followed by his suite. But this was only a small part of what happened that day, and it took just a few hours out of the three months covered by the chronicle.

Since Book I centers on Selim with whom the Jewish merchant and courtier had spent a significant amount of time, we can be certain that Almosnino refers to his host as he writes, "When I conducted negotiations at his court while he [Selim] was a prince, I was assured and thoroughly informed by someone who knew it very well and spoke with him many times." (100). Almosnino cites his sources on a wide range of subjects, without naming them but most often referring to his informants as "competent people" close to the court. On the subject of Suleyman's death, he cites various alleged diagnoses but concludes that the true reason must have been blood loss caused by dysentery, as he learned from someone who really knew the cause (62). This information could have been conveyed to him by Nasi or, perhaps, directly either by Joseph Hamon, who had replaced his father, the famous Moses Hamon, as the Sultan's personal physician, or by another doctor, Judah de Segura, both of whom Almosnino knew personally.

In the sermon he delivered in March 1568 at the Salonican Talmud Torah, with the purpose of giving members of various congregations an account of the delegation's mission, Almosnino thanks, aside from Nasi, "the wise R. Judah de Segura, who helped us with the imperial treasurer," "the clever and influential R. Abraham Salama; in his great kindness he interceded for us with the grand mufti," "the wise R. Meir ibn Sanche," and "the blessed . . . physician R. Joseph Hamon." As Almosnino informs his listeners, the first three on his list served as the delegation's "spokesmen before His Excellency the grand vizier."[35] Meir ibn Sanche (Bensanchi) was a "wealthy Constantinople scholar and businessman . . . an old friend of the Nasi family . . . who combined profound talmudic learning with considerable literary skill and was a member of the famous Poetical Academy of Salonica," where his family members continued to reside.[36]

Thus, all of Almosnino's informants (possibly with the exception of ibn Sanche) were close to the court, where they had acquaintances among various grandees, bureaucrats, and other insiders who served as their sources of privileged information. Furthermore, one of Almosnino's contacts, most likely Abraham Salama, had access to some Ottoman chronicles and was able to read them. We learn about it thanks to Almosnino's attack on Joseph Ha-Kohen's work.

Almosnino was familiar with Ha-Kohen's *Divrei ha-yamim* and probably met the author during the latter's stay in Salonica in 1544–1547. He obviously expected some of his readers to know his predecessor's version of Ottoman history, which is why, even as he acknowledged that the digression was out of place, Almosnino decided to expose Ha-Kohen's errors. Thus, he rather irreverently claims that the "modern [author] named Ha-Kohen who wrote a general chronicle" should not be considered an authority on the sultans' chronology, because he is confused even about the number of Suleyman's horses and the sultans' names. Worst of all, Ha-Kohen added to the list a non-existent one (87–88). He mentions someone called Kyerí who, as Almosnino points out, never existed, because "it is known for certain that after Ildirim Bayezid Han reigned Mehmed Han Gazi in the year 804 [1402]" (90).[37] Ha-Kohen was indeed wrong. He might have borrowed this incorrect information from Ramberti's *Libri tre delle cose de Turchi* that also appeared in Venice, in 1539, a few years before Ha-Kohen's *Divrei ha-yamim*. According to Ramberti, Bayezid I was followed by "Kiris Celeby, or, as others wish, Calepino, who lived about six years."[38] In reality, both "Celeby" and "Calepino" are forms of *çelebi*, a honorific term that can be translated as "gentleman." "The Gentleman" was the appellation of Mehmed I (r. 1413–1421), which means that the two "names" referred to the same person.[39]

To prove that he is right, Almosnino not only goes into chronological details, but proudly announces that he has checked the information in the Ottoman chronicles (to which he refers as *tavarih otoman* instead of *Tevarih-i Al-i Osman*) with the help of an "esteemed friend experienced in reading and writing Turkish" who confirmed what he had already known (88). (The use of an Ottoman source explains why Almosnino cites the Islamic calendar for his chronology, though he does not seem to know how it relates to the other ones.)

However, he used help from his informants not only to check facts from the past. He also relied on his patrons' accounts of events that took place in the capital during his stay there, which determined not just his interpretations but, in some cases, even his special vantage point as a narrator vis-à-vis his objects of description. It is precisely this optical angle that reveals the spectator's physical position and, therefore, his source. While Almosnino's chronicles say very little about Jews, Book I mentions Jews only a few times and contains two episodes in which they participate. Both of them, I believe, were related to the author by Nasi, although in the first case this is not immediately obvious.

The first event is a parade of the guilds preceding Selim's coronation on December 5, 1567. Almosnino claims that the morning of the sultan's entry into the capital, around two hundred thousand people came to greet the new king outside the city that he was going to enter through the Edirne Gate. (See map 4.1 in the next chapter.) Among them were "Jews, Greeks, and Europeans (*frankos*) residing in Constantinople, many of whom presented him with brocades and damasks made in the city"; they covered the king's passage with fine purple and red scarlet cloth and blessed him in loud voices to which "infinite people responded amen, as it is the same in their languages and in Turkish, which cracked the skies" (79).[40]

Since this "long shot" is taken outside the city walls, Almosnino who, as he explains, was inside, could not have seen this picture. Then we see a close-up of the sultan who stops his horse to listen to these blessings and shows great contentment with the "courteousness and reverence" expressed by his subjects' gifts and with the "great love" conveyed by their blessings (80). Obviously, the sultan's happy expression could have been seen only by someone riding near him. The next long shot shows "other inhabitants of Constantinople, including Muslims,

Christians, and all other nations" throwing in front of Selim all sorts of silks and brocades (80). This is done by "different guilds which they call *rufetes*," and the members of each guild carried their own gifts. And the Jews, who had already welcomed Selim with their separate presents, also greeted him as members of all those guilds because they belonged to various professions.

Almosnino, who stayed indoors, concludes that it was "admirable to see so many people together outside the city" welcoming the arrival of their new king (80). In other words, he relates someone else's report on this display of popular enthusiasm, conveying his informant's satisfaction with Jewish participation in it. What the Salonican traveler did see were the crowds surrounding the sultan which, on his way to the palace, rode down the street past the shop from where Almosnino was watching. He saw various military units and grandees accompanying Selim, and his very detailed but rather naive descriptions of their uniforms and arms are clearly firsthand. By contrast, the rest of his long account of the procession is presented from the vantage point of a person able to see the sultan's face ("he was very upset judging by the look on his face" [96]) and hear his conversations with courtiers and janissary *agas* (commanders), some of which are reported as indirect speech. Finally, the account of the janissaries' mutiny during the festivities is interrupted by a proleptic reference to the events of the following days, all of which would have been relayed to Almosnino by an eyewitness with connections at the court. At first, we get a detailed report on how Sokollu Mehmed Pasha, the grand vizier, was injured by a janissary, and then learned that as a result, he was unable to attend the Divan for a few days (95). It is safe to assume that the person riding near Selim was Joseph Nasi, and that the representation of many events we find in this book reflects both his visual and mental perspectives. Hence, the first chronicle is anything but an unbiased or independent account of a perceptive traveler, as is claimed by many scholars.

Nonetheless, even though one should not overestimate the value of *Crónica* (with the exception of Book IV) as a source on Ottoman history, the account of the guilds parade related to Almosnino by an eyewitness presents historical interest as it is arguably the earliest mention of Jewish membership in guilds, which were originally Muslim urban institutions.[41] Sixteen years later, however, at least two Ottoman sources—

Gelibolulu Mustafa Ali (d. 1600) and the anonymous *Surname-i Humayun* (Imperial Festival Book)—mention the participation of Jewish and Christian craftsmen in the procession during the imperial circumcision festivities of 1582.[42] In fact, while this genre soon became popular in Ottoman literature, Almosnino's description of artisans' processions predates most Ottoman accounts and is the only known one in Ladino.[43] While Ottoman writers usually aimed at producing comprehensive and meticulous reports, Almosnino's (or, rather, Nasi's) goal was not only to demonstrate the affluence of Ottoman Jews, their high visibility, and their loyalty to the sultan, but, even more important, to assert their integration into the Ottoman Empire. They are shown to be like everyone else in their admiration for the new sultan, but a little more generous, because they give him presents as a religious group and as members of the guilds.

Given that in the sixteenth century the population of Constantinople *intra muros* surpassed 250,000, Almosnino's figures for the crowds in the streets are not a great exaggeration.[44] However, in the middle of that century, Jews formed a small minority of the city's population: around 18,000, and most of them were poor.[45] In other words, either the participation of Jews in the procession was exaggerated by Almosnino, or they were indeed overrepresented.[46] In any case, their alleged high visibility is meant to assure readers that the capital's Jews are prosperous, useful, and faithful Ottoman subjects happily partaking in the imperial celebration and, in unison with all other communities, blessing their new ruler.

Servants of Kings

A report on the other "Jewish" event concludes the first chronicle, which gives it particular prominence and clearly demonstrates Nasi's role in shaping the book. It is an account of Joseph Nasi's appointment as the Duke of Naxos (101–102) which, in a nutshell, formulates the social agenda of Ottoman court Jews.

This account, unlike the description of the coronation parade, is terse and entirely based on its protagonist's words. Almosnino explains that in addition to daily wages (*ulefa*) of fifty-five aspers that Joseph Nasi was receiving as Prince Selim's courtier (*müteferrika*) and the twenty-five aspers paid to his brother, Samuel Nasi, Prince Selim had promised to have his father make Don Joseph the Duke of Naxos and all adjacent islands in the Aegean (the Cyclades).[47] As soon as Selim became ruler, even before the official succession, he confirmed his promise in Filipopoli (Plovdiv) where Nasi had joined him. The new duke kissed the sultan's hand and went off to "put in order his estate, or dukedom, or sanjak" where he was free to do what he pleased. Furthermore, as "a sign of affection," Selim gave him full control over all ships carrying wine to Black Sea ports, which frightened all his competitors (101–102). (No doubt, the latter "honorific and useful" privilege was granted to Nasi as the wine provider for the prince later known as Selim the Drunkard.)

Almosnino concludes that Selim rewarded Nasi just like he rewarded all his other slaves, "in accordance with their worth and merit, not only the Muslims of his nation, but also those of other faiths, heeding only to reason and gratitude toward those who loved him and faithfully served him" (101).[48] The fact that in the Ottoman Empire, advancement was typically based on merit rather than rank or wealth amazed many Europeans. Busbecq writes that among the Turks "no value is attached to anything but personal merit." When the sultan assigns administrative positions, he

> pays no attention to wealth or the empty claims of rank, and takes no account of any influence or popularity which a candidate may possess; he only considers merit and scrutinizes the character, natural ability, and disposition of each. Thus each man is rewarded according to his merit.[49]

Although Almosnino's message to readers is similar to Busbecq's observation, he is somewhat insincere. First of all, he knows very well that while many Ottoman officials, including some of the grand viziers he portrays in *Crónica*, come from Christian villages, all of them had to convert. Thus, he says that Ibrahim Pasha, Suleyman's most famous grand vizier, was of humble Greek origin. When he protests Suleyman's order to execute him despite his earlier vow, the sultan responds that he promised not to kill him only while Ibrahim remained Muslim, and now he considers him a heretic (153). Even some Jewish physicians faced the requirement to convert, which Almosnino would have known very well.[50] Thus, Nasi, a non-Muslim sultan's favorite, was an exception rather than the rule.

Second, in Book III, which was not commissioned to him, and is based on his own impressions of Constantinople, Almosnino is much more skeptical. He observes that people's positions, ranks, and wealth "are attained at this court randomly and without any real grounds, everything depends on the turn of the celestial wheel . . ." (221–222). Yet, since Book I is in essence Nasi's educational project, Almosnino closes it by declaring that his promotion proves that the sultan is a "generous lover of virtue and justice and extremely merciful as is required of such a great ruler of such a great state" (102).

The story of Nasi's appointment, like the account of Jewish participation in the guilds parade, is intended to show that Jews play a noticeable role in the empire, including its economy. In this case, however, the author goes beyond recounting facts, and directly encourages readers to serve the sultan, claiming that in the public sphere Jews are like "other nations," differing from Muslims only in terms of religion, which is visible chiefly during holidays and in some private practices. This idea is implicitly but consistently affirmed throughout the other books of *Crónica*. Thus, Almosnino explains that he is writing Book II at the time of "forced leisure because today, on Thursday, the first day of Iyar 5327 of the Creation [10 April 1567], begins the Turkish Easter (*pascua de los turkos*), which they call Bayram and hold in very high esteem" and are going to celebrate with great joy in all parts of the empire (108).[51] As for the capital's Jews, Book III tells us that most of them (undoubtedly, an exaggeration) "fast every Rosh Hodesh eve *(first day of the Hebrew month)* and spend the whole day, from morning till night, at the synagogue praying and reading the Scriptures with their tefillins and tallliths on, like on Yom Kippur."[52] On the other hand, all Jews, while dealing with the Turks, abstain from wine, because their counterparts "do not want the people they talk with to drink wine or smell of it." These Jews drink wine only at their leisure when they return home (217).

As for legal status, the Salonican delegation insists that the authorities are obliged to grant the Jewish community the same tax privileges as other communities, because the Jews of Salonica are "as free as the Muslims and the Christians" (241). While in this particular case the complaint was legitimate, Almosnino and his readers knew only too well that, as *zimmis*, i.e., "tolerated" non-Muslims, Jews and Christians had an inferior status marked by the *cizye* (poll tax).[53] The only way to legal equality was conversion, of which Almosnino was reminded by an official.

Book IV, and thus *Crónica* as a whole, closes with a dramatic scene that takes place at the Divan on the day when the delegation finally receives a positive answer. One of the viziers, pointing to an old Christian who was converting to Islam at that very moment, offered to grant Almosnino's request and liberate the community from the poll tax if the Jews of Salonica also converted. In response, the Salonican rabbi, fighting fear and tears, requested only what was legally due to his community. After this exchange was repeated three times, the pasha exclaimed, "Those people are not like Christians who easily understand the truth; they will not do it even if you kill them" (267). The request, however, was granted. Thus, it was Almosnino's steadfastness that finally decided the matter.

It is impossible to tell how much of this really happened, though the triple repetition of the exchange is certainly a literary device. But the factual truth is less important than the message of this story: even though, unlike Christians, Ottoman Jews will never convert, they are heard at the Divan and can win a legal case if they are persistent. In other words, conversion is not the only option for those Jews who want to succeed in the Ottoman Empire. The first prerequisite for success, according to Almosnino, is being faithful to the sultan; the second condition is, apparently, becoming educated about the greatness of the empire, for the purpose of which he wrote Book II.

Another aspect of this story is Almosnino's attitude toward Ottoman Christians. He never shows any anti-Christian sentiment, whether he talks about Europeans or their Ottoman coreligionists, but as the episode related above demonstrates, he not only considers Ottoman Christians inferior to Jews, but attributes this view to the authorities. In fact, Book IV contains a story that directly proclaims the superiority of the Jews and establishes their place in the hierarchy of Ottoman religious communities: below Muslims, but above Christians.

Almosnino claims to have witnessed this event, which, to my knowledge, is not mentioned by any other source. According to him, after Suleyman's death, the Greek Patriarch—to whom the deceased king had given "an absolute power to dismiss or appoint metropolitans and collect money in all parts of the empire from which they pay the tax to the king so that he would allow them to continue practicing the prescriptions of their law"—wanted Selim to renew the royal decree.[54] When he saw Joseph Nasi, who followed the new sultan to Constantinople and who was known to have been close to him for a long time, the Patriarch went to see the Jewish courtier. The Patriarch handed him a thousand *sultani* (the same sum Nasi wanted to charge the Salonican community) and Suleyman's decree begging him, at his feet, to have it renewed by Selim.[55] Don Joseph, "as he admits, did it more because of his [the Patriarch's] confidence in him than for the profit he got." When Nasi returned with good news, he had the Patriarch come again and gave him a new decree "wonderfully adorned with gold." The delighted Patriarch bent to kiss his hand, which Nasi did not let him do "out of courteousness," but later received from him another "magnificent gift" (242).

Almosnino tells this story to chastise the Jewish leadership in Salonica for being less reasonable than Christians and not taking advantage of Nasi's position. The latter allegedly said that he would have much rather helped the Jewish delegation because this concerned "his people which he always wanted to benefit" and because the Jews had offered to pay him five thousand ducats after the matter was settled (i.e., five times more than the Patriarch's initial gift) but then changed their minds (242). (This comment, together with the one Nasi made earlier about the Patriarch's confidence in him, suggests that the story was not entirely made up.)

This episode is striking because it mirrors the story of Nasi's appointment in Book I, and together the two show how Almosnino (and, we can assume, his patrons) saw the distribution of power from the top down. The new sultan makes Nasi Duke of Naxos, for which the latter kisses his hand. Then he, in turn, gets a renewal of the Patriarch's license to appoint metropolitans, for which the grateful Christian tries to kiss his hand. Interestingly, while in the first episode Nasi is described as one of Selim's slaves, in the second, his name is followed by *yarum hodó* (may He exalt his majesty), a blessing used for monarchs. Regardless of whether this may have been a coincidence, the two stories related by Almosnino demonstrated to readers that, unlike Christians, Ottoman Jews were "servants of kings and not servants of servants."[56]

This message was not lost on Abraham Danon who included the second story in his above-mentioned publication in *El Tyempo*, where he explained that Joseph Nasi enjoyed the "extraordinary benevolence of Sultan Suleiman the Lawgiver and, especially, his son Sultan Selim II."[57] Danon was among the proponents of Jewish political integration who believed in teaching Ottoman Jews how to become loyal imperial citizens. As Julia Phillips Cohen's insightful analysis demonstrates, proving allegiance to the empire required "reinforcing and propagating the myth of their [the Jews] special connection to the Ottoman Empire" and entailed competing with other groups.[58] Almosnino's account of Nasi's influence at the court, his power to help Christians maintain their privileges, and his gracious treatment of their Patriarch perfectly served Danon's educational goal as it emphasized that the Jews had a special place in the empire already in the sixteenth century.

In fact, as Cohen reminds us, "the narrative of a special Ottoman-Jewish relationship" dates back to the early modern period, when various Jewish chroniclers praised the sultans for accepting Iberian exiles.[59] Kapsali's *Seder Eliahu Zuta*, first published in full in 1869 by Moses Lattes, while initially somewhat misunderstood, profoundly influenced the perception of the Ottomans' attitude toward the Jews and supported the special relationship myth.

The difference between Kapsali's and Almosnino's historical methods and literary styles (obviously associated with the language each of them used) is brought into sharp relief by the description of Mehmed's encounter with Moses Kapsali (the author's great-uncle) whom, it was later claimed, he appointed Chief Rabbi of the Ottoman Empire. Unlike the dry and informative account of Nasi's appointment, Kapsali's story uses mythological and fairytale tropes that make it impossible to establish what actually happened and what legal consequences this event had.[60]

When, sitting on his throne, Mehmed the Conqueror asked his ministers about the judge of the Jews, they described him as "an old man, an ascetic, who fasts all the days of the year . . . whilst he labors in Torah. . . . When he was brought in front of the king, the latter addressed him as '*Hoca*' ('my teacher' in the language of Togarmah [Turkey]) and spoke graciously to him. Even though the Rabbi did not know the language of Togarmah and the king had not met him previously, nevertheless the king relied upon reports he heard from all that the Rabbi's name was like pure oil, for in friendship and in esteem, he turned not to bribes."

And so the sultan ordered his servants on duty at the royal gate to put him on a horse and take him to his home. [61]

Stylistic differences aside, the two men are rewarded for completely different virtues. Unlike Nasi who accepted gifts even from his coreligionists (which was probably common practice) and was made Duke of Naxos for his loyalty to the prince, Kapsali is appointed or, more precisely, confirmed in his position, for being a righteous Jew and an incorruptible judge.[62] While in *Crónica*, Jews appear as sultans' servants, Kapsali presents the sultans as instruments of redemption who therefore serve the Jewish people. In addition, Kapsali was an ardent admirer of the kabbalah and believed in messianic calculations, which is why he proclaimed that during the rule of "the tenth king of the Turks," i.e., Suleyman, the people of Israel would be saved.[63]

As I already said, Almosnino's view of Jewish history could not have significantly differed from those of his contemporaries. Besides, his approach to history was also far from scientific. He, too, was fond of magic numbers. In the last section of Book III, he discusses at length the magic power of certain numbers and their significance for the Jewish people.[64] This is why he is particularly annoyed by Ha-Kohen's flawed list of sultans. Pointing out that Suleyman is the tenth Ottoman sultan, he interprets some of his actions and certain events that happened during his reign, as well as the number of his viziers and even horses, as perfect by relating them to the number ten (87). Yet he never mentions anything related to messianic expectations. Besides, given the purpose of his chronicles, if Suleyman had been the eleventh sultan, Almosnino would have found some special meaning in this number as well.

The fundamental difference between *Seder Eliahu Zuta* and *Crónica* is their goals and target audiences, which determined each author's approach. *Seder Eliahu Zuta* was written for traditionally educated Jews, more precisely, for Romaniots who, as was mentioned in chapter 1, had been deported from various places as part of Mehmed II's resettlement policy continued by Bayezid II and Suleyman. Kapsali's goal was to console those and all other Jews in their recent tribulations and to help them to "accept the yoke of the kingdom of God."[65]

Almosnino, never alluding to any past troubles, wanted not only to reassure Sephardim that they were living in the right place (the Great Empire) at the right time (the Suleymanic Age), but also to encourage them to serve the Sultan. To achieve this goal, he had to write in Ladino and be specific. It is also important to emphasize that to use a modern term, most of Almosnino's protagonists were removed from readers by only two or three handshakes, as is evident from his sermon.

No doubt, *Crónica*'s target audience was essentially the same (but probably larger) as that of his epistles, namely, educated men not fluent in Hebrew, mainly ex-*conversos* who were generally known for high social mobility and who, therefore, were more inclined to check out new opportunities. Nonetheless, some readers were expected to know Hebrew, which is why Almosnino warns "those who might see or read it" about the errors in Ha-Kohen's book (87).

Nasi's comment that the Patriarch's confidence in his influence mattered to him more than gifts, suggests that court Jews did not take their proximity to the center of power for granted. Evidently, it is their wish to maintain and strengthen their influence at the court that motivated them to commission Almosnino to write the first chronicle.

The Second Chronicle

The second chronicle was written between April 10 and 24, 1567, during the holiday of Bayram, when Almosnino and his friends were unable to attend to their affairs at the court. In other words, he had four months to prepare for this job and two weeks for writing. He states that this chronicle was commissioned by "some gentlemen from this noble city and famous place," who, having seen the record of Suleyman's death and Selim's succession he had produced on the request of his "intimate friends," were so impressed that he was again urged to write and disseminate an account of "the power and excellence of Sultan Suleyman . . . worthy of eternal memory, for those who want to enjoy it [the memory]" (107). Unable to excuse himself or disobey their orders, "despite being very busy with the petition of our republic," he decided to avoid the vain joys [Bayram festivities] and produce a brief general summary (107).

In fact, Almosnino also agreed to write the first chronicle instead of participating in the coronation celebration and despite being "very busy with the affairs of our republic of the noble city of Salonica," which left him no time for a longer account (78). As in the case of the epistles, despite being busy with more important matters, Almosnino cannot excuse himself from the job and agrees to produce a short work (though Book II is more than twice as long as Book I). However, while the epistles were produced for laudable didactic purposes, and the first chronicle was aimed at informing his readers about the greatness of the Ottoman Empire and encouraging them to serve the sultan (i.e., had an educational or even propagandistic goal), the second chronicle was proclaimed to have been written for the enjoyment of potential readers who might be interested in the "memory" of Ottoman kings. It is obvious, however, that his busy friends would not have wasted their time helping him write something they considered unimportant. Hence, we should not be misled by the word "enjoy" (*gozar*). In his preface to the Hebrew version of *Amadís de Gaula* discussed in chapter 1, among the three reasons for reading books, Eliezer Soncino mentions "gratification of the spirit":

> A person is grieved by the cares of daily life, so in his leisure time he seeks after stories, fables and other vanities, which are of no other use than to gratify his spirit. This is what we find among readers of chronicles, the book of Ben Gurion, and other such works.[66]

One should bear in mind that in the sixteenth century, *Sefer Yosef Ben Gurion*, or *Yosipon*, a popular Jewish history attributed to a Joseph Ben Gorion, who presumably wrote it in Southern Europe in the eleventh century, was believed to have been produced by Josephus and hence, taken seriously. In fact, in 1510 in Constantinople, it was "brought to print" by the well-known Sephardi scholar Tam ibn Yahya ben David.[67]

Therefore, the introduction to *Amadís* reflects the attitude of sixteenth-century Jewish readers to *all* works of "history," whether (pseudo) scholarship or fiction. Gutwirth points out that the "medieval notion of the function of history, to delight and instruct . . . was still alive in fifteenth-century Spain," when chronicles of certain events were written because they were deemed "fit for remembrance."[68] In the sixteenth century, this perception of historiography hardly differed from what it had been in previous centuries. A "historical work was regarded as something pleasant and diverting in moments of leisure, and at best a source of moral uplift."[69] For this reason, Jewish scholars felt the need to apologize, in the introductions to their works, for dealing with history, let alone the history of gentile nations.[70]

Almosnino's first excuse is that he produced his chronicles under pressure and at a time of "forced leisure" (107). In addition, he repeats four times that he writes only about things "worthy of eternal remembrance" (78, 107, 109, 205). Even so, the chronicle of Suleyman's reign was a daring enterprise at a time when the opinions of halakhic literature on works on the history of "gentile nations," described as "books of wars," were still divided "as to whether one is permitted to read them, and when, and in what language."[71] Almosnino's second chronicle can certainly be described as a "book of wars," because wars among "gentiles" is one of its chief topics. In general, it has more in common with Pulgar's *Crónica de los altos y muy esclarecidos reyes católicos* than with Sefer Ben Gurion, because it deals with events of the recent past and interprets them from a particular political perspective. We do not know which Castilian chronicles Almosnino might have read, but, as was mentioned in chapter 2, Pulgar's work was likely to have been available to him. Yet, like Yosipon, Almosnino's chronicle contains some fictional stories, albeit very few.

Having agreed to write a chronicle of Suleyman's reign, Almosnino had to find an adequate form, since a simple day-by-day account, like in the first chronicle, would not have worked to tell the history of a forty-six-year period. Even more important was the decision regarding which events should be included and what aspects of Suleyman's reign should be emphasized. No doubt, Almosnino's patrons significantly influenced his choices and supplied most of the information needed for his work, but, as we will see, in this case, the Salonican traveler did his own research on Ottoman architecture. Furthermore, the rather sophisticated structure of the book and some of its features indicate that Almosnino had a lot more freedom for literary creativity here.

Book II can be divided into three parts. The first part is a summary of sixteen Ottoman wars waged during Suleyman's reign. The second part contains information on his grand viziers, admirals, janissary *agas*, *beylerbeys* (governors general), and grand muftis. The third section, the most original part of the second chronicle, is dedicated to Ottoman architecture of the Suleymanic age and, regardless of its purpose, can be described as a travelogue.

In the introduction to Book II, Almosnino declares that he will give a brief summary of facts he knows very well. A more detailed account of noteworthy events of Suleyman's reign about which he has heard can be found in "their chronicle . . . which, they say, is very long, so that including them here would make it inappropriately verbose" (107). Thus, Almosnino claims to have some knowledge of the court chronicle, even though, as he notes, it is not yet available to the public. At another point, he says that those who want to know everything in detail will easily learn this from

> [their] special chronicle which, it is said, very soon will become available to them, in accordance with their ways and customs, which is that after a king's death they divulge his chronicle and pass it to the scribes and allow everybody wishing to copy it to do so, and many people copy it. (172)

The Salonican rabbi must have received this rather inaccurate information from the same friend who had checked the sultans' chronology in the Ottoman chronicles referred to as *tavarih otoman* (88). Yet, this person would not have read the official chronicle. Because the sixteenth century saw a proliferation of historiographic works in Ottoman Turkish and Persian, in an attempt to control historical ideology, Suleyman established around 1550 the position of court historiographer in charge of writing a history of the Ottoman house in Persian panegyric verse.[72] Through the end of the century, official chronicles were written in Persian or Arabic, which made them accessible only to the Ottoman elite "who could afford to commission them or might have a chance to read or listen to a recitation of them."[73]

Therefore, most likely, Almosnino's friend (probably Abraham Salama, who knew Turkish) saw the *Tevarih-i Al-i Osman*, histories of the Ottoman house written in simple Turkish that would have been accessible to him but were not official Ottoman chronicles.[74] Perhaps an investigation of those documents could explain some of the oddities of Almosnino's account, which is still rather accurate in general terms. In many cases, as I will show, it indeed reflects official ideology, but this is accounted for by the proximity of Almosnino's informants to the court.

As in the first chronicle, Almosnino sometimes indicates that certain facts were related to him by "a competent person," but Nasi is no longer his main source, because most of the events described in the second chronicle occurred long before he immigrated to the empire. In fact, Almosnino relays some privileged information about the 1539 fire in Constantinople that was conveyed to him at that time by someone "who knew it very well," as the Salonican rabbi happened to be in the capital for "personal matters" (155). In connection with the 1525 execution of Ahmed Pasha, governor of Egypt, Almosnino says that he had heard about its true cause "long ago from a very competent person" (148).

In a few cases, he cites a "very competent person" (probably always the same one), who saw the information in question in writing. For example, talking about the number of mosques built by Suleyman, Almosnino cites "a very competent person who had seen it written in detail" (202). Sometimes, he discloses his informants' sources stating, for instance, that he was informed "by a person of great authority who had heard it from the *kapi aga* [the guard of palace eunuchs] who died in the last war" (188). All of this means that his connections among court Jews began to form rather early, and he was probably introduced to Nasi by a mutual acquaintance when the latter needed to find a rabbi for the new Portuguese congregation in Salonica.

Almosnino's accounts of Suleyman's wars reflect official ideology, and portray the sultan as victorious, wise, and magnanimous. This is especially evident in the representations of Suleyman's failures. Thus, rather than saying that he failed to capture Vienna in 1532, Almosnino explains that Suleyman decided to go back in order not to overburden or put the local population at risk (113). His failure to take Corfu in 1537 is blamed on the treachery of his grand vizier, Ayas Mehmed Pasha, who allegedly convinced the sultan to stop the siege (115, 154).

The most telling example of Almosnino's loyalty to the Ottomans is the conclusion of his rather lengthy account of the conquest of Rhodes (1522), which he presents as one of the greatest victories in the world and a crushing defeat of Christendom (110–111). Unlike Kapsali who sees the capture of Rhodes as a crucial act in the messianic drama, i.e., from a Jewish perspective, Almosnino is aware of its strategic and economic significance for the Ottoman Empire.[75] He reports on Suleyman's decision to develop the island's economy by means of population transfer, and its consequences:

> And since it appeared to the king that few people would go to live there because it was a small island, which did not have enough food for them,

> he ordered to bring there exiles (*surgunes*) from all parts and of all nations with very good and permanent guards; and they live there today in tranquility and without fear. (111)

As was discussed earlier, Mehmed II's policy of forcible repopulation of his capital, known as *sürgün*, left Salonica without Jews until new immigrants began to arrive in the 1490s. "All nations" transferred to Rhodes in 1522 included Salonican Jews, namely, about a hundred and fifty of the richest and most respected families from Almosnino's hometown.[76] This was a large number for the time, and Almosnino certainly knew both about the hardships the exiles had endured and the losses suffered by the Salonican community. Furthermore, he would have read the responsa written by well-known Salonican rabbis that dealt with numerous legal complications caused by this event.[77] Writing forty-five years later, he obviously preferred to focus on the happy existence of the exiles' descendants, but his comment on their living in tranquility and without fear makes it clear that he was aware that earlier, the deportees had been afraid of their guards who were constantly present.[78]

However, it is not only Suleyman's wars per se that prove his greatness, but also the number of his wars. According to Almosnino, the tenth Ottoman sultan personally led ten wars, but since in reality it was thirteen, he adds Suleyman's three "extra" campaigns to those waged by his grand viziers.[79] Moreover, the number of Suleyman's grand viziers is also declared to be ten, though to reach this result Almosnino had to count Rustem Pasha twice, since he held this office twice. Some information on the viziers and their relations to the sultan's family was recounted in the first chronicle. In the second one, we find detailed portrayals of some of the grand viziers and anecdotes from their lives.

History and Stories

The longest among these stories is the account of Suleyman's favorite, grand vizier Ibrahim Pasha, which cannot, however, claim veracity. This is a very long narrative (135–154) with an extremely complicated but skillfully constructed plot centered on the relationship between Suleyman and Ibrahim. It starts with Selim I's decision to poison Suleyman, his only son. Saved by Ibrahim Pasha, Suleyman swears not to execute him even if one day he deserves it. As soon as he becomes the next sultan, Suleyman appoints Ibrahim as grand vizier, but, many years later, having learned of his favorite's treason, he ends up breaking this promise.

This story is similar to modern historical novels in that it includes three, at least, partly made up murder plots that develop against the background of the Ottoman capital in the sixteenth century. Thus, having mentioned that Ibrahim "built himself a mansion in the ancient Hippodrome, one of the largest squares in the universe," Almosnino offers a first-hand description of the two obelisks and the Serpentine Column standing there (144). At another point in the story, he describes the famous forty-day festival that marked the circumcision of Suleyman's three sons (1530), which the sultan watched from Ibrahim's palace (145–146). Finally, after Ibrahim is executed, the sultan orders the removal from the Hippodrome the bronze Hercules (that had miraculously survived there for so long), because he claims, it was worshipped by his grand vizier who looked at it through his mansion's window (155).

Attempting to establish which facts found in this "novel" are true would be a waste of time. Almosnino obviously constructed it from elements preserved by popular memory, which he acknowledges, saying that the story of Ibrahim's execution has two versions (153) and (as in a postmodernist novel) recounts both. Furthermore, there is an obvious chronological error: the circumcision festival of 1530 takes place before the rebellion of the governor of Egypt which, in reality, happened five years earlier. The "novel" also includes a few common fairytale motifs and even some biblical elements. Thus, Ibrahim's feast is reminiscent of the one in the Book of Esther, and his relationship with Iskender Çelebi, the sultan's faithful servant, brings to mind that of Haman and Mordechay who refused to bow to him.

Notably, the story about Ibrahim Pasha does not have any moral to it, not even a postponed one appearing at the end of the chronicle, as in the case of Mustafa's execution account (discussed below). It commends loyalty, but, as in fairy tales, it is taught as a human virtue rather than an allegiance to a specific authority.

It seems obvious that the Ibrahim Pasha story was indeed intended to entertain readers and "gratify their spirit," just like the Ladino rewriting of *Orlando Furioso* or the Hebrew versions of *Amadís* and *Celestina*. We should add to this list Bernardim Ribeiro's chivalric novel *Menina e*

Moca published in Portuguese in 1554 by Abraham Usque, at the same press as the Ferrara Bible and Samuel Usque's *Consolation for the Tribulations of Israel*.[80] Thus, the fact that Almosnino wrote an entertaining secular story is not surprising. After all, Joseph Tsarfati, the translator of *Celestina* was also a scholar.

What may indeed surprise the modern reader is that Almosnino includes this thriller in what he considers a work on Ottoman history. In the introduction to the second chronicle, he declares that he will write "a history of the victory that occurred" (*una istorya de la vitorya ke ubo*) (107), that is, a history of *real* events. However, as Barbara Fuchs notes, "the Spanish term historia, which today means both history and story, only gradually and conflictingly acquired the second meaning in the early modern period."[81] In other words, genre boundaries between a (chivalric) novel and historiographic prose were still very blurry.[82] It is clear that Almosnino did not see the genre difference between a history of Suleyman's wars (the veracity of which he proclaims more than once) and half-fictional (as he knew) stories about the sultan's relationships with his courtiers.

One can say of the bulk of Almosnino's two chronicles that he only edited and organized material received from his informants that they, in turn, had received from others. By contrast, the account of Almosnino's encounters with the grand mufti, a true historical and memoiristic gem, is all his own and even reveals a side of his personality that is not visible in his other texts.

Danon included this episode in his publication because, while the excerpt on Nasi and the Greek Patriarch demonstrates that Jews had more influence at the court than Christians, the story of Abu-Suad (Ebus-su'ud) presumably testifies to the mutual respect between Muslims and Jews.

Having discussed the first of Suleyman's grand muftis, Almosnino turns to the second one, appointed by him in 1545, Ebus-su'ud Efendi, or Hoca Çelebi (1490–1574). This Sheyh ul-Islam was not only a renowned Quran exegete, but also a famous jurist who put together the *Kanunname* (collection of edicts, law code) of Suleyman the Lawgiver, which joined the *sharia* and Ottoman administrative code.[83] Since the grand mufti was "the final earthly authority in the interpretation of the Sacred Law as completed by Mohammed the Prophet," the sultans indeed stood up to greet the grand muftis, as Almosnino notes with regard to Suleyman (177).[84] Moreover, the latter addressed Ebus-su'ud as "my companion in the mystic state," "my friend in my bosom," and "my comrade on the path of truth."[85]

It was therefore a great honor for the Salonican rabbi to be introduced to Ebus-su'ud on business, and even more so to be invited by him again for a philosophical discussion. Almosnino's portrayal of the grand mufti is full of infinite and sincere admiration, which contrasts in marked ways with his formulaic praises of the sultans. He declares, on the basis of their conversations, that Ebus-su'ud is the most knowledgeable grand mufti who is superior to all his predecessors and who will never be surpassed by any other (177). We learn that six (seven, according to Cansino's version) years earlier the mufti, who had heard about Almosnino's arrival in the capital, invited him to discuss some matters related to the houses he owned in Salonica that were apparently rented to some Jews (178). It will be remembered that in his sermon Almosnino thanks Abraham Salama for ensuring the support of the grand mufti. Hence, it is likely that Salama was the one who made the connection already in 1561, because Ebus-su'ud was looking for someone he could put in charge of his property. Evidently, Almosnino was only a one-time intermediary, or he would not have tried to avoid seeing the mufti later (which he did out of modesty). We can assume that Salama also served as an interpreter during the conversations between the two scholars, because Almosnino's very limited Turkish would not have allowed him to discuss philosophical or scientific matters.

Having entrusted the business of the houses to Almosnino, Ebus-su'ud, known for his respect for "scholars of all faiths," "with eyeglasses in his hand," asked Almosnino whether he agreed with Aristotle's theory of vision or with that held by Galen (178). At first, the Salonican rabbi was too shy to express his own opinion, but then, urged by his host, spoke in favor of Aristotle's idea. Proponents of Aristotle's view believed that the object emits rays to the eye (intramission), while Galen's followers claimed that it is the eye that sends rays to the object (extramission). As Almosnino points out, the former idea, in a revised version, was widely accepted in European universities.

Then the mufti asked about certain propositions formulated in Alhazene's celebrated work on optics, *Kitab al-Manazir*, translated into Latin as *De aspectibus* or *Perspectivae*, where this eleventh-century Muslim scientist, combining elements of Galen's, Aristotle's, and Euclid's teachings, formulated his own intramission theory, further developed by Roger Bacon.[86] The mufti obviously expected his visitor to have read the Latin translation available in various forms in Europe, which was indeed familiar to Almosnino. This episode shows that Ebus-su'ud perceived his guest as a Westerner, that is, a non-Christian European, and it is possible that other educated Muslims, based on their experience, saw Sephardi Jews the same way.

In 1566, when Almosnino came to Constantinople with the Salonican delegation, the mufti who must have learned about it from Salama invited him again for a philosophical conversation (though the delegation's concerns would have also been discussed) and asked him to return another time. But Almosnino, who appears to have been a person of great humility, felt that it was inappropriate for him to disturb such an important and busy man.

A Panegyric of Suleyman

This story marks the transition to the last section of Book II that also is largely based on Almosnino's first-hand information. In fact, he declares that he will speak mainly as an eyewitness (*testigo de vista*) (180), which was a term frequently (and polemically) used by sixteenth-century Castilian authors to claim that their stories were not fictional.[87]

As is well known, the Ottoman style of architecture had reached its classical stage by the 1550s, expressing the official ideology of the mature Ottoman Empire.[88] It is astonishing that Almosnino, a rabbi from Salonica, which could not boast any such edifices, was acutely aware of the significance of Suleyman's architectural project and chose it as a lens through which to show readers the sultan's greatness as he understood it.

Apparently, he realized that Suleyman's architectural patronage was his most important accomplishment in the 1550s, a less eventful period of his reign than previous ones. Furthermore, Almosnino starts and ends this section of his second chronicle by emphasizing that Suleyman not only funded the construction of new buildings across the empire, but also set an example for his family members and courtiers, strongly encouraging architectural patronage among them (179, 203).

All three structures described by Almosnino—one religious and two civic—were built by Sinan (1490–1588), the chief imperial architect appointed to this post by Suleyman in 1538. Each of the three accounts starts with a description of the building in question, discusses technical difficulties faced and overcome by Sinan, relates at least one anecdote to illustrate Suleyman's wisdom, and ends with information about the cost of construction.[89]

Almosnino begins with "the largest of the Ottoman building enterprises," the Suleymaniye complex, constructed between 1550 and 1557 on the Third Hill in Constantinople.[90] This was a perfect choice for his purposes. Even *tabakatü'l-Memalik ve Derece-Mezalik* (The Echelons of the Dominions and Hierarchies of the Professions), one of the most authoritative Ottoman histories, ends with a description of the Suleymaniye, which its author, Celalzade Mustafa (c. 1490–1567) considered the zenith of Suleyman's reign.[91]

Almosnino briefly mentions it in the first chronicle in connection with Suleyman's burial, but it seems that by that time, he not yet visited or been inside. Now his enthusiastic firsthand account is full of praise but is also thorough and specific. One of his goals is to acquaint readers who have not been inside a mosque (the majority of his readers) with its interior elements (such as the *qibla*, *mihrab*, and *minbar*) and explain their functions. Then, the narrator moves outside to describe at length the marble fountain for ablutions and elegant minarets, and goes on to discuss other structures in the courtyards of the Suleymaniye complex, including four general *medreses*, a Quran school for boys, a hospital, soup kitchen, *caravanserai*, and some other buildings.

Introducing his readers to the social, religious, and educational functions of these institutions, Almosnino reveals an impressive familiarity with the Muslim system of education, including curricula and the appointment of teachers. It seems that he was aware of the educational reforms carried out by Suleyman, which centralized education in the empire. The sultan even created a list of books to be studied in the highest grades of medreses.[92] The colleges of the Suleymaniye complex described by Almosnino "came to occupy the most prestigious position" in the hierarchy of Ottoman medreses.[93]

Almosnino also praises the system for teaching medicine and taking care of patients, and warns his readers that very soon Muslims will

FIGURE 3.1.
Mausoleum of Sultan Suleyman. Public Domain.
Library of Congress Prints and Photographs Division.

not need foreign doctors (185). This account concludes with a report on various expenses associated with the construction of the Sulemaniye complex and its functions.

The Suleymaniye section includes a rather lengthy anecdote about the sultan's visit to the construction site before the mausolea for his wife and himself were built. Sinan allegedly wanted to show the sultan the

FIGURE 3.2.
Suleymaniye Mosque. Public Domain.
Library of Congress Prints and Photographs Division.

spot where he was planning to erect a mausoleum for Suleyman but did not dare to say this directly. So he took Suleyman's prayer rug and put it in the assigned spot. The sultan understood what that meant and in tears, praised God for allowing him to see his burial place (182). A shorter vignette demonstrates Suleyman's love for his wife.

The second structure described by Almosnino is the Constantinople aqueduct built in the fourth century AD, during the reign of the Roman emperor Valens. It was rebuilt and expanded in every period of Constantinople's history, including the reigns of Mehmed II and Beyazid II. In 1553, Suleyman commissioned Sinan to add two more lines to the aqueduct and reconstruct a few arches that collapsed during the 1509 earthquake.[94] In Almosnino's words, "this magnanimous king" asked

FIGURE 3.3.
Valens/Sinan Aqueduct. Public Domain.
Library of Congress Prints and Photographs Division.

Sinan to build an aqueduct because he saw how much the people in the capital needed water (188).

Allegedly, Sinan's construction soon failed, and everyone was afraid to let the sultan know, until one of his courtiers eventually did. The wise ruler rejoiced at this news because he had been worrying that some disaster might happen after his death, and now he was sure the aqueduct would be rebuilt in his lifetime. Sinan indeed finished his work in 1564. This story (apparently made up) was intended to demonstrate Suleyman's wisdom and concern for his people. In addition to giving readers the impression that Sinan built the aqueduct from scratch, Almosnino's account includes another anecdote about Suleyman and Sinan, which serves the same purpose.

The third of Sinan's works discussed in the architecture section is the Çekmece Bridge (1555–1567), about twenty-five miles from the Old

FIGURE 3.4.
Büyükçekmece Bridge (now Kanuni Sultan Suleyman Bridge).
The first two (counting from the East) of its four sections.
Photo by Rebekah Bob-Waksberg.

City, which in Almosnino's time was rather far from Constantinople. This four-part bridge crossed an inlet called Lake Büyükçekmece spanning three artificial islands. According to Almosnino, the first bridge collapsed because its foundation had been placed in a swamp, which prompted Suleyman once again to praise God for allowing him to erect a new bridge for his people (197). Yet in reality, the first bridge was constructed in Roman times, and, before having Sinan build a new one, Suleyman ordered him to investigate flaws in the ancient structure.[95]

By June 1566, when the Salonican delegation was approaching the capital, work on the bridge had not been completed, so Almosnino had a chance to see its construction in progress. He proudly says that he dismounted the horse and inspected the site that he found impressive and could describe as an eyewitness (200).

One cannot fail to notice that the organization of material in these three accounts is similar (albeit simpler) to what one finds in *Seyahat-name* (The Narrative of the Travels) by the famous Ottoman traveler Evliya Çelebi (1611–1682). Very often, detailed descriptions of edifices in his book are followed by anecdotes and conclude with reports on construction costs. Furthermore, the vignettes included in Almosnino's discussions of architectural works, as well as the story about Ibrahim Pasha, are obviously borrowed from the same popular tradition as Evliya's anecdotes. In fact, Evliya's description of the Sulemaniye includes an anecdote (incidentally a Judeophobic one) about the sultan and the construction of the Jewel Minaret.[96]

I suggest that not all of these similarities are coincidental; rather, they demonstrate that Almosnino and the court Jews, his informants, were more immersed in Ottoman culture than we usually assume. Yet one textual similarity between the two accounts of the Suleymaniye, in fact, masks a contrast between them. Describing the four huge columns supporting the main dome of the mosque (shown on fig. 3.1), Almosnino says that those who have traveled all over the world have not seen anything comparable (180–181). As I suggested earlier, he is referring to European travelers who wrote about the Suleymaniye. Evliya, in turn, claims to have met ten Franks (Europeans) at the Suleymaniye who were utterly amazed by what they saw and stated "in the whole of Fringistan [Europe] there was not a single edifice which could be compared to this."[97]

Paradoxically, this coincidence reveals the difference between the two authors' attitudes toward Europe. For Evliya, Europe is the antagonist par excellence whose inferiority he is always happy to confirm. For Almosnino and many of his coreligionists, especially those who had spent time there, Europe remains—despite the persecution—an important point of reference, which is why he wants to assert the Ottoman Empire's *cultural* superiority. I believe that the section on architecture, as well as the thorough rendering of his conversation with Ebus-su'ud, intend to prove that their new homeland can not only protect Jews but also produce high culture.[98]

The need for such assurance is proven by the words of the European-educated Daniel de Ávila Gallego, an ex-*converso* physician, who tells Salonican Jews in 1601 that "their works in the fields of medicine and philosophy are nowhere near what their ancestors produced in the golden age (*dorados tiempos*) of peace and tranquility in their natural hemisphere."[99] Since they had left it, he claims, their creativity lost its clarity and suffered from the slimy commerce of the "barbarous peoples in whose kingdoms we are living."[100] This attitude, rooted in notions of Europe's geographic and cultural superiority, mixed with pride in the accomplishments of Iberian Jews, is akin to the sentiment expressed in the writings of European Christians, such as Busbecq's letters, or even more so, the work of Pierre Gilles, who laments the fate of Constantinople's Greeks who are "for a vast distance . . . encompassed on all sides" by "those barbarians."[101] We may assume that Gallego was not the only one who looked down on the Turks, and that not everyone shared the gratitude expressed by some rabbis.

Almosnino's representation of Islam, which says next to nothing about the essence of this religion but emphasizes its philosophical character, is to show that it is a serious intellectual enterprise. He even resorts to Maimonides's authority to prove his point. Discussing subjects studied at the *medreses*, which include law, grammar, and logic among others, Almosnino says that "Moshe Rabbenu Cordobi" had a high opinion of the Arabic treatises on logic, as he indicated in the epistles to his son (187). The grand mufti is described as a scholar who is competent in various fields of knowledge and open to European scientific ideas.

In addition, Almosnino stresses the charitable aspect of Islam. According to his sources, 6,004 mosques were built during Suleyman's reign, most of which were surrounded by complexes that provided food for the hungry and travelers who were staying there. Buildings such mosque complexes, Almosnino explains, is "considered among them a laudable thing" (202).

The architecture section concludes with an explanation of why Suleyman was so keen on architectural enterprises. Almosnino believes that the sultan had two goals in mind. The first and main one was to benefit the people, especially the poor and needy who would use new mosques, fountains, bridges, and roads. The second goal, common to all kings and great men, was to gain fame and be remembered after his death. Almosnino finds the second purpose the most laudable because Suleyman's example will motivate successors to continue his work, at least for the sake of glory if not for the good of their subjects (202).

In addition to his architectural achievements, Suleyman allegedly increased the population of Constantinople and its surroundings ten times because, according to Almosnino, people came "under his wings" not only from all parts of the empire but also from most parts of the world, learning that he was a just, merciful, and kind ruler (203–204). These virtues earned him the help of Providence, and it was not coincidental that God wanted him to be the tenth sultan, which made "this extraordinary master and absolute king" superior to all the kings who came before him and those who will come after (204).

But more than any other of Suleyman's accomplishments, Almosnino valued the security he ensured for his subjects and the "stability and protection of this kingdom" (205), which had brought so many Jews "under his wings." We read that having captured Belgrade (1521), the sultan made it so safe that the city's population began to grow and its commerce to thrive, because Jewish, Muslim, and Christian merchants were going there from all parts of the empire (110).

However, in rare cases when his subjects were harmed, the sultan was sure to punish the culprits. After some janissaries, who had taken advantage of their *aga*'s absence from the city, broke into several Jewish and Christian houses, Suleyman had the *aga* executed for leaving his regiment for one night (170).

A Mirror for Princes

The colophon of Book II has only one purpose: to praise Suleyman for murdering his own children for the sake of his subjects' safety. According to Almosnino, when he ordered those executions, Suleyman's intentions were holy. Although this made him appear a "cruelest slaughterer who slaughtered his own sons and grandsons" ("not only his adult sons who might have been suspected or presumed to be disobedient, but his innocent grandsons"), this showed his "sincere intention to ensure peace and serenity in his kingdom," because if there had been two contenders for the throne, his innocent subjects would have suffered (207).

Kapsali, who casts Mehmed the Conqueror as a messianic figure, feels the need to justify his notorious cruelty. Having recounted a few stories that demonstrate the sultan's brutality in various circumstances, he concludes: "Many such cruel deeds did he do . . . for he was cruel to the wicked but merciful to the righteous."[102] Almosnino, by contrast, rather than finding justification for Suleyman's cruelty to the innocent, simply pronounces his actions "heroic and deserving eternal remembrance, felicitous fame, and perpetual glory" (206).

In the introduction to Book II, the author promised to tell his readers how Suleyman, thanks to his justice, reason, and compassion, ensured a peaceful life for his people, not only during his reign but also in later centuries, by making struggles between his sons impossible (109). In fact, the story of Prince Mustafa's assassination is told twice: the first time in the context of the ninth war (the third campaign against the Safavid Empire, 1553–1555), during which it happened, and then in the section on grand viziers, because it involves Rustem Pasha.

The story of Suleyman's eldest son was well known, and Almosnino could have heard it from any of his acquaintances in the capital. Mustafa, the sultan's son by a concubine, enjoyed the admiration of the janissaries and the support of many grandees who saw in him a welcome replacement for his aging father. It is believed that Suleyman's wife, Hurem Sultan (known in Europe as Roxelana), who wanted one of her own sons to succeed their father, conspired with Rustem Pasha, her son-in-law, to persuade the sultan that Mustafa was plotting to usurp the throne. The prince's execution provoked such indignation in the army that Suleyman had to dismiss from office Rustem Pasha who was blamed for this injustice.

Almosnino's first account of these events is brief and does not go into Suleyman's motives (119–121). The second version of this episode (162–163) is much more revealing. Having learned that Prince Mustafa had the "fantasy" of replacing his father in his lifetime, Rustem Pasha, characterized as the most efficient grand vizier, convinced Suleyman to execute his son. For having insulted his father and being disobedient, Rustem argued, he deserved to be considered an enemy and a traitor and, therefore, was legally qualified for execution. By being merciful to his son, claimed Rustem, Suleyman would become "his own cruel enemy and that of his kingdom," because if he did not kill him, he would not be able to prevent disorder and would eventually lose Constantinople and his throne to Mustafa (163).

Later in the book, Almosnino mentions that Bayezid, the younger of Suleyman's two surviving sons, started a war against his brother, Selim

(164–165). What he does not say is that in 1559, Bayezid, who fled to Persia, was murdered there, together with his four sons, on Prince Selim's orders, which made the latter the only heir to Suleyman's throne.[103] Almosnino either did not know what exactly happened, or chose to attribute this "heroic deed" to Suleyman rather than to his son, the ruling monarch.

The execution of the sultans' family members was not a new practice in the Ottoman Empire. Moreover, Mehmed the Conqueror's *Kanunname* states: "The majority of Legists have declared it allowable, that whoever among my illustrious children and grandchildren may come to the throne, should, for securing the peace of the world, order his brothers to be executed" (*Kanun* of the Security of the Throne).[104] This practice was known and abhorred in Europe. Mustafa's execution was treated in Italian fiction and drama as the tragedy of an innocent prince.[105] But diplomats who had spent some time in the Ottoman Empire took it for granted and continued to regard Suleyman as a just monarch. Although one Venetian ambassador called him "the crudest and most irreverent father," others admired him for his "intimate knowledge and strict application of the law" and explained that he murdered his sons because they had challenged his authority.[106] Even Busbecq, whose detailed version of Mustafa's assassination is similar to Almosnino's (since the two were obviously based on the same Venetian accounts), while less forgiving in general, almost justifies Suleyman's deeds. He believes that Suleyman had no choice because this was the law of the country: "The Turks tolerate no rival to the throne . . . Sultans of Turkey are thus compelled to stain their hands with their brothers' blood and to inaugurate their reign by murder."[107]

Almosnino, however, went much further. He obviously found this practice commendable, because the stability of the Ottoman regime and relative safety that Jews found in the empire made it so attractive to Jews who had always suffered as a result of wars between European monarchs. Some of Almosnino's readers might have heard about Mustafa's execution, but it is clear that his goal was not to justify this cruelty in their eyes but, instead, to reassure them that the sultans would not spare their own flesh and blood for the sake of their subjects' protection.

I suggest, however, that, aside from Almosnino's concern for his coreligionists' safety, this blatant endorsement of filicide is justified by his political philosophy, a key term of which is *republika*. He uses it in two senses, both of which are attested in sixteenth-century Castilian. The first meaning is "commonwealth," i.e., "a body of people composed of one or more nationalities usually with its own territory and government (law) that will benefit all the citizens of the commonwealth."[108] That is why Almosnino refers to the Jewish communities of Salonica and Constantinople as "republics" that exist within the Ottoman Empire. His primary loyalty is to his "noble republic," his fatherland (*patria*) for which he would die "a hundred thousand deaths [rather than] say anything that might harm it" (265).

The second meaning is close to the Latin *res publica*, literally "public matter." A current dictionary lists this definition as the fifth meaning of the word, but in the sixteenth century, it was used more frequently than today.[109] This is what *republica* means in "matters of the court and the republic" (166) and "sustaining this kingdom and the republic" (204).

Almosnino's civic ideal is putting the common good ahead of one's private interests, thus serving the commonwealth. He praises the fortitude of those who, as described by historians and chroniclers, put their lives at risk "during wars and military campaigns in which one defends his republic at the time and in the way required of him" (*Rejimyento*, fol. 46b). As for governments, they cannot be effective if they are concerned with their own interests rather than the common good (*byen komun*) (*Rejimyento*, fol. 121A). Almosnino agrees with Aristotle that a bad king or tyrant is particularly dangerous when he administers justice because he has great power, but cares more about his own good than that of the "republic" (*Rejimyento*, fol. 121a).[110] However, he believes that a king who is not more concerned about the common good than about his own interests is usually not of royal lineage but "has risen by luck" (*Rejimyento*, fol. 120b).

Suleyman, who descended from Osman and cared about sustaining the kingdom and the common good, sacrificed his own sons and grandsons for the peace and safety of his subjects. In the case of Mustafa's execution, he would have preferred to be merciful, but had to agree with Rustem that it was necessary to kill him to save the kingdom.[111] For all of this, the tenth Ottoman sultan should be not only praised but also "held as a mirror in which [everyone] must look in order not to go astray from the way of life" (205).

In other words, Almosnino, having recounted Suleyman's heroic and admirable deeds, declares that his chronicle is a biography of a great man meant to be used as a Mirror for Princes, a category of didactic literature aimed at giving moral and political guidance to rulers and ministers. Although some classical and biblical texts are considered Mirrors for Princes, this type of literature became popular in Europe during the medieval and early modern periods, while in the Middle East, works of advice were produced mainly between the ninth and nineteenth centuries.[112]

We cannot establish with certainty which "mirrors" were familiar to Almosnino, but he must have read the *Secret of Secrets*, produced in the mid-tenth century in Baghdad under the title *Kitab sirr al-asrar* and later widely known in Europe as *Secretum secretorum*, a book styled as Aristotle's advice to Alexander the Great.[113] Translated into Latin in Iberia, it spread from there to Europe and was later translated into many other languages. In 1200, Yehuda al-Harizi translated it into Hebrew.[114] We can also assume that Almosnino, who had written a commentary on al-Ghazali's *Intentions of the Philosophers*, would have known his *Counsel for Kings* (late eleventh century), which had a significant influence on subsequent advice literature.[115] Castilian authors also produced many "mirrors," some of which would have been available to Almosnino.[116] For instance, he could have read Antonio de Guevara's *Libro áureo del emperador Marco Aurelio* (Golden Book of Emperor Marcus Aurelius) (1529) or its later version, *Reloj de príncipes* (Dial of Princes) (1539), which were extraordinarily popular across Europe in the sixteenth century.

It is clear that Almosnino was familiar with some works that had "mirror" in their titles. In the West, "the first mirror-titled book with a political focus" was the anonymous *Speculum regum* (The King's Mirror), written in Norway before 1260.[117] But Almosnino seems to have misunderstood the meaning of *speculum*, which in such titles connotes survey, a magic mirror that shows all of the prince's responsibilities. But it is also possible that he intentionally changed its meaning to denote a model, looking at which—as if in a mirror—the ruler would see how he differed from Suleyman, and thus correct his ways. In fact, since the Mirrors for Princes category is not constituted by formal features but only by the subject and purpose, it includes texts of various genres. Hence, biographies of famous men to be imitated or rejected are also considered "mirrors." In *Rejimyento*, Almosnino cited Plutarch's *Parallel Lives*, and he probably knew other works that fit the category, such as Suetonius' *Lives of the Twelve Caesars* and Guevara's *Década de los Césares* (Lives of the Ten Roman Emperors), which imitated the former two.

As we have seen, Book II consists of miscellaneous elements united by the author's objective, namely, to present Suleyman and his rule as perfect and worthy of imitation, which is why it *appears* to be a Mirror for Princes. Almosnino's praise of Suleyman's cruelty toward his sons means that his "mirror," like Machiavelli's *Prince* and some other works of this type, values the ruler's political efficiency and success more than his virtue. Indeed, despite calling Suleyman kind and merciful, Almosnino shows that the sultan was often devious and manipulative but always successful. Thus, when he decided to kill Ibrahim Pasha but felt bound by his promise not to do so, he managed to get the grand mufti's permission by posing his question in such a way that the latter unknowingly sanctioned the execution.

And yet there is a crucial difference between Almosnino's second chronicle and the "mirror" literature. Such works were usually produced for a specific addressee, often at the accession of a new monarch, and in any case, with the expectation that they would be read and used by rulers. The Salonican rabbi, however, could not have expected the new sultan, Selim II, or any other monarch to read his work. Rather than instructing rulers, it aimed at educating subjects: Ottoman Sephardim. It seems that he made his second chronicle look like a Mirror for Princes because, as a reader of European literature, he felt that this category best fit his subject.

The Language of the Chronicles

The richness of *Crónica*'s vocabulary, reflecting the great variety of subjects covered in the book, shows not only that its author was a reader of Castilian literature but also that he expected his audience to know these words. That he produced his book largely for those who had spent years in Europe is evident from his use of Christian dates (except for the years) in addition to Hebrew ones and European toponyms, followed by corresponding Ottoman ones. For instance, he refers to Greece as Gresya adding, "which they call Oromeli" (72). On one occasion, he uses "Babel," the Hebrew term for "Babylon," and explains it as follows, "the populace (vulgo) usually calls it 'Babylonia,' and they [the Turks] call it 'Baghdad'" (113). "The populace" obviously refers to Christians, or Europeans; the term was used in Europe to refer to Baghdad, although Babel is about 100 kilometers from it. In 1553, for example, the Venetian ambassador to Constantinople talks about "Babylon, which they call Baghdad."[118]

In addition to toponyms, Almosnino's educated readers were expected to learn from *Crónica* the most useful Ottoman administrative and military terms, some of which, especially from the latter category, would have been new to Almosnino himself. This was evidently an important element of the educational project devised by Nasi and his circle, although, having immigrated to the Ottoman Empire as an adult, he would not have known all of those terms himself. It is therefore likely that Almosnino gave his lesson to Ottoman Sephardim with the help of his "esteemed friend," who was expert in reading Turkish. It must be emphasized that nowhere does Almosnino discuss the need to learn this language as such, and Book IV makes it clear that his own knowledge of it was quite limited. In any case, the first language ex-*conversos* had to master was Hebrew.

We do not know for sure whether Almosnino indeed read Arabic, but he probably knew the Arabic script (used by Ottoman Turkish). Thus he should have had no difficulty transcribing new words into Hebrew characters when he saw them in writing. But it is also possible that he spelled them phonetically from his friend's dictation. Pilar Romeu, who published the list of Turkish words found in *Crónica*, believes that Almosnino's purpose was to make the text comprehensible for readers.[119] Yet this is clearly not the case, because, as Romeu herself points out, Almosnino always offers either a Ladino equivalent or translation, which shows that he could have done without the Turkish terms. Moreover, the explanation always precedes the term in question, which, therefore, can be easily removed. Finally, Book III, which was not intended for educational purposes, contains only one Turkish term—*divan*—which was known to readers anyway and thus is not explained.

Another feature confirming that this was a concerted educational effort is the consistency with which Turkish words are introduced: either by "which they call . . ." or "which is . . ." For example, the term *kundak* (the stock of a gun) is explained as follows: *palo en ke esta puesta la eskopeta, ke elyos yaman kundak* (the pole on which a gun is placed which they call *kundak*) (95); *bas defterdar* (administrator of finances, treasurer) is introduced as *eskribano mayor en la puerta del gran senyor, ke elyos lyaman bas defterdar* (the head clerk at the Grand Senyor's Porte whom they call *bas defterdar*) (72).

In addition to military and administrative terms, Almosnino introduces his readers to some of those related to Islam. For instance, he explains *giblah* as follows: *onde endresen su orasyon, ke elyos lyaman kibela, ke es el enfrente de Kordoba i la Meka, onde esta sepulkro de su profeta* (where they direct their prayers, that they call *kibela* which faces Córdoba and Mecca where their prophet's tomb is) (181).

A few Turkish words, however, appear without any explanations (for instance, *sicil* [court record]), which suggests that they were already familiar to Sephardim. A comparison with Turkish words in Benaim's corpus of responsa confirms this. Yet the two lists barely overlap. And almost none of the words introduced in *Crónica* is found in later texts. This fact indicates that the plan to teach Sephardim military and administrative terms that would presumably help them serve the empire, came to nothing.

Conclusion

We have seen that while revealing certain affinities with several European accounts of the Ottoman Empire, Almosnino's chronicles differed from them in terms of perspective and attitude toward the Ottomans. Instead of hostility mixed with awe of the "Grand Turk," Almosnino's account of events that shocked Europeans expressed unconditional admiration for Suleyman, and profound gratitude to Selim. Unlike a conventional travelogue produced by an outsider with the purpose of conveying new knowledge to other outsiders, *Crónica*, written by a self-identified insider, is intended for other insiders, trying to convince them that Ottoman sultans would always ensure the safety and welfare of their subjects.

As far as literary form, the first two books of *Crónica* display some features of such European genres as the travelogue, the Mirror for Princes, and the Castilian chronicle. Yet Almosnino's chronicles are so eclectic that formal criteria are hardly applicable to them. Instead, it makes more sense to describe them from the standpoint of their purpose and subject matter, because this is what determined the author's literary choices. Thus, while the two chronicles offer engaging accounts that include amusing anecdotes about historical figures and firsthand descriptions of architectural sites, these elements of the travelogue and Mirror for Princes are there to assert the superiority of Ottoman high culture and the wisdom of Suleyman's rule. As for the obvious genre similarity with Pulgar's chronicle, Almosnino's work, while serving a political purpose, is entirely apologetic. At the same time, his praise of Ottoman sultans has nothing in common with the messianic interpretation of their role proclaimed by contemporaneous Jewish historiography, but rather, repeats the official version of events related to him by court Jews.

Therefore, in terms of their purpose, Almosnino's chronicles (the second in particular) are a didactic panegyric meant to educate readers about the Ottoman Empire and reassure them that it was ruled by merciful monarchs who rewarded loyalty. In terms of content, they should be described as an Ottoman history for Sephardi Jews. For us, however, they are an important source on the political aspirations of Jews close to Selim II's court and, therefore, on Jewish history.

Having found themselves in a new and much more favorable political situation, some Sephardim hoped to replicate and cultivate in the Ottoman Empire the royal alliance familiar to them from Iberia. This is why Nasi and his circle wanted Almosnino to educate Sephardim about their new homeland and encourage them to serve the Porte. Well-read in European literature, he was able to talk to his readers in language and terms they understood. No doubt, a lot of what he wrote could have been conveyed in religious language, but court Jews, as well as the majority of ex-*conversos*, were used to thinking about political matters in secular terms. Thus, Nasi made a perfect choice for his assignment and made Almosnino the first Jewish political writer in the Ottoman Empire.

However, the economic decline of the Jewish community and accession of Murad III (r. 1574–1595), during whose reign the women of the harem gained significant influence on state policy, rendered earlier aspirations untenable. Hence, *Crónica*'s message quickly became outdated and irrelevant. Later, Cansino definitively turned Almosnino's work into a travelogue.

Notes

1. See n. 112 in chapter 4. The historian Jonathan Ray also described Almosnino as "one of the keenest observers of Sephardic society during this formative period." (*After Expulsion* [New York, 2013] 82–83.)

2. Emmanuel, *Histoire des Israélites de Salonique*, 181.

3. Romeu, "Introduction," 15–16.

4. Molho, "Dos obras maestras," 100.

5. Romeu, "Introduction," 23. On the differences between the two texts, see her "Diferencias y paralelismos entre la *Crónica de los Reyes Otomanos* de rabí Mosé ben Baruh Almosnino y los *Extremos y Grandezas de Constantinopla* de Iacob Cansino," *Proceedings of the 3rd International Congress of Misgav Yerushalayim* (Jerusalem, 1994), 189–200.

6. Abraham Danon, "Abu Suad i rabi Moshe Almosnino," *El Tyempo* (April 17, 1902, 5–6).

7. Danon refers to Almosnino's work as *Kronika turka* and to Book II as *Kompendyo universal*, which is how Almosnino describes it himself at the beginning of this book. It is unclear, however, why Danon did not mention his discovery anywhere. This publication remained unnoticed by scholars, who continued to identify Almosnino's work with the Cansino edition. I am grateful to Julia P. Cohen for bringing this important text to my attention.

8. Romeu, "Introduction," 15.

9. Ibid.

10. On these taxes, see Minna Rozen, "Individual and the community," 254–257.

11. This was a large sum. For comparison, a high-ranking treasurer who served as the governor of Constantinople in Suleyman's absence was paid 6,000 ducats per year. (Albert Howe Lybyer, *The Government of the Ottoman Empire in the Time of Suleiman the Magnificent* [Cambridge, MA, 1913], 169.)

In this chapter and the following one, numbers in parentheses refer to the pages in Moises Almosnino, *Crónica de los reyes otomanos* (Barcelona, 1998).

12. Lucette Valensi, *Birth of the Despot: Venice and the Sublime Porte* (Ithaca and London, 1993), 73.

13. See, for instance, Laura Alcoba, "La Question du pouvoir au miroir ottoman," *Littérature et exotisme, XVI–XVIIIè siècles*, ed. Dominique de Courcelles (Paris, 1998), 17–34.

14. Valensi, *Birth of the Despot*, 11.

15. Caroline Finkel, *Osman's Dream: The History of the Ottoman Empire, 1300–1923* (London, 2005), 127.

16. Pierre Gilles (Petrus Gyllius), a French humanist, author of *The Antiquities of Constantinople* (1561), visited the Ottoman capital in 1544–1547. Nicolas de Nicolay, a French geographer, followed the French ambassador to

Suleyman's court in 1551. His best-known work is *Quatre premiers livres des navigations* (1568), quoted in this book more than once.

17. Benedetto Ramberti, *Libri tre delle cose de Turchi* (Venice, 1539), 11b.

18. Lybyer, *The Government of the Ottoman Empire,* 315.

19. Ibid., 316. Yaari, *Hebrew Printing,* no. 135. See "Bibliography" in A. Asher, ed. and trans. *The Itinerary of Rabbi Benjamin of Tudela* (London and Berlin, 1840), vol. I, 2–3.

20. On these two editions, see Yaari, *Hebrew Printing,* no. 135.

See "Bibliography" in A. Asher, ed. and trans. *The Itinerary of Rabbi Benjamin of Tudela* (London and Berlin, 1840), vol. I, 2–3.

21. Marcus Nathan Adler, trans. *The Itinerary of Benjamin of Tudela: Critical Text, Translation, and Commentary* (New York, 1907), 12.

22. Ramberti, *Libri tre*. Lybyer's translation of the book in *The Government of the Ottoman Empire,* 251.

Giovanni Antonio Menavino, *Trattato de costumi et vita de Turchi* (Florence, 1548) 155. (I have used the first edition, which would have been less easily available to Almosnino.) Nicolay probably got the story from Menavino. (*Les quatre premiers livres des navigations et pérégrinations de Nicolay* [Lyon, 1568], 100.)

23. Andrew Wear, "The Spleen in Renaissance Anatomy," *Medical History* 21 (1977): 43–63.

24. Although he might have also included those Jews who had spent time in Europe.

25. Finkel, *Osman's Dream,* 127.

26. Ramberti, *Cose tre,* 11b. Nicolay must have borrowed it from him. (*Les quatre premiers livres des navigations,* 63)

27. Ogier Ghiselin de Busbecq, *The Turkish Letters* (Baton Rouge, 2005), 40.

28. Roth, *Doña Gracia,* 184.

29. Quoted in Rozen, *Istanbul,* 43.

30. Ibid.

31. See the editorial in the first issue of *El Jurnal isrealit* (December 27, 1860, 1).

32. Yosef Yerushalmi, *Zakhor: Jewish History and Jewish Memory* (Seattle, 1998), 65.

33. Quoted in Charles Berlin, "A Sixteenth-Century Hebrew Chronicle of the Ottoman Empire: The *Seder Eliyahu Zuta* of Elijah Capsali and Its Message," in *Studies in Jewish Bibliography History and Literature in Honor of Edward Kiev,* ed. Charles Berlin (New York, 1971), 21–44, 24.

34. Yerushalmi, *Zakhor,* 65. For a detailed discussion of Hakohen's work, see, for example, Isidore Loeb, "Josef Haccohen et les Chroniqueurs Juifs," *Revue des Etudes Juives* 16 (1888): 28–56.

35. Saperstein, "Moses Almosnino: Sermon on *Eleh Fequde,*" 225–226.

36. Roth, *The Duke of Naxos,* 165

37. Here Almosnino is wrong. 1402 is when Beyazid I was captured, which effectively ended his reign followed by an interregnum through 1413, when Mehmed I was enthroned.

38. Ramberti, *Cose tre*, 14a.

39. Lybyer, *The Government of the Ottoman Empire*, 243.

40. The scarlet cloth was an expensive fine woolen fabric of various colors.

41. For information on Ottoman guilds and literature on this subject, see Rozen, *Istanbul*, 62–64.

42. Derin Terzioğlu, "The Imperial Circumcision Festival of 1582: An Interpretation," *Muqarnas* 1 (1995): 84–100, 95. Jews of Spanish origin are mentioned there also as dancers and performers.

43. Ibid., 90.

44. Haul Inalcik, "Istanbul: An Islamic City," Journal *of Islamic Studies* 1 (1990): 1–23, 12.

45. Rozen, "Contest and Rivalry in Mediterranean Maritime Commerce in the First Half of the 18th Century: The Jews of Salonika and the European Presence," *Revue des Études Juives* 147 (1988): 309–352, 310. Yaron Ben-Naeh's figure, 30,000, is an exaggeration. ("Istanbul," in EJIW).

46. Evliya Çelebi, known for his Judeophobia, claims in his famous account of the procession of the guilds: "As Jews are the most despised of all men, they pass the very last of the whole procession." [Evliya Efendi (Çelebi), *Narrative of the Travels in Europe, Asia, and Africa*, vol. 2 (London, 1968), 248.] Nonetheless, he mentions them as members of at least eight guilds.

47. Asper (the European term for *akçe*) was a silver coin that in the 1560s, contained 0.61 grams of silver. Ramberti says that 1,000 aspers = 20 ducats. (Ramberti in Lybyer's *The Government of the Ottoman Empire*, 243.) For comparison, according to Ramberti (i.e., around thirty years earlier), the chief gardener earned 50 aspers per day, and the chief cook who supervised fifty cooks was paid 40 aspers. (Ibid., 245.)

48. Technically, all Ottoman subjects, grandees included, were considered sultans' slaves. However, it is not clear whether Almosnino was aware of this because in another place he says that Selim was greeted by "all people, his slaves, subjects, and grandees" (119).

49. Busbecq, *The Turkish Letters*, 60.

50. On Jewish physicians and literature on the subject, see Rozen, *Istanbul*, 24 n. 26.

51. "Easter" was a common European translation of [*Ramadan*] *Bayram*.

52. *Rosh Hodesh* is the first day of the Hebrew month.

53. On the *zimmet* (*dhimma*), see Rozen, *Istanbul*, 16–18.

54. In 1544, Suleyman's *firman* granted the Ecumenical Patriarch territorial jurisdiction referring to him as "the actual patriarch of the well-guarded Istanbul and of the countries and areas that depend on it." (On the Patriarch's titles and the *firmans* conferring them in the sixteenth century, see Paraskevas

Konortas, "From *Ta'if e* to *Millet*: Ottoman Terms for the Ottoman Greek Orthodox Community," in *Ottoman Greeks in the Age of Nationalism: Politics, Economy, and Society in the Nineteenth Century,* eds. Dimitri Gondicas and Charles Issawi (Princeton, NJ, 1999, 169–179, 174.)

55. The *sultani* is an Ottoman gold coin, first minted during the reign of Mehmed II and discontinued in the late 17th century. It weighed about 3.45 grams, i.e., close to the Venetian ducat.

56. The expression coined by Yerushalmi in his "'Servants of Kings and Not Servants of Servants': Some Aspects of the Political History of the Jews," Tenenbaum Family Lecture Series in Judaic Studies delivered at Emory University, February 8, 2005 (Atlanta, GA).

57. Danon, "Abu Suad i rabi Moshe Almosnino," 5.

58. Julia Phillips Cohen, *Becoming Ottoman* (Oxford, 2014), 17.

59. Ibid., 1.

60. Benjamin Braude, "Foundation Myths of the *Millet* System," in *Christians and Jews in the Ottoman Empire vol. 1*, eds. Benjamin Braude and Bernard Lewis (New York and London, 1982), 69–88, 79–80.

61. Quoted in ibid., 80.

62. Ibid.

63. Berlin, "A Sixteenth-Century Hebrew Chronicle," 24.

64. On the role of numbers in Jewish magic, see Joshua Trachtenberg, *Jewish Magic and Superstition: A Study in Folk Religion* (New York, 1939), 117–120.

65. Quoted in Berlin, "A Sixteenth-Century Hebrew Chronicle," 27.

66. *Amadís de Gaula*, trans. Alan Astro and Nathan Snyder (Constantinople, 1540), 2.

67. Yaari, *Hebrew Printing*, no. 128.

68. Gutwirth, "Expulsion from Spain and Jewish Historiography," 143.

69. Yerushalmi, Zakhor, 69.

70. Ibid., 67.

71. Ibid.

72. On the proliferation of historiographic works in Ottoman, see Robert Mantran, "L'historiographie ottomane à l'époque de Soliman le Magnifique" in "Soliman le Magnifique et son temps," *Actes des IXè rencontres de l'École du Louvre, 7–10 mars 1990*, ed. Gilles Veinstein (Paris, 1992), 25–32. On the position of court historiographer, see Cornell H. Fleisher, "The Lawgiver as Messiah," in ibid., 150–178, 172.

73. Finkel, *Osman's Dream*, 100.

74. Fleischer, *Bureaucrat and Intellectual in the Ottoman Empire* (Princeton, 1986), 239.

75. See Berlin, "A Sixteenth-Century Hebrew Chronicle," 38.

76. This figure is cited in the document quoted in Hacker, "The Sürgün System and Jewish Society in the Ottoman Empire during the Fifteenth to the Seventeenth Centuries," in *Ottoman and Turkish Jewry: Community and Leadership* (Bloomington, 1992), ed. Aron Rodrigue, 1–66, 27.

77. Ibid., 28–30.

78. This confirms Hacker's conclusions on the deportation to Rhodes based on very few primary sources. (Ibid., 27–30.)

79. On Suleyman's wars, see Mesut Uyar, Edward Erickson, *A Military History of the Ottomans: from Osman to Atatürk* (ABC-CLIO, 2009).

80. See Macedo, "A Sixteenth Century Portuguese Novel and the Jewish Press."

81. Barbara Fuchs, "Don Quijote and the Forging of National History," *Modern Language Quarterly* 68, no. 3 (2007): 395–415, 398.

82. For a discussion of this question in 16th-century Castilian literature, see David Mañero Lozano, "Historiografía novohispana y prosa de ficción del Siglo de Oro," *Criticón* 106 (2009): 79–97.

83. See, for example, Fleischer, "The Lawgiver as Messiah." On Ebus-su'ud's role, see Colin Imber, *Ebus-su'ud: The Islamic Legal Tradition*, (Stanford, 1997).

84. According to a European traveler, "Bayezid II was accustomed to stand to receive the Mufti, and to give him a seat above his own." (Quoted in Lybyer, *The Government of the Ottoman Empire*, 209.)

85. Shahab Ahmed and Nenad Filipovic, "The Sultan's Syllabus: A Curriculum for the Ottoman Imperial medreses Prescribed in a fermān of Qānūnī I Süleymān, Dated 973 (1565)." *Studia Islamica*, nos. 98/99 (2004), 183–218, 192.

86. On theories of vision, see David C. Lindberg, *Roger Bacon and the Origins of Perspectiva in the Middle Ages* (Clarendon Press, 1996).

Not surprisingly, Cansino understood that the word *perspektiva* referred to the title of Alhazene's book and capitalized it in his transliteration. (*Extremos y grandezas*, 142.) But more than two and a half centuries later, Abraham Danon failed to understand what *perspektiva* meant here and explained it to his readers as "the science called 'perspective' (seeing from afar)." ("Abu Suad i rabi Moshe Almosnino," 5.)

87. See Mañero Lozano, "Historiografía novohispana," 88–89.

88. See Gülru Necipoğlu, "A Canon for the State, A Canon for the Arts: Conceptualizing the Classical Synthesis of Ottoman Arts and Architecture," in *Soliman le Magnifique*, 195–216.

89. In this connection, Gutwirth suggests that Almosnino "is devising a series of questions which resound with the modern reader: How much did the building in Constantinople cost? Where did the materials originate? How did the materials arrive in Constantinople? What is their function? Whom do they benefit?" ("*Acutissima patria*: Locating Texts before and after the Expulsions," *Hispania Judaica* 8 [2011]: 19–38, 33.) I do not think Almosnino devises any questions, let alone modern ones. Instead, he informs the readers how much Suleyman spent to benefit his subjects. In fact, Evliya does the same thing with the purpose of impressing his readers with the greatness of Ottoman sultans and their cities.

90. Necipoğlu, "The Süleymaniye Complex in Istanbul: an Interpretation," in *Muqarnas* 3 (1986): 92–117.

91. Kaya Şahin, "Imperialism, Bureaucratic Consciousness and the Historian's Craft": in *Writing History at the Ottoman Court*, eds. H. Erdem Çipa and Eniine Fetvaci (Bloomington, 2013), 39–57, 50.

92. Shahab and Filipovic, "The Sultan's Syllabus," 1.

93. Ibid., 187.

94. See Gülru Necipoğlu, *The Age of Sinan, Architectural Culture in the Ottoman Empire* (London, 2005), 141.

95. Ibid., 140–141.

96. Evliya Efendi, *Narrative of the Travels*, vol.1, 78–79.

97. Ibid., 81.

98. I am surprised by Gutwirth's interpretation of the architecture section: "The section on the buildings of Constantinople is clearly a courtly writing: courtly because it deals with the Sultan and his servants/courtiers; courtly, because it is connected to the rest of the work as an example or component of the chronicle of the reign of the Sultan Selim II [*sic*] . . . ; courtly, also, because he constantly mentions sources of information that come not from popular sectors but from the highest ranks of the empire." I define it as a didactic panegyric of Suleyman. Even more surprisingly, Gutwirth claims that Almosnino fashions himself as a courtier. ("*Acutissima patria*," 32.)

99. The use of the term "golden age" in reference to the pre-1492 Jewish existence in Spain and the idea of the corrupting influence of the East on Jewish creativity, might have appeared in Jewish vernacular literature for the first time, but they certainly would be repeated by many Jews in the centuries to come.

100. Gallego, *Dialogo del colorado*, fol. 1. The term "hemisphere" is one of the very few allusions to the Americas in sixteenth-century Sephardi literature.

101. Pierre Gilles, *The Antiquities of Constantinople* (New York, 1988), 62.

102. Quoted in Berlin, "A Sixteenth-Century Hebrew Chronicle," 29.

103. Finkel, *Osman's Dream*, 141. For more on this subject, see, for example, Alan Fisher, "Süleyman and his Sons" in *Soliman le Magnifique*, 117–126.

104. Quoted in Lybyer, *The Government of the Ottoman Empire*, 94.

105. See Zahit Atçıl, "Why Did Süleyman the Magnificent Execute His Son Şehzade Mustafa in 1553?" *The Journal of Ottoman Studies* 48 (2016): 67–104, 69.

106. Quoted in Valensi, *Birth of the Despot*, 38.

107. Busbecq, *The Turkish Letters*, 30.

108. *The Merriam-Webster Unabridged Dictionary Online* (accessed October 11, 2014).

109. República 5. Causa pública, el común o su utilidad. Diccionario de la lengua española 23d ed.

A search for *república* in http://www.corpusdelespanol.org/ shows seven tokens in the fifteenth century and 1614 in the sixteenth. Many are used in the sense of *res publica* (accessed May 11, 2013). I am very grateful to Vincent Barletta for this search. Incidentally, in chapter 1 of *Don Quixote* (1605), we read that the ingenious hidalgo decided to become a knight-errant not only for the sake of his own glory but also to serve "his republic" (*para el servicio de su república*).

110. Cf. Aristotle, *Pol.* v. 10, 1311a3–5. (Curiously, Almosnino notes that Selim II is not a tyrant and does not want to be taken for one [99].)

111. Needless to say, today historians discuss Suleyman's actions and their consequences from a different perspective. Still, recent historiography has argued that the Ottoman household had gained full dynastic legitimacy as a result of Suleyman's "lifting the Ottoman dynasty out of the realm of competition by executing Mustafa, who had . . . been used by politically active janissaries, bureaucrats, and scholars." (Atçıl, "Why Did Süleyman the Magnificent Execute His Son?" 98.)

112. For a discussion of this question, see Linda T. Darling, "Mirrors for Princes in Europe and the Middle East: A Case of Historiographical Incommensurability," in *East Meets West in the Middle Ages and Early Modern Times* (Berlin and Boston, 2013), 223–242.

113. Ibid., 233.

114. Moses Gaster, "The Hebrew Version of the Secretum Secretorum: A Mediaeval Treatise Ascribed to Aristotle," *Journal of the Royal Asiatic Society* (Oct. 1907): 879–912.

115. Darling, "Mirrors for Princes in Europe and the Middle East," 224.

116. See María Angeles Galino Carillo, *Los Tratados sobre educacion de principes (siglos XVI y XVII)* (Madrid, 1948).

Needless to say, Shem tob de Carrión's *Proverbios morales* is also an example of advice literature.

117. Darling, "Mirrors for Princes in Europe and the Middle East," 229.

118. Valensi, *Birth of the Despot*, 46.

119. Romeu, "Turquismos en la Crónica de los Reyes Otomanos," 100.

FOUR

The First Ladino Travelogue

ALMOSNINO'S TREATISE ON THE EXTREMES OF CONSTANTINOPLE

Book III of *Crónica* (henceforth, *Extremes*) is one of the most misunderstood works of Ladino literature. This misinterpretation was largely a consequence of its first appearance (albeit in adapted form) as the opening part of Cansino's volume entitled *Extremos y grandezas de Constantinopla*, discussed in chapter 3. As will be remembered, since that moment, Almosnino's multi-part and multi-genre work has been known as a travelogue. The third part of the full version in particular has been invariably described as a picturesque travel account of Constantinople.

In this chapter, I will show that what has been erroneously taken for a trustworthy description of the Ottoman capital is in fact an idiosyncratic representation of the city in the form of a medieval treatise on its alleged climatic, socioeconomic, and moral extremes. Furthermore, rather than conveying Almosnino's impressions in his own terms, this account heavily depends on several intertexts, including works by Hippocrates, Aristotle, Maimonides, Ibn Sinna, and other classical and medieval authors.

As will become clear, due to its intertextuality, this work cannot be treated as a reliable source on Constantinople.

The Purpose of Extremes

Book III and Book IV of *Crónica*, as we know, were produced at the same time but belong to different genres and serve different purposes. Book IV is a thorough account of the delegation's activities written for those Salonicans who would have been interested in what exactly the delegation did in the capital and why it took it so long to achieve the desired result. In the sermon mentioned in chapter 3, which Almosnino delivered at the Talmud Torah in March 1568, soon after his return to Salonica, he is clearly trying to defend himself from "slanderers" who accused him of procrastinating in Constantinople "not in order to attain our charter of liberty, but rather to profit in my business affairs!"[1] In fact, he indirectly acknowledges having done business there by promising to offer "in sacrifice to God" the material benefit accrued on this trip.[2] There is no information on the commercial activity in which he was engaged, but given how much he says about the capital's goldsmiths and their problems, it is possible that Almosnino had some commercial interest in the jewelry business. In any event, he indignantly refutes all accusations. Marc Saperstein suggests that one of the functions of Almosnino's sermon was to "quell opposition in his own community."[3] But the "malicious" letters to which Almosnino alludes might have been sent to him while he was still in Constantinople, so it is possible that he produced Book IV, at least in part, for the purposes of self-justification. In his sermon Almosnino refers to it as the Ladino report confirming his words.[4] Book IV is of great interest as a primary source and merits a thorough examination by historians, but since its specific audience and purpose make it irrelevant for my study, I will not discuss it here.

Books III and IV, unlike Almosnino's other vernacular works, were neither commissioned to him nor were answers to anyone's questions. Though they were also written at a time of leisure, during the holiday of Sukkot, Almosnino does not mention this as an excuse for writing a vernacular work. In the introduction to these two Books, he makes it clear that this was his own decision:

> I thought it would be good to write an account of some of the extremes without a mean found in the city of Constantinople and of the immense travails that we endured on our journey in the service of God and our republic, and of the six conjunctions in which we failed to conclude our affair.[5] (207)

Out of the three topics listed in the introduction—the extremes without a mean found in Constantinople, the efforts and failures of the Salonican delegation, and the six missed opportunities to reach its goal—the latter two are discussed at length in Book IV, whereas the first one is the sole subject of Book III. In other words, Book III is not a narrative of specific events but rather, an attempt to make sense of what Almosnino knew about Constantinople, where these events had taken place, and to articulate this in a suitable form.

It is also noteworthy that *Extremes* is by no means a physical description of Constantinople, let alone a picturesque one. Indeed, there are only two pictures: rainwater gushing down the steep streets of Constantinople and collecting waste (no. 2), and smelly houses crammed together along narrow streets with women shouting from their doors and windows (no. 25). Furthermore, the only adjective denoting color used in *Extremes* is "black," to describe rotten grapes.

Nevertheless, even after *Crónica* was published in full, it continues to be perceived as a single text and treated as an ad hoc travel account akin to those produced by sixteenth-century European travelers. For instance, in his brief discussion of *Crónica* as a whole, Eleazar Gutwirth suggests "it recalls travel literature with its characteristic features: descriptions of cities, its informal character and personal anecdotes. It is a genre that flourished in the sixteenth century. It was intensely cultivated by travelers to the Ottoman Empire."[6]

The reason it never occurred to scholars to question the definition and nature of *Extremes* has to do with a general problem in the field of Sephardic Studies where Hebrew and vernacular works are dealt with by different groups of scholars. Hebrew-text specialists work only on high culture and are not interested in vernacular literature, whereas Ladino literature specialists, almost by definition, focus on popular culture. As a result of this compartmentalization, students of Almosnino's Hebrew works barely mention his *Rejimyento* and usually do not know anything about *Crónica*. Since *Rejimyento* is known as a semi-religious work and *Crónica* as a whole is believed to be a travelogue with elements of a chronicle, Spanish scholars (almost the only ones who have worked on the latter) were not interested in the former, while the few students of *Rejimyento* apparently found *Crónica* irrelevant to their subject.[7] Hence, none of the scholars of Almosnino's vernacular works thought of putting *Rejimyento* and the third part of *Crónica* side by side and comparing the two texts. Yet, as I will show, they have the same philosophical foundations and are based on the same classical and medieval writings.

Regimens of Health

Extremes, like *Rejimyento*, has a clear structure. The introduction is followed by twenty-six sections presenting and explaining the alleged extremes of Constantinople. The conclusion announces that the author has to stop because he cannot surpass the number twenty-six, which stands for the name of God (231).[8] All sections (except no. 1) start with the claim that a given aspect of the city's life is characterized by two extremes. The sections conclude with an explanation of this opposition, sometimes followed by a description of another pair of extremes brought about by the first one. This structure is reminiscent of Parts Two and Three of *Rejimyento* where, following Aristotle's *Nicomachean Ethics*, each chapter deals with two moral extremes.

Yet, even though the underlying notion of Book III is that happiness is found in the mean between two extremes, only a few of its sections deal with virtues and vices, while many more are concerned with material aspects of life in Constantinople that cannot be changed through moral behavior, since they are caused by the geographic or socioeconomic environment. Obviously, unlike *Rejimyento*, *Extremes* is not a work on ethics per se, even though a few sections deal with virtues and vices. Instead, this book demonstrates what happens to the bodies and minds of those who are forced or choose to live in extreme conditions. Thus, despite being descriptive rather than prescriptive, *Extremes* is similar to medieval regimens of health in that it serves as a warning to people who do not follow those regimens.

Treatises on health, usually in the form of counsel to lay people, were very popular in the medieval and early modern periods. They were based on the assumption that the health of body and mind were interconnected and achieved through the appropriate regulation of ways of living.[9] This view was held by physicians and philosophers at least since Hippocrates' *Airs, Waters, Places* and *Regimen in Health* that described regulatory factors, the balance of which was essential for maintaining one's health and preventing disease. Galen, who wrote a commentary on *Airs, Waters, Places* and further developed Hippocrates' teaching, called these factors (or causes) *sex res non naturales*: "six non-naturals."[10] He considered health a natural state, seeing disease as unnatural and described these six factors as "non-naturals," i.e., neither in accordance with nature nor contrary to it, since they can lead both to health and disease depending on whether they are used properly.[11]

The six non-naturals are air, food and drink, exercise and rest, sleep and wakefulness, excretion and retention, and accidents of the soul (i.e., emotions). It was believed that they could affect the human body to the point of altering the balance of what were considered primary qualities (hot, cold, moist, and dry), which, in turn, could change the balance of humors (four bodily fluids) thus causing diseases.

In the ninth century, Hunayn ibn Ishaq translated into Arabic Galen's *Ars Medica* and produced a compendium of his works, many of which did not survive in their original Greek versions. Ibn Ishaq's translations made Galen's work available, among others, to Ibn Sinna (Avicenna) whose *Canon of Medicine* was translated into many languages, including Hebrew.[12] The *Canon* combined Aristotle's and Galen's ideas. According to Ibn Sinna, factors that could change or maintain the state of the human body included food and drink, air, water, seasonal changes, localities of residence, exercise and repose, age, sex, occupation, customs, race, and evacuation and retention. Maimonides incorporated in his *Regimen of Health* and *Treatise on Asthma* the teachings of Hippocrates, Galen, and Ibn Sinna. He instructed his patients on how to cure and prevent many diseases by using pure air and water, baths, exercise, and a healthy diet. Similar to Ibn Sinna, Maimonides emphasized the role of the environment, particularly one's living conditions, for the preservation of health.

In addition to the treatises mentioned above, which are cited in *Rejimyento*, Almosnino would have known such popular regimens of health as *Epistola super regimen sanitatis*, a work by Petrus Hispanus (thirteenth century) presented as an epistle to various famous people (mentioned in previous chapters), *Regimen sanitatis salernitanum*, a hygienic treatise in verse produced in the twelfth or thirteenth century, allegedly by a member of the Salernitan School of medicine and translated into many languages including Hebrew, and *Secretum Secretorum* discussed in chapter 3. Being a Mirror for Princes, it included a regimen of health supposedly written by Aristotle for Alexander to instruct him on diet and personal hygiene. It was the Middle Ages' best-known treatise on health and clearly a bestseller, judging by the fact that there were around five hundred versions of it in Latin alone.[13] Its short version is essentially a manual of hygiene. Regimens of health continued to be produced in the sixteenth century. Thus, Almosnino's contemporary, Ioannes Katschius, wrote *Nonnulla de regimine sanitatis, juxta sex res non naturales*, a treatise devoted specifically to the six non-naturals.

As will be remembered, the Hebrew title of *Rejimyento* is *Hanhagot ha-haiim* (The Regimen of Living), even though it does not correspond to the definition of Hanhagot literature that deals with small details of everyday life. It seems that Almosnino chose it because this was the closest translation of the Ladino title, *Rejimyento de la vida*, which is much more appropriate and indeed perfectly matches the book's content. *Rejimyento* is an ethical treatise divided into three parts, the first of which is a regimen of health, the second deals with moral virtues, and the third with intellectual ones.[14]

It was common practice to discuss ethical precepts together with medical ones, because hygiene was considered "an ethical activity, for it both reveals and reinforces a properly functioning hierarchy within the individual."[15] Thus, combining ethical and hygienic treatises within one book was not unusual. In fact, a Middle English translation of *Secretum secretorum* describes it as "The Book of Good Governance and Guiding of the Body," because it includes both a regimen of health and ethical and political advice.

As was discussed in chapter 2, among Almosnino's friends and mentors there were at least three famous physicians: Aron Afia, Daniel ben Perahya Hacohen, and Amatus Lusitanus. Moreover, in addition to his general interest in science, Almosnino himself had some practical knowledge of medicine, so that during the delegation's trip he was able to diagnose one of his colleagues with a lethal heart condition (240). It is therefore not surprising that he, too, decided to produce a regimen of health. He instructs his nephew on proper conduct with regard to ten (his favorite number again!) everyday activities: eating, drinking, sleeping, being awake, lying down, getting up, walking, sitting, speaking, and being silent (fol. 12a). He obviously skips some of the six non-naturals and adds a few of his own (for instance, sitting or speaking), but this was common for regimens of health. *Secretum Secretorum*, for example, provides guidance in fifteen activities, including sex and choice of clothes.

There is a more fundamental similarity between *Rejimyento* and *Secretum Secretorum*. Once again, Almosnino presents his work as a Mirror, which is stated on the title page: "Book entitled *The Regimen of Living*, which can be truly called a mirror for the wise and fortunate." The publishers of the romanized Amsterdam edition agreed that reading Almosnino's work is like looking in "a crystalline mirror" that allows one to correct his errors and get rid of his vices.[16] It would be a stretch to say that teaching his nephew, Almosnino saw himself in the role of Aristotle guiding Alexander, but there is no doubt that he followed *Secretum secretorum* and similar Mirrors as a model for his *Rejimyento* which, while addressing Moses Garson, was intended for all those who wanted to be wise and happy.

Talking about health in *Rejimyento*, Almosnino directly cites or mentions Hippocrates' *Aphorisms*, Aristotle's *Problems*, (which he had earlier translated from Latin, cf. fol. 25a) and *Meteorology*, Galen's *Ars Medica*, Ibn Sinna's *Canon of Medicine*, and Maimonides's *Regimen of Health* and *Treatise on Asthma*. As I will show, *Extremes* is based on the same canon of classical and medieval works on medicine and health, even though they are not directly cited.

Still, despite the similarities, *Extremes* is not a health regimen, and it does not contain a single recommendation or exhortation. Instead, its sections dealing with climate and diseases nos. 1, 2, 3, and 26) are closest to a genre related to health regimens, the medical topography (a term first used in 1843[17]). Such topographies, most of which were produced in Europe between the seventeenth and twentieth centuries, described specific geographic locations (usually cities) from the standpoint of their presumed influence on inhabitants with the purpose of fighting epidemics and improving people's health.

Hippocratic in essence, they dealt with climate, soil, water, air, flora, people's temperaments, living conditions, and common diseases. Spanish scholars created a large corpus of medical topographies, the earliest of which, a topography of Saragossa published in 1575, is attributed to Benjamin of Tudela.[18] The second, *Sevillana Medicina* by the convert Juan de Aviñón (mentioned in the prologue as Moses ben Samuel de Roquemaure), was written no earlier than 1420 but first published in 1545.[19] Whether Almosnino read *Sevillana Medicina* or not, it is clear that his work belongs to the same medieval–early modern Iberian tradition.

The Non-Naturals of Constantinople

In the introduction to *Extremes*, Almosnino says he will present what he saw in the capital as a few universals that will allow his readers to understand the particulars. This is a reference to Aristotle's idea laid out in his *Categories* and further developed in *The Metaphysics*. Aristotle believed that "each category contains a hierarchy of universals and particulars, with each universal being 'said of' the lower-level universals and particulars that fall beneath it."[20] Thus, if climate is the highest universal in a category, then the lower and subordinate universals are winds, rains, air, etc., which can be described as "general and corruptible [i.e., changeable] ones." As we will see, for Almosnino, many things, including diseases and conception, are related to climate and second-level universals. And it is the particulars, such as *north* wind and *humid* air, that have a direct effect on the lives of Constantinople's residents. But, as we are informed already in the introduction, everything in the capital, including universal and particular cases and all its foundations, goes "contrary to nature" (209). Thus, *Extremes* presents a series of twenty-six things that go wrong in the Ottoman capital.

The first two sections apparently follow Hippocrates' *Airs, Waters, Places*, where we read:

> when one comes into a city to which he is a stranger, he ought to consider its situation, how it lies as to the winds and the rising of the sun; for its influence is not the same whether it lies to the north or the south, to the rising or to the setting sun.

It is also important to learn about "the winds, the hot and the cold" (*Aër.*, I).[21] Accordingly, sections 1 and 2 of *Extremes* deal with the situation of Constantinople, its climate, air, and waters. Those who have not been to the capital learn that it is a big city surrounded by two seas, situated on a few hills, and open to winds from the north and west. When it rains the streets are very wet, but after the rain stops they quickly become very dry. Although this triviality couched in terms of extremes without a mean does not provide any information about the city, no. 2 is of great interest for the modern reader, because it immediately exposes Almosnino's method in this book, the nature of the facts he uses to prove his theory, and one of the key sources of his philosophy.[22]

The true meaning and function of no. 2 become clear if nos. 1 and 2 are *read* as one unit. To begin with, these sections illustrate the ancient theory of four elements and qualities embraced, with some variations, by all medieval scholars. Aristotle relates the four classical elements of which everything terrestrial is made to two of the four primary qualities: fire is hot and dry, air is wet and hot, water is cold and wet, and earth is dry and cold (*Meteor.* I. 2, 339a 16–19).[23] Almosnino demonstrates that the climate of Constantinople has all four qualities: the winds are cold and hot, rains make the soil wet, but later it dries up. Yet there are only three elements—air, water, and earth—whereas fire is conspicuously absent from *Extremes*. I find a plausible explanation in Aristotle's idea expressed in his *Meteorology* (extensively cited in *Rejimyento*):

> When the sun warms the earth the evaporation which takes place is necessarily of two kinds . . . One kind is rather of the nature of vapour, the other of the nature of a windy exhalation . . . Of these the windy exhalation, being warm, rises above the moister vapour. (*Meteor.* I. 4, 4341b 8–13)

Aristotle calls the warm and dry element "fire" "for there is no word fully adequate to every state of the fumid evaporation" (*Meteor.* I. 4, 341b 15–16). Hippocrates speaks not about fire but rather of heat which, together with abrupt temperature changes, he considers a cause of disease (*Aph.*, III, 1).[24]

Almosnino not only accepts Aristotle's exhalation theory summarized above, but also uses his language to speak about climate and natural phenomena. For instance, the following explanation is obviously phrased in terms of Aristotle's *Meteorology*:

> And the reason why the north wind is colder there than in other parts of our land is that it comes directly from the Black Sea which cools it beyond natural due to the exhalation of the vapors rising as a result of the continuous movement of the flow. (no. 1)

Aristotle writes: "The north wind . . . coming from moist regions, is full of vapour and therefore cold" (*Meteor.* I. 10, 347b 40–42). As we now see, section two of *Extremes*, which appears trite, should be understood in the context of Aristotle's *Meteorology* and in relation to the following statement in particular: "After rain the earth is being dried by its own heat and that from above and gives off evaporation which we saw to be the material cause of wind" (*Meteor.* II. 4, 360b 30–32).

The interaction between earth, water, and air is important for Almosnino as he is particularly interested in the quality of air and its "corruption" caused by contact with the other two elements. In fact, the verb "corrupt" and its derivates are among Almosnino's favorite terms, borrowed from Aristotle. "The Philosopher" says that the four elements account for all "coming to be" (generation) and "passing away" (corruption) (*On Generation and Corruption.* II. 1). Each element can change (corrupt) into two others with which it shares a property.[25] Thus air, which is moist and warm, can change into water, which is moist and cold.

In the case of Constantinople, its air is "predisposed to corruption" because it is surrounded by seas, which makes the air exceedingly humid. In addition, it interacts with earth, which is cold and dry, but in this city it gets humid: "And because the air is thin and the earth is humid, the air easily corrupts" (no. 26). This was a commonly accepted view formulated by Ibn Sinna, among others, who stated that "damp soil favours putrefaction, with ultimate pollution of the air."[26]

Air cleanliness was believed to be important for human health. For instance, Maimonides quotes Galen on the subject: "Says Galen: taking care of cleanliness of the surrounding air which enters the body is no less important than watching any other matter which is exposed to corruption by contact."[27] "The concern for clean air [Maimonides continues] is the foremost rule in preserving the health of one's body and soul."[28] In Almosnino's system, however, air is not only a non-natural but also a "lower universal" subordinate to climate. And the humid air of Constantinople is a particular that affects the health of its residents, women's fertility, and living conditions for its Jews.

Section 3 is based on the miasma theory that had been accepted by scholars at least since Hippocrates' time. It was believed that corruption of air was the primary cause of epidemics (which was allegedly confirmed by the Black Death in the fourteenth century).[29] For instance, Juan de Aviñón, who dedicates a few chapters to the air of Seville, states that there are three ways of air transformation: natural, non-natural, and counter-natural. The natural change is the kind that comes with each of the four seasons. The non-natural change takes place in the same way all year round. "And the counter-natural [change] happens when the air corrupts, which brings epidemics and [high] mortality."[30]

Throughout the later Middle Ages and Renaissance, plague tracts, that is "manuals of advice on how to cope with the pestilence . . . enjoyed widespread popularity."[31] To those who had not yet caught the disease, they offered regimens to minimize the chances of being stricken. Most recommended purifying the air by burning wood and using herbs.[32]

Thus Almosnino repeats a commonplace when he says "whenever it [air] corrupts all kinds of diseases occur." This happens because the air of Constantinople is prone to corruption, "and when it gets corrupted, it corrupts suddenly and in the extreme."

In the sixteenth century, due to the expansion of Ottoman territories and growing maritime trade, Constantinople became a hub for infection transmission and was stricken by plagues more frequently than before.[33] Almosnino happened to visit the capital several times during a severe plague wave (1552–1567), whose devastating impact is described by Busbecq.[34] There was indeed a seasonal pattern in plague epidemics, which had nothing to do with air "corruption," but with rising temperatures that provided more favorable conditions for sustaining outbreaks. Thus, in Constantinople "plague would typically start in April or May, peak in August and September, and recede in November and December," but could return the following spring.[35]

In no. 26, Almosnino returns to the effect of the thin and rare air of Constantinople, but now he claims that it is beneficial for quick conception, which explains why women in the capital give birth every year. However, epidemics caused by air corruption take the lives of many children. Almosnino poignantly conveys the anxiety of the first generations of Ottoman Sephardim faced with high infant mortality following the expulsion, and their fear of not having any descendants.[36] Section 26 is the only place where he shows emotion, interjecting superstitiously, "*has ve-shalom*" (God forbid).

The most important recommendation provided in plague tracts was to flee the city and remain in a village to avoid the pestilential atmosphere. This was common practice in Almosnino's time. In fact, during the epidemics of 1546 and 1564 in Salonica, he, too, stayed in nearby villages, Pelestria and Levadia, where he produced a few of his works.[37] But, despite these precautions, plagues were brutal to children and the elderly. The famous Sephardi poet Saadia Longo, in his eulogy for the victims of the 1541 epidemic in Jerusalem (which Almosnino would have read), says that there was not a single household untouched by death. "People abandoned the city and wandered from place to place," but death found and struck innocent children. "It snatched them from the mother's bosom, it devoured the father's heart; a consuming fire consumed them."[38]

According to Almosnino, air corruption in Constantinople is exacerbated by the adversities of city life, a topos of medieval and Renaissance health regimens. Thus, Maimonides observes that the "town air is stagnant, turbid and 'thick,' the natural result of its big buildings, narrow streets, the refuse of its inhabitants, their corpses and animal carcasses, food gone bad and the like."[39] Almosnino confirms that in Constantinople sewage is thrown into courtyards and remains there until it is washed off by rain meanwhile "corrupting" the air (no. 2). The description of dismal living conditions in Jewish neighborhoods might have reminded some of his readers of what Ibn Sinna and Maimonides found particularly detrimental for one's health. He tells us that in many houses

> ground-floor rooms are very dark, and there is no wind from anywhere, as there are buildings on all sides and no space between them. And because the service spaces are inside the houses and the sewage thrown down [from the top floor] goes to the bottom level inside, as there is no other place or empty space in the building, the bottom stories are very smelly. And because the city is very humid, in winter when the moisture freezes, it gets colder, and the closer to the ground the more humid it is. (no. 22)

No doubt, while writing these lines, Almosnino kept in mind his predecessors' recommendations. Ibn Sinna cautions against the overcrowding of houses: "It is not sufficiently realized that the befouling of the air through lack of air-space between the houses is as dangerous as close contact with the organic emanations from the human body."[40]

Maimonides admits that it is hard for those who grew up in cities to live in the country, but at least they should

> choose for a residence a wide-open site, facing the north-east . . . Living quarters are best located on an upper floor, giving on a wide street exposed to the north wind . . . Toilets should be located as far as possible from living rooms.[41]

In *Regimen of Health*, he gives similar instructions adding "the dwelling place should be a tall building and should have a wide court, traversed by the north wind and accessible to the sun, because the sun dissolves the putridity of the air, thins it, and clarifies it."[42] Ibn Sinna explains "north wind . . . makes septic pestilential atmosphere healthy."[43] Almosnino, indeed, confirms that in Constantinople "the best lodgings are built on the top floor so that they would be open to the north wind, which is salubrious" (no. 22).

* * *

Almosnino's description of Constantinople and its non-naturals covers every issue deemed important by Hippocrates, who sees climate as but one aspect of a city's existence:

> Having inquired into the waters and geography of the place, one should ask about the mode in which the inhabitants live, and what their pursuits are, whether they are fond of drinking and eating to excess, and given to indolence, or are fond of exercise and labor, and not given to excess in eating and drinking. (*Aër.*, I)

We learn from the introduction to *Extremes* that all non-naturals work to the detriment of Constantinople's residents, owing to the pressures of a big city, which also happens to be a "city of the court which has innumerable people and grandees" (no. 22). Most sections on people's everyday activities evidently deal with the Jews whose conditions are even more "unnatural," since they struggle (not always successfully) to preserve their way of living while interacting with the Muslim majority.

In eating, a second non-natural, the Jews of Constantinople go to extremes: "Some people eat a lot in the morning, and others have a lot very late, almost at suppertime, both in summer and in winter" (no. 14). Almosnino emphasizes the fact that these people ignore seasonal differences because since Hippocrates, it has been taken for granted that "with the seasons the digestive organs of men undergo a change" (*Aër.*, II).

Furthermore, this regimen is precisely the opposite of what is recommended by Maimonides:

> It appears that those who are used to eating mornings and evenings, fare best when taking their meals, in wintertime, two or three hours

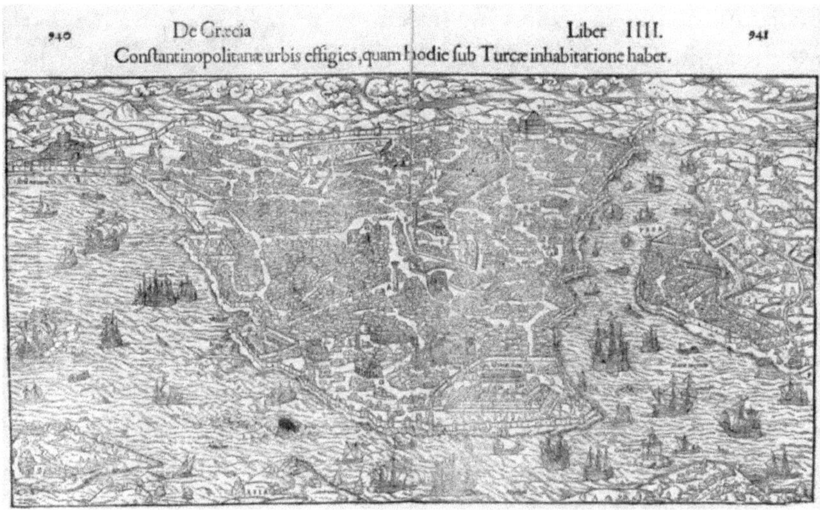

FIGURE 4.1.
Map of Constantinople. Drawn by a European traveler in 1550. Public Domain. *Library of Congress Prints and Photographs Division.*

> after the coming of day . . . In summer one should take one's meal five hours after sunrise . . . The evening meal, accordingly, should be taken long before the end of the day.[44]

We can assume that the people who have meals at odd hours are indeed the Jews, because they cannot eat (except for small snacks [no. 13]) outside their homes since they require kosher food. However, merchants cannot go home to eat in the middle of the day, because some of them conduct affairs with grandees (who can eat wherever they want) and others own shops or do business in Galata (no. 14).

At the time, Constantinople was situated only on the southern shore of the Golden Horn, a channel that was not crossed by a bridge until the mid-nineteenth century. The neighborhood on the northern shore, opposite Constantinople, inhabited mainly by Christians, was called Galata. When it became too small for its residents, Galata moved up to the Pera plateau. But even before this, Europeans tended to refer to Galata as "Pera" (see fig. 4.1).

In Almosnino's day, many Jewish residents of Constantinople owned shops in Galata. But it had not always been this way. When around 1170,

Benjamin of Tudela visited Byzantium, he learned that Jews had been expelled from Constantinople to "Pera," where they were allowed to own houses and where they had a cemetery. When "they visit Constantinople for purposes of trade," they have to travel by water.[45]

Sometime between 1455 and 1472, the Rabbanite Jews and Karaites of Galata were transferred to Constantinople, and until the middle of the sixteenth century, few Jews settled there.[46] Nicolas de Nicolay, who was in Pera in the early 1550s, famously recalls seeing very few Jews there.[47] But the following passage from the *Viaje de Turquía*, which was based on a few eyewitness accounts produced in the 1540s–early 1550s, offers more information on the Jews than Nicolay (always quoted in this connection): "The Jews do not have houses in Galata, but they have shops where they stay all day, and at night they close their shops and go to Constantinople to sleep."[48]

In the 1550s–1560s, following an influx of ex-*conversos* fleeing the newly established Portuguese Inquisition and persecutions in Italy, more Jews settled in Galata.[49] Some started building houses and opening shops where they traded with Europeans who lived nearby and whose languages they spoke. One of the new Jewish residents of Galata was Gracia Nasi. According to a European traveler, she did not "live in Constantinople among the Jews, but in Galata in a country home and garden for which she is said to pay a ducat a day rent."[50]

As we learn from *Extremes*, in 1567 most Jewish merchants still resided in Constantinople, while many of them owned businesses in Galata or had certain jobs there (for instance, at the customs house), where they were busy until nighttime (no. 14).[51] And because one had to take a boat to get there, merchants indeed spent a lot of time commuting back and forth, which apparently affected their eating routines.

In addition, Almosnino mentions two factors that had an effect on the diet of Constantinople's residents, regardless of their religion. First, the poor cannot afford sufficient food because provisions in the capital are often too expensive (no. 11), while others imitate the eating habits of grandees (nos. 5 and 6). Second, Almosnino clearly believes that certain foods should be eaten only when they are in season, which means in accordance with nature. Otherwise they may "corrupt" in one's stomach, causing disease (no. 7). Ibn Sinna, in fact, claims "the origin of all sickness is indigestion, that is to say, corruption of the meat in the stomach."[52]

As for drinking wine, alcohol was prohibited by Islam. Yet physicians had always considered wine beneficial for one's health, which is why Ibn Sinna favored it: "Wine is very efficient in causing the products of digestion to become disseminated through the body."[53] Hence, it is not surprising that Maimonides recommends wine to a Muslim ruler, noting "if taken in moderate measure and at the right time it is beneficial in many respects to both body and soul."[54]

In addition to religious prohibition, alcohol was repeatedly banned by several sultans, including Selim II who, as will be remembered, was known to be a heavy drinker himself. Nevertheless, in certain periods, wine was available in Constantinople, especially to non-Muslims, the existence of wine houses providing a source of income for the treasury as well as the city's police.[55]

According to Almosnino, the Jews of Constantinople sometimes drink wine "in great quantities, and sometimes they do not have it with their meals at all" (no. 13). Besides, very often the wines they drink are extremely bad, because the good kinds are not always available or affordable (no. 8). Although they could usually have wine at home or in Galata, where wine houses always existed, when Jews dealt with Muslims they could not drink or even smell of alcohol (no. 13). (The latter observation is confirmed by Busbecq who also notes that Turks cannot tolerate the smell of wine.)[56] To make up for this forced abstinence, some Jews drink excessively in their free time (no. 12).

In addition to disrupting their eating and drinking routines, the busy life of the capital's merchants who work far from their neighborhoods also affects their sleep, because "most days they do not come home for the night" (no. 12).

The last one on the list of Galenic non-naturals—accidents of the soul—was believed to impact the movement of bodily heat and spirit inward and outward, thus affecting one's physical and mental health. Almosnino does not deal with emotions per se, but he is interested in the means of reaching the desirable state of gladness used by Constantinople's residents. Medieval regimens of health, among other things, recommend "delightful books" and "pleasant sounds," "mutual argumentation with kindred minds . . . contact with curious things . . . meeting friends and friendly surroundings."[57] Needless to say, wine was considered a powerful "gladdening agent."[58]

The importance of reading "delightful books" as a means of gaining a cheerful disposition was emphasized by the plague tracts mentioned before.[59] In fact, the introduction to the Hebrew translation of *Amadís de Gaula* discussed in chapter 1 also declares "gratification of the spirit" a legitimate purpose of reading: "A person is grieved by the cares of daily life, so in his leisure time he seeks after stories, fables and other vanities, which are of no other use than to gratify his spirit."[60] The Salonican rabbi, however, does not mention reading as a leisurely activity of Constantinople's Jews, and, as we know, there was not much for them to read in Ladino. Curiously, those who use their free time to study the Scriptures are referred to as *letrados*, which probably means "literate in Hebrew" (no. 12).

While conversation with friends is on the list of healthy recreations and, according to Almosnino, is one of the "duties of friendship," "some people are extremely talkative and can talk for a long time about all sorts of things" (no. 10). In *Rejimyento*, Almosnino introduces a "regimen for speaking and not speaking," and in *Extremes* he relates chattiness to idleness, which he finds particularly detrimental for women, some of whom become dissolute and even talk to strangers because of "constant idleness without a minute of work" (no. 25). In addition, living in narrow streets without courtyards between houses, the women have no place to relax and spend hours by doors or windows chatting with neighbors and passersby.

Men do not get enough exercise either, which they need when they come home after a day of work, because the capital (apparently unlike Salonica) does not offer adequate public spaces or opportunities for physical activities (no. 10).[61] Deprived by the city of healthy recreations (except for taking walks), Constantinople's Jews use their leisure to make up for the days when they had no time for entertainment. And in recreations, including "eating, drinking, taking walks, and all other kinds of pleasures," they are also extreme (no. 12).

We can only guess what those other pleasures, enjoyed in the extreme, are and why they increase one's appetite for wine and food (no. 13). Most likely, this is a reference to playing cards, a most popular pastime among Sephardim. The rabbis tried to ban gambling, and in some Constantinople communities it was allowed only on certain days, but in others no restrictions could be imposed.[62] Games of chance were so pervasive that even pious men indulged in them on some occasions.[63] Another amusement Almosnino would not have approved of was visiting coffeehouses, which were first launched in Constantinople around 1555.[64] Most of the rabbis did not ban coffee, and some even found it useful, but going to coffeehouses was considered inappropriate because they offered other, more sinful amusements, such as puppet shows and male prostitution.[65]

Finally, even innocent entertainments were considered beneficial only as long as they were enjoyed in moderation and led to moderate gladness, which brings "natural heat to the outer parts of the body and makes the blood purer; it sharpens one's wit and makes the understanding more capable."[66] Emotional excesses and extremes, on the contrary, were considered dangerous for one's health. Thus Maimonides warns "when people indulge to excess, in headlong pursuit of pleasure, which sometime happens with the ignorant and the foolish, they too invariably fall sick and may even sink altogether."[67]

* * *

Thus, Almosnino explores every point that according to Hippocrates, a traveler ought to investigate when he comes to a new city. We learn that some of Constantinople's residents eat and drink to excess and at the wrong time, some of them work extremely hard while others are indolent and not fond of labor, and those who require exercise do not have an opportunity for it. On top of this, the climate in the Ottoman capital is extreme, and the air corrupts very easily, causing epidemics that take the lives of many children. Low houses built in narrow streets and without courtyards are smelly and stuffy, too cold in winter and too hot in summer.

This kind of inquiry, says Hippocrates, is necessary, because "if one knows all these things well . . . he cannot miss knowing, when he comes into a strange city, either the diseases peculiar to the place, or the particular nature of common diseases." Moreover, "one must be acquainted with each particular, and must succeed in the preservation of health" (*Aër.*, II). In other words, one should be able to diagnose the city's diseases and take measures not to contract them, if not cure others. Not a physician, Almosnino is not very interested in bodily illness and simply states, "pestiferous apostomes, and pestilential fevers, and drowsiness, and other similar ones" strike at the same time (no. 3). His chief concern is the city's all-encompassing disease diagnosed already in the introduction to *Extremes*: contrary to nature, the capital's residents constantly "move from one extreme to the other without ever passing through or being in the middle." And, as was said before, it is the state of disease that is considered to be "contrary to nature."

We find out that Almosnino himself is "ailing from the travails and passions" endured by the others in this city. Having "left the extreme of quietness and tranquility and fixed state of intense contemplation," he was "transferred to the extreme of a continuous and variable movement, full of tribulations and labors" (209).

If we keep in mind that the third of Galenic non-naturals commonly known in English as "exercise and rest" is called in Latin *motus et quies* (movement and quietness), we will see that Almosnino describes his way of living in the capital as anomalous and unnatural, hence, unhealthy. Yet he hopes to recover in God's compassion and benevolence (231).

In his sermon, Almosnino reiterates that on this trip he was often sick. Moreover, he explains that the "one who is always on the move is unable to think systematically or philosophically" for which one has to be still and engage in "tranquil contemplation."[68] Therefore, if it had not been for the needs of his republic, he would not have stayed for so long in Constantinople, where he was thrown by his "adverse and sinister destiny."

The Social and Moral Extremes of Constantinople

Almosnino does not limit his representation of Constantinople to the functions of non-naturals, but extends his analysis to the social, moral, and even economic aspects of its life. In these areas, he does not always find sufficient support in earlier authors, which is why he tries to extrapolate from Aristotle's idea of extremes and a mean onto phenomena and events to which it does not apply. Hence, certain sections of *Extremes* are rather puzzling and hard to interpret. For instance, the explanation of why coins in Constantinople are either new and shiny or old and clipped (no. 23) does not make much sense, if only because what is taken for granted first needs to be established as fact.[69] Section 24 is a mini-treatise on how to achieve the desired goal at the court, which can be done not only by bribes but also by negotiating without any intermediaries and keeping everything secret. While this conclusion is, no doubt, based on Almosnino's own experience, the framework used to describe it is inadequate.

Since Aristotle was interested in the rich and the poor only from the point of view of different political constitutions, his writings did not provide any support for Almosnino's economic theories, which are rather confused and self-contradictory.

Thus, according to him, prices in Constantinople are affected both by its geographic situation and social composition. Section 4 explains fluctuations in the prices of provisions according to their availability: when the west wind blows, many provisions are brought to the city, and the prices drop. But no. 5 tells us the opposite: "what is abundant costs very much, and what is lacking is very cheap, unlike in other places." And this is so because everyone wants to eat the same things as the grandees. And since there are many grandees and many who want to imitate them, a lot of provisions are brought to the city and prices are high. Almosnino's account of people's economic conditions in no. 9 also lacks logic and contradicts common sense. We learn that "only very few people do not have positions at the court or sinecures from the king or his courtiers, which allow them to make as much money as they want," while no. 22 appears to indicate the opposite.

Another socio-economic issue brought up in *Extremes*, the question of status and power, had particular significance in the Ottoman context. As was discussed in chapter 3, many Europeans, including Busbecq, were impressed by the Ottoman practice of assigning administrative positions based solely on the person's merit rather than blood or lineage. Almosnino also praised it when it was Joseph Nasi who was appointed Duke of Naxos by Selim II. But in *Extremes*, presenting life in Constantinople in general terms, he offers a more cynical explanation of the courtiers' rise and fall: "Since all these favors are attained at the court by chance and without any natural causes, everything depends on the turn of the celestial wheel, which is never still . . ." (no. 17). A century later, Sir Paul Ricault, a British diplomat who spent a great deal of time at the Ottoman Court, made a strikingly similar observation. He was astounded by

> how men are raised at once by adulation, chance, and the sole favour of the Prince, without any Title of noble Blood, or the motives of previous deserts, or former testimonies and experience of parts and abilities, to the weightiest, the richest, and most honourable charges of the Empire; when I consider how short their continuance is in them, how with one frown of their Prince they are cut off.[70]

Needless to say, Almosnino was aware that this practice was the opposite of what Aristotle recommends, saying that all governments should "give moderate honor for a long time rather than great honor for a short time. For men are easily spoilt." And if someone has received many honors at once, they should be taken from him gradually (*Pol.* V. 8, 1308b 14–17).[71] In addition, in *Extremes* the issue of status and honor has an ethical dimension. Almosnino directly condemns Constantinople where "people's worth is almost always measured not by their character but solely by their position, connections, and influence at the court." Aristotle, in the *Nicomachean Ethics*, acknowledges that this is often the case, yet "in truth the good man alone is to be honoured," because "honour is the prize of virtue, and it is to the good that it is rendered" (*EN*, IV. 3, 1124a 25–26).[72]

In the next four sections, Almosnino continues to describe the residents of Constantinople from the perspective of Aristotelian virtues, starting with friendship. In *Rejimyento* he deals with this in great detail (Part Three, chaps. 4–7) following Books VIII and IX of the *Nicomachean Ethics*. In addition, his analysis of friendship depends heavily on Cicero's *On Friendship*. In fact, Almosnino begins his discussion by citing Cicero who declares "without friendship life cannot be" (*De Amicitia*, 23).[73] Almosnino agrees that friendship is "necessary for sustaining human life because nobody would agree to live without friends with whom he can converse" (fol. 107b).[74] In accordance with "the Philosopher," he divides friendship into three species: friendship of virtue, friendship of pleasure, and friendship of utility (fol. 6b). He refutes the view that something can change, or even end a true friendship, because this kind of friendship is eternal. Aristotle sees a potential danger in a social difference between friends, believing that "friendship implies likeness and equality" (*Pol.* III. 16, 1287b 34). Cicero, on the contrary, argues that "those who are superior ought, undoubtedly, not only to waive all pretension in friendly intercourse, but to do what they can to raise their humbler friends to their own level" (*De Amicitia*, 20).

Siding with Cicero, Almosnino claims that because friendship is in the heart, it cannot "corrupt," even if one friend rises to the status of prince or grandee, and the friends are no longer equal or alike (fol. 115ab). However, this is not true of "common friendships." So, in case a friendship is gone due to changes in people's lives or habits, Cicero recommends that great care should be taken "lest there be the appearance, not only of friendship dropped, but of enmity taken up; for nothing is more unbecoming than to wage war with a man with whom you have lived on terms of intimacy" (*De Amicitia*, 21).

Thus, the friendships Almosnino found among residents of Constantinople go against his fundamental convictions rooted in the works of Cicero and Aristotle. Those who only recently appeared to be loyal friends, all of a sudden, "full of cruel hatred, harm each other as much as they can" (no. 18). People move from friendship to enmity so quickly because these relationships are not friendships of virtue (or true ones) but those of utility. And, as we know, in the capital people are "in constant movement and are rapidly transferred from one extreme to the other, which is true for their positions and ranks as well as wealth and poverty."

Yet even "the friendships between the grandees and other influential people in the capital are not steadfast . . . since these people think they do not need one another." Hence, while very briefly, the rich help the rich and the poor help the poor, having no common grounds, people cannot form strong relations or brotherhoods.

This last comment seems to be a direct critique of Constantinople's Jews whose alleged practice is incompatible with Almosnino's social program that is formulated in his sermon. Concerned about the allotment of the tax burden in Salonican congregations, he proclaims that to ensure the wellbeing of the people "the great men of the community" must bear the financial burdens of "the lesser ones, who pay them proper respect . . . Each person must recognize his own status, and the lesser people must obey the greater ones."[75] It is therefore possible that the critique of Constantinople's Jews was meant to be a lesson for Salonicans.

Although at first glance, the next three sections (nos. 19–21) appear to discuss only the religious practices of the capital's Jews, in reality they go far beyond their specific topics and are also concerned with Aristotelian virtues and ways of becoming virtuous. In fact, Almosnino himself indicates that no. 21 is related to no. 9, which talks about people's economic conditions and attitudes toward money. Indeed, no. 21 deals not only with alms collected in synagogues, but also, together with nos. 9 and 19, with generosity (or liberality) and its opposites, prodigality and stinginess. Almosnino discusses this subject in philosophical terms in *Rejimyento*, Part Two, chap. 7, which is a rendering of Aristotle's idea (*EN*, IV. 1, 1120b–1122a).

Aristotle defines generosity with regard to giving and taking wealth (though mainly giving) as a mean between the excess of prodigality and the deficiency of stinginess. Following Aristotle, Almosnino explains that a generous person gives to the right people, the right amounts, and at the right time (fol. 66a), whereas a prodigal one will give more than appropriate, in the wrong place, and in the wrong way (fol. 70b). Such a person is unable to take care of his own property and will quickly spend all his money. Still, Almosnino says, at this time when everyone covets money, prodigality is "much less bad" than stinginess because it is corrected by old age or poverty (fol. 70b), (an idea found in Aristotle).

Another important characteristic of a generous man, discussed by Aristotle, is that he gives the right amount with pleasure and will be moderately pained if he has given "in a manner contrary to what is right and noble . . . for it is the mark of virtue both to be pleased and to be pained at the right objects and in the right way." The prodigal person not only gives money in the wrong way and for the wrong objects, but also, "is neither pleased nor pained at the right things or in the right way." Still, the prodigal man is closer to being virtuous than the stingy one and "if he were brought to do so by habituation or in some other way, he would be generous" and would give to the right people.

As for stinginess, Aristotle says that it occurs in different forms: "some men go to excess in taking, others fall short in giving." Some others claim to save money so that one day they would not be forced to do something disgraceful. The worst kind will rob or do other shameful things and "would put up with a bad name for the sake of gain." It is evident that nos. 9, 19, and 21 illustrate Aristotle's argument by showing that Constantinople's Jews are not generous: "the majority are prodigal, and the rest are extremely stingy" (no. 9). Indeed, those who have big incomes throw away their money, without any pain. In section 9, we find that the prodigal give away money for unspecified purposes, whereas in section 21 Almosnino states that money is collected at synagogues for charitable purposes, which means that it goes to the right cause. It appears, therefore, that prodigal people err by donating too much at all times and in all places "without zeal or pain." In addition, they "spend more of their wealth in the service of God than on their own needs" (no. 19), which is likely to change when they get old or cannot provide for themselves. Some of those who do not give anything are forced to be stingy to survive (no. 9), while others do not make any donations because of stinginess and vanity (no. 21). The worst category is the wicked, whose members harm others to extort money from them (no. 19).

Almosnino's explanation of virtuous behavior and its opposite is also borrowed from Aristotle: some people are accustomed to making large donations, while for others it is not giving that has become a habit (no. 21). Likewise, people who spend a lot of time dealing with grandees have formed a habit of skipping prayers (no. 20). Indeed, according to Aristotle, "moral virtue comes about as a result of habit," hence, we "are made perfect by habit" (*EN*, II. 1, 1103a 15).

Furthermore, Almosnino argues that both vice and virtue are deliberately chosen and turned into habit by repetition. Thus, "the good people are so good because, despite having opportunities to be evil they chose to be good," whereas the evil, once they have chosen an evil course, "habit makes them even more vile and wicked" (no. 19).

The first impression one gets from reading *Extremes* is that Almosnino disparages the Jews of Constantinople because their conduct and relationships are "contrary to nature" and go against the basic principles of morality. But, even though he focuses only on what goes wrong in their community, he claims at the beginning of the sections dealing with morality that the majority are virtuous. In other words, what one finds in Almosnino's book is not a characterization of people but of the city that is out of balance on all counts, from climate to mores.

Extremes as a Historical Source

Robert Dankoff begins his brilliant analysis of Evliya's *Narrative of the Travels* by proposing to "see it first of all, not as a source, but as a text, i.e., a reflection of the mind of the author."[76] For my part, I suggest that one cannot use such a complex work as *Extremes* (even if it is just the size of a section of Evliya's book) without first approaching it as a reflection of Almosnino's thinking. To establish how accurate his evidence may be, one needs to understand what he wants readers to believe and what means he employs to convince them.

The message of *Extremes* formulated in the introduction is simple and clear: in the capital, everything goes contrary to nature, and those who stay there become ill. Thus, *Extremes* in its peculiar way, corroborates the account of the delegation's hardships related in Book IV, chronologically and in plain language. The sermon (preserved in Hebrew but most probably delivered in Ladino) tells the same story by means of biblical exegesis.[77]

The sermon analyzes Psalm 107, a song of thanksgiving to God for guiding those who got lost in a desert, for liberating prisoners, healing the sick, and rescuing those who nearly perished at sea. The preacher announces that all of this happened to him on that journey:

> I went to sea when we traveled to Bursa; I traveled dangerous paths by land from there to Kara Hisar and Karamürsel; I fell sick on several occasions; I was frequently imprisoned, though not in an actual jailhouse, in chains of poverty.[78]

Moreover, Almosnino adds that being on a ship, he also felt like a prisoner, and the motion made him sick, so that he "reeled and staggered like a drunkard" (Ps 107: 27). Even this excerpt shows that the sermon combines biblical metaphors (usually explicated) with straightforward explanations and specific information (e.g., geographic names). In the introduction to *Extremes* (clearly meant to be read rather than heard), Almosnino presents the same events using various literary means:

> Navigating the gulf of the sea and ailing from the travails and passions endured by those in this noblest city of Constantinople . . . mandated by the divine providence, by my sins, and by my adverse and sinister destiny, or cruel fate . . . which united in order to shoot at me their

poisonous arrows of cruel hatred that sufficed to tear me away from my continuous study and permanent contemplation.

Extremes is a third and, obviously, the most elaborate version whose literary character and stylistic features are manifest already in the introduction. It is characterized by convoluted syntax (simplified in my translation out of necessity), use of binary synonyms ("adverse and sinister destiny, or cruel fate," "zeal and love," and a few others), and Spanish literary clichés. The most obvious example of the latter (found twice, with slight variations) is: *mi adversa i sinistra fortuna o kruel fado . . . se juntaron para tirar kuentra mi las pesoñosas saetas de odyo kruel . . .*" This formulaic language is mocked already in *Celestina* where Calisto's speech parodies the courtly love discourse. For instance, when his beloved sends him away, Calisto laments, "*Iré como aquél contra quien solamente la adversa fortuna pone su estudio con odio cruel*" (I will go as someone whom adverse destiny has singled out with its cruel hatred) (Act I, Scene 1).

In addition to these literary features, even the rhythm and alliterations used in the introduction (reminiscent both of Castilian poetry and rabbinic writings) suggest to the reader that the book is going to be something more imaginative than a simple record of facts: "*Andando navegando en el golfo del mar i mal de los trabajos i pasyones ke padesen.*"[79]

Furthermore, Almosnino's statement that the book will describe "some of the extremes without a mean found in the city of Constantinople" makes one suspect that the author will see extremes wherever he looks, which immediately puts into question his credibility as a source. As Dankoff notes with regard to Evliya, notorious for his exaggerations, "Where we do detect dissimulation, there has to be a motivation for it."[80] The opposite may also be true, at least, in Almosnino's case: when there is a motivation, there will have to be dissimulation. Almosnino's desire to make us believe that Constantinople is a city of extremes sometimes prompts him to make absurd statements, for instance, about no one in the whole city having a headache (no. 3) Such bizarre assertions should have alerted scholars who take Almosnino's words at face value.

The first and easiest thing to check is Almosnino's statements about Constantinople's climate, which he considers key to understanding most of its other extremes. Even though average temperatures in this city have changed over the last four-and-a-half centuries, its climate remains hot-summer Mediterranean. This means that it is mild, i.e., not characterized by sharp weather changes in one day, or extreme temperatures in winter or summer. In fact, contradicting himself, Almosnino describes it as temperate several times. Curiously, the climate of his native Salonica is also hot-summer Mediterranean and differs from that of Constantinople only by being drier.

Almosnino explains alleged weather extremes by the interchangeable influence of the north and west winds, which is supposed to be "obvious and evident to those who are observant" (no. 1). In other words, in the sixteenth century, the age of revolutionary experiments, Almosnino continues to employ one of Aristotle's methods of argumentation, namely, appealing to everyday experience and observation.[81] The phrase "it is obvious/evident" is used in *Extremes* nine times, though in most cases what is presumed to be obvious is either wrong or requires substantiation. For example, more than two winds are common in Istanbul (Constantinople): northeast winds prevail in summer, whereas in winter, it is either northwest, or north, or southwest.[82]

Almosnino's evidence in *Extremes* is unreliable for two reasons. First of all, by applying the concept of the mean to areas to which it is not applicable and trying to fit various social, economic, and natural phenomena into the Procrustean bed of his "extremes," which also had to match the precepts of dietetics, he was forced to distort many facts, sometimes to the point of absurdity. Second, while having firsthand information on the subjects related to his mission, Almosnino was still a visitor to the capital (albeit a frequent one), with very limited knowledge of Turkish and personal contacts only among the Jews. As a result, almost the only trustworthy information found in *Extremes* is that which does not interest the author and remains on the periphery of his attention.

In some cases, this information is corroborated by other sources. Thus, claiming that food prices are always extreme, Almosnino notes in passing that this is not true for meat. Because the taxes negotiated by the Salonican delegation included the provision of sheep to the capital, he knew why there was never a shortage of meat. The suppliers are required to bring a certain amount, "and there is a sufficient number of experienced people in charge of this who are severely punished if there is not enough meat" (no. 4). Meat was supplied to Constantinople mainly from the empire's European territories, and in times of shortage, the government often resorted to forced purchases or fixed prices. This happened, for instance, in Almosnino's time, when suppliers of sheep were unwilling to comply with Suleyman's policy in 1545.[83]

The main claim of no. 23 is certainly wrong: it cannot be true that all coins in Constantinople were either very good or very bad. Nevertheless, the details mentioned by Almosnino are accurate. He says that a lot of coins are "paid out at the court on the day of the Divan," and that in Constantinople "only those coins that come from the Treasury are good." Indeed, on the days when the Divan convened, which happened four times a week in the sixteenth century, the public treasury adjacent to Divan Hall would be opened in order to pay troops and civil servants. But before the coins were distributed, they would be weighed and tested in a special furnace for metal content.[84] Almosnino undoubtedly had many opportunities to see this with his own eyes during his negotiations at the court.

In some cases, however, the Salonican rabbi is confused or misinformed. For example, in no. 8 he wants to juxtapose good wines brought from other places with bad ones produced in the city. Many physicians, Ibn Sinna among them, suggest that wines with a good aroma and taste are the most beneficial.[85] Therefore, Almosnino claims that local wines are "made from black raisins or rotten grapes that nobody likes because they smell of mold and have a bad taste." For this reason, they are "consumed right after being made." Yet what he calls rotten ("corrupted") grapes are the so-called "suspended grapes," often preserved with mustard seed to be used out of season.[86]

And "bad wine" was not a wine but a "delicious drink" which, according to Busbecq, was called Arab sorbet and prepared as follows: "They take raisins and have them ground up, and, when they are ground and pounded, they throw them into a wooden vessel" where they are left to ferment in water.[87]

> If you taste it when it is beginning to ferment, it would seem insipid and disagreeable owing to its excessive sweetness; but afterwards it takes on a somewhat acid flavour, and if mixed with something sweet it is very pleasing to the palate.
>
> Yet it, indeed, has to be consumed within three or four days, because later it gets sour and affects one like wine, which is banned.[88]

Such errors, unimportant as they may appear, together with the lack of corroborating evidence, make *Extremes* problematic as a source. Hence, when it is hard to tell truth from fiction, one has to rely on the internal logic of the text, keeping in mind the author's determination to describe every phenomenon in terms of extremes.

Section 25 is among the most confusing. Almosnino tells us that "the virtuous women, who are the majority . . . do not speak to any men no matter how close they are to the family and are not even seen by them." These "virtuous and honorable ones, who are the majority, are forced to stay in their rooms completely secluded" doing handwork, because all housework is done by hired maids or slaves. Since it is clear from the context that Almosnino is talking about Jewish women, this statement seems to suggest that Constantinople Jewish homes, like Muslim ones, had a special room in which male visitors were received.

Based on this text, Minna Rozen indeed concludes that in Constantinople Jewish houses were divided into the men's section open to all visitors (*selamlik*) and the women's section (*haremlik*) accessible only to immediate family.[89] She further claims that being virtuous meant being rich:

> Since women of good quality [*sic*] . . . were considered to be those who kept indoors and avoided any contact with men outside the family circle, and since only the rich could maintain such a lifestyle, being rich also meant being an honorable and decent woman. Being poor immediately cast doubt on a woman's virtues and chastity. In addition, such women were usually hidden from the public eye.[90]

Yet contemporaneous responsa contradict Rozen's claim that "virtuous" Jewish women stayed in their rooms and did not see men. Many testimonies make it clear that not only unmarried women of various means freely socialized with men inside and outside their houses, often without any family members around, but even married women talked to men at home and outdoors. Thus, the witnesses' testimonies in a responsum of Rabbi Elijah ben Hayyim relate various situations at the house of a well-off Jew, where a married woman is in the same room not only with her husband's brother, but also with a male friend and a scribe.[91] It is true that, according to Almosnino, those virtuous women had maids, slaves, and wet nurses (no. 26), but even people of middling income had slaves.[92] Besides, these women lived in houses that had no courtyards and were built on narrow streets not inhabited by the rich. As for wealthy Jewish women not being seen by men, Rozen herself contradicts Almosnino and her own conclusion by stating "Hebrew sources attest to the penchant of Jewish women for expensive clothes," which were repeatedly banned by the sultans' firmans.[93] Naturally, this became a problem precisely because those women appeared dressed up in public.

Most important, however, is that by describing some women as virtuous and others as dissolute, Almosnino by no means pronounces a moral judgment but rather, creates the two extremes necessary to get his point across. And because in his construction it is always the majority who has to be pious and well-established, he also declares in no. 25 (even twice) that virtuous women are the majority. If we believe Almosnino when he says that most women were secluded in their rooms, we must accept his other assertions, for instance, that "the majority of Constantinople's inhabitants were grandees" (no. 5). Given what Almosnino tells us in other "extremes" and what he wants us to believe, it is reasonable to assume that in the capital some well-off Jews who had contacts with Muslims tried to imitate the ways of the land and indeed had their wives stay in their rooms while there were male visitors in the house. This practice apparently appealed to Almosnino and fit his construction (though the richest Jewish woman in the empire and patroness of his congregation, Gracia Nasi, was a prominent public figure). Still, it is unlikely that many Jewish houses would have designated rooms for receiving male visitors, *selamlik*, which in Turkish homes were frequently located on the upper floor or in a separate structure over the stables.[94]

It is clear that in *Extremes* the lifestyle question is closely related to the living conditions of the capital's Jews. But Almosnino's description of Jewish houses has also been misunderstood by Rozen and interpreted as a social issue. Section 22 talks about the houses in *la juderiya*, i.e., the Jewish neighborhood, though there were a few of those in the capital, and they significantly differed from one another.

Typically, in Constantinople, each religious community occupied a specific area in the residential quarters (*mahalle*) around a church, mosque, or synagogue. There were also mixed neighborhoods. In Almosnino's time, the majority of Constantinople's Jews lived in "a trapezoid-shaped area formed by Eminönü, Sirkeci, Tahtakale, and Mahmut Paşa." A smaller number settled in Balat and Hasköy, while others resided on

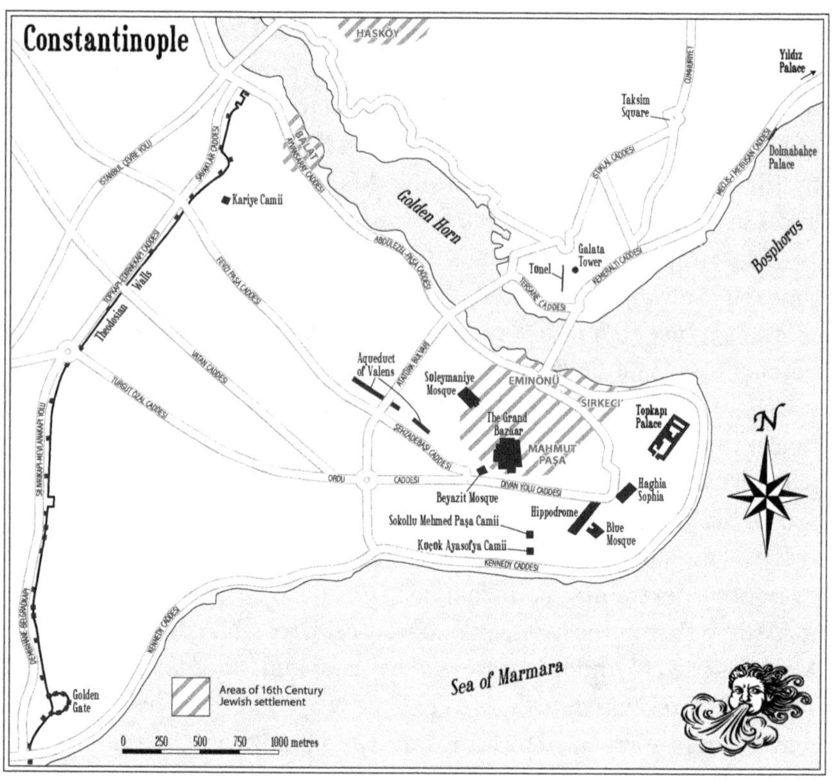

MAP 4.1.
Map of present-day Istanbul.
By Martin Lubikowski, ML Design, London 2016.

the shore of the Marmara Sea and in several villages along the Bosphorus on both the European and Asiatic sides (see map 4.1). Sephardim lived in most of these neighborhoods and, some of them, in Galata.[95]

Thus, Almosnino could have described various quarters of Constantinople and its environs, but he chose the most densely populated neighborhood, the trapezoid, which was the city's business center. He probably referred to it as *the* Jewish neighborhood, because around 60% of the capital's Jewish population had homes there.[96] We can tell that Almosnino is talking about the trapezoid from his description of the narrow streets and houses without galleries or courtyards, which were not common in other parts of Constantinople. Since the business district was more densely populated than the rest of the city, inhabitants there constructed more compact dwellings.[97] These houses, probably of Byzantine origin, were remnants of the pre-conquest period.[98]

The typical sixteenth-century home in the capital had "an average of 2.57 habitable rooms, in addition to a courtyard, latrine, and well."[99] In most districts, houses were built in a rectangular shape around a courtyard and usually had semi-open galleries or verandas. When owners wanted to enlarge their dwellings, they built additional structures, either on the ground level, if there was space, or on the upper floor.[100] In the commercial section of Constantinople, however, "courtyards, *soffas* [covered verandas] and *zulles* [galleries] are comparatively rare; dwellings are more compact, and service spaces, such as kitchens and latrines, are typically located on the upper floors."[101]

This is precisely the kind of structure Almosnino describes in no. 22. And he accurately notes that those houses are "very narrow, and there is not enough space to build patios or even verandas, which is why they expand more in height than in length or width" (no. 25). Not all Jewish homes in the trapezoid were old, narrow, and smelly. Some were luxurious, such as the mansion owned by Moses Hamon, and rather big two- or three-story buildings with many rooms and courtyards that were rented out to a few Jewish families.[102] But these houses were of no interest to Almosnino. As we have seen, he presents the dwellings of Constantinople's Jews in such a way that they would appear the exact opposite of what regimens of health recommended, and thus would demonstrate that in Constantinople everything is "counter-natural."

Needless to say, here Almosnino is not interested in social differences. Besides, as we have seen, inhabitants of narrow houses are not poor. Some deal with the grandees, others trade with Europeans in Galata, and those who are helped by their wives (presumably a minority) probably have shops in the neighborhood. Furthermore, there are no grounds for concluding, as Rozen does, that "the upper floors were occupied by the rich; the lower floors, by the poor."[103] People of various means shared the bigger houses mentioned above, but most of the narrow ones were occupied by one family, and it was slaves who usually lived in the ground-floor rooms.[104]

Finally, it is incorrect to conclude that, according to Almosnino, to be poor also meant "to be more exposed to maladies."[105] As has been shown, he claims that all inhabitants of the capital are exposed to disease when the air corrupts, which is why he does not empathize with the poor more than with the rich. Besides, he emphasizes several times that there are very few people who "earn their living by working hard" and live in misery (no. 9). In other words, Almosnino was not an advocate of social justice.

Conclusion

As we have seen, *Extremes* could not have served as a guidebook to Constantinople. It does not even mention by name a single place or building in the city. Instead, *Extremes* conveys the author's idiosyncratic vision of the Ottoman capital, which is often contradicted by facts. Nevertheless, it fits into the travelogue category, which is not constituted by formal features and comprises all representations of geographic locations regardless of factual veracity, the author's purpose, or literary method. Indeed, scholars have described such different works as the straightforward travel account by Nicolas de Nicolay, the fantastic *Book of Eldad the Danite*, Petrarch's allegoric description of his (probably fictional) ascent of Mont Ventoux, and even Orhan Pamuk's *Istanbul: Memories and the City* as travelogues, although the latter portrays the author's own hometown.

It is clear from the second chronicle that Almosnino was familiar with several sixteenth-century European (and likely Benjamin of Tudela's) accounts of Constantinople. Having visited the Ottoman capital many times and spent there, all in all, a few years, he evidently wished to convey his own vision of that city to his readers, many of whom would have been familiar with existing travelogues of Constantinople. But the European travelogue as a genre was both alien to the Salonican rabbi and inappropriate for him. Therefore, he chose a literary strategy in which he was most experienced, namely, intertextuality, which is the most salient feature of *Extremes*.

Intertextuality is a constitutive principle of the majority of rabbinic writings, something Almosnino produced most of his life. At least some intertexts in rabbinic writings are always explicit, since most of them are either commentaries, interpretations, or expositions of earlier texts. Although some of the quotes are not identified or do not even appear in full, they are obvious to intended readers.

Despite its use of intertexts, however, *Extremes* differs from rabbinic writings both in its subject matter and in its exclusive reliance on secular literature. Unlike in *Rejimyento*, the texts are never cited, although most belong to one corpus, namely, health treatises. Aristotle's works, while forming a separate corpus, are closely related to the first by providing a theoretical foundation for it. Since the idea that the health of body and mind is governed by proper regulation of living had long become an axiom by Almosnino's day, the teachings of Hippocrates, Galen, Ibn Sinna, and Maimonides had fused in the minds of lay people to such an extent that most of his readers would not have been able to identify every source.[106] Nonetheless, they would have had no difficulty understanding *Extremes* the way it was intended and would have immediately recognized cues found in the introduction (such as references to "extremes without a mean" and that which was "contrary to nature"). Furthermore, in the sixteenth century, this corpus was still shared by Jews, Christians, and Muslims, and served as a common intellectual space for scholars of various faiths. This allowed Almosnino to address both readers who had always lived as Jews and ex-*conversos* who had been educated at Christian institutions in Europe.

As for literary form, instead of producing a travel narrative, Almosnino came up with a structure suitable for a scholarly treatise. *Extremes* indeed combines features of the health treatise, ethical literature, and even medical topography. As we know, rabbis used the vernacular almost exclusively for didactic purposes. Almosnino's travelogue is certainly a work of didactic literature. In fact, one may understand *Extremes* as an extension of *Rejimyento* that persuasively illustrates the dangers of extremes, including those one cannot avoid.

Needless to say, *Extremes* is not the only travelogue that misrepresents the object of its description. The same was done, for example, by the author of *Viaje de Turquía*, which is based on real travel accounts. Thus, the author draws an idealized picture of the grand mufti and the *ulema* to emphasize the inferiority of the Pope and the Catholic Church. But while the literary device employed by the author of *Viaje* is timeless and thus easily comprehensible to the modern reader, the same cannot be said of Almosnino's strategy. Cansino, undoubtedly, was aware of intertextual references found in the book, and many of his Christian readers would have also recognized several allusions. But taking *Extremos y grandezas de Constantinopla* as a regular travelogue in an exotic land produced by a native, readers had no way of telling truth from fiction and no reason to question the veracity of Constantinople's extremes. Twentieth-century scholars, also misled by Cansino's arrangement of Almosnino's work and apparently uninterested in *Rejimyento*, missed the subtexts and referred to the author as a keen observer, *costumbrista*, and *colorista*.[107]

Finally, can we consider *Extremes* a literary expression of the author's frustration with the city where he had wasted so much time and endured so many "travails, tribulations, and calamities?" This is possible, although in the final section of *Extremes* Almosnino directly blames the delegation's misfortunes only on Salonican leaders and delegation members rather than on the city or its inhabitants. In any event, Almosnino's work is by no means a panegyric of Constantinople, even in Cansino's version, as suggested by Gutwirth, who sees *Crónica* as a single text.[108] One point is indisputable: the first Ladino travelogue presents the capital as an exceptional city where everything goes "contrary to the common order and manner of things."[109] To understand *Extremes* the way the author intended it and effectively use it as a historical source, one must approach it as a text deeply rooted in the medieval scholarly tradition and dependent on numerous subtexts obvious to its target audience.

Notes

1. Saperstein, "Moses Almosnino: Sermon on Eleh Fequde," 229.
2. Ibid., 230.
3. Ibid., 229.
4. Ibid., 223.
5. "Conjunction" is an astrological term referring to an apparent proximity of two planets that are said to be in conjunction when they are in the same zodiac sign or in adjacent ones.

Book III (*Extremes*) is quoted from my translation in the Appendix.

6. Gutwirth, "*Acutissima patria*," 30.
7. For a list of the most important among them, see introduction, n. 15.
8. The numeric value of the Hebrew letters *yod heh waw heh* representing God's name is 26 (10+5+6+5).
9. On these theories and the regimens of health, see Klaus Bergdolt, *Wellbeing: A Cultural History of Healthy Living*, trans. Jane Dewhurst (Cambridge, UK, 2008).

10. Although the original is not extant, its Hebrew version produced in 1299 by Solomon ha-Me'ati has survived and was even translated into Latin in the sixteenth century. (See Abraham Wasserstein, ed. and trans., *Galen's Commentary on the Hippocratic Treatise Airs, Waters, Places in the Hebrew Translation of Solomon ha-Me'ati* [Jerusalem, 1982]).

11. For a short summary of Galen's *non naturales*, see Saul Jarcho, "Galen's Six Non-Naturals: A Bibliographic Note and Translation," *Bull. Hist. Med.* 44, no. 4 (1970): 372–377.

12. See Benjamin Richler, "Manuscripts of Avicenna's *Kanon* in Hebrew Translation: A Revised and Up-to-Date List," *Koroth* 8, nos. 3–4 (1982): 145–168.

13. Glending Olson, *Literature as Recreation in the Later Middle Ages* (Ithaca and London, 1982), 53.

14. For a discussion of the book's structure and content, see Zemke, "Introduction," in Moshe ben Baruk Almosnino, *Regimiento de la vida*.

15. Olson, *Literature as Recreation*, 54.

16. Quoted in Zemke, "Introduction," in Moshe ben Baruk Almosnino, *Regimiento de la vida*, 11.

17. Juan Casco Solís, "Topografías médicas: Revisión y cronología," *Asclepio* 53, no. 1 (2001): 213–243, 114 n.1.

18. Ibid., 229.

19. Ibid. Here the dates are 1393 and 1547, respectively. Gutwirth believes that it was written between 1374 and 1381 ("Acutissima patria," 26). However, the author mentions the epidemic of 1420 (Juan de Aviñón, *Sevillana Medicina*, 36). The title page of the 1885 edition indicates that the first appeared in 1545.

20. Marc Cohen, "Aristotle's Metaphysics," *The Stanford Encyclopedia of Philosophy*. Summer 2014 Ed., ed. Edward N. Zalta: http://plato.stanford.edu/archives/sum2014/entries/aristotle-metaphysics (accessed September 9, 2014).

21. Trans. T. Francis Adams.

22. I refer to the sections of *Extremes* by their numbers in order to help the reader identify them in my translation in the Appendix.

23. Trans. E. W. Webster.

24. Trans. T. Francis Adams.

25. Only the fifth element, ether, of which the heavens are made is not "corruptible," which is why Almosnino sees his future life as "permanent and everlasting," as opposed to "this corruptible" one (209).

26. *The Canon of Medicine of Avicenna*, trans. Oskar Cameron Gruner (New York, 1973). Henceforth, *Canon* followed by the number of the respective section. Here, 178.

27. *The Medical Writings of Moses Maimonides. Treatise on Asthma*, ed. and trans. S. Muntner (Philadelphia, 1963), 73.

28. Ibid., 74.

29. See *Encyclopedia of Public Health*, ed. Lester Breslow (New York, 2001), "Miasma Theory."

30. *Sevillana Medicina*, 18.

31. Olson, *Literature as Recreation,* 166.

32. Ibid., 167.

33. See Nükhet Varlik, *Plague and Empire in the Early Modern Mediterranean World: The Ottoman Experience, 1347–1600* (Cambridge, 2015), 160–184.

34. Busbecq, *The Turkish Letters,* 180–190.

35. Varlik, *Plague and Empire*, 18.

36. For an insightful discussion of this question, see Joseph Hacker, "Superbe et désespoir: L'existence sociale et spirituelle des Juifs ibériques dans l'Empire ottoman," *Revue historique* 578 (1991): 261–293.

37. According to Emmanuel, Almosnino wrote *Pirqe Mosheh* in Pelestria, during the plague of 1546. *Tefillah le-Mosheh* was finished during the plague of 1564, in Levadia. (*Histoire des Israélites de Salonique,* 177–178.)

38. Quoted in ibid, 279.

39. Maimonides, *Treatise on Asthma*, 74.

40. *Canon*, 332.

41. Maimonides, *Treatise on Asthma*, 74–75.

42. Maimonides, *Two Treatises on the Regimen of Health*, trans. Ariel Bar-Sela, Hebbel Hoff, and Elias Paris (Philadelphia, 1964), 27.

43. *Canon*, 314.

44. Maimonides, *Treatise on Asthma*, 130–131.

45. *The Itinerary of Benjamin of Tudela*, 11–12.

46. Rozen, *Istanbul*, 55.

47. Nicolas de Nicolay. *Les Quatre premiers livres des navigations et pérégrinations orientales.* (Lyon, 1568), 77.

48. *Viaje de Turquía*, 826.

49. See Rozen, "Public Space and Private Space Among the Jews of Istanbul in the Sixteenth and Seventeenth Centuries," *Turcica* 30 (1998): 331–346, 334.

50. This information is found in the journal of Hans Dernschwam, who stayed in Constantinople in 1553–1555 as a member of the Austrian diplomatic mission. Despite his Judophobia, Dernschwam is a rather reliable source on the capital's Jews. Quoted in Yaron Ben-Naeh and Giacomo Saban, "Three German Travellers on Istanbul Jews," *Journal of Modern Jewish Studies* 12, no. 1 (2013): 35–52, 38.

51. On those jobs, see Stéphane Yérasimos, "La communauté juive d'Istanbul à la fin du xvie siècle," *Turcica* 27 (1995): 101–130, 130.

52. *Canon*, 245.

53. Ibid., 802.

54. Maimonides, *Treatise on Asthma*, 31–32.

55. See for example, Ebru Boyar and Kate Fleet, *A Social History of Ottoman Istanbul* (Cambridge, UK, and New York, 2010), 195–198.

56. Busbecq, *The Turkish Letters*, 154.

57. Books and music were recommended by "Aristotle" to "Alexander." (M. A. Manzalaoui, ed., *Secretum Secretorum. Nine English Versions* [Oxford

and New York, 1977], 9.) The other means of reaching an emotional balance were suggested by Ibn Sinna. (*Canon*, 1109.)

58. Ibid., 104.

59. See Olson, *Literature as Recreation*, 169.

60. *Amadís de Gaula*, 2.

61. Almosnino says that Constantinople's Jews are deprived of *panina* (216), but the meaning of this word is unclear. He uses it again when he talks about the production of broadcloth in Salonica. But there its meaning is clear as it obviously derives from *paño* (broadcloth) (*Crónica*, 245). Romeu's suggestion that it may mean "patio" does not seem plausible. (Ibid., 308.)

62. Cf. Document 4 in Rozen, *Istanbul*, 314.

63. See "Gambling," *The Jewish Encyclopedia.*

64. Ralph S. Hattox, *Coffee and Coffeehouses: The Origins of a Social Beverage in the Medieval Near East* (Seattle and London, 1985), 77.

65. See Elliott Horowitz, "Coffee, Coffeehouses, and the Nocturnal Rituals of Early Modern Jewry," *AJS Review* 14, no. 1 (Spring 1989): 17–46.

66. A medieval treatise quoted in Olson, *Literature as Recreation*, 50.

67. Maimonides, *Treatise on Asthma*, 37.

68. Saperstein, "Moses Almosnino: Sermon on *Eleh Fequde*," 237.

69. Moreover, one is tempted to suspect that the author added some sections and divided others in order to have twenty-six of them.

70. Paul Rycault, *The Present State of the Ottoman Empire* (New York, 1971), 3.

71. Trans. Benjamin Jowett.

72. Trans. W. D. Ross.

73. Trans. Anthony Everitt.

74. Aristotle says something similar (*EN*, VIII. 1, 1155a), but does not mention conversation, which Almosnino obviously values above all other "duties of friendship."

75. Saperstein, "Moses Almosnino: Sermon on *Eleh Fequde*," 238. In Salonica, the poor were usually willing to submit to the rule of the wealthy, if the rich promised to fulfill their communal responsibilities in accordance with their wealth. But many rich members of the community refused to recognize their duties. (See Rozen, "Individual and Community in the Jewish Society.")

76. Robert Dankoff, *An Ottoman Mentality: The World of Evliya Çelebi* (Leiden, 2004), 10.

77. On the language of Jewish sermons, see Saperstein, "Introduction to his anthology," *Jewish Preaching, 1200–1800*, 39–40.

78. Idem, "Moses Almosnino: Sermon on *Eleh Fequde*," 237.

79. Gutwirth also points to an instance of paranomasia (here *mar* and *mal*). ("Acutissima patria," 36.)

80. Dankoff, *An Ottoman Mentality*, 153.

81. Pedro Mejía, whose discussion of natural phenomena also largely depends on Aristotle, on the contrary, suggests a few experiments that involve

putting one's hand in hot water or covering snow with straw. (See *Silva de varia leccíon*, III, 21.)

82. See, for example, "Climate of Istanbul" in *Digital Print of Europe Comenius Partnership Project 2012–2014*: http://mebk12.meb.gov.tr/meb_iys_dosyalar/34/02/972859/dosyalar/2013_12/25115535_climateofistanbul.pdf (accessed May 15, 2014).

83. See Boyar and Fleet, *A Social History of Ottoman Istanbul*, 160–161.

84. See Gülru Necipoğlu, *Architecture, Ceremonial and Power, The Topkapı Palace in the Fifteenth and Sixteenth Centuries* (Cambridge MA, 1991), 87.

85. *Canon*, 802.

86. Busbecq, *The Turkish Letters*, 54.

87. This must be the drink that Evliya calls *assilma*, which the translator explains as a wine made of suspended grapes. (Evliya Efendi, *Narrative of the Travels*, vol. 2, 245.)

88. Busbecq, *The Turkish Letters*, 53.

89. Rozen, "Public Space," 343; *Istanbul*, 218.

90. Ibid., 220.

91. Benaim, *Sixteenth-Century Judeo-Spanish Testimonies*, 324–27.

92. See Yérasimos, "Dwellings in Sixteenth Century Istanbul," in *The Illuminated Table, the Prosperous House: Food and Shelter in Ottoman Material Culture*, eds. Suraiya Faroqhi and Christoph Neumann (Istanbul and Würzburg, Germany, 2003), 275–300, 294.

93. Rozen, *Istanbul*, 20.

94. Yérasimos, "Dwellings," 279.

95. Rozen, *Istanbul*, 55–60. For a detailed discussion of various Jewish neighborhoods and their demographics, see Yérasimos, "La communauté."

96. Ibid., 124.

97. Idem, "Dwellings," 291.

98. Ibid.

99. Ibid., 293.

100. Ibid., 292.

101. Ibid., 293.

102 Yérasimos, "La communauté," 127–128.

103. Rozen, "Public Space," 338.

104. Busbecq says that in the house where he was staying only the upper story was inhabited (Busbecq, *The Turkish Letters*, 93).

105. Rozen, "Public Space," 338.

106. It is possible that in some cases I, too, took one health regimen for another or missed some.

107. Pascual Requero, "Las 'Crónicas otomanas' de Moisés Almosnino," 76; Romeu and Hassán, "Apuntes sobre la lengua de la Crónica," 162; Romeu, "Introduction," in Almosnino, *Crónica de los reyes otomanos*, 34.

108. Gutwirth, "*Acutissima patria*," 30, 33. As we saw, Almosnino's praise of the city's architecture in the second chronicle is specifically intended to serve as further proof of Suleyman's wisdom, rather than to glorify Constantinople.

109. On later travelogues, see Borovaya, *Modern Ladino Culture*, ch. 2; Olga Borovaya, "Shmuel Saadi Halévy/Sam Lévy Between Ladino and French: Reconstructing a Writer's Social Identity" in *Modern Jewish Literatures: Intersections and Boundaries*, eds. Sheila Jelen, Michael Kramer, and L. Scott Lerner (Philadelphia, 2010), 83–103.

FIVE

Rabbis and Merchants

NEW READERS, NEW EDUCATIONAL PROJECTS

In the final section of chapter 1, I discussed the decline of Ladino literature at the turn of the seventeenth century caused by the disappearance of its audience, resulting from the end of the *converso* immigration and the economic crisis. In this chapter that covers the period between the 1600s and the 1860s, I will briefly outline the development of Ladino literature after a long hiatus, namely, its re-emergence for the benefit of a newly "discovered" audience, followed by the birth of another readership and modern forms of literary production. I will also show that contrary to common belief, Almosnino continued to be remembered and relevant in the eighteenth century. Since this is just a synopsis, I will briefly look at literary texts, dwelling mainly on their authors and addressees, as well as socioeconomic and political factors that had an impact on the trajectory of Ladino literature. Yet the first question I have to answer is why, in the early modern period, no vernacular literature emerged in Izmir, a Jewish community that did not suffer from the general economic downturn but rather, benefited from it.

The Jewish Community of Izmir

At the time when the Jewish communities of Salonica, Safed, and Manisa involved in textiles production experienced economic and cultural crisis, and Constantinople Jews had lost their prominence, a new community emerged in Izmir, a port city on the western Anatolian coast of the Aegean. For a long time, Izmir's chief function had been supplying agricultural products to the capital. While the Ottomans were neither willing nor capable of doing much for the city's development, English, Dutch, French, and Venetian merchants who began to arrive there in the 1620s soon turned it into a bustling port city. Izmir's population grew from a couple of thousand inhabitants at the turn of the seventeenth century to 35,000 or 40,000 in 1640.[1]

Izmir was unique among Ottoman cities not only in that it was to a large extent, created by Europeans; it was different on a more fundamental level. Daniel Goffman has shown that "in a manner strikingly similar to the city-states of the Hanseatic League or Renaissance Italy there arose in seventeenth-century western Anatolia a vigorous and innovative pocket of laissez-faireism within the strictly static Ottoman economy and society."[2] While not a free port, Izmir enjoyed light taxes that made it even more attractive for merchants.[3] This economic development had important sociodemographic consequences for the local Jewish community, shaping it in such a way that it resembled those of European port cities.

In general, Izmir's demographics did not differ markedly from what we find in other large Ottoman cities. There were Muslims, who formed a bare majority, Greeks, Armenians, local Jews (Romaniots and Sephardim), and Europeans (Jews and Christians).[4] In the sixteenth century, Izmir, a village, was of no interest to Sephardi refugees, and local Romaniots had been transferred to Constantinople. That is why the first Jewish community was established there only in 1605, when the town began to attract work migrants from other parts of the empire.[5] By 1660, according to Ottoman tax registers, it had more than two thousand members. However, it must be remembered that until 1831, Ottoman censuses counted only males.[6] Therefore, taking into account the tendency of Ottoman Jews to report lower figures to the authorities for tax purposes, we can assume that the total Jewish population was larger, probably around 4,500.[7] In any case, by the 1660s, the Jews of Izmir formed nine or ten congregations.[8]

In the 1680s–90s, there was a small wave of emigration from Iberia caused by a renewed persecution of *conversos*, many of whom were sentenced to death and executed during large *autos-da-fé*.[9] Previously, most *conversos* had preferred Amsterdam, but starting in 1672, "Dutch trade entered a process of permanent decline which was to have devastating consequences for the [Jewish] community . . . the 'Portuguese' community was hit especially hard."[10] Izmir, by contrast, offered new trade opportunities and, therefore, attracted some wealthy merchants who left the Peninsula in the last two decades of the seventeenth century. Western Sephardim founded a few congregations that were among "the largest, richest, and most influential ones in the city."[11] In the seventeenth century, a significant number of Jews in Izmir served as consular dragomans, brokers, and factors of foreign companies, which gave them the protection of their respective states. For European merchants it was desirable to hire them because in certain periods, particularly in 1610 and 1650, almost all customs agents in Izmir were Jews.[12] Therefore, Christian traders hoped that their factors would protect them from excessive taxes through connections with their coreligionists among customs officials.

The presence of foreigners in the Ottoman Empire was regulated by the capitulations, treaties between the Porte and European states that "exempted Europeans from paying head taxes and granted them lower customs duties than those paid by Ottoman subjects." They also guaranteed "the right to religious worship, protection from arbitrary seizure of their goods, full autonomy in the adjudication of commercial and civil disputes, and ample jurisdiction over criminal cases."[13] As was mentioned earlier, the first to obtain capitulations were France and Venice, followed by England, Holland, Genoa, and Tuscany (when it became part of the Habsburg Empire). Starting in the 1620s, there was "a significant increase in the number of Jews bearing identification from an Italian state while trading in the Empire under French protection."[14] In the 1670s, this number grew even larger, because France succeeded in negotiating lower customs duties than Venice in 1673, and in 1669 Marseilles was granted special status that allowed it to dominate trade between Europe and the Ottoman Empire in the last quarter of the seventeenth century.[15]

The capitulations thus created a new category of Jews referred to as "Francos" who came mainly from Italy and resided in the Ottoman Empire as foreign subjects.[16] Because in the seventeenth century, Sephardi Jews in Italy continued to speak Portuguese and at least read Spanish, which had acquired the status of a semi-sacred language, they had no difficulty communicating with Ladino speakers.[17] Nevertheless, they did not join local Sephardi communities if only to avoid the taxes. In Izmir, starting at least in the 1670s, Francos had their own congregation called *Kahal orhhim* (Congregation of visitors) or *Forasteros* (foreigners).[18]

The First Vernacular Books in Izmir

While the presence of Francos did not have the same stimulating effect as the mass immigration of Iberian Jews, they had—often to the chagrin of local rabbis—a considerable impact on the intellectual and social life of Ottoman Jews by serving as a link to Europe. Francos introduced new styles, forms of entertainment, and, eventually, educational institutions. One of the most important innovations brought to Izmir by European Jews was a Hebrew press (the first printing press ever in the city) that was established in 1658 by Abraham Gabay who came from Livorno, where he had worked at his father's printing shop. The latter, Jedediah Gabay, was the son of Isaac ben Solomon, author of popular commentaries, who was a typesetter at a famous Venetian press. In 1650, Jedediah purchased the type and ornamentation from its owner and founded the first Hebrew press in Livorno.[19] This became possible thanks to the support of the Grand Duke of Tuscany who believed that "the entire nazione ebrea of Livorno, and hence the economy of the Tuscan state, would benefit from it," due to the community's close relations with the Jews of the Levant.[20] Gabay received an exclusive privilege to print Hebrew, Latin, and vernacular books, which he enjoyed between 1650 and 1657. The majority of his books, however, were in Hebrew since he published mainly rabbinic writings.

When his son, Abraham Gabay, moved to Izmir, he brought with him most of the typographical equipment from Jedediah's shop, which is how a Latin font reached this Ottoman city.[21] As far as we know, Abraham's press produced only two books in Spanish (that were bound together), both published earlier in Europe: Menasseh Ben Israel's *Esperança de Israel* (The Hope of Israel) and *Apologia por la noble nación de los judíos* (Apologia for the noble Jewish nation) by an Edward Nicholas.[22]

The Hope of Israel was written by Menasseh Ben Israel, a renowned Sephardi rabbi of *converso* origin, author of numerous books, and founder of the first Hebrew press in Amsterdam (1626). His interest in the kabbalah and messianic ideas led him to believe that an important element in hastening the Messiah's coming was the readmission of English Jews, which he fervently advocated.[23] *The Hope of Israel*, first published in Amsterdam in Hebrew and Latin, later appeared in London in an English translation (1652) and made a considerable impression on Christian millenaries. The second book in Gabay's volume was written by Edward Nicholas who issued it in London in 1649 under the title *An Apologia for the honourable nation of Jews, and all the sons of Israel*. It also called for the readmission of Jews to England.[24]

On the first page of his volume, Gabay explains that he decided to publish these books in memory of Menasseh Ben Israel who was a great scholar and a good friend of his father's.[25] (Cecil Roth, based on indirect evidence, suggested that the two men might have visited London at the same time, in 1655.[26]) The volume also includes three sonnets and a eulogy in praise of Menasseh Ben Israel, composed by two local physicians of *converso* origin, which, in Jacob Barnai's opinion, points to more profound reasons for this publication. One of the authors of these messianic poems appears to have been a key figure among Shabbetay Zvi's close friends, which provides a direct link between him, his close associates, and the printing of *Esperança de Israel* in Izmir.[27] Moreover, Barnai suggests that Christian messianic hopes, presumably espoused by "agents of various European Levant companies stationed at Smyrna," which included many fervidly religious men, were transmitted to local Jews by Portuguese *conversos* who served as a "meeting point" between them.[28] Gershom Scholem believes that the Gabays, both father and son, were personally involved in the Sabbatean movement, though it seems that he confuses the two and their places of residence.[29] Still, this might have been true for both.

We know for certain that Abraham Gabay continued to produce Hebrew books in Izmir through 1675, though in 1660 he briefly left for Constantinople, where he also printed a few books.[30] A French traveler reports that during his trip to the Ottoman Empire in 1674–1675 he met a Jewish printer named Abraham Gabay who served as an interpreter for Augustine Spinola, the ambassador of the Republic of Genoa in the Ottoman capital.[31] In 1684 or so, Gabay established a printing press in Salonica, "the first in that city in thirty years."[32] However, ten years later, it was taken over by the *Talmud Torah*, because he was unable to maintain it. Nevertheless, Gabay continued to operate the press and printed three Talmudic treatises in the early eighteenth century.[33]

Thus, the three crowns, originally the mark of the sixteenth-century Venetian printer whose press was acquired by Abraham Gabay's grandfather, traveled through Livorno, Izmir, and Constantinople, eventually appearing on the title pages of books published in Salonica.[34] The history of the Gabay family and its press, symbolized by the trajectory of this emblem, demonstrates that in the seventeenth century Italian and Ottoman cities and Amsterdam formed one cultural space where typefaces, texts, printing houses, and printers moved freely from one place to another, producing books in the main Jewish languages of the time, namely, Hebrew and Spanish. To print a book in Ladino would have meant drastically limiting the press's audience and market.

Curiously, the same French account states that in Constantinople Gabay owned a "printing press in which there are fonts of letters in the Slavic, Armenian, Hebrew, Greek, and Latin languages. He has printed numerous books in the latter three languages."[35] In Gabay's time, Armenian books were imported from Amsterdam and Italy, since the printing press established in Constantinople in 1567 was short-lived.[36] There is no evidence that Gabay traveled to Rome or Amsterdam where he could have purchased an Armenian typeface. As for Cyrillic printing, in the sixteenth and seventeenth centuries, Slavic books were produced in Serbia and Wallachia but also brought from Italy.[37] In any case, there was no audience for them in Constantinople. Greek books, too, were imported from Italy, because there was no Greek press in the Ottoman Empire at the time. It appears highly unlikely that Gabay would have owned Greek or Armenian fonts (let alone a Cyrillic one) since he was not a hired compositor, but a Jewish publisher and thus would not have wanted to print Christian literature. However, since he had a Latin typeface in Izmir, he would have brought it to Constantinople and might have produced new books in Latin script. The fact that none of them is extant does not mean they were not printed. After all, only one copy of *Esperança de Israel* has survived, and it could have been lost as well.

What makes this account questionable yet at the same time important for us is that it is strikingly similar to the three statements of sixteenth-century travelers quoted in chapter 1. It is also noteworthy that neither one cites a single book title or gives any other specific information, while claiming that the Jews printed numerous books in non-Jewish languages. So, most likely, this seventeenth-century traveler simply repeated what his predecessors had written, because the notion of Ottoman Jews printing books in various languages in an empire where, allegedly, no other books were produced seems to have become a topos of the genre, just like the story of the sultan's footmen without spleens.

However, even one extant Spanish volume is enough to raise a few questions, the first about its target audience. Evidently, Gabay believed that in Izmir there were enough people able to read a book in Latin script. Indeed, there were the Francos, recent Iberian refugees, and local Jews who worked as agents of foreign companies. Barnai's hypothesis that Shabbetay Zvi would have been familiar with *Esperança de Israel* is plausible given that his father and two brothers, as is well known, were brokers for English merchants and could have taught him the Latin alphabet.[38] Finally, it is possible that this volume would have attracted even some Christians in a city where no other books were published.

A second question is whether these were the only European books that reached the Jews of Izmir. If a Jew from Livorno brought two Spanish books and a Latin typeface to print them, someone else could have brought other books for those who knew the Latin alphabet. Furthermore, just like rabbinical works, these books could have been copied by hand or even transcribed into Hebrew characters. We must keep in mind that works printed by the Jews of Amsterdam or Italy and even by Christian printers for western European Jews were usually written in Spanish or, rarely, Portuguese. Hence, language per se was not an obstacle for Jews who wanted to read those books. It was the alphabet that would have been a barrier. However, in the commercial circles of Izmir, there were many Jews who could read books out loud.

Thus, while in the sixteenth century those who knew the Latin alphabet had to unlearn it, in later times, there were always some Jews who were willing to rediscover it. We even have a business letter written by a local agent to the English consul in Aleppo, which was most likely produced in Izmir in the early seventeenth century.[39] While the letter is written in Ladino, the address is inscribed in Italian. We can assume that the author had some knowledge of the Latin alphabet but not enough to write a letter. Even if the address had been written by another person, this was probably also a Jew familiar with both alphabets.

Surely, such people could not have been numerous, but enough to make the rabbis worry. Thus, Elijah Ha-Kohen, a prominent rabbinic authority in Izmir, proclaimed in his *Shevet Musar* (1712) "there is no one more foolish than the one who studies foreign books, that is, books of the gentiles," because "all their laws are the opposite of the Law of Moses."[40] This does not tell us which "gentile books" were read by the Jews of Izmir, but it is safe to assume that Ha-Kohen was referring to European fiction. It will be remembered that in the mid-seventeenth century a rabbi in Venice condemned those who, on the Sabbath, read Ariosto's *Orlando Furioso*, which was translated into Castilian in Spain and later, probably in Turkey, transcribed by hand into Hebrew characters.[41] This is an example of not only the rabbis' reaction to "Gentile" literature but also of what kind of books might have been available in Izmir.

A third—and the most relevant to this study—question related to the publication of the only surviving vernacular volume produced in the seventeenth century is why no works in *aljamiya* appeared in Izmir. Although there were still new immigrants in need of re-education, their numbers were small, and obviously, the available books sufficed. Some books would have been brought in from Salonica, since a few Salonican rabbis had moved to Izmir. Also, reprints made in Venice would have been easily available in Izmir. In addition, as we know, most seventeenth-century immigrants left the Iberian Peninsula because they feared for their lives, not because they were eager to practice normative Judaism. Hence, we can assume that most would not have been interested in reading religious literature beyond liturgical texts. Finally, Gabay, who was not a local rabbi but a European publisher, was not interested in producing Ladino books, and there was no other printing press in Izmir until 1728.

We must also remember that a major factor affecting the rabbis' state of mind around the time of Gabay's operation in Izmir was the Sabbatean crisis. Having proclaimed himself the Messiah in Gaza in May 1666, Shabbetay Zvi returned to Izmir, his hometown, in the fall of that year.[42] The events surrounding his return shook not only thousands of Izmir's Jews but also Christian merchants from Europe. He had followers both among the rich and the poor, and most rabbis became his followers, some of them out of fear. Shabbetay Zvi's actions and messianic claims caused disruption in the city's life and trade and led to tremendous excitement all over the diaspora. In September 1666, faced with a choice between death and conversion to Islam, he chose the latter and was followed by a few hundred supporters. The consequences of this debacle for the Jewish world were momentous and long lasting.

Despite the fact that paradoxically, messianic excitement had less of an impact on the economic situation of Izmir's Jews than on that of Jews in other places, it was one factor that led to the community's economic decline.[43] More important, however, in the late seventeenth century, for various reasons that were not always clear, a considerable number of foreign merchants decided to stop trading in western Anatolia. One of the consequences of their withdrawal was an escalation of "the rivalry between Ottoman subjects and communities who vied for control of this lucrative commerce with each other as well as with outsiders."[44] This competition resulted in the commercial rise of the Greek community in Izmir and the empire in general at the expense of its rivals.[45] In the eighteenth century, Ottoman expansion to territories previously belonging to Persia increased trade with the East. "Armenians, who had established themselves as merchants and tradesmen along the route from Persia to Constantinople, gained influence because of this expansion of Ottoman trade."[46] As for the Jews, the connections they had were mainly in Italy, which no longer played a central role in international trade. Due to these circumstances, by the end of the eighteenth century, Armenians and Greeks took over international commerce in Izmir.

Though some Jews continued to serve as tax collectors, factors for foreign companies, and consular dragomans, they lost their prominent positions and were impoverished by the devastating earthquake of 1772. In the eighteenth century, like the city's population as a whole, the Jewish community diminished. Yet in the following century it began to grow again, and it is not coincidental that Izmir became the birthplace of the first Ladino periodical.

The Francos

There were Francos in many Ottoman cities, but in the eighteenth century their largest colony was in Salonica. According to Minna Rozen, "their choice of place was related to their early identification of Macedonia as a possible source of the agricultural produce that was in demand in Europe."[47] The first newcomers from Livorno were either merchants who had not prospered at home and wanted to try their luck in the Levant, or sons or poor relatives of successful Livornese families.[48] Thanks to their strong commercial ties with prosperous firms, these Francos, typically Tuscan subjects trading under French consular protection, quickly gained control of trade between Salonica and Italy, which made them wealthy.

Yet, even after many years in Salonica, they did not identify with local Jews to whom they felt superior, or with European states that granted them protection, and certainly not with the Ottoman Empire. Hence, as in the case of Izmir, they were unwilling to join the local community and refused to contribute to charitable causes. For instance, in the late 1740s, some Salonican Francos refused to contribute to funds raised for the Holy Land, even though this went against the agreement that the community had reached with them in 1730.[49]

This attitude is explained by the fact that "their affinities lay with the community of Spanish-Portuguese Jews who left Portugal in the wave of immigration that occurred in the seventeenth century" and settled in western Europe.[50]

There, they adopted the habits and tastes of wealthy classes of European Christians and, despite being criticized by rabbis for their laxity, they were not inclined to change their ways. Their acculturation to "Christian gentility" is best illustrated by their surviving portraits. For instance, "in the 1760s Isaac Medina of Livorno was depicted in a stylish cloak and periwig holding a sheet of music, in a composition reminiscent of Vivaldi's iconic portraits."[51]

The influence of foreign Jews on their Ottoman coreligionists would have been limited because they socialized separately. Yet business must have brought some together. The following lines from Huli's story of the Tower of Babel from *Meam Loez* indicate that he expected some of his readers (surely only males) to have a certain familiarity with the languages spoken by foreign Jews: "For you must have noticed that the languages of the world differ from one another. For example, the Portuguese and the Calabrians, although it is one language, there is a difference in the words they use."[52] It is through those male contacts that western influence spread among Sephardim.

As foreign subjects, Francos visibly differed from local Jews by the way they dressed, including a hat or a wig, and their facial hair, which was shaved or cut with scissors.[53] The latter, somehow associated with drinking non-kosher wine, was a constant point of contention with local rabbis. In the early 1720s, a Livornese rabbi reported that "whenever tensions ran high in the cities of the Ottoman Empire between the local Jews and those of the West European merchant class . . . the latter would be scoffed at for shaving their beards and drinking 'wine of the gentiles.'"[54] Elliott Horowitz is right in his explanation of what made Francos resist the rabbis' demands to stop grooming their beards with scissors, as they did in Europe: "they were Europeans in both their self-image and public identities, and they resisted being 'Orientalized.'"[55]

The European fashion of trimming hair and shaving the beard with a razor was adopted by some Ottoman Jews who considered those who followed the rabbinic ban obscurantists. Thus, in 1763, a rabbi wrote about a certain man who, having been rebuked by a barber for obeying the rabbis and keeping the corners of his hair long, agreed to have them shaved with a blade.[56]

Among the Francos' other "bad" habits was reading secular books. Although the rabbis found "gentile" literature dangerous, they never mentioned foreign Jews as its source. They were even less likely to admit that they suspected that some newcomers were secret followers of Shabbetay Zvi, because Sabbateanism was pervasive among European Jews, rabbis, and laymen alike.

For a long time after the messianic crisis, it was believed that the best way to bury Sabbateanism was concealment. "[The] bans that had been pronounced against mentioning Sabbatai Zebi or his adherents were still considered to be in effect in the eighteenth century, and this contributed to the atmosphere of taboo that surrounded the subject."[57] Among Jews of the Ottoman Empire, where the messianic drama took place, and where some Christians wrote about it in prose and rhyme, the taboo was not broken until the nineteenth century, which is why we can only speculate about the movement's influence and the rabbis' misgivings.[58]

As far as we know, there was only one open confrontation, and it did not involve local rabbis. In 1709 in Constantinople, Abraham Yizhaki, the Chief rabbi of the Sephardi community in Jerusalem, together with two other emissaries from the Holy Land, issued a general ban against

Nehemiah Hiya Hayon, an itinerant kabbalist born in the Ottoman lands. Accusing him of crypto-Sabbateanism, they demanded that those who had his works burn them.[59]

Europe, on the contrary, witnessed a series of violent anti-Sabbatean polemics, the first of which erupted in 1713 around Hayon, thus shattering "the uneasy silence."[60] Italian Jews participated in these controversies on both sides. In fact, Hayon had established contacts with Italian Sabbateans already in his youth.[61]

Thus, Francos were familiar with various heterodox ideologies related to Sabbateanism and were likely to have embraced some of them. This must have been of great concern to Ottoman rabbis who had enough trouble dealing with local Sabbateans, but this subject was not to be discussed in writing. Curiously, they never directly blamed foreign subjects for any transgressions or deviations in observance among Ottoman Jews. Instead, as we will see, they warned their flocks against the dangers associated with Europeans, such as "foolish books" and Christian beliefs.

It appears that the story about a fake Jew in Huli's *Meam Loez* on Exodus is a warning against those "gentiles" who only pretend to be Jews.[62] A certain *goy* dressed as a Jew used to go to Jerusalem to celebrate Passover. A sage who noticed the man's ignorance with regard to *kashrut* realized that he was an impostor and thought of a way to outsmart him. As the man was leaving for Jerusalem again, the rabbi instructed him to say to the Jews there that he would like to buy a lamb to eat its tail (which must not be eaten but instead has to be burned). When the impostor betrayed himself, the Jews of Jerusalem killed him. The story following this one tells of a true convert to Judaism who asks Maimonides whether he is permitted to say blessings and prayers that include the words "God of our fathers" since his father was a Christian.[63] Maimonides replies in the affirmative, explaining that Abraham's generation was the first to convert, and all Jews were their descendants. By juxtaposing a genuine convert and an ignorant impostor masquerading as a Jew, Huli teaches his readers not to trust those who only appear to be Jews, and to be tolerant to converts.

The rabbis had another reason to present Francos in a negative light. Local Jews could become Francos by serving as factors or dragomans for foreign companies, thus acquiring protégé status, and eventually becoming subjects of European states. They could also buy exemption patents (*berats*), which granted non-Muslim Ottomans tax exemptions and the option to use European law. Some bought a few *berats* to have more legal choices.[64] This undermined the rabbis' control over local Jews and caused financial losses for their communities.[65]

The rabbis' mistrust of Francos as agents of the West proved to be founded. The first Ladino periodicals and earliest European-style Jewish schools were established or sponsored by Francos whose ancestors had come to the empire in the seventeenth or eighteenth centuries, and by foreign protégés. Those literati, educators, and community leaders, while holding foreign citizenship, belonged to the most mobile and progressive segment of the Ottoman Sephardi community.

The "Vernacular Rabbis"

We have seen that at the turn of the seventeenth century Sephardi rabbis and printers stopped producing Ladino books because their target readership had disappeared. The traumas of expulsion and mass conversions had been dealt with, and rabbis turned to other subjects on which they deliberated in Hebrew. Fundamental theological questions raised by the messianic movement could not be discussed by mainstream rabbis in *any* language. Throughout this entire time there had existed a potential Ladino readership because as in all communities where the language of religion differs from the vernacular, a large number of people were illiterate in the "holy tongue." This was true for almost all women and a significant number of men, mainly among the poor. But even though their numbers were by far larger than those of the ex-*conversos*, because of their low social role, their education was not of great importance to the rabbis. In the eighteenth century, however, some rabbis came to the conclusion that large sectors of the Sephardi population had only nominal Jewish education and, for the first time, began to produce Ladino books for mass consumption. In other words, they were the first educators to "discover" the mass audience that had always been there.

Matthias Lehmann, in his pioneering study of rabbinic vernacular literature, interprets its emergence largely as a response to what "vernacular rabbis" (as he dubbed them), in the wake of the Sabbatean movement, perceived as an educational crisis. However, rather than seeing it as a reaction to a new situation, Lehmann argues that it is the transformation of the rabbis' own ideology that shaped their new educational ideal rooted in the Lurianic thought spread by the Sabbatean movement. This accounts for the rabbis' sense of responsibility for the masses since they believed "[t]he restoration of the divine order is a collective effort of all Jews carried out by scrupulously fulfilling the religious commandments."[66]

In general, I agree with Lehmann and find his argument convincing, especially because it shifts the focus from social reality to its observers, an issue that has barely received any attention. At the same time, I think he underestimates the significance of Sabbateanism and its consequences for Ottoman Jews in the eighteenth century and, therefore, the rabbis' efforts to battle them. Lehmann suggests that by the time rabbinic vernacular literature emerged in Constantinople, the impact of Sabbateanism there had been largely overcome, although in Izmir its sympathizers "continued to hold key positions in the community and in 1731 edited the three-volume ethical work *Hemdat Yamim* with clear Sabbatean tendencies."[67]

However, this influential work was printed by Jonah Ashkenazi, the same Constantinople printer who, a year earlier, had published the first volume of *Meam Loez*. It is entirely possible that Ashkenazi was attracted to some form of Sabbateanism but, as in the case of Elijah Ha-Kohen, this was fully compatible with his passion for educating the masses in Orthodox Judaism.[68] On the other hand, he could have been among those critics of Sabbateanism who were interested in Sabbatean literature and took it very seriously. As Maoz Kahana's text analysis persuasively shows, viewed as an 'error' and a 'stumbling-block' of central importance to the continued existence of Judaism and its literature, the study and scrutiny of Sabbateanism became almost compulsory, as the movement demanded 'rectification' and 'sweetening,' and sometimes even acceptance and enrichment.[69]

Furthermore, we have no evidence that Sabbateanism had lost its sway in the capital, or that crypto-Sabbateans in Izmir did not have counterparts in Constantinople, where Abraham Yizhaki banned Hayon's writings. While we cannot assess the impact of Sabbateanism on the Sephardi masses, it is hard to imagine that in the 1730s popular religiosity and beliefs were the same as before 1665. Besides, given the presence of ubiquitous crypto-Sabbatean preachers, there is no reason to assume that only orthodox rabbis had an influence on the general public. After all, Jacob Frank, who was considered in his native Podolia a reincarnation of Shabbetay Zvi and who led his followers to convert to Catholicism in 1756–1760, grew up in Turkey and later visited several times.[70]

Huli's teacher, Juda Rosanes (1657–1727), chief rabbi of Constantinople, was known as an enemy of crypto-Sabbateanism both in the empire and in Europe.[71] Whether because of his influence or for another reason, Huli saw the messianic drama as an earthshattering, albeit unmentionable event. In the Hebrew introduction to the first volume of *Meam loez*, he states that sometime after the appearance of *Shulchan Aruch* (1565), a "series of disasters" befell the people of Israel (iii).[72] Among the consequences lamented by Huli are the absence of true scholars and great "spiritual poverty among the foolish and ignorant masses" (ii–iii). It seems obvious that the disasters are the Khmelnitsky massacres and the Sabbatean crisis. It is also possible that the masses are called "foolish" because they had taken Shabbetay Zvi for the Messiah. Perhaps, as Lehmann suggests, the new vernacular authors indeed did not directly respond to "a perceived post-Sabbatean threat to traditional authority," but they definitely had to fight the spiritual consequences of the Sabbatean "disaster."[73]

In fact, some of the rabbis' concerns specifically related to the Sabbatean teachings are found in their texts. For instance, in the Ladino introduction to *Meam Loez*, Huli warns readers not to depart from what the Gemara (the second part of the Talmud) requires in anything at all: "And if someone contradicts the Gemara, do not pay attention to him, even if he offers many proofs to support his opinion."[74] Further along in the same introduction, Huli insists on the need to know the positive and negative commandments, which in another context, would not necessarily point to an anti-Sabbatean endeavor.[75] Yet, together with his reference to someone who will make an effort to disavow the Gemara, it does bring to mind the "New Law" proclaimed by Nathan of Gaza (Shabbetay Zvi's prophet), in which the old positive and negative commandments were abolished.

Among other things cancelled by Shabbetay Zvi was the fast of the Ninth of Av, which he turned into a celebration of his birthday. It seems that the rabbis found it difficult to make people properly observe this day of mourning again. We see that Abraham Asá's *Sefer Tsorrche Tsibbur* (Book of the requirements of the community, Constantinople 1733) chastises those men who on "this bitter day do forbidden things and sin. They dress in white, ride horses, swim, smoke, and laugh, without any understanding of its meaning" (142a).

In addition to Sabbateanism, there were other concerns that motivated the "vernacular rabbis" to produce a new literature. Lehmann's general explanation of what brought Ladino rabbinic literature into existence cannot be disputed: it was the discrepancy between the rabbis' new educational ideal and the alleged ignorance of the Sephardi masses. Furthermore, since Huli's claim about their intellectual and spiritual decline cannot be taken at face value, since starting at least with Maimonides and through the end of the nineteenth century, rabbis made the same complaint using similar words, the only reliable evidence we have is related to the creators of Ladino rabbinic literature themselves.

The second educational project undertaken by Sephardi rabbis differed from the first, among other things, in that it was initiated by a small group of men who had a common understanding of the problem and tried to solve it by acting as a team, at least for a while. At first, it consisted only of three people who happened to be in Constantinople in the first third of the eighteenth century. It is likely that initially, the key role in this endeavor belonged to Jonah ben Jacob Ashkenazi (d. 1745) who, as his nickname indicates, came from Eastern Europe, from a town not far from Lemberg, a city known at the time as a center of Hebrew book printing. In 1710, he established a printing press in the Ottoman capital, which for two years he ran together with a Jew from Vienna.[76] In 1728, Jonah Ashkenazi founded a press in Izmir (the first after Gabay's departure), where, using the font he had engraved in 1710, he printed Hebrew books in partnership with David Hazan, until the latter moved to Palestine in 1739.[77]

It appears that in 1727–1728 Jonah Ashkenazi helped set up the first Ottoman printing press for which he cast the letters. He must have been the man described by an Ottoman official as "the Jew named Yuna, who possesses all the important elements needed for printing, is knowledgeable in the art of printing, and is an expert in the art of tools, implements, and requisites."[78] Because of this, together with his son, he was exempted from the poll tax.[79]

Although in certain periods Jonah Ashkenazi thrived, employing up to fifty workers at his shops, one can gather from the introductions to his publications that at other times he lost books at sea and in numerous fires, and experienced financial troubles that delayed the appearance of several volumes of *Meam Loez* and made him ask for donations from readers.[80] Nevertheless, between 1710 and 1745, Ashkenazi's two presses produced around 125 books in Hebrew and Ladino. Moreover, together with a Venetian printer, Benjamin Rossi, he printed the first complete Ladino Bible. Ashkenazi was passionately dedicated to making Hebrew literature available to Ottoman Jews which, having mastered their vernacular, he expressed in programmatic introductions to some of the books he printed. After his death, the press passed to his sons and grandsons who, between 1745 and 1778, printed another fifty-five volumes.

By far the most famous among the "vernacular rabbis" was Jacob ben Meir Huli (c. 1689–1732) who came to the Ottoman capital from Jerusalem with the intention of publishing the writings of his maternal grandfather, a renowned rabbi (which he accomplished in 1727).[81] Huli's father came to Palestine from Europe at the age of fifty and, until his death, led a pious life in Safed (x). In 1714, Huli became close to Judah Rosanes, who appointed him judge on a rabbinic court.[82] After Rosanes's death, Huli prepared for publication his teacher's famous commentary on Maimonides's *Mishneh Torah* (Constantinople, 1731).[83]

The first volume of *Meam Loez*, a commentary on Genesis, appeared in 1730. Unlike later *Meam Loez* authors, Huli received generous financial support that allowed Jonah Ashkenazi to print a thousand copies of the volume, a large number given the size of the Sephardi community.[84] Huli died in 1732 having written only a part of his commentary on Exodus (up to 26:33), which came out posthumously in 1733, with Ashkenazi's introduction. Isaac ben Moses Magriso completed the commentary on Exodus (1746) and wrote commentaries on Leviticus (1753) and Numbers (1764), all three published by the Ashkenazi press.

Huli's work became immensely popular: his Genesis went through nine editions between 1730 and 1897, and his Exodus was reprinted seven times between 1733 and 1868.[85] Huli not only started one of the most important and most voluminous series in Ladino literature, but his own text

ספר
מעם לועז
חלק שלישי ספר ויקרא
יצחק מאגריסו
נדפס פה
קושטאנדינא

FIGURE 5.1.
Meam Loez Leviticus. Constantinople, 1753. Title page. Public Domain.
The Sephardic Studies Digital Library and Museum, University of Washington.

had a lasting influence on subsequent rabbinic and secular production in terms of language, genre, and method. *Meam Loez* was continued, albeit much less brilliantly, by another ten authors through the end of the nineteenth century.

The third participant in the project was Abraham ben Isaac Asá (c. 1710–c. 1780), the only native of Constantinople.[86] Virtually nothing is known about him. Despite being a generation younger than the other two, Asá (as far as we know) was alone in producing the first vernacular work since the turn of the seventeenth century. It was *Sipur Malkhe Otmanlis* (History of the Ottoman kings, 1728), a Ladino version of the respective chapters from Joseph Sambari's *Divre Yosef.* Ashkenazi must have acquired the manuscript in 1714 in Egypt, Sambari's home country. (In 1767, it was printed by Jonah's sons as *Deklaro del Reyno de Otmanjik i su grandeza* [A story of the Ottoman reign and its greatness].)

A year later, Ashkenazi's Polish competitor in Constantinople, Benjamin Peretz, printed *Letras de Rabi Akiba* (Alphabet of Rabbi Akiva), Asá's Ladino adaptation of the Midrash *Otiyyot de-Rabbi Aqiva*, a well-known mystical work. Given the wide interest in mystical literature and popularity of the Hebrew original, we can assume that this publication was expected to be a commercial success. In fact, on the title page, the publisher advertises it as a book translated from Hebrew "to be read by everybody, rich and poor, as well as by rabbis and judges."[87] This is the first reference to the demographics of the Ladino-reading audience we find in the eighteenth century.

During the fifty years of Asá's activity, the Ashkenazi press and its competitors printed an astonishing number of his translations of Hebrew texts on various subjects, which form a "library of Jewish knowledge," as Lehmann described it.[88] With help from Jonah Ashkenazi and his partner, Benjamin Rossi, Asá produced the first full edition of the Bible in Ladino. This version of the Pentateuch (1739) is still similar to the Constantinople Bible (1547) and is also printed in square letters with vowel points.

However, starting with the Prophets (1743), the biblical text was for the first time printed in Rashi script, which average people apparently found easier to read.[89] Most important, this translation is much more readable than that of the Pentateuch. Finally, in 1744, Asá produced a

בע"ה
חלק ראשון
מהארבע ועשרים
והוא חמשה חומשי
תורה
עם לעז ופירוש רש"י ז"ל מוגהה
בעיון נמרץ ומנוקדה מכל סיג
וחלאה למען ירוץ הקורא בו:
נדפס
בקושטנדינא
אשר תחת ממשלת אדוננו המלך
שולטן מחמוד ירום הודו:
בשנת יי' צבאות יגן עלימו לפ"ק
בדפוס המחוקק והמדפיס סה"ר יונה בכמה"ר
יעקב זלה"ה

FIGURE 5.2.
Abraham Asá's translation of the Pentateuch. Constantinople, 1739. Title page.
Public Domain. *Beinecke Library, Yale University.*

volume that included all five Scrolls in Hebrew and Aramaic accompanied by Ladino translations both of the Hebrew text and the Targum. Asá's version is not only highly readable but also is written in a lively style. It is Asá's Five Scrolls, rather than the Bible as a whole (as is often claimed), which became so popular and was reprinted multiple times in the nineteenth century.

The Useless Books

The Hebrew introduction to the first volume of *Meam Loez* served as a manifesto of the new educational movement. In fact, Ashkenazi's and Asá's introductions to Ladino books published after Huli's death are either short variations on this programmatic text or include excerpts from it.

Huli's Hebrew text obviously intended for rabbis, both supporters and detractors, explains his reasons for starting a vernacular commentary on the Pentateuch. One of his major objectives, stated in the opening lines, is "Judaizing" the "uneducated masses" to turn them into the children of Israel. Needless to say, he is not talking about re-educating *conversos* but rather of providing a basic Jewish education to Jews ignorant in Judaism. In the eighteenth century, this automatically meant people illiterate in Hebrew, i.e., men and women of lower classes with little or no education, often unable to read even Ladino.

"Meam Loez" is an allusion to Ps 114:1 and literally means "from a people of strange language," i.e., speakers of a vernacular. By giving this title to his commentary, Huli announced that it was intended for those who did not know Hebrew. Anticipating the ire and derision of those who would censure him for using the vernacular and producing "women's knowledge," he finds support in the works of Jewish commentators before him. Huli reminds his critics that Maimonides and Saadia Gaon used Arabic to teach Judaism to those who did not know Hebrew. But his ambition and audacity go much further. Among his predecessors, he names Moses who was ordered by God "to write down on the stones the words of the Law in a clear manner" (vi). While this daring comparison was likely to prompt even more indignation, Huli's interpretation of Moses's job, with an emphasis on clarity, shows that he saw the production of his own exposition of the Law as God's assignment.

In the Ladino introduction to *Meam Loez*, written for all readers, Huli presents the history of Judaism largely as a constant rewriting of earlier Bible commentaries that was called for by the insufficient education of ordinary people. The only exception is the work of Moses who first had to formulate what God had told him, and then, because the words on the tablets were "short and very sealed," he had to explain them in the Torah. Among Moses's successors, Huli particularly admires Maimonides whose *Mishneh Torah* made all other books superfluous: having read the *parasha* and Maimonides's respective commentary, one "did not need to read any other book." This is precisely what Huli aspired to accomplish by producing *Meam Loez* which, indeed, covered all fields of knowledge he deemed important. In an effort to replace all other Ladino texts available to his audience, Huli had gone through at least 217 rabbinic sources to provide an adequate education and laudable entertainment for "all men and women and the youth of Israel," (iv) (that is, children old enough to enjoy a tale and learn a simple lesson).[90]

In the Ladino introduction, Huli shows his readers in a simple way why they need his commentary. Having stated that the world has declined to "such a degree that very few people are able to read a biblical verse correctly," he explains that one has to learn the Scriptures not to fail the test on Judgment Day:

> One will be asked, "What have you learned during all these years in that world?
>
> Tell us what you have learned and understood from the weekly *parasha* and *haftorah*—because one is obliged to read and understand them." And, surely, one will be very embarrassed not to know what to answer, and will have to say, "Oh, what shame. Oh, what ignominy!"

Huli claims that Sephardim hunger for learning, but the lack of appropriate reading material and the reality of everyday life make studying impossible. When after returning from their shops, the men open even an easy Hebrew book, they do not understand what it says and fall asleep. They would gladly study early in the morning, but having nothing to read, they waste "this time of clarity in mundane conversations." And those who do not work because they are old or sick are locked in their homes without anything useful to read.[91] In addition, Huli worries that while their Hebrew books are "collecting dust," Sephardim may stumble upon useless or even harmful books. He tells his audience about three Ladino books from the sixteenth century that apparently were still available but inaccessible to the unlearned. The first two books (both mentioned in chapter 1) are *Mesa de el alma*, a Ladino version of *Shulchan Aruch*, and *Obligasyon de los korasones*, a translation of ibn Paquda's *Hovot ha-levavot*. Both were printed in block letters with vowel points, which in the sixteenth century was considered the most accessible form of print. Huli, however, declares them useless for linguistic reasons. Having referred to the language of these works as "Ladino," he goes on to say that the translator of ibn Paquda's book wrote it in "his idiom, in Spanish words which are very difficult and incomprehensible for the people in these parts of Turkey, Anatolia, and Arabistan."[92] The next sentence is of particular importance for my study. It is often quoted and systematically misinterpreted by historians, scholars of Sephardi literature, and linguists who use it to prove that by the eighteenth century, Almosnino's language had become obsolete and his work irrelevant.[93] The following words typically introduce discussions of *Meam Loez*, presumably explaining why Huli had to produce his Bible commentary: "The book written by our master and teacher Moses Almosnino of blessed memory, called *Rejimyento de la vida*, is a very enlightening book, but its idiom is incomprehensible."[94]

I suggest that this statement about Almosnino's book cannot be taken as evidence on its language. Even less so can one draw general conclusions about eighteenth-century Ladino, as does Coloma Lleal who claims that Huli's words "clearly capture" "the situation of rupture with the Spanish literary norm."[95].To begin with, Huli's linguistic expertise is questionable, which is obvious from his explanation that the *Ladino* translation of ibn Paquda's book is unintelligible for most readers, because it is written "in *Spanish* words." Besides, as will be remembered, he believed that Calabrian and Portuguese were one language. More important, Huli's argument is not about language per se.

The true purpose of this section of his introduction is to show to the rabbis that the Ladino works of his predecessors, excellent and enlightening as they may be, are inadequate for mass education. Huli is particularly keen on proving the uselessness of Almosnino's book. The first problem he mentions is a technical one, allegedly encountered by readers of all three books: it is their spelling (*solotreo* [*sic*]), which he considers correct but no longer comprehensible. The difficulty was probably caused not by the unstable orthography but, at least in Almosnino's case, had to do with the way of printing.

Unlike the other two books, *Rejimyento* was printed in unvocalized Rashi script with inconsistently used *matres lectionis*. John Zemke explains that in the sixteenth century neither author nor readers "required a consistent spelling system" and that "unpointed *aljamiya* was read in the same fashion as unpointed Hebrew: a reader recognizes a known word form."[96] This means that reading *Rejimyento* required a vocabulary of philosophical and scientific terms far beyond that of the petty merchants and their wives who formed Huli's intended readership.

In fact, the second problem discussed by Huli is the lack of general understanding of the text, because the unlearned "do not understand his words to which they are not accustomed." Moreover, they do not understand "the meaning of what he says [*sus ablas*] which, being very short, require a lot of studying." Obviously, here *ablas* does not refer to words or sentences (since one can call Almosnino's sentences very short only as a joke). Hence, this probably means that his ideas are not sufficiently explained. Huli indeed says that to "understand what he [Almosnino] wanted to say, one has to know how to study, as he intended to be short by conveying a lot of knowledge in few words."

The adjectives Huli uses to prove that the three Ladino books are incomprehensible for the masses—*karo*, *serado*, and *ondo* (difficult, sealed, profound)—appear in his introduction whenever he needs to explain why his predecessors had to produce a new commentary. In every case, he says that the world had declined, and the words of the available commentary had become incomprehensible. Evidently this does not refer to linguistic problems as such, since Moses had to write the Torah to explain the Ten Commandments, because "the words of the Law are very sealed and short (*las ablas de la Ley son muy seradas i kortas*)." It is precisely these adjectives that Huli uses to describe Almosnino's *Rejimyento* (*sus ablas son muy seradas; las ablas, ke son muy kortas*). Thus, his writing is too dense, which "is not useful for the common people, because they cannot spend a whole day trying to understand one thing." This last comment, in a way, contradicts what Huli considers the book's third problem, namely, that it is so short that it will be finished very quickly thus leaving the people without anything to read once again.

This lengthy discussion of *Rejimyento* and the fact that it is cited together with adaptations of *Shulchan Aruch*, the most authoritative legal code of Judaism, and *Hovot ha-Levavot*, described by Joseph Dan as "the most important and influential work of Jewish philosophical ethics," is ample proof that it was still available and continued to be relevant for some readers, if only for the rabbis.[97]

No doubt, *Rejimyento* was unintelligible for the masses unfamiliar with Aristotle, Plato, and even Maimonides, but this was also true at the time of its production, since it was intended for educated young men. In fact, to use its glossary one had to know Hebrew.

It seems that scholars have begun to treat Huli's words as linguistic evidence rather recently. At any rate, in 1948, Michael Molho was aware that Almosnino's work was intended for a small audience:

> Despite its lively style, *Rejimyento de la vida* is not a popular work accessible to every reader, which is why it did not become a favorite of the general public. Judging by its literary structure and scholarly content characterized by philosophical contemplations, this masterpiece was intended for educated people able to appreciate the author's talent and his manner of writing.[98]

Indeed, if the problem had been a purely linguistic one, the "vernacular rabbis" could have adapted *Rejimyento*, as was done in its Romanized edition (Amsterdam, 1729). (See fig. 5.3.)

Furthermore, in 1749, Asá produced a new translation of *Ora Chayim* (manner of life), the same section of *Shulchan Aruch* that Meir Benveniste adapted under the title "*Mesa de el alma*."

Yet *Rejimyento* and *Obligasyon de los korasones*, complex ethical works that talked about abstract virtues and spiritual commandments and were intended for individual reading, were either not published in the Ottoman Empire again (the former) or not until 1898 (the latter).[99] Instead, they were replaced with straightforward religious education and clear guidance offered by *Meam Loez*, which was appropriate for reading out loud in a group setting. To sum up, the fact that Huli went to such lengths to prove the obvious, namely, that *Rejimyento* could not serve the purpose of mass education, testifies to Almosnino's high prestige, which made it impossible to reject his work without a thorough justification.

TRATADO PRIMERO
DEL REGIMIENTO DE LA VIDA.

CAPITULO I.

Se trata el gran provecho que alcançan los Moços de acompañar con los buenos; muestra como los bienes se reparten en tres especies; Espirituales, Corporales, y Exteriores; se propone una duda por que viene bien al malo, y mal al justo? y se responde.

Na coza universal, que alos Moços conviene mucho atender en el principio dela jornada de su vida, te quiero antes de todo dezir; por que es mucho menester que seas en ella advertido; y es, que pues saliste debaxo de las alas de tu Madre, procures de acompañarte con los buenos, y virtuozos, huyendo a rienda suelta como de enimigos, de los malos, y viciozos; por que nó solo és menester que nó se quiebre el hilo del buen regimiento de la niñés, sinó que continuamente se siga su beatissimo camino, hasta qué con la perfecta continuacion, llegue ál verdadero conoscimiento del bien, y mal; y nó sese hasta que se haga en el fixo, y firme el buen habito, sin rezelo de corrupcion alguna; por que nó bastan todas las buenas costumbres dela niñes para rezistir a los tempestuozos vientos de los apetitos, en la flor de la juventud si nó sigué assi bien hasta acabár de efectuárse el fruto con los firmes habitos, y si de otro modo lo hizieres, perderás todo quanto de tu Madre hás aprendido, y yo te hé enseñado.

De lo dicho nacio aquel proverbio antiguo que se suele dezir; *No Con quien nasces sino con quien pasces*; que en dezir, *nó con quien nasces* denota el ser con quien nasce necessario; por lo qual fue menester advertir que nó basta que aquella compañia del nascimiento sea buena si la que despues della succede nó la confirma; por que pará corromper lo acostumbrado dela niñés un solo vicio, o compañia de un solo viciozo basta; mas para confirmár el bien

A contra

FIGURE 5.3.
Moses Almosnino, *Regimiento de la vida*. Amsterdam, 1729. First page of chapter 1. Public Domain. *Jewish National and University Library (Jerusalem).*

A New Calamity

In the Hebrew introduction, Huli mentions another category of "useless" Ladino books:

> And now a calamity has spread: [Jews] buy perverse books written by liars, invented by non-Jews. They waste time on vanities and jokes, which

> is a shame for the people of Israel. For this reason, the earth is sad, and the Jews complain because we are considered stupid, and the Torah is thrown in the corner because nobody understands it, and the whole people of Israel is lamenting a great lamentation. (iii)

We remember Elijah Ha-Kohen calling readers of non-Jewish books fools. But Huli takes the problem much more seriously and declares that it is one reason why he decided to undertake his Bible commentary (iv). Huli was not the only "vernacular rabbi" concerned about the "new calamity."

In 1743, Ashkenazi published Asá's translation of *Sefer ben Gorion*, which, as will be remembered, was printed in Hebrew in Constantinople in 1510 and must have been quite popular in the empire, like in other countries. In his introduction, Asá complains that no one knows the history of the world because books on history are not available, which prompted him to translate this one into "clear Ladino," so that it could be read both by rabbis and laymen:[100]

> It is also true that I have seen people who waste money commissioning others to write stories (*dan a eskrivir istoryas*) for leisurely reading, and all those tales are lies and vainglories, and no benefit comes out of this. And they say that they do this because they cannot find true stories for reading, and that if they had such true stories that talk about the past they would certainly prefer to read those.[101]

Strikingly, these and similar complaints are found in rabbinic writings long before Ladino *belles lettres* first appeared in print. From what the rabbis say, it is clear that made-up "gentile" stories of the past were chivalric novels translated into Ladino and sold in manuscript. We know that European Jews were reading chivalric novels already in the thirteenth century, and the rabbis lamented this in similar words.[102] As for Ottoman Jews, r. Menahem de Lonzano, a renowned scholar and poet from Jerusalem, censured for the same practice some Sephardim of Constantinople, where he spent a few months in 1573–1574. According to him, instead of studying the Torah at least on the Sabbath, they were "drawn to words of falsehood like *Amadís* and *Palmerin Silistri*, stories of wars among Gentiles."[103]

Minna Rozen's assumption that "the reference to Palmerin and Amadis . . . is apparently taken directly from *Don Quixote de la Mancha*," is wrong, because the first volume of Cervantes's novel first appeared in 1605, i.e., about thirty years after Lonzano wrote these lines.[104] His statement is of great interest to us precisely because it is not taken from a book but based on his own observations. I suspect that the second title should be translated from Hebrew as "Palmerin of Silistra" and that it was given to the novel by analogy with "Palmerin of England." This may suggest that it was a local adaptation of *Palmerin*, since Silistra is a town and area in Bulgaria, then an Ottoman province. In any case, it is clear that some Ottoman Jews had access to European fiction already in the sixteenth century, let alone in the following one.

Until recently, one could only speculate about the nature of books condemned by Huli and Asá without any hope to find the actual texts, because, needless to say, those stories were not printed or kept in *genizas*. Hence, it is almost a miracle that a significant fragment of a chivalric novel produced in Ladino in the first half of the eighteenth century has survived until this day.[105] Paleographic analysis of this unique manuscript conducted by Alla Markova demonstrates that it was produced by a professional scribe for a well-off patron, able to pay for his work and for rather expensive paper. The scribe's errors and corrections make clear that he copied the text from another manuscript.[106]

It is noteworthy that the text is written in unvocalized Sephardi cursive, and the orthography is still rather unstable.[107] Moreover, a word can be spelled in different ways on the same page.[108] Yet, there is no reason to believe that this created a reading problem.

Although Markova was unable to identify the novel on which the Ladino rewriting was based, she has convincingly shown that the original was produced by a Spaniard. Most important, one can see that it was adapted for a Jewish audience and along the same lines as nineteenth-century Ladino rewritings.[109]

On the basis of evidence gleaned from Asá's introduction and Markova's analysis, we get a much better idea of the production of "useless" books in the eighteenth century. Some people would bring European novels to the empire, where others adapted them in Ladino. Then scribes copied them from the original manuscript, and the translator or someone else sold the copies to those who had "commissioned" the novels (if the latter was indeed true and they were not produced for sale in the first place).

The originals were most likely brought by Francos who might have been asked to do so. Local protégés who knew foreign languages and needed money would have served as translators. Obviously, we have no information on the numbers of readers of those novels. However, we know from the practice of collective reading in the nineteenth century that one copy could have sufficed for ten or fifteen people, most of whom, at least in the eighteenth century, would have been illiterate. In any case, the number of manuscript copies of those novels could not have been large due to their prohibitive price.

Of course, Jewish religious authorities tried to ban fiction in all epochs, at least its reading on the Sabbath, to make sure their flocks would read the Torah.[110] But "vernacular rabbis" apparently had an additional reason to resent European novels. Talking about the nineteenth century, Lehmann suggests that it is "the challenge posed by the acculturation of both Jews and non-Jews to a European-inspired culture" that leads the rabbis to protest against secular fiction.[111] In other words, they feared secularization that would undermine their authority.

It appears, however, that in the 1730s, when foreign novels had become popular enough to be described as a "calamity," the rabbis were not so worried about cultural assimilation (which was hardly a danger), but they feared that those books would transmit Christian beliefs. We do not have a great deal of evidence of this, but it is quite important. The first piece of evidence is Jonah Ashkenazi's introduction to the Ladino Pentateuch. This text is so striking that it is worth quoting a long passage:

> And in the whole Law, only the name of Israel is mentioned, and no other nation, even though Christians say that God abandoned us and took them instead, saying that we had sinned. But we can easily respond to them: they could say such things if God had achieved something by taking better people instead of us. But this is not so, as we see that those who say that God abandoned us and took them instead are much worse sinners who do not perform a single commandment of the Law (in particular, the commandment of circumcision or rules and injunctions of the Law which God told them to perform). So, why would God who knows the future abandon us without gaining anything? And knowing that this is not so but that they found themselves in power because of our sins, they are wondering why the Master of the Universe left them in exile for so long despite their having such a holy law; and thus . . . they say that he abandoned us.[112]

Ashkenazi concludes by saying "the uncircumcised" chose the wrong law. It is remarkable that this passage appears near the beginning of the introduction, even before the explanation of what one is required to read to fulfill the commandments. This is a short and simply formulated anti-Christian polemic intended for all those who open the Ladino Bible.

A year later, in 1740, Ashkenazi reprinted a work of Jewish apologetics, *Fuente klara*, which, as was previously mentioned, first appeared in Salonica in 1595. The first edition targeted an ex-*converso* audience, but in 1740s very few converts came to the Ottoman Empire to become Jews. The last *converso* emigration from Spain, caused by new *autos-da-fé* in the first quarter of the eighteenth century, was very small, and most of the refugees went to Europe. Given his financial straits, it is unlikely that Ashkenazi would have printed a book meant for such a miniscule audience.

How do we explain the rabbis' concern about the influence of Christianity in a Muslim empire? It is well known that Jews had strained relationships with Greeks and Armenians, exacerbated by economic rivalry that was inauspicious for the Jews. Hence, there was no danger of Sephardim being converted by local Christians, and they had very little contact with European Christians. Missionaries, who were active in the Ottoman Empire in the eighteenth century, were Catholics, mainly Jesuits, who had no interest in converting Jews. In the nineteenth century, however, there was a large number of Protestant missionary societies that came to convert Sephardim, but they proved unsuccessful. A number of missionaries stated that the conversion of Jews was a difficult task, and very few of them changed their religion.[113]

Thus it seems that in the rabbis' minds, it was European fiction that served as a medium for spreading Christian beliefs because it propagated the wrong values, "opposite to the Law of Moses." It is not surprising that in the fragment examined by Markova, all Christian terms are substituted with Jewish ones (e.g., priests become "sages"). But, unlike nineteenth-century Ladino *belles lettres*, this fragment is purposely anti-Christian. For instance, there is "the cave of very false gods of Muslims and Christians (*de moros o de kristyanos*)." And "sage Martin made enchanted arms for twenty knights, so that they would wage a war against Christendom."[114] Since the action in the novel takes place in the

Ottoman Empire, the *moros* (the Castilian but not Ladino term for "Muslims") would have come from the Spanish original, while Christians were added in the adaptation. These additions and revisions must have aimed at proving the novel's anti-Christian thrust.

Although there is no (and there may never be) conclusive evidence, I would cautiously suggest the following: Jonah Ashkenazi's emphasis on apologetics and the fact that Huli cites the "new calamity" among the reasons that prompted him to start *Meam Loez* point not only to the popularity of foreign novels, but also to the rabbis' fear that they might spread Christian beliefs.

Meam Loez, a School for the Whole Family

Huli states in both introductions that his goal is not only to explain the biblical text and the commandments but also to provide pleasant and edifying reading for the whole family "on the holidays and the Sabbath." This means that *Meam Loez,* which was always read aloud, had to include some sections to engage all members of the family at the same time. Explanations of Hebrew verses were probably meant only for men, as were "the precepts interesting for all heads of households" (iv).

As for women, one can tell from Ashkenazi's long justification of female education in his introduction to the Ladino Pentateuch that it continued to be a contentious point. He insists that women must study the Torah in translation

> because if they do not know the precepts, how will they observe the Sabbath and the rest of the commandments? How will women learn to perform a commandment if they do not read about it? How will they learn that there is such a commandment in the Law? . . . And if they read and do not understand what can they learn?[115]

Moreover, he declares that the words of the Gemara that forbid teaching the Torah to women "relate only to the depth or secrets of the Law."

On the other hand, Asá's *Sefer Tsorche* Tsibbur, a book of precepts for Jewish men, treats women only as tools for performing male commandments, which is particularly evident when it talks about sex. So, despite being concerned about women's education, "vernacular rabbis" continued to view them only as wives and mothers and did not hesitate to call them foolish. For instance, we read in Huli's story of Adam's fall that the Serpent knew that Eve, "being a woman, had little wit and would soon agree to his counsel."[116] In the account of the offering of Isaac, Abraham takes it for granted that "the intelligence of women is slight."[117]

To make *Meam Loez* appealing and comprehensible to a "dim-witted" female audience, Huli sometimes addresses women directly to discuss their household duties, but more often he includes them in the general audience, sometimes together with children.[118] Since the subject of children's audience has not been studied so far, I will demonstrate at some length Huli's method for engaging and teaching his youngest addressees.

Obviously, *Meam Loez* was designed to be heard more than read. Or, more precisely, Huli intended it to be read by somewhat educated men, whom he addresses in the Ladino introduction, to an illiterate audience.[119] This way the first thousand copies of Genesis would have reached no less than 10,000 people, that is, at least a third of Constantinople's Jews.[120] Huli constructs his discourse and organizes the commentary so that it would be comprehensible not only to better educated men who read it aloud, but also to their least learned listeners. For instance, as Ora Schwartzwald has observed, Hebrew terms, unless they are well known, are translated into Ladino, and often by two or three synonyms.[121] This is important, since in public reading, one cannot revisit an unclear passage.

In general, Huli's commentary contains many elements of oral communication.[122] For example, he often introduces a new subject by saying, "As you [plural] will/must know . . ." which allows the person reading out loud to direct the listeners' attention as needed.[123] Thus, the story about the Tower of Babel quoted above begins as follows: "You must know that until then everyone spoke Hebrew and did not know any other language."[124] Annette Benaim, who studied sixteenth-century Ladino responsa discussed in chapter 1, concluded that the language of Huli's *Meam Loez* is "very similar in style, in its use of Hebraisms, in its rhythm, in its syntax, morphology and phonology" to that of the oral testimonies.[125]

Perhaps the most effective device for oral teaching is storytelling, which was widely used in Ladino *musar* (ethical) literature. The two types of short didactic stories, whose goal is to illustrate proper moral behavior, are *mashal* and *maaseh*. The former is a parable or allegory, a story that has an anonymous protagonist and is always fictional. The latter is an *exemplum*, i.e., a moral anecdote that illustrates a good or bad moral behavior and purports to be a true story about real people.

Almosnino's *Rejimyento*, the first Ladino *musar*, contains a significant number of such stories, mainly parables, most of them borrowed from rabbinic sources.[126] Usually, he does not tell the story in full, but only alludes to it or summarizes its content in a few words, expecting the reader to remember the rest.

Although *Meam Loez* is not a *musar*, it often functions as one. Besides, as we will see, Huli uses stories to illustrate precepts of the Law. Since he modified original stories, mostly taken from rabbinic writings and cited on the margins, an analysis of these changes puts in sharp relief his own message that can differ from that of the original, and reveals his literary devices. Huli masterfully constructs his stories to engage various groups of listeners to ensure that all family members participate in the study, even though a lot of his material would have been incomprehensible or boring for children.

I suggest that the account of Noah's hardships in the ark (based on a *midrash*) told by his son was meant primarily to educate children, while entertaining their parents. It is a *maaseh* (*exemplum*) showing how Noah and his son Shem tended to the animals during the flood.

Shem, the narrator, being a model son, helps his father take care of animals in the ark, at the same time learning about nature. At first, not knowing what a certain animal would eat, they noticed that it picked up a worm that had fallen out of a pomegranate. So they ingeniously put some grains in water to grow larvae for the animal. Feeding all the creatures was difficult because they ate at different times. Once, when Noah was late with the lion's food, it bit him on the leg. Listeners learn that he deserved it for failing to perform God's commandment: "You are to take every kind of food that is to be eaten and store it away as food for you and for them" (Gen 6:21). This is both an explanation of a verse from Genesis and a straightforward lesson where a failure to observe the Law is followed by immediate and evident punishment.

Young listeners also receive a few lessons in natural sciences, including medicine. To prevent the lions from eating other animals, God gave them a fever that made them "low-spirited": "You will observe this in sick people who go without food because their fever sustains them."[127] Noah himself became sick several times. "The dampness was so great that he developed dysentery with bloody discharges." This diagnosis is followed by what sounds like a conversation between curious children and their teacher:

> And you will ask, "On the contrary, would not the ark be hotter than a bath, since the water was boiling hot?" And although we stated above that the water round the ark was cold, without doubt God worked this miracle for love of him [Noah], and it was a great boon, but doubtless the miracle was not meant to hurt him by making him ill with the cold.[128]

Finally, there is a little vignette that seems to offer a lesson in model behavior that is immediately and generously rewarded. Noah makes the phoenix immortal, because it refuses to take food to make his life easier: "I see how much you have to do and it seems a shame to give you trouble."

Some of Huli's stories indeed can teach and entertain the whole family at the same time. The following story from Exodus is listed in the index (put together by Ashkenazi) at the end of the volume as *mashal*, but in the body of the book it is introduced as *maaseh*. In reality it is both, which is why it is so effective. It is a story about a king's daughter locked up with her maids inside a castle with an enchanted door.[129] The king promised to give her as wife to the man who would find the door, enter the castle, pick the right key from a bunch, and unlock all the doors to the rooms until he saw the princess. He could also achieve this by getting her to open a window and show him the door. And many men from the four ends of the earth came to the castle but failed to find the door. They would serenade the princess in the hope that she would look out of the window, but very soon they would despair and go back.

One day, a clever man came to the castle and decided to spend forty days and forty nights there, hoping that he would find the door or have an opportunity to talk to the princess. After many attempts, he finally discovered a window, opened it, and pleaded with the princess. Seeing how much he had struggled out of love for her, she encouraged him to continue. When he eventually reached her room, she was very happy and called her father who gladly accepted the man as his son-in-law and revealed to him many more secrets.

Huli borrowed this *mashal* from a Hassidic source (which only the person reading aloud would see in the margins) where it served as an allegory of Torah study in pursuit of its mysteries. While preserving this obvious meaning, he expanded the story, added numerous details, and created suspense. As a result, it became a long and thrilling story for both children and adults. It is remarkable that Huli added, albeit a little awkwardly, some elements of the chivalric novel, evidently, in an attempt to replace "useless" books. Thus, he talks about a castle, apparently without having a clear idea of what it is, because his "castle" is a big house in the middle of a square. In addition, although it is called "enchanted," there is no explanation of who enchanted it and why. The princess is touched by the man's love, though, as in chivalric novels, he is in love with her without ever having seen her. Finally, instead of immediately opening the door for him, the princess encourages him to win her hand through his own efforts. In other words, here, as in many chivalric novels where the knight faithfully serves his courtly lady, the woman controls the love relationship. Thus an allegory is turned into an enjoyable story meant to inspire adults to study the Torah, teach children to persevere, and entertain the whole family. It is evident that Huli's didactic goals in this *maaseh* are defined by the lowest educational common denominator of his audience. The more advanced among readers of *Meam Loez* would have wanted to learn more and would have turned to Asá's translations, which (with the exception of the Bible and the prayer book) were intended for a more limited audience.

"Vernacular rabbis," however, had yet another tool for mass education that was appropriate for family reading, namely, *koplas* (couplets). Thanks to their simple rhymes, *koplas* could be easily memorized and recited even by the illiterate. While *koplas* as a genre go back to the pre-expulsion period, they were first published, as mentioned before, in the sixteenth century by Eleazar Soncino. In the eighteenth century, they were reprinted and transmitted in print, until some entered the oral tradition.[130] Initially, they were composed by rabbis for Jewish holidays, especially Purim, but later their topics went beyond religion. The most famous eighteenth-century edition is *Koplas de Yosef ha-Tsadik* by Abraham de Toledo, published in Constantinople in 1732.[131] Asá's *Tsorche Tssibbur*, whose subtitle is *Dinim kojidos de libros de konsuelos* (Rules gathered from books of consolation), and which appeared a year later, belongs to the same genre, because it has the same purpose to teach precepts of Judaism by presenting them in the form of couplets.

Yet the scope of Asá's work goes far beyond that of any other *koplas*. He announces at the outset that he has translated into Ladino the laws of Judaism to make them available to "sons, fathers, and grandfathers" who do not know Hebrew.[132] Asá effectively relayed a significant part of *Shulchan Aruch*, whose sixteenth-century Ladino version, proclaimed incomprehensible by Huli, he replaced in 1749 with his *Shulchan ha-melech*. Because of its subject matter, *Tsorche Tsibbur* contains a great number of Hebrew words, phrases, and formulas, which required of readers a limited knowledge of Hebrew. We can assume, therefore, that Asá's addressees knew enough to understand religious terms and prayers but were unable to read a Hebrew book. It is for this better educated male audience that Asá produced his translations of Elijah Ha-Kohen's *Shevet Musar* (1842), *Sefer Ben Gorion* (1843), and Isaac Aboab's fourteenth-century ethical treatise *Menorat ha-Maor* (1762).

"In the Sight of the Nations"

In the so-called "golden age" of Ladino literature, David Attias, author of *La Güerta de Oro* (Livorno, 1778), claimed that young Ottoman Jews had nothing to read because, unlike all "other nations," Sephardim did not print any useful books "in our Levantine Spanish language: not historical accounts ancient or modern, nor any book on geography or other sciences, not even books dealing with commerce."[133] In his opinion, books produced by the rabbis were boring and could not satisfy the needs of the time, since "everything there deals with the Law and is in the holy tongue, which only few understand."[134] In Attias's view, the rabbis do not realize that young people are more alert now than earlier generations, and that "not all of them are inclined toward studying the Torah, and to see and hear always the same things repeated and repeated all over again."

This bold pronouncement appeared in print only because *La Güerta de oro* saw light outside the Ottoman Empire, where all book publishing was controlled by rabbis. It was published by a Christian printer in Livorno where, after 1743, the final decision to permit the printing of a book was granted either by Tuscan authorities or the lay leadership of the community.[135]

David Attias, an Ottoman Jew born in Sarajevo, moved to Livorno no later than 1769.[136] There, he tells us, he received his education and, following his passion, became a merchant. Like all Sephardi vernacular authors, he felt the need to educate Ottoman Jews and do so in the "Levantine language," "for there are a lot of people who do not understand the real Spanish language." According to Attias, young people want to learn new things and read new books written in a "language and script that they understand, in witty and enjoyable language, but which are at the same time intelligent." In other words, they do not understand Hebrew, cannot read square letters, and, it seems, do not find the available amusing stories "intelligent." (The latter comment might have been a reference to chivalric novels.) Like Huli, Attias declares that the new generation is eager to learn but has nothing to read.

The rationale for Attias's educational program is announced by the book's motto that is later repeated in the text. It is the second part of a biblical verse, Deuteronomy 4:6, which I am quoting in full:

> (a) Keep therefore and do them [God's statutes, i.e., the commandments] for this is your wisdom and your understanding in the sight of the nations, which shall hear all these statutes, (b) and say, "Surely this great nation is a wise and understanding people."

Thus, unlike the rabbis, Attias does not tell his intended readers, identified as young merchants, that they will be punished in the world to come if they do not perform the commandments. Instead, he warns them that if they try to do business in Europe, they will always be "in the sight of the nations" who are superior to Ottoman Jews and will scorn them for their ignorance. The only remedy, therefore, is to read and learn. Matthias Lehmann, author of the only study of Attias's work, notes in this connection:

> *La Güerta de oro* echoes a common theme in the writings of the early *Haskalah*, namely the frustration with being perceived as ignorant by Christian society and eager to restore the place of the Jews in a world of knowledge.[137]

But what was a common theme for European Jews was news to Ottoman Sephardim. On the other hand, even Huli, as we know, lamented the fact that Christians considered Jews stupid. Attias, however, was the first in the long line of Sephardi literati who *constantly* felt being "in the sight of the nations" and wrote about it. Moreover, as far as we know, he was the first Ladino author to report an encounter with Judeophobia and partially blame the Jews for it. He says that while God wanted the Jews to be seen as a wise people, "because of our sins," "the nations" consider them "the most ignorant and evil people," who "know only one science: to trade and cheat."[138]

Yet Attias is almost equally frustrated by the superiority of European Jews who look down on "Levantines." In fact, as Lehmann observes, it is often impossible to tell whether he talks about Jews or Christians, all of whom he calls "Europeans" (*frankos*).

La Güerta de oro introduced many things in Ladino literature for the first time, because it was the first work whose author was not a rabbi. Hence, Attias did not consider Hebrew a viable language of communication, but, instead, explained why he was not writing in "real Spanish." Like his predecessors, he translated and summarized in Ladino some of the texts he found important, but all were originally written in European languages. He claims to know French, Latin, Italian, Turkish, Serbian, and a few other languages, mentioning in passing that he knows a little (*algo de*) Hebrew.

La Güerta de oro reveals the author's familiarity with some works of Italian and French literatures (such as Jean de La Fontaine's fables and Pietro Metastasio's poetry) and books on etiquette that were then popular in Europe. Lehmann notes that Attias also quotes *Le parfait négociant* by Jacques Savary, "a seventeenth century classic of mercantilism."[139]

Attias's book is an anthology that includes treatises and letters on such wide-ranging subjects as commerce, astrology, physiognomy, education of children, European etiquette, causes of infertility, and many other topics, but no religious ones.[140] The most revolutionary innovation of *La Güerta de oro* is the author's advice to Sephardim to learn foreign languages, which rabbis tried to oppose even a century later. For instance, in 1876, one of them wanted to ban language instruction in schools, because it led to reading "books about the religions of the nations of the world, and [about] natural philosophy, which is forbidden because it contradicts knowledge of the Divine."[141]

Attias, however, believed that basic knowledge of Italian was the minimum requirement for any merchant trading in Europe, which is why the first chapter of *La Güerta de oro* is an Italian lesson. He teaches his readers not only the Latin alphabet, but also, using Ladino words as examples, explains Italian sounds. Charts with letters and sounds are

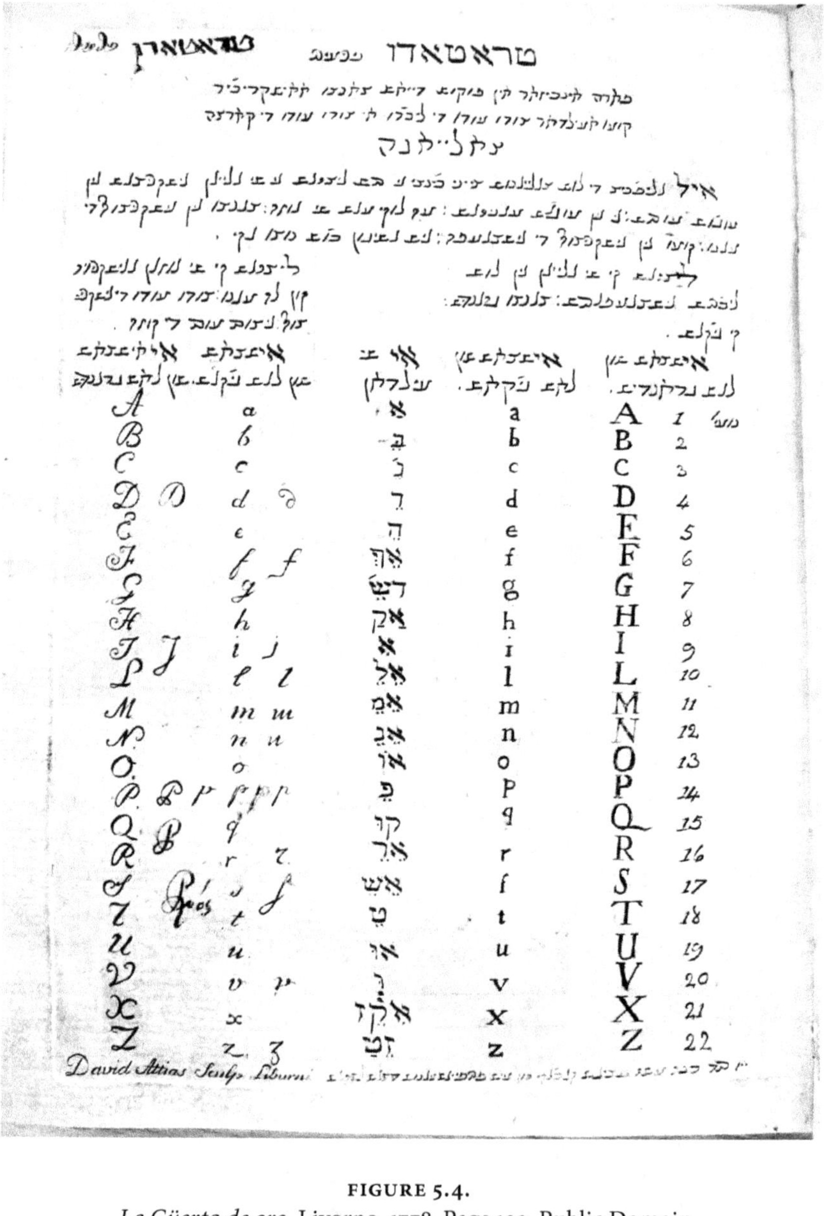

David Attias Sculp. Liburni

FIGURE 5.4.
La Güerta de oro. Livorno, 1778. Page 12a. Public Domain.
Jewish Theological Seminary.

followed by Italian dialogue and a list of proverbs. While his pedagogical methods are imperfect, his endeavor is astonishing.[142]

His approach to education drastically differs from that of the "vernacular rabbis." While they aimed at fully controlling what their audiences read and believed, explaining everything they deemed important in their own words, Attias never patronizes his readers and encourages them to study on their own. Having taught them letters and sounds, Attias concludes that now they can learn Italian without him: "Everybody needs to have the desire to persevere in this, because you will not find a better teacher than your own desire."[143] Attias claims to have produced his book for the benefit of "a friend of his in the East," but he hopes that it will be "useful" to all those Levantines who care about their property, the joy of their hearts, and the knowledge of what they do not yet know."[144] It should be noted that while writing for literate male readers, he encourages them to read parts of his book to their wives and fiancées (if they are illiterate). Although his attitude toward wives' education does not essentially differ from the rabbis' approach, he has a separate (and philosophically profound) chapter that tells a mother what she should teach her son.

It is common in the scholarly literature to compare Attias to nineteenth-century Sephardi westernizers and present his work as a precursor of the Ladino press. However, Attias differs from most later literati no less than he resembles them, and his book has affinities only with the early Ladino press, because he was not interested in mass education, and did not aim at making his readers good Jews or good Ottoman subjects, but rather, good Jewish merchants. Besides, his attitude toward Europe is not the uncritical admiration of nineteenth-century westernizers, but the respect of someone who recognizes the merits of a rival and wants to prevail. At the same time, one cannot deny Attias a certain idealism and a *Haskalah*-inspired faith in education as a means of battling Judeophobia. (Later, this idea was espoused by the Alliance Israélite Universelle, a philanthropic organization founded in Paris in 1860 for the purpose of "reforming" Jews and thus overcoming antisemitism.) What later Ladino literature did have in common with *La Güerta de oro* is that it always existed in the presence of an imaginary European observer, whether Jewish or Christian, since the perspective was often the same.

As in the case of Almosnino's *Crónica*, the significance of *La Güerta de Oro* for Ladino literature is negligible at best, since we do not even know how many copies of the book reached its addressees. However, Attias's work is important for my study, because it indicates that in the last quarter of the eighteenth century the Ladino-reading public was not homogeneous, and there were men interested in "useful" vernacular literature. Although they could not have been numerous, like the ex-*conversos*, those men were the most socially mobile and interested in change.

The Emergence of the Ladino Press

It is not coincidental that the first extant announcement of a Ladino periodical appeared in 1842, because the Ladino press emerged as a consequence of two historic events that took place in 1839 and 1840 and impacted the lives of Ottoman Jews in different ways. On November 3, 1839, the *Hatt-i Sherif* of Gülhane (the Noble Rescript of the Rose Chamber) proclaimed the beginning of the *Tanzimat*, a series of reforms aimed at transforming the Ottoman Empire into a modern state.[145] The rescript guaranteed the life, honor, and property of all subjects without distinction of race or religion, thus implying equality between Muslims and non-Muslims. Some Sephardim concerned about the diminishing role of their community welcomed the reforms as an opportunity for its advancement. Aware that Jews continued to lose out to other Ottoman communities in the economic sphere, they believed that commercial information and modern instruction, together with their anticipated new legal status, would improve Sephardim's financial prospects.

The second event was a prolonged crisis caused by the blood libels in Damascus and Rhodes, both of which erupted in February 1840.[146] Although the Porte eventually intervened on the side of the Jews, this happened chiefly under pressure from England, whose government acted in response to the appeals of some influential British Jews and the press campaign they organized. Awareness of new persecutions and the realization of the newspapers' power led to an unprecedented rise of Jewish journalism in the 1840s in various parts of the world.[147]

The importance of the press for building international Jewish solidarity became evident also to some Ottoman Jews, including the chief rabbi of Izmir, Pinchas de Segura. In a sermon delivered in honor of Sir Moses Montefiore's visit in October 1840, he emphasized the role played by "written works and letters" in rescuing the Jews of Damascus and Rhodes.[148] In addition, as a result of closer contacts between Ashkenazim and Sephardim during the blood libels, many European Jews became aware of the poverty and "backwardness" of their Ottoman coreligionists. Their compassion notwithstanding, the former did not hesitate to let the latter know what they thought in the pages of their newly established periodicals. Thus, the early Ladino press (1840s–1860s) appeared in response to the need of the merchant class for economic information, a growing sense of Sephardim's ignorance in religious and secular matters unacceptable in the new circumstances, and—in the words of an Anglo-Jewish newspaper—a desire to join "the great chain of communication . . . between Jews all over the world."[149]

To create the first Ladino periodical in the Ottoman Empire, however, it was necessary not only to find resources and a printing press not controlled by the rabbis, but—much more important—to make sure there would be a reading public interested in something they had not seen before. It is not surprising, therefore, that the first attempt to create a Sephardi newspaper failed. Nevertheless, the same person made another courageous attempt and succeeded.

This man, Rafael Uziel (1816–1881), was a merchant and member of a Franco family that had come to Izmir from Livorno in the seventeenth century. He held Tuscan citizenship and possibly not only visited Livorno, but also studied at its Talmud Torah.[150] Of all Sephardi journalists, Uziel had the closest cultural affinity with Attias and was the likeliest person to have read his work, but his concerns went beyond the interests of the merchant class.

Livorno, "a major center for the production and dissemination of economic information," even in Attias's time, had weekly bulletins that contained "updates on prices, currency exchange rates, insurance premiums, and stock values."[151] In the Ottoman Empire, such information became available only in the nineteenth century thanks to European newspapers, the first of which, *La Gazette française de Constantinople*, came out in 1796.[152]

In Izmir, French-language periodicals first appeared in the 1820s. Since Jewish merchants who traded with Europe or other parts of the empire needed to have commercial information and updates on port traffic, we can assume that some were able to read French. The fact that in the 1840s *L'Écho de l'Orient*, a local French-language newspaper, frequently printed local and international Jewish news confirms this assumption. Hence, only those Jewish traders who did not know European languages would have been interested in a Ladino periodical as a source of commercial information. But they would not have been the most successful ones and thus might have found the rather expensive subscription to Uziel's projected newspaper unaffordable.

Indeed, Uziel's first publishing endeavor failed, because he did not garner enough subscriptions. *La Buena Esperansa* (The Good Hope) scheduled to appear in the summer of 1842 did not go beyond the prospectus. While the prospectus is not extant, it was summarized in a German Jewish periodical that states that the forthcoming Judeo-Spanish weekly will contain:

> commercial news, exchange rates, port traffic updates, and advertisements of auctions and sales, as well as political news from all parts of the world, and finally, articles that aim at spreading light and knowledge among the Jews of the Turkish Empire.[153]

The same paper quoted two Ladino sentences from the prospectus:

> And we will often publish things necessary for success with which few people of our nation in these parts are familiar. But the sages in our parts of Turkey do not waste or employ their time on such things, nor do they study, and this is so because of the great poverty and a great lack of money in these parts.

Clearly, Uziel addressed the same audience as Attias, namely, "all those Levantines who care about their property . . . and the knowledge of what they do not yet know."

We have no information on the press that printed the prospectus of *La Buena Esperansa*, but we can be sure that it was the same one that in 1845–1846 printed *Shaarei mizrach*, the first Ladino newspaper.[154] This press was run by an English Protestant, G. Griffith, who had a Rashi typeface because missionaries published Christian literature in Ladino. Between 1841 and 1844, there was just one Jewish printer in Izmir, Shmuel Hakim, and he probably did not have a Rashi font since he printed only

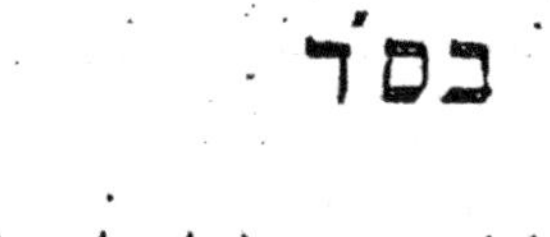

FIGURE 5.5.
Shaarei mizrach. Masthead. Public Domain.
Ben Zvi Institute Library (Jerusalem).

Hebrew books. But he would not have agreed to print a newspaper in any case, because as we know, no book could be printed without the approval of the rabbis, and they would not have consented to a periodical, let alone one that criticized them.

Regardless of whether Uziel had close connections with the missionaries, as suggested by Dov Cohen, Griffith would have been willing to print a Ladino newspaper, because missionaries supported the secularization of Ottoman Jews, believing that it gave them better chances to convert them.[155]

Uziel's second undertaking was successful. On December 29, 1845, the first issue of *Shaarei mizrach Las Puertas de Oriente* (The Gates of the East) saw light. According to the editor, the circulation of this bimonthly was under 100 copies (no. 2, 17), but it had distributors in other Ottoman cities. Curiously, in the top right corner of *Shaarei mizrach* one finds the letters *bet, samech, daled*, an acronym for the Aramaic expression meaning "with the help of the heavens." At the time, this acronym was commonly used in private correspondence. Its appearance in Uziel's periodical might have been a way of affirming that despite the paper being printed at a Christian press, its publisher was a pious Jew. In addition, the newspaper's motto was a biblical verse accompanied by its Aramaic translation from Targum Jonathan. (See fig. 5.5.)

Published in the early years of the *Tanzimat*, *Shaarei mizrach* was intended to be not only a commercial bulletin but also a tool of Jewish education, thus challenging the rabbis' monopoly in this sphere. This was the beginning of intense competition between rabbis and westernizers for Ladino-reading audiences, which lasted for about fifty years.

Uziel was well informed, both about the circumstances of the two blood libels and the actions of European Jews, through Isaac Pincherle, a Triestine merchant who had resided in Izmir since 1829. Pincherle was directly involved in rescuing the Jews of Rhodes and personally knew Montefiore. In fact, Uziel probably met the English philanthropist himself during the latter's visit to Izmir. In any case, in 1842, Montefiore welcomed Uziel's plan to establish a Ladino periodical, and was aware of the appearance of *Shaarei mizrach*. (In February-March 1846, *The Jewish Chronicle* published at least three advertisements urging the English-speaking public to subscribe to "The Gates of the East.")

Judging by the materials Uziel published in his paper, Isaac Pincherle and his brother must have shared with him the Jewish periodicals they received from Europe, namely, *The Voice of Jacob*, *The Jewish Chronicle*, and *Les Archives Israélites*. Thus, Uziel had access both to local and international business-oriented newspapers (e.g., *L'Écho de l'Orient* and *Chambers's Edinburgh*) and some European Jewish periodicals, all of which helped him create his own paper.

The eight pages of *Shaarei mizrach* were divided into two parts. The first started with the editorial discussing a biblical verse or a religious question. It was followed by a lengthy section on Ottoman news, after which there would be a rather long article on natural history or sciences. Then came international and local Jewish news and, sometimes, a sensational crime report. The second part had commercial information that included wholesale prices, exchange rates, and port traffic updates.

It must be emphasized that the biblical title and mottos of Uziel's newspaper, its abundant use of biblical and rabbinic quotes (in Hebrew with Ladino translations), and, particularly, his editorials on faith were certainly not just a means of "proving his unquestionable loyalty to Judaism" in view of his connections to the missionaries.[156] This was in fact a crucial element of his program to transform Ottoman Sephardim into modern Jews by providing them with both secular and religious education in the new spirit. It is noteworthy that he relates, with cautious sympathy (which would not have endeared him to the rabbis), an article from *L'Impartial de Smyrne* on reforms of Jewish practices in Berlin (no. 2; 3).

An adherent of the *Haskalah*, Uziel explains that God endowed man with intelligence that he is obliged to use to get closer to his creator. Furthermore, God gave the Jews the title of "a wise and understanding people," and they have to deserve the right to be called this name by learning and educating their sons. Yet at present, "the other nations despise us saying, 'Where is your wisdom?'" and the Jews of Europe are wondering why Sephardim are behind all other nations. Uziel urges his "brothers" to teach their sons more things than their fathers had taught them, because the world has changed since then. Their sons should learn not only the Law of Moses but also sciences, languages, and other alphabets, which will awaken their minds and will enable Sephardim to follow the way of "the most civilized nations of Europe" (nos. 3; 17, 4; 25, 9; 65). One of the ways to achieve this, according to *Shaarei mizrach*, was to take advantage of state educational institutions, which included the medical school, the artillery school, and some others that opened to non-Muslims.[157]

"The other nations" that Uziel constantly mentions in his newspaper are not European Christians ("the nations"), but other *millets*, i.e., the religious communities of the Ottoman Empire. Nos. 8 through 11 provide long accounts of the sultan's trips to various cities in the European part of the empire with high proportions of Christians. These events give Uziel an occasion to offer his readers civic education. With astonishing insightfulness, he describes Abdulmecid's reforms as "extraordinary deeds in the eyes of history" (no. 9; 65). He quotes Reshid Pasha, architect of the *Tanzimat*, who declares that now "we are all the subjects of the same empire, children of the same country. We are all fellow-countrymen and fellow-citizens." Hence, we must "endeavor with all our energy to contribute to the common good of our common country" (no. 9; 66).

Shaarei mizrach reports that during his visit to Edirne the sultan invited religious leaders of "all the nations" to his palace. Addressing them on behalf of the sultan, Reshid Pasha said that "all his subjects without exception enjoy equal protection in accordance with our holy laws, which support the rights and beliefs of every person" (no. 9; 65). Uziel's accounts of how inhabitants of each city greeted the sultan in various languages, all of them shouting "amen" and throwing flowers on the road in front of him immediately bring to mind Almosnino's first Ottoman chronicle. Moreover, Uziel also provides a list of troops accompanying the sultan with their Turkish names. Yet a more profound similarity between the two authors separated by three centuries is their civic enthusiasm at two crucial points in the history of Eastern Sephardim: their settling in the Ottoman Empire as *zimmis* with significant internal autonomy and the abolition (albeit until 1856 only on paper) of *zimmet* (the *dhimma*). Yet it is noteworthy that unlike his predecessor who called *patria* only Salonica, i.e., his community, Uziel applied this term to the whole empire.

No doubt, on December 12, 1939, he was among those who attended the historic event reported by many European periodicals:

> The Hatti Scheriff was promulgated at Smyrna with great pomp on the 12th ult. in presence of the Governor, the Mollah, the Mufti, the Ulemas, the Greek and Armenian Archbishops, the Great Rabbi of the Jews, all the European Consuls, the garrison, and an immense concourse of people.[158]

The difference between Almosnino and Uziel is that the former was commissioned to produce chronicles by a small group of court Jews connected to the center of power through personal ties, whereas the latter was the first Jewish intellectual to establish a direct formal relationship with the state by officially licensing his newspaper, as was required by the decree of 1841.[159] Like Almosnino, Uziel addressed the most active and enterprising members of his community hoping to educate them and prepare them to work for the benefit of their homeland. However, in 1846 in Izmir this audience was too small to keep a Ladino periodical going. As a result, *Shaarei mizrach* closed in November of that year, leaving its editor with a large debt.[160]

Nevertheless, other early Ladino periodicals continued to address educated male readers engaged in trade and financial activities and able to read some Hebrew. The second newspaper, *Or Israel* (The Light to Israel, Constantinople, 1853–1855), was edited by Leon Hayim de Castro, a member of an influential Franco family.[161] The two extant issues deal only with secular matters, such as the Crimean War and some financial news. De Castro had the same representative in Bucharest as Uziel. The short-lived *El Dragoman* (The Translator, Vienna, 1856), edited by Joseph Calvo, was the first periodical targeting Ottoman Jews but published outside the empire.

The first long-lived Ladino newspaper, *El Jurnal israelit* (Constantinople, 1860–1873), was edited by Yehezkel Gabay.[162] It served as the organ of the *Meclis pekidim* (the lay council of notables in charge of communal affairs), which consisted of leading figures of the Constantinople community, mainly Francos, headed by Abraham de Camondo, an Austrian subject, the most influential Jew in the empire. *El Lunar* (Moonlight, Salonica, 1864–1865), an encyclopedic monthly almanac, aimed at enlightening its readers in various fields of knowledge without moralizing.[163] Its editor, r. Judah Nehama (probably an English protégé), was a scholar, educator, and social activist.

El Verdadero progreso israelita (The true Jewish progress, 1864), while intended for Ottoman Jews, came out in Paris, presumably because its editor, Ezra Benveniste, who came from Jerusalem, wanted to be close to the Alliance Israélite Universelle, which gave it some funding.[164] Initially, this newspaper included a page in French, and it always printed some articles in Hebrew, since Benveniste was interested in religion no less than Uziel. In fact, the latter was its correspondent in Gallipoli, while Nehama was its representative in Salonica.

Conclusion

The second period in the history of Ladino literature started with an audacious educational project that targeted a large and partly illiterate audience of both sexes with the purpose of making them better Jews. Given that the early *Meam Loez* volumes and Asá's translation of the Five Scrolls were reprinted even in the nineteenth century, we can conclude that "vernacular rabbis" initially managed to reach mass readerships, even if their works did not replace European novels. However, the authors of all later *Meam Loez* commentaries, starting with Magriso (during his work on Leviticus, published in 1753), experienced financial difficulties and complained that people did not buy enough books to support printing.[165] In the nineteenth century, things got much worse.[166] This may suggest that Huli's volumes sold so well because Sephardim enjoyed his work, and not because they were interested in Bible commentaries as such. Another reason why rabbis who wanted to continue the series, just like Uziel, did not get enough subscriptions was general poverty among Ottoman Jews.

It is clear that in the eighteenth century there already were people who were not satisfied with having only religious books and who craved practical secular knowledge that would help them in trade. This kind of reading, however, did not become available until 1846. Convinced that educated young men would help the Jewish community catch up with other *millets* and thus earn the respect of Europeans, the first Sephardi journalists started their own educational endeavor, which initially did not have much impact on the community, because their periodicals were read by very few people. For the same reason, they were not economically viable. Only by turning to mass audiences and publishing serialized novels suitable for collective reading, did Sephardi literati achieve modest commercial success and significantly contribute to the westernization of their community. But this did not start until the 1870s. By addressing Sephardim of both sexes and all ages, westernizers effectively moved into the territory of the "vernacular rabbis," who responded by persecuting and even excommunicating them. This clash of two educational ideals first announced by David Attias ended in the victory of secularization and secular literature.

Though the status of Hebrew was never challenged directly, secularization and westernization (which came hand-in-hand with it) undermined the prestige of the culture it represented, so that by the last third of the nineteenth century its functions had been limited to liturgy and religious education. Under such circumstances, one would expect the vernacular to assume the functions no longer performed by the H language (the language of high culture), but this did not happen in the case of Ladino. As we know, its high register had disappeared by the turn of the seventeenth century, together with the genres that required it. In addition, in the 1740s, after the appearance of Asá's Prophets and the Five Scrolls, it became clear that the calque style of Bible translations could never be used again. Having written hundreds of pages in the only available register, *ladino klaro*, "vernacular rabbis" effectively made it the language of mass education and popular literature, with which it became associated forever.

Hence, even when Hebrew was used only for religious purposes, Ladino, due to its low social prestige, did not become a vehicle of high culture. As a result, this function was assigned to French, whose presence in the Sephardi community expanded, thanks to the growing number of Alliance Israélite Universelle schools. By the early 1890s, young Sephardi literati began to produce newspapers and books in French for intracommunal purposes, that is for educated Jews who knew Hebrew but chose to read and write in French.

This turned the diglossic situation into a triglossic one, with two H languages. Thus, four hundred years after the expulsion, French became a second ethnic marker of Sephardi Jews.[167] As we will see in the epilogue, in the twentieth century, those Sephardi authors who admired Almosnino's "Spanish," discussed his work mainly in French.

Notes

1. Daniel Goffman, "Izmir: From Village to Colonial Port City," in *The Ottoman City between East and West. Aleppo, Izmir, and Istanbul*, eds. Daniel Goffman, Edhem Eldem, and Bruce Masters, (New York, 1999), 79–134, 89.

2. Ibid., 89–90.

3. Goffman, *Izmir and the Levantine World, 1550–1650* (Seattle and London, 1990), 84.

4. Goffman, "Izmir: From Village to Colonial Port City," 95.

5. Ibid., 98.

6. Fuat Dundar, "Empire of Taxonomy: Ethnic and Religious Identities in the Ottoman Surveys and Census," *Middle Eastern Studies* 51 (2015): 1, 136–158, 147.

7. Rozen uses a tax evasion rate of 20 percent for the Jewish population of Constantinople. (Rozen, *Istanbul*, 50.)

8. Barnai, "Organization and Leadership in the Jewish Community of Izmir in the Seventeenth Century," in *The Jews of the Ottoman Empire*, 275–284, 277.

9. In Spain, 1680 marked the climax of the Spanish Inquisition's persecution of Portuguese "new Christians." At the *auto-da-fé* in Madrid, on June 30, 1680, 118 *conversos* were sentenced in actuality or in effigy. At least twenty-one were executed (an all-time record), and eight burned alive. (Antonio Jose Saraiva, *The Marrano Factory. The Portuguese Inquisition and Its New Christians, 1536–1765* [Leiden, Boston, and Köln, 2001], 216–217.)

10. Miriam Bodian, *Hebrews of the Portuguese Nation* (Bloomington, 1997), 156–157.

11. Barnai, "Christian Messianism and the Portuguese Marranos: The Emergence of Sabbateanism in Smyrna," *Jewish History* 7, no. 2 (1993): 119–126, 121.

12. Goffman, "Izmir: From Village to Colonial Port City," 100.

13. Trivellato, *The Familiarity of Strangers*, 115.

14. Rozen, "Strangers in a Strange Land: The Extraterritorial Status of Jews in Italy and the Ottoman Empire in the 16th to the 18th Centuries," in *Ottoman and Turkish Jewry: Community and Leadership*, ed. Aron Rodrigue (Bloomington, 1992), 123–166, 147.

15. Trivellato, *The Familiarity of Strangers*, 115, 100.

16. The term "Franco" is used somewhat differently by different scholars, and its meaning in Ladino was not always the same. I use it only to refer to the Jews residing in the Ottoman Empire while holding foreign citizenship, regardless of whether they were born in Europe or the empire. Most, but not all, Francos born abroad came from Livorno.

17. On the status of Spanish, see Cecil Roth, "The Role of Spanish in the Marrano Diaspora," in *Studies in Books and Booklore: Essays in Jewish Bibliography*, ed. Cecil Roth (Westmead, 1972), 111–120; Minervini, "*Llevaron de acá nuestra lengua. . .*"

18. Barnai, "Organization and Leadership in the Jewish Community of Izmir," 277.

19. Marvin J. Heller, *Printing the Talmud; A History of the Individual Treatises Printed from 1700 to 1750* (Leiden, 1999), 328.

20. Francesca Bregoli, *Mediterranean Enlightenment, Livornese Jews, Tuscan Culture* (Stanford CA, 2014), 183.

21. Heller, *Printing the Talmud*, 328.

22. Abraham Yaari, "Hebrew Printing in Izmir," *Aresheth* 1 (1958): 97–222, 100 (Heb.).

23. See Cecil Roth and Adri K. Offenberg, "Manasseh (Menasseh) ben Israel," *Encyclopaedia Judaica.*

24. Roth, "The Marrano typography in England," in *Studies in Books and Booklore*, 1–11, 2.

25. See the facsimile in Yaari, "Hebrew Printing in Izmir," 102.

26. Roth, "The Spanish Press in Smyrna," in *Studies in Books and Booklore*, 23–26, 26.

27. Barnai, "Christian Messianism," 121.

28. Ibid.

29. Gershom Scholem, *Sabbatai Sevi: The Mystical Messiah* (Princeton, 1973), 150.

30. Yaari, "Hebrew Printing in Izmir," 101; Heller, *Printing the Talmud*, 328.

31. Quoted in Hacker, "Authors, Readers, and Printers," 18.

32. Heller, *Printing the Talmud*, 328.

33. Ibid. 330.

34. Ibid., 330–331.

35. Quoted in Hacker, "Authors, Readers, and Printers," 18.

36. Réné Bekius, "Polyglot Amsterdam Printing Presses 1620s–1720s: Armenian and Jewish Printers Compared," in *Printing and Publishing in the Middle East*, ed. Philip Sadgrove, *Journal of Semitic Studies*, Supplement 24 (2008): 23–64, 56.

37. See Aleksandar Fotić, "Belgrade: A Muslim and Non-Muslim Cultural Centre (Sixteenth-Seventeenth Centuries)," in *Provincial Elites in the Ottoman Empire*, ed. Antonis Anastasopoulos (Rethymno, 2005), 51–75.

38. Barnai, "Christian Messianism," 121.

39. For the text and a brief discussion, see Bernard Lewis, "A Letter from Little Menachem," in *Studies in Judaism and Islam*, presented to Shelomoh Dov Goitein, ed. Sh. Morag et al. (Jerusalem, 1981), 181–183.

40. Quoted in Matthias Lehmann, "A Livornese 'Port Jew' and the Sephardim of the Ottoman Empire," *Jewish Social Studies* 11, no. 2 (2005): 51–76, 59.

41. Minervini, "An *Aljamiado* Version of 'Orlando Furioso,'" 192.

42. For a short version of Shabbetay Zvi's biography, see Scholem, "Shabbetai Zevi," *Encyclopedia Judaica*. An account of the Sabbatean movement in the Ottoman context is found in Cengiz Şişman, *The Burden of Silence: Sabbatai Sevi and the Evolution of the Ottoman Dönmes* (Oxford, 2015), chs. 1–2.

43. Goffman, *Izmir and the Levantine World*, 92.

44. Idem, "Izmir: From Village to Colonial Port City," 110.

45. Ibid., 123.

46 Fatma Müge Göçek, *East Encounters West: France and the Ottoman Empire in the Eighteenth Century* (New York and Oxford, 1987), 123.

47. Rozen, "Salonica," *EJIW*.

48. Rozen, "Contest and Rivalry in Mediterranean Maritime Commerce in the First Half of the Eighteenth Century: The Jews of Salonika and the European Presence," *Revue des Etudes Juives* 147, nos. 3–4 (1988): 309–352, 329.

49. See Lehmann, *Emissaries from the Holy Land: The Sephardic Diaspora and the Practice of Pan-Judaism in the Eighteenth Century* (Stanford, CA, 2014), 92.

50. Rozen, "Contest and Rivalry," 351.

51. Trivellato, *The Familiarity of Strangers*, 86. See illustrations there.

52. Cynthia Crews, *Extracts from the Me'am Lo'ez (Genesis) with a Translation and Glossary* (Leeds, 1960), 21. My translation.

53. See Matthew Elliot, "Dress Codes in The Ottoman Empire: The Case of the Frank," in *Ottoman Customs: From Textile to Identity*, eds. Suraiya Faroqhi and Christoph K. Neuman (Istanbul, 2004), 103–123.

54. Elliott Horowitz, "The Early Eighteenth Century Confronts the Beard: Kabbalah and Jewish Self- Fashioning," *Jewish History* 8, nos. 1–2 (1994): 95–115, 101.

55. Ibid., 105.

56. Joseph ben Isaac Moses Montequio, *Sefer Ketonet Yosef* (Salonica, 1763). The passage relating this incident is found in *Sephardi Lives: A Documentary*

History of the Ottoman Judeo-Spanish World and its Diaspora, 1700–1950, eds. Julia P. Cohen and Sarah A. Stein (Stanford, CA, 2014), 34. Introduced and translated by Matt Goldish.

57. Elisheva Carlebach, *The Pursuit of Heresy* (New York, 1990), 166.

58. For instance, a well-known Armenian author, Eremya Chelebi Komurjian, Shabbetay Zvi's contemporary, wrote a long narrative poem and a short rhymed one about him. Eremya is very sympathetic with the Jews but, naturally, is hostile to the pseudo-messiah. Some Sabbatean texts were translated into Armenian and Greek. (See "Introduction" in *Eremya Chelebi Komurjian's Armeno-Turkish poem "The Jewish Bride,"* eds. Avedis K. Sanjian and Andreas Tietze (Wiesbaden, 1981), 27–29.

59. Carlebach, *The Pursuit of Heresy*, 167.

60. Ibid., 86.

61. Ibid.

62. Aitor García Moreno, ed. *Relatos del pueblo ladinán (Me'am Lo'ez de Éxodo I)* (Madrid, 204), no. 13, 54–55.

63. Ibid., no. 14, 56–57.

64. An innovative article by Cihan Artunç argues that a wider range of legal choices had a higher value than the potential financial gains, which explains why some people purchased more than one *berat*. ("The Price of Legal Institutions: The *Beratlı* Merchants in the Eighteenth-Century Ottoman Empire," *The Journal of Economic History* 75, no. 3 [2015]: 720–746.)

65. See Eyal Ginio, "Jews and European Subjects in Eighteenth-Century Salonica: The Ottoman Perspective," *Jewish History* 28, nos. 3–4 (2014): 289–312.

66. Lehmann, *Ladino Rabbinic Literature and Ottoman Sephardic Culture*, 34.

67. Ibid., 38.

68. On Elijah Ha-Kohen, see Scholem, "Elijah Ha-Kohen Itamari and Sabbateanism," in *Alexander Marx Jubilee Volume on the Occasion of His Seventieth Birthday*, Jewish Theological Seminary (New York, 1950), 451-470. (Heb.)

Among Ashkenazi's most famous volumes is the *Tikkunei Zohar* (an appendix to *Zohar*), which became a standard edition of this text. Ashkenazi acquired the original in Egypt, where he traveled in 1714 in search of manuscripts for printing, and he published it in 1719. The following year, he traveled back to Poland and then to Holland, where the followers of Shabbetay Zvi continued to be active. (Yaari, "Ashkenazi, Jonah ben Jacob," *Encyclopedia Judaica*).

69. Maoz Kahana, "The Allure of Forbidden Knowledge: The Temptation of Sabbatean Literature for Mainstream Rabbis in the Frankist Moment, 1756–1761," *Jewish Quarterly Review* 102, no. 4 (2012): 589–616, 615.

70. On Frank, see Pawel Maciejko, *The Mixed Multitude: Jacob Frank and the Frankist Movement* (Philadelphia, 2009).

71. "Judah ben Samuel Rosanes," *The Jewish Encyclopedia*.

72. The Hebrew introduction to Genesis is divided into ten sections, which I cite by Roman numerals. See David Gonzalo Maeso and Pascual Recuero, eds.

Me'am Lo'ez. El gran comentario bíblico sefardi (Granada, 1969), vol. I: *Beresit* [Genesis], parte 1, 41–46.

73. Lehmann, *Ladino Rabbinic Literature, 38.*

74. The Ladino introduction to *Meam Loez* as a whole is cited from: David Gonzalo Maeso and Pascual Recuero, eds. *Me'am Lo'ez. El gran comentario bíblico sefardí* (Madrid, 1964), Vol. 0 (Preliminar): Prolegommenos, 142.

75. Ibid., 147.

76. Leah Bornstein-Makovetsky, "Ashkenazi, Jonah ben Jacob," EJIW.

77. Yaari, "Hebrew Printing in Izmir," 97.

78. Göçek, *East Encounters West*, 115. A French missionary states that in 1729 the Ottoman press "was run by a wretched Polish Jew who knew very little Turkish." (Ibid., 114.)

79. Ibid.

80 Abraham Haim and Yaacov Geller, "Istanbul. Hebrew Printing," *Encyclopedia Judaica.*

81. Meyer Kayserling, Louis Ginzberg, and Lazarus Grünhut, "Yakov Culi," *The Jewish Encyclopedia.*

82. Ibid.

83. Ibid.

84. See Lehmann, "Culi (Hulli), Jacob ben Meir," EJIW. For comparison, the first Turkish press produced 500 copies of most of its volumes, though in a few cases this number came up to 1,000 and 1,200. (William J. Watson, "Ibrahim Muteferrika and Turkish Incunabula," *Journal of the American Oriental Society* 88, no. 3 [1968]: 435–441, 437.) In Amsterdam, in 1676, only one printer produced 6,000 copies of the Yiddish Bible. (Bekius, Polyglot Amsterdam Printing Presses, 35.)

85. Lehmann, "Culi (Hulli)."

86. Idem, "Assa, Abraham Ben Isaac," EJIW.

87. See Yaari, *Hebrew Printing in Constantinople*, no. 324.

88. Lehmann, "Assa, Abraham Ben Isaac."

89. In the introduction, Ashkenazi explains that the readers asked him to use Rashi letters. (Quoted in Romero, *Creación literaria*, 40.)

90. On Huli's sources, see ibid., 88.

91. *Me'am Lo'ez*, vol. 0, 147.

92. Ibid. I translate *luzio* as "enlightening" following John Zemke. It makes more sense than the usual "clear." (Zemke, "Introduction" in Almosnino, *Regimiento de la vida*, 1.)

93. For instance, Lleal, *El judezmo*, 27; Lehmann, *Ladino Rabbinic Literature*, 34; Zemke, "Introduction," 1; Romero, *Creación literaria*, 84.

94. *Me'am Lo'ez*, vol. 0, 147.

95. Lleal, *El Judezmo*, 27. To make her point more convincing, Lleal connects this passage to the next one where Huli talks about Hebrew books being neglected by those who cannot read them. By skipping the sentence in between, she makes it appear as if Huli continues to discuss vernacular texts.

96. Zemke, "Introduction" in Almosnino, *Regimiento de la vida*, 15.

97. Dan, *Jewish Mysticism and Jewish Ethics*, 25.

98. Molho, "Dos obras maestras," 99.

99. Molho, *Literatura sefardita de Oriente*, 229.

100. Asá, like other "vernacular rabbis," uses the term *Ladino klaro* in reference to the spoken register when he wants to indicate that the text in question is not written in the calque language of the Bible translations. Therefore, it does not express Asá's pride in his language, as suggested by Quintana. ("From Linguistic Segregation outside the Common Framework of Hispanic Languages," 709.)

101. Moses Lazar, ed. *The Five Ladino Scrolls: Abraham Asá's Versions of the Hebrew and Aramaic Texts* (Culver City, 1992), 6, 8.

102. See "General Introduction" in *King Artus: a Hebrew Arthurian Romance of 1279*, ed. and trans., with cultural and historic commentary by Curt Leviant (New York, 1969).

103. Quoted in Rozen, *Istanbul*, 268.

104. Ibid., 269.

105. See Alla Markova, "Un fragmento manuscrito de una novela de caballerías en judeoespañol," *Sefarad* 69, no. 1 (2009): 159–172.

106. Ibid., 167.

107. Ibid., 166–167.

108. Ibid., 170.

109. On Ladino rewritings of European novels in the nineteenth century, see Borovaya, *Modern Ladino Culture*, chs. 3–4.

110. Maimonides, for instance, says that it is a "sheer waste of time" to read any of the histories of the Arabs "or books of song and similar works, which neither possess wisdom nor benefit anybody." (Quoted in Leviant, "General Introduction" in *King Artis*, 57.)

111. Lehmann, *Ladino Rabbinic Literature*, 143.

112. Ashkenazi, "Hakdamah del estanpador" in *Tanach: Arbaa v'esrim* (Constantinople, 1739), 1a.

113. Mehmet Ali Dogan, "Evangelizing the Jews: Western Missionaries and their Encounters with the Sabbatean/Dönme Community in the Ottoman Empire," *International Journal of Turcologia* 9, no. 18 (2014): 65–82, 69–70, 75–76.

114. Markova, "Un fragmento manuscrito," 169.

115. Ashkenazi, "Hakdamah del estanpador," 2b.

116. Crews, *Extracts from the Me'am Lo'ez*, 33.

117. Ibid., 42.

118. On Huli's advice to women, see Alisa Meyuhas Ginio, "Everyday Life in the Sephardic Community of Jerusalem According to the *Meam Loez* of Rabbi Jacob Kuli," *Studia Rosenthaliana* 35 (2001): 133–142.

119. On this subject, see Quintana, "Sobre la transmisión y el formulismo en el Me'am Lo'ez de Yacob Juli," in *IJS Studies in Judaica 3: Proceedings of the Twelfth British Conference on Judeo-Spanish Studies, 24–26 June 2001*, eds. Hilary Pomeroy and Michael Alpert (Leiden, 2004), 69–80, 69–70.

120. According to an Ottoman register, there were 8,000 Jewish taxpayers in the capital in 1690 (Göçek, *East Encounters West*, 117), which means roughly 20,000 Jews. Yaron Tsur, without citing his sources, states that there were 30,000–40,000 Jews in Constantinople in the eighteenth century. ("Dating the Demise of the Western Sephardi Jewish Diaspora," in *Jewish Culture and Society in North Africa*, eds. Emily Gotreich and Daniel Schroeder (Bloomington, 2011), 93–107, 99.

121. Schwarzwald, "Le style du *Me'am Lo'ez*: une tradition linguistique," *Yod (nouvelle série)* 11/12 (2006–2007): 77–112, 105.

122. See ibid.; Quintana, "Sobre la transmisiôn y el formulismo en el Me'am Lo'ez de Yacob Juli," in *IJS Studies in Judaica 3: Proceedings of the Twelfth British Conference on Judeo-Spanish Studies, 24–26 June 2001*, eds. Hilary Pomeroy and Michael Alpert (Leiden, 2004), 69–80, 77–80.

123. Quintana points out that vernacular testimonies in Sephardi responsa often start with *savras senyores* addressed to the members of the court. (Ibid., 76.)

124. Crews, *Extracts from the Me'am Lo'ez*, 36.

125. Benaim, *Sixteenth-Century Judeo-Spanish Testimonies*, 187.

126. Romeu, "Ejemplificar con el ejemplo: *mesalim* y *ma'asiyot* en el *Regimiento de la vida* de Moises Almosnino," *Orientalis* 17–18 (1999–2000): 315–322.

127. Crews, *Extracts from the Me'am Lo'ez*, 35.

128. Ibid.

129. *Relatos del pueblo ladinán*, no. 31, 78–80.

130. On the *koplas*, see Romero, *Creación literaria*, 141–176.

131. Ibid., 143.

132. Abraham Asá, *Sefer Tsorche Tsibbur: Dinim kojidos de libros de konsuelos* (Constantinople, 1733), 1a.

133. Unless otherwise indicated, *La Güerta de oro* is quoted, with minor changes, from "David Attias," trans. by Lehmann in *The Jew in the Modern World: A Documentary History*, eds. Paul Mendes-Flohr and Jehuda Reinharz (New York, 2010), 445–446.

134. From what Attias tells us, we can infer that he was either unfamiliar with vernacular rabbinic literature or did not see much difference between it and the Hebrew writings, because all those books talked about the Law.

135. Bregoli, *Mediterranean Enlightenment*, 181.

136. Jean-Pierre Filippini, *Il Porto di Livorno e la Toscana (1676–1814)* (Naples, 1998), vol. 3, 107.

137. Lehmann, "A Livornese 'Port Jew,'" 61.

138. David Attias, *La Güerta de oro*, (Livorno,1778), 4a.

139. Lehmann, "A Livornese 'Port Jew,'" 58.

140. *Anthologia* means "flower garden" in Greek. Poetic anthologies and collections of stories in Castilian and Ladino were commonly called "huerta/guerta" (lit. "garden").

141. Isaac Akrish, *Sefer kiryat arba* (Istanbul, 1858). This excerpt appears in *Sephardi Lives*, 124–125. Introduced and translated by Matt Goldish.

142. See my translation of this chapter at *The Digitized Ladino Library* at the Sephardic Studies Project at Stanford University (http://ladino.stanford.edu).

143. Attias, *La Güerta de oro,* 12b.

144. Ibid.

145. See Onur Yildirim, "Hatt-i Sherif of Gulhane (Tanzimat Fermani)," EJIW.

146. On these blood libels, see Jonathan Frankel, *The Damascus Affair: Ritual Murder, Politics, and the Jews in 1840* (Cambridge, 1997).

147. See Baruch Mevorakh, "The Influence of the Damascus Blood Libel on the Development of the Jewish Press in 1840–1846," *Zion* 23–24 (1958–1959): 46–65 (Heb.).

148. "A Sermon Delivered at the Great Synagogue of Smyrna on the arrival of Sir Moses and Lady Montefiore in that City," 3 (Heb.) (Montefiore Endowment 03144).

149. *The Voice of Jacob,* July 8, 1842, 142. The article welcomed the first attempt to create a Ladino newspaper.

150. I discuss both of Uzeil's projects in detail in Borovaya, *Modern Ladino Culture,* 25–37. Here, I only highlight the main points relevant to this study without proving my conclusions.

151. Trivellato, *The Familiarity of Strangers,* 170.

152. Bernard Lewis, *The Muslim Discovery of Europe* (New York, 1982), 304.

153. *Die Allgemeine Zeitung des Judentums,* July 23, 1842, 39–40.

154. Yaari, "Hebrew Printing in Izmir," 108.

155. On Uziel's possible contacts with the missionaries, see Dov Cohen, "Un bien conocido negociante i luchador comunal," in *La Presse judéo-espagnole, support et vecteur de la modernité,* edited by Rosa Sánchez and Marie-Christine Varol Bornes (Istanbul, 2013), 231–252, 240–241.

In 1850, an American missionary wrote about the Jews of Salonica, "when their eyes first open to the light of modern science, and they discover that their rabbis are but men, and not the wisest men either," they are "in a danger of infidelity." (Dogan, "Evangelizing the Jews," 73.)

156. Cohen, "Un bien conocido negociante i luchador comunal," 241.

157. On this subject, see Aron Rodrigue, "From *millet* to Minority: Turkish Jewry in the 19th and 20th Centuries," in *Paths of Emancipation*, eds. Pierre Birnbaum and Ira Katznelson (Princeton, 1995), 238–261, 245.

158. *The Times,* January 6, 1840, 4 col. D.

159. See Siren Bora, "Formation of the Jewish Press in Izmir: The First Jewish Newspaper *Üstad,*" *Tarih ve Toplum* 127 (1994): 18–22, 19 (Turk.).

160. See Uziel's letter in *Les Archives Israélites*, May 27, 1847, 549–550.

161. On *Or Israel*, see Borovaya, *Modern Ladino Culture*, 37–39.

162. On this periodical, see ibid., 39–43.

163. On Juda Nehama and *El Lunar*, see ibid., 78–81.

164. On this newspaper, see Annie Bellaiche Cohen, "Un Journal judéo-espagnol: *El Verdadero Progreso israelita* à Paris, en 1864," in *La Presse Judéo-Espagnole, Support et Vecteur de la Modernité*, 37–51.

165. See Romero, *Creación literaria*, 91–93.

166. Ibid., 95–102.

167. See Rodrigue, "From *millet* to Minority," 253. On the use of French by Sephardi literati, see Borovaya, "Shmuel Saadi Halevy/Sam Lévy Between Ladino and French: Reconstructing a Writer's Social Identity," in *Modern Jewish Literatures: Intersections and Boundaries*, eds. Sheila Jelen, Michael Kramer, and L. Scott Lerner (Philadelphia, 2011), 83–103.

Epilogue

MOSES ALMOSNINO, A RENAISSANCE MAN?

I.

Joseph Nehama, a well-known Salonican historian, called Almosnino "a true Renaissance man."[1] Another scholar born in Salonica, Isaac Molho, referred to him as "a humanist."[2] A third twentieth-century author from the same city, Michael Molho, characterized him as "a profound humanist of the Renaissance age."[3] Although Nehama was an anti-Zionist, Isaac Molho a Jewish nationalist, and Michael Molho a Hispanophile, all three described their celebrated compatriot in terms of European culture, effectively presenting this Ottoman rabbi as a European author. Almosnino earned these "honorifics" thanks to his two Ladino works praised by Spanish Christians, one of whom insisted on the purity of his language. In the final pages of this book, I will explain what made Almosnino a European in the eyes of these and other intellectuals of their generation, and brought him new fame.

In the nineteenth century, when the chief concern of European Jews was emancipation, "Jewish history rose to affirm the Europeanness of Jews, and through this affirmation set out to prove their worth as citizens of their respective countries."[4] This was the social agenda of the *Wissenschaft des Judentums*, a movement of German Jewish scholars advocating a scientific approach to Jewish history. From their perspective, Ottoman Sephardim could not be considered Europeans despite their Iberian origins, because they resided in the lands of Islam. The article "Turkey" in Theodore Singer's *Jewish Encyclopedia* (1901–1906), which epitomized the *Wissenschaft* ideology, explained that the descendants of Spanish luminaries had degenerated as a result of their isolation from Europe, "the low grade of civilization" in Turkey, and "the despotic rule of centuries."

As Devin Naar has shown, the desire "to strengthen their position within the Ottoman Empire and to elevate their status in the eyes of world Jewry" from the late nineteenth through the first third of the twentieth centuries motivated a number of Sephardi intellectuals to engage in historical writing.[5] They aspired to produce a history of Ottoman Jews that would counter the narrative created by European Jewish scholars, who emphasized how far they "had tragically fallen from the heights attained by their ancestors in the golden age of medieval Spain."[6] In the process of recasting their history in the Ottoman lands, Sephardim "repositioned the image of Salonica and its storied Jewish past and presented it as an idealized symbol of the broader Ottoman Jewish experience."[7]

Not surprisingly, Moses Almosnino, a famous Salonican scholar, eloquent preacher, and influential community leader, became an important protagonist of all histories of Ottoman Jews. Even a newspaper article on the history of Turkish Jews that appeared in *El Tyempo* mentioned him together with Samuel de Medina, Mordechai Matalon, and Joseph Forman, among other celebrated scholars who supported and propagated education in the sixteenth century.[8]

Needless to say, all works on Salonica's history dedicated a great deal of space to Almosnino. The first among these studies to appear in an academic journal was Abraham Danon's "La Communauté juive de Salonique au XVIè siècle" (The Jewish community of Salonica in the sixteenth century) (1900–1901), which, while largely dependent on published works, used numerous communal records and rabbinical documents, many of which were signed by Almosnino.[9]

Curiously, while Danon mentions the Cansino edition, he does not use it as a source and misspells its title (*Extremos y grandezas de Constantinopoli*), which suggests that he had not seen the book himself.[10] Yet, as will be remembered, he owned or had access to a full *Crónica* manuscript, two excerpts from which he published in *El Tyempo* a year later. In view of the problems faced by Ottoman Jews at that moment, he chose to demonstrate the influence of Joseph Nasi at the court and the respect with which he was treated by the Greek patriarch, as well as the importance of Almosnino himself, who was held in high regard by the grand mufti. Introducing these two episodes, Danon proudly emphasized that the information provided by Almosnino was unknown to Graetz or Steinschneider.[11]

Moïse Franco, in his *Essai sur l'Histoire des Israélites de l'Empire Ottoman depuis les origines jusqu'à nos jours* (1897), talks about Almosnino's trip to the capital, his activities in Salonica, his preaching, and writings.[12] Having mentioned his Hebrew works, Franco turns to *Rejimyento*, saying that Almosnino "wrote his masterpiece in such pure Spanish that according to the Spanish scholar Sánchez, this work could be considered one of the rarest in Castilian."[13] As far as I know, this was the first reference to Sánchez's characterization of *Rejimyento* (quoted in the introduction). As it appeared in many other works after Franco, Sánchez's words require a brief examination.

One must keep in mind that the Spanish *raro* has more meanings than the French and English *rare*, respectively. In addition to "unusual," "exceptional," "infrequent," and "extraordinary" denoted by *rare*, *raro* also signifies "strange" and "odd," which at least today is its first meaning. Sánchez refers to *Rejimyento* as *una de las más raras* [*obras de la lengua castellana*] (no. 263), which means "one of the most unusual (or "oddest") works written in Castilian."[14] In another section, he calls it *el más raro y singular* [*libro*] (no. 260), which means "the most unusual and peculiar book."[15] It is noteworthy that Sánchez did not know where and when this book was published, which is why he must have found it especially strange. Finally, these characterizations of *Rejimyento* are not related to what the Spanish cleric says about its language, which is discussed in a separate section (no. 262). Thus, though it is true that Sánchez's "review" of *Rejimyento* is positive, he does not say that it is exceptionally good because of its pure language, as Franco and others claim.

It is not clear what exactly Sánchez meant by "its Castilian is pure." Perhaps, he expected a rabbinical work to have many Hebraisms, and *Rejimyento* has very few. There may be another explanation. The nineteenth-century Spanish scholar José Amador de los Rios, whose work is discussed below, as a Romantic, had a predilection for medieval literature. Hence, he favored the "purity" of the somewhat archaic language of

Moses Pinto Delgado, a renowned ex-converso poet who lived in Amsterdam, over the style of "such venerated talents as Lope de Vega and Góngora who distorted the language and flooded our Parnassus with excesses."[16] It is possible that Sánchez, a publisher of medieval Castilian texts, also preferred Almosnino's "natural and simple style," to that of later Baroque literature.

It is likely that the article "Moses b. Baruch Almosnino" in the *Jewish Encyclopedia*, which cites Sánchez, was also written by Franco. In any event, this reference in both publications was meant not simply to boast of Almosnino's having been noticed by a Christian authority, albeit unknown to Jewish readers, but more important, to announce to European Jews that Sephardim once spoke "pure Spanish." To understand the full meaning of this message, we have to put it in the context of the language discussion between European and Ottoman Jews, which started in the 1840s in the wake of the Damascus and Rhodes blood libels.

In 1845, Rafael Uziel complained in the first issue of *Shaarei mizrach* that "one of the passions of our brothers in Europe is saying that, among many other things, Ottoman Jews lack a language of their own." He explained that this Spanish language that we speak in Turkey is not learned from grammars or dictionaries, but only as a heritage of our fathers [i.e., orally]. The day our ancestors left Spain, they broke away from the real Spanish language and began to speak as they wished, because they had so many things to think about other than their language. He added that "the knowledge of real Spanish was lost among them."[17]

The fact that the first issue of the earliest Ladino newspaper opens with a lengthy statement about the Sephardi vernacular addressed mainly to European Jews points to the urgency of the subject in conversations between Ottoman Jews and their European coreligionists. It is clear that both the language discussion and its terms were imposed on Sephardim from the outside. Thus, the use of "corrupted Spanish," as their language was commonly referred to, was seen as proof of Sephardim's intellectual and moral degradation. Ironically, the Anglo-Jewish *Voice of Jacob* that welcomed the appearance of *Shaarei mizrach* shows that the author was not sufficiently informed about the paper's content and unknowingly confirmed Uziel's words. He expresses the hope that the periodical will be useful for "our backward brethren in Asia" despite its strange appearance. But then he corrects himself.

> We may be wrong, however, in giving an opinion, founded on European views. Perhaps the very jargon in which the publication is written, so unpleasing to a person of education, the very medley of subjects so strange to a methodical mind, may be best calculated to benefit a mass that understands no other language, and that, but for the interest felt in the commercial part, would not feel inclined to read any such publication.[18]

What exactly made Ladino so "unpleasing?" Clearly, not only its being "a mixture of old Spanish and Hebrew," as it was often characterized. The fact that almost all descriptions of the Sephardi vernacular in the European Jewish press mentioned that it was written in Hebrew characters suggests that Ashkenazim had been under the impression that Sephardim not only spoke Spanish but also used the Latin alphabet, i.e., a European script. Thus, from the standpoint of those journalists who *saw* Ladino texts, it was the Hebrew characters, and Rashi script in particular (mentioned in this article), that patently testified to the corruption of Spanish. It confirmed Sephardim's backwardness, because it reminded European Jews of Yiddish, against which they had been fighting since the *Haskalah*. This is why the article "Judaeo-Spanish" in the *Jewish Encyclopedia* (possibly written by Danon) assured readers, most of whom would have had no idea about Ladino, that "Judaeo-German" was "much more corrupted."

The article "Turkey" in the same encyclopedia applied to *Wissenschaft*'s concept of Sephardi history as a course from grandeur to decline, which shaped the attitudes of many Sephardi intellectuals, including Danon, to their mother tongue, once a great language and now a "corrupted *patois*."[19] This article written by two English scholars claimed that initially, Iberian exiles "preserved their mother tongue in its original purity," but after about a century, "through the intermixture of words from Hebrew and other tongues, the language degenerated into a jargon."[20]

The only evidence proving that Sephardim once spoke pure Castilian mentioned in the article (and Danon's essay) comes from "Gonsalvo de Illescas," a Spanish writer of the sixteenth century [who] says that he met Jews in Salonica who spoke Castilian with as pure an accent as his own." Although the article does not directly cite Heinrich Graetz, the most important German Jewish historian in the nineteenth century, but merely includes his work in the bibliography, we can be sure that the author borrowed this information from him. Graetz, who uses the quote from "Gonsalvo" de Ilescas, did not read the work of this church historian, but found his account in a book by Amador de los Ríos, *Estudios históricos, políticos y literarios sobre los judíos de España* (Historical, political, and literary essays on the Jews of Spain) (1848). In a footnote, Amador quotes Gonzalo de Illescas, a sixteenth-century Spanish historian, author of the multi-volume *Historia pontifical y católica* (first published in 1564).[21]

During his trips to Venice and Rome in the 1550s, this scholar met many Jewish refugees who

> took from here our language and still preserve and willingly use it, and it is true that in the cities of Salonica, Constantinople, Alexandria, Cairo, and other centers of trade as well as in Venice everything is bought, sold, and negotiated only in Spanish. And in Venice I knew many Jews from Salonica who, even at a young age, spoke Castilian like me or better.[22]

Graetz obviously liked the quote that so well fit his idea of Spanish Jews' attachment to Castilian, and translated it, somewhat loosely, into German.[23] Among other things, he dropped the words "in Venice" from the sentence "And in Venice I knew many Jews from Salonica." In addition, Graetz misspelled the scholar's name turning "Gonzalo" into "Gonsalvo."

The authors of the article "Turkey" did not read the quote in its original version, but translated it into English from Graetz's German version, turning *aus Salonichi* (from Salonica) to "in Salonica." This inaccuracy changed the statement in such a way that it now appeared to be the traveler's account of his visit to this city (which presumably emphasized Salonica's importance). The scientific value of de Illescas's statement, quoted from the original or from Graetz and almost always out of context, by a great number of scholars until this day, is questionable, but this is not relevant to my study. What matters here is that it was the only "evidence" on the subject of language purity available to European scholars. This is why Sánchez's praise of Almosnino's work was so valuable to Sephardim.

However, Franco and Danon, proud of their community's past glory, had nothing positive to say about the present state of its language or literature. In an article in the French-language Jewish periodical, *Le Journal de Salonique*, Franco wrote that Sephardim who have the honor of counting among their ancestors . . . Judah Halevy, ibn Ezra, ibn Gabirol, and Maimonides, who were born on the Spanish soil and wrote in the purest Hebrew and the most perfect Arabic, these Sephardim—I say—since their immigration to the East adopted only such literary tools as two jargons, Chaldean Hebrew and Judeo-Spanish.

He went on to claim that Sephardim used them to produce only religious literature and translations of novels, biographies, and poems from different languages.[24]

Franco approves only of those Sephardi literati who chose to write in other languages, such as French, German, Hebrew, Turkish, or Greek. It is not surprising, therefore, that he is not very proud of *Meam Loez*, "revered by the Jews of the Orient . . . as much as the Bible, if not more."[25] He not only distances himself from those Jews, but even sounds like a European ethnographer or traveler describing some indigenous population. He undoubtedly valued Almosnino's *Rejimyento*, praised by a European author, much more.

It is important to emphasize that despite being proud of Almosnino's "pure Castilian," Franco reminds his coreligionists about their connection to the so-called golden age of Iberian Jewry, naming among their ancestors authors who not only wrote in Arabic or Hebrew, but even condemned Jews who used the Romance.[26] Carmoly, Almosnino's first biographer, while acknowledging that his style both in Hebrew and Spanish was "as pure as it was polished and elegant," likens his Hebrew poetic style to that of "the old Hebrew poets of Spain."[27] In 1887, *El Luzero de la pasensia* (Turnu Severin), the first Ladino periodical to use the Latin alphabet, claimed that Danon's Hebrew works proved that Sephardi Jews were the true heirs of their medieval "Spanish ancestors," such as ibn Gabirol and Maimonides.[28]

II.

In the twentieth century, it was not Hebrew but Spanish that was declared the main link between Ottoman Jews and their "old homeland," though not the medieval Iberia of their ancestors, but the Golden Age Spain that had no Jews. Historians seem to have missed this change all the more easily because both Sephardim and European scholars at the time failed to distinguish between Spain and Iberia.

While French and German Jewish intellectuals considered Ladino a contemptible jargon testifying to Sephardim's degradation, some Spaniards were thrilled to learn that they still spoke a variety of Castilian. After the abolition of the Inquisition in Spain (1834), at least two Spanish scholars showed interest in the history of Iberian Jews, which led to the production of a few studies on this subject. The first history of Spanish Jews published on the Peninsula was Adolfo de Castro's *Historia de los judíos en España, desde los tiempos de su establecimiento hasta principios del presente siglo* (A history of Spanish Jews from the time of their arrival until the beginning of this century) (1847). A year later, José Amador de los Ríos published his *Estudios históricos, políticos y literarios sobre los judíos de España* (mentioned above), which was translated into French in 1861 and, unfortunately, eclipsed de Castro's work. Amador's famous three-volume *Historia social, política y religiosa de los judíos de España y Portugal* came out in 1875–1876. Senator Ángel Pulido, who, at the turn of the twentieth century, initiated a famous campaign of *philosefardismo*, acknowledged that these works had a strong influence on him. Even though this interest in Iberian Jews had to do with Spain's own political and cultural problems, these works and Pulido's activities, to some extent, counterbalanced *Wissenschaft*'s disparaging attitude toward Ottoman Jews and their language.

El Verdadero progreso israelita (Paris, 1864), which was close to the Alliance Israélite Universelle, published a few installments from *Istoriya de los judyos de Espanya*, described by the editor as a translation of a work by "Don Hosef Amador de los Rios."[29] This adaptation was produced by Meir Judah Caplan, an Ashkenazi Jew who had spent many years in Spain and Latin America.[30] Three weeks before this serialized publication began, the paper printed Caplan's "Letter to the Editor" that insisted that Sephardim needed to be taught modern Spanish. Caplan declared that their "slightly corrupted Spanish" was preserved by God as "a tie that had forever connected them to Europe":

> In his wisdom and infinite mercy, God left them . . . as the last resort (*tabla de salvasyon*) their beloved language, which they brought from Spain, one of the richest, noblest, and most advanced in Europe. Transplanted to Asia, these Jews kept in Europe a deep root which is their language.[31]

At the turn of the twentieth century, similar ideas, although expressed in secular terms, were formulated by Ángel Pulido, who together with a few other Spaniards, aimed at establishing connections between Spain and the descendants of Spanish exiles, whom he called "Spaniards without a homeland."[32] Some Sephardi intellectuals, who found this project attractive, maintained correspondence with Pulido, parts of which he published in his two books: *Los israelitas españoles y el idioma castellano* (Spanish Jews and Castilian) (1904) and *Españoles sin patria y la raza sefardí* (Spaniards without a homeland and the Sephardi race) (1905). Of course, this correspondence centered on their language, which was recognized by both sides as Sephardim's connection to Spanish soil, indeed their roots in it. Some Ottoman Jews began to present Ladino as medieval Spanish, claiming that it sounded exactly the same, a belief held by many people for a long time. José Estrugo, who was born in Izmir and visited Spain (which he considered to be Sephardim's "Jerusalem or spiritual Zion") concluded, "we are like live phonograph records for the scholars of old Spanish."[33]

For the first time, many Sephardim felt proud of their language, which was particularly important for Salonican Jews who, after the annexation of their city by Greece in 1912, suffered under exclusivist Greek nationalism that grew more aggressive in the 1930s. The notion that they constituted a living museum of the Spanish Golden Age helped them battle "the widely held assumption that the Jews of Salonica had long since fallen from grace, transformed into backward Oriental Jews, and had relinquished all connection to their ancestors' medieval glory."[34]

This is the main reason why the third generation of Ottoman-born scholars, as Julia Cohen and Sarah Stein defined them, had a more positive view of their language than Franco (1864–1907) and Danon (1857–1925).[35] In addition, most of them personally witnessed hardships endured by their community unknown to previous generations and wanted to uplift its morale through their writings. (Needless to say, the destruction of Salonica had a much stronger impact on the survivors' attitude to Ladino.) Among those scholars were Joseph Nehama (1880–1971), Michael Molho (1890–1964), Isaac Molho (1894–1976), and Isaac Emmanuel (1899–1972).

Pride in Salonica's Spanishness permeates works on its history produced by these authors. A chapter in the best known among them, Joseph Nehama's *Histoire des Israélites de Salonique* (1935), entitled "Salonique. Ville juive et espagnole" (Salonica. A Jewish and Spanish city), states that in the sixteenth century Castilian was the "official language" of Jewish Salonica.[36] Michael Molho's *Kontribusyon a la Istorya de Saloniko* (1932), one of the few works he wrote in Ladino, claims that in sixteenth-century Salonica, which had "the character of a Spanish city . . . one heard the harmonious sounds of the language of Cervantes."[37] In another essay, he even says that "the language of Cervantes remained intact among Spanish Jews through the end of the sixteenth century."[38]

Sam Lévy, a Salonican journalist who once actively corresponded with Pulido, wrote after World War II that "in 1898 Spanish visitors to Salonica were amazed to hear its Jewish inhabitants speak the language of Lope de Vega, García Calderón, Cervantes Saavedra, and other contemporaries of Don Quixote."[39] Although Lévy apparently believed that Don Quixote was a real person and confused García Calderón, one of Peru's presidents and his own contemporary, and Pedro Calderón de la Barca, who lived in the seventeenth century, the message is clear: the Sephardi vernacular spoken in the nineteenth century was the language of the Spanish Golden Age.

Molho, however, hardly literally meant that in the sixteenth century Ottoman Jews used the language of *Don Quixote* (first published in 1605). Rather, he implied that they spoke the language of the Spanish Renaissance and, therefore, had a share in Spain's great cultural legacy. Thus, the previously cherished ties to the golden age of Iberian Jewish creativity were replaced with a proclaimed connection to the Golden Age of Castilian literature. And who could embody this connection better than Almosnino? This is why his fame reached its highest point (at least after his death) in the twentieth century.

Isaac Emmanuel, author of yet another *Histoire des Israélites de Salonique* (1936), made an important contribution to Almosnino scholarship, since he had first-hand knowledge of relevant communal records. Besides, unlike other Sephardi scholars, he had received a formal education in Europe where he experienced "a continued lack of respect among European Jews for their 'Oriental' brethren."[40] Emmanuel's treatment of Almosnino's work reveals his concerns, yet also demonstrates an academic (rather than emotional) approach to the texts he discusses. He states that Almosnino's command of Castilian was as good as that of "any Christian cleric in Spain at that time." To prove his claim, the scholar quotes Sánchez's characterization of Almosnino's style.[41] To demonstrate the purity of his language and the later deterioration of

Castilian, Emmanuel cites a passage from the original edition of *Rejimyento* in Rashi script and invites readers to compare it with the Amsterdam edition in Latin characters quoted on the same page.[42] In addition, Emmanuel provides a list of all non-Jewish authors cited in *Rejimyento.*

Finally, Emmanuel does what no one had done before him: he quotes one of the Catholic censors who allowed the publication of Cansino's *Extremos y grandezas de Constantinopla.* Fray Gerónimo de la Cruz praises Almosnino's work, saying that it has only one flaw, namely, that it was written by a man of another faith.[43] Thus, both of Almosnino's major vernacular works were approved by Spanish clerics.

According to Michael Molho, Almosnino wrote in "correct and perfect Hebrew which reflected his outstanding erudition, but he also wrote in an impeccable Castilian, which earned him a place of honor in the pantheon of Spanish literature."[44] In other words, one hundred years after Carmoly compared Almosnino to medieval Hebrew poets, Molho emphasized that it was his Spanish and not Hebrew that connected him to Iberia, and specifically to late-Renaissance Christian Spain, hence, to modernity. This was the ultimate proof that Ottoman Sephardim, some of whom at the turn of the twentieth century had begun to call their vernacular "Castilian," belonged to great European civilization. Hence, their most celebrated author, a polymath who lived in the Renaissance age, could be called a Renaissance man. This mattered to modern Sephardi intellectuals, assimilationists, and Jewish nationalists alike, because, as Aron Rodrigue put it, all of them believed that "Jews belonged to the West."[45]

Notes

1. Joseph Nehama, *Histoire des Israélites de Salonique* (Salonica, 1935), vol. III, 80.

2. Isaac Molho, "Un humaniste séfardi de Salonique: Moshe Barouh Almosnino (1518–1581)." *Otsar Yehude Sefarad* 7 (1964): 49–68.

3. Michael Molho, "Dos obras maestras," 98.

4. Aron Rodrigue, "Salonica in Jewish Historiography," *Jewish History* 28 (2014): 439–447, 440.

5. Devin Naar, "Fashioning the Mother of Israel: The Ottoman Jewish Historical Narrative and the Image of Jewish Salonica," *Jewish History* 28 (2014): 337–372, 337.

6. Ibid., 338. (Naar obviously means the so-called golden age of Iberian Jews in the medieval period, when Spain as a state did not yet exist, rather than the Spanish Golden Age, i.e., sixteenth-seventeenth centuries.)

7. Ibid., 339.

8. David Fresco,"Los judyos de Turkia, 5.

9. Abraham Danon, "La Communauté juive de Salonique au XVIè siècle," *Revue des* Études *Juives* 40 (1900): 206–230; 41 (1900): 98–117, 250–265. Here, 40; 209.

10. Ibid., 41; 99.

11. Danon, "Abu Suad i rabi Moshe Almosnino," 5.

12. Franco, *Essai sur l'Histoire des Israélites de l'Empire Ottoman*, 77–78.

13. Ibid., 78.

14. Tomás Antonio Sánchez, *Colección de poesías castellanas*, vol. I, 187.

15. Ibid., 185.

16. José Amador de los Ríos, *Estudios históricos, políticos y literarios* (Madrid, 1848), 510.

17. "Hakdamah del komponedor," *Shaarei mizrach*, December 29, 1845, 1.

18. "Gates of the East," *The Voice of Jacob*, February 13, 1846, 80.

19. Danon, "La Communauté juive," 40; 209.

20. "MM" stands for Joseph Jacobs and Mary W. Montgomery. Joseph Jacobs was President of the Jewish Historical Society of England and Corresponding Member of the Royal Academy of History, Madrid. I thank Julia Phillips Cohen for this information.

21. Amador de los Ríos, *Estudios históricos, políticos y literarios*, 510.

22. Gonzalo de Illescas, *Historia pontifical y católica* (Barcelona, 1606), Parte 2, Book 6, 109.

23. Heinrich Graetz, *Geschichte der Juden von den* ältesten *Zeiten bis auf die Gegenwart* (Leipzig, 1866), vol. IX, 13.

24. M[oïse] F[ranco], "La littérature actuelle des Israélites d'Orient," *Le Journal de Salonique*, July 6, 1905, 2.

25. Franco, *Essai sur l'histoire des Israélites de l'Empire Ottoman*, 122.

26. See Wacks, "Toward a History of Hispano-Hebrew Literature," 183.

27. Carmoly, *La Famille Almosnino*, 11, 17.

28. Quoted in Naar, "Fashioning the 'Mother of Israel,'" 352.

29. The editor, Ezra Benveniste, tried to "correct" the Ladino spelling to make it look like Castilian. Among other things, he often used *chet* instead of *gimel* to replace the Ladino sound [j] with the Castilian [h], as in this case. Such changes often led to hypercorrection, e.g., *Haustria* for *Austria*. The first writer to do so as far as I know, was David Attias.

30. Annie Bellaiche Cohen mistakes him for the author, because on p. 47 it says *kompuesto por Meir Yehuda Kaplan*. ("Un Journal judéo-espagnol: *El Verdadero Progreso israelita* à Paris, en 1864," in *La Presse judéo-espagnole, support et vecteur de la modernité*, 37–51, 49.)

31. M[eir] J[udah] C[aplan], ["A letter to the Editor"], *El Verdadero progreso israelita*, September 30, 1864, 33–34, 34.

32. On Pulido and his campaign, see for example, María Antonia del Bravo, "Angel Pulido y el sefardismo internacional," *Hispania Sacra* 92 (1993): 739–762; Michael Alpert, "Dr. Angel Pulido and Philo-Sephardism in Spain," *Jewish Historical Studies* 40 (2005): 105–119.

33. José Meir Estrugo, *El Retorno a Sefard: Cien años después de la inquisición* (Madrid, 1933), 81–82. It is interesting that to give an example of the [j] sound in Ladino, Estrugo mentions the title of a book he owns, "*El Regimiento de la vida* (by rabbi Moses Almosnino) published in Constantinople [*sic*] in 1547 [*sic*]." I thank Devi Mays for bringing this text to my attention.

34. Naar, "Jewish Salonica and the Making of the 'Jerusalem of the Balkans,' 1890–1943," (PhD diss., Stanford University, 2011), 127.

35. Julia Phillips Cohen and Sarah Abrevaya Stein, "Sephardic Scholarly Worlds: Toward a Novel Geography of Modern Jewish History," *The Jewish Quarterly Review* 100, no 3 (2010): 349–384, 359.

36. Nehama, *Histoire des Israélites de Salonique*, vol. II, 33.

37. Michael Molho, *Kontribusyon a la Istorya de Saloniko* (Salonica, 1932), xii. I thank Devin Naar for making this excerpt from Molho's work available to me.

38. Molho, "Dos obras maestras," 98.

39. Sam Lévy, *Salonique à la fin du XIXè siècle: Mémoires* (Istanbul, 2000), 37.

40. Naar, "Jewish Salonica," 170.

41. Emmanuel, *Histoire des Israélites de Salonique,* 181.

42. Ibid., 180.

43. Ibid., 181.

44. Molho, "Dos obras maestras," 98.

45. Rodrigue, "Salonica in Jewish Historiography," 445.

APPENDIX.
[*THE EXTREMES OF CONSTANTINOPLE*]

Moses Almosnino

As all of this is over, I thought it would be good to write an account of some of the extremes without a mean found in the city of Constantinople, and of the immense travails that we endured on our journey in the service of God and our republic, and of the six conjunctions in which we failed to conclude our affair. May God in his mercy help us to succeed during the seventh one, as we hope.

Navigating the gulf of the sea and ailing from the travails and passions endured by those in this noblest city of Constantinople who have affairs at the court of the Grand Signor, may God sustain him; mandated by divine providence, by my sins, and by my adverse and sinister destiny, or cruel fate (all of them necessary, in my view), which united in order to shoot at me their poisonous arrows of cruel hatred that sufficed to tear me away from my continuous study and permanent contemplation; and now day and night, continuously moving with the zeal and love required to achieve the desired goal for the benefit of our noble republic; seeking and considering the most suitable means of reaching the goal of this affair; having to speak with many different people (because often in this affair, unfortunately or providentially, the fulfillment of our hope was deferred from one day to the next); I found that similarly to how I left the extreme of quiet and tranquility and fixed state of intense contemplation in the service of God and for the sake of his Holy Scriptures worthy of perpetual glory in this corruptible transitory life and even more so in the future permanent and everlasting life in eternity; similarly to how I was transferred to the extreme of a continuous and variable movement, full of tribulations and labors, enduring many calamities without any respite but the glory of hope in the accomplishment of this affair (which I have always regarded as supreme happiness and glorious prize and a reward for the work of my whole life); similarly, I discovered in every person I spoke with in this city and in every particular occurrence I saw there that—contrary to nature—all of them move from one extreme to the other without ever passing through or being in the middle.[1] This is true of affairs and those who conduct them, and the means by which they are conducted, as well as of all the customs and universal and particular cases in this city and of all its foundations.

For this reason, I hope that what we have been unable to achieve and accomplish during this time of negotiations, which lasted almost a year and a half, despite all possible diligence and passion and fervor as well as fatigue of the body and spirit and great danger to us, will be accomplished without any fatigue or labor, only through divine help and providence, which will be the ultimate extreme. May it be so, amen.[2]

And with this hope, I will relate here some of the universals through which one will be able to understand many other particulars, and thus also the extreme of our past travails during the conjunctions when we failed to conclude our affair. I will do all this briefly with God's help.

1.

I found that the first extreme, climate, is the most universal one, to which all lower and lesser things, general and corruptible ones, are related and subordinated.[3] And I found that weather changes happen there both in summer and in winter in one of two extremes each in its proportion: it is either excessively hot or considerably cold. And most of the time this happens within a very short interval, in a few days. Both in winter and summer, there will be a very hot day and then a cold one, and sometimes in one day or one instant the two extremes switch and the weather changes from one to the other.

And the reason for this is obvious and evident to those who are observant; this happens due to the existence of different winds. Experience makes it clear that, when the north wind blows, both in winter and summer, the air cools down very much and everyone is cold.

And the reason why the north wind is colder there than in other parts of our land is that it comes directly from the Black Sea which cools it beyond normal due to the output of the vapors rising as a result of the continuous movement of the current.

And when the hot west wind that comes from inland blows, it is insufferably hot all the time.

2.

When it is raining, and particularly if the rain is heavy, it is completely impossible to walk on the streets because of the extreme abundance of water and mud that is there all the time while it is raining. And as soon as it stops raining, the streets are turned to the other extreme, becoming dry and cleaner than before the rain.

And the reason for this is that almost the whole city is either elevated or low, as it has many hills and very high places. And since all the streets are paved with cobblestone, when the rain water comes down, even if there is very little of it, because the city is very big, all the time while it is raining, streams are rushing down the streets to the sea, which is the lowest place, taking with them all the sewage from the streets and courtyards that is thrown there on purpose, so that it would be washed off. And when the water is gone, as we have said, the streets are washed and are cleaner than before and dry.

3.

In this city, I have never seen a middle ground between health and sickness. Sometimes, it is very healthy with no one in the whole city having even a headache, and sometimes it is stricken with diseases, most of them contagious, like pestiferous apostomes and pestilential fevers and drowsiness, and other similar ones. And, when one strikes, so do the others.

And the reason for this, in my view, is because the air of this illustrious city is very thin and rare, on account of being surrounded by the Mediterranean Sea and the Atlantic.[4] As a result, the air is exceedingly humid and is predisposed to corruption. And when it gets corrupted, it corrupts suddenly and in the extreme, which is why whenever it is corrupted all kinds of diseases occur, like those mentioned above and other similar ones. And at the time when the air is not corrupted, as it is so thin and rare, it is very salubrious, and all inhabitants of this city are very healthy.

4.

Provisions of all kinds are constantly in one of two extremes: either very expensive or very cheap, with the exception of meat because those who bring it are required to provide the necessary amount, and there is a sufficient number of experienced people in charge of this who are severely punished if there is not enough meat, which is why there is never a shortage of it. But everything else is constantly in one of the two mentioned extremes.

And the reason for this is that all provisions are brought from outside the city, and most of them come by sea when the west wind blows. During this time, many provisions arrive in great quantities. And though there are very many people and the city is very big, when provisions come in such quantities from many places, the prices go down. And those who bring the provisions cannot hold on to them because they know that the north wind will return. And it often happens that, when the north wind suddenly comes, there is still a lot of fruit on the ships, and, in order to make it back safely, the merchants throw the merchandise into the sea, where it is picked up by the people coming in boats. And when the north wind blows for a few days and no ships come, the prices go through the roof. And because there is always one of the two winds, there is always one of the two extremes.

5. & 6.

There are always another two extremes in what concerns all kinds of provisions: what is abundant costs very much, and what is lacking is very cheap, contrary to the common order and manner of things. And this is true for fruit and fish, as well as for meat.

And the universal reason for this is that everyone wants to eat the same thing as the others, and since the majority are grandees, the rest do not want to appear inferior to them. As for fruit, when its season starts, everyone wants to enjoy it, because, as has been said, the majority are grandees. And those who are not, want to appear as such, and there is enough of both kinds, which is why a lot of fruit is brought to the city. But no matter how much fruit there is at the beginning of the season there is too little of it compared to the number of consumers. And when there is little fruit, which happens at the end of the season, everyone is tired of it, and because no one wants to appear so low as to want fruit, it is very cheap.

As for fish, when it is abundant, if it is in season, many people eat it, and when it is not in season, no one wants it, and those who eat it are considered inferior and are pronounced base and vile. Aware of this, the merchants bring very little fish to the market, and because no one buys it, fish costs very little, almost nothing.

And the same happens with meat. In winter, everyone eats mutton, and because of this, very few cows are slaughtered, and very few people buy beef, and because of this, mutton, which is plentiful, is very expensive, and beef, which is scarce, is cheap. And in summer, it is the opposite.

7.

For the same reason, in the case of fish, there are two more extremes. Though at the fish market there are equal quantities of all sorts of fish, certain kinds are very expensive while others do not cost anything. And those that at one point are very expensive, at other times do not cost anything, and those that were very cheap become very expensive, which is unbelievable.

And the reason for all this is that no one wants to buy fish that is not in season, because every kind of fish has its time, and most people are aware of this as in its season fish is more tasty and fatty, and the kind that is not in season is very lean and tasteless. It is believed that fish that is not in season is very harmful and corrupts in the stomach causing many troubles and diseases. And because of this, everyone stays away from it and does not want it for any price, with good reason.

8.

The wines sold and drunk in the city are in two extremes: there are extremely good ones, such as malvesies and perfect muscatels from Candia [Crete], and others from other places which are no less perfect as far as their color, aroma, and flavor are concerned. And there are others, made from black raisins or rotten grapes that no one likes because they smell of mold and have a bad taste.

And the reason for this is as follows. Since inside the city wine is banned and forbidden by the king and his judges, one is forbidden not only to make it but even to buy amounts of grapes that appear to be larger than one can eat.[5] Hence, the wine made in the city has to be produced from the grapes obtained little by little which, by the time they are used, get spoilt, and most of them become rotten, so the wine comes out bad as far as its color, aroma, and flavor are concerned. This is why it is consumed right after being made. And it is produced mostly from raisins because it is very difficult to make wine from such grapes and there will be very little of it.

The wines coming from outside the city are perfect.[6] Since it is possible to bring them into the city only if one has very good connections and is able to pay a great deal of money, merchants import only the most perfect wines from Candia and other places that produce wines of equally high quality, which allows them to ask for their wines as much as they want and thus cover the expenses and make up for the great risk they took to bring them.

Because of this, there are two extremes in the wines made in the city: when grapes are scarce, a lot of wine is made, and when grapes are abundant, very little wine is made.

And the reason for this is as follows. Since wine is banned and one is not allowed to make it, when, early in the season grapes begin to ripen and there is still little of them, the authorities do not prohibit selling grapes in large quantities as they are not yet afraid that people will make wine. At this time, everyone buys grapes and makes as much wine as possible, because one can do this without any danger or fear of getting into trouble. And when during the time of harvest grapes are abundant, city authorities fear that people would make wine, and those who buy grapes are watched and warned. At this time, very few dare to make wine, only those who have connections or do not care about the risk.

9.

As far as their economic conditions and habits are concerned, most people are constantly in one of two extremes: the majority is wasteful, and the rest are extremely stingy, though there are very few of them.

And the reason for this is that only very few people do not have positions at the court or sinecures from the king or his courtiers, which allows them to make as much money as they want, and, since they have large incomes and make great profits, they give away money extravagantly and without pain. And those who do not have a pension or an income from the king or a sinecure from his courtiers, though there are very few of them, earn their living by working hard, and, since the expenses are extraordinary and impossible to avoid and provisions are usually very expensive, one has to be very stingy.

10.

Some people are extremely talkative, and others do not talk at all, some are completely idle and others are very busy.

And the reason for this is that those who are involved in business with the grandees, and most are, have to wait a long time for their attention in order to get the profit they expect, and thus they have very little time to talk with anyone.

And those who are not involved in such affairs and do not study most of the time stay in their houses idly because this city does not offer any public recreations in which people can engage after their workday is over. And for this reason, those who have finished their affairs are idle and willing to talk with their friends for pleasure and can talk for a long time about all sorts of things.

11.

The conditions described above cause two more extremes among the inhabitants of this city: some of them enjoy an extremely good life in great abundance, and others live in extreme poverty, misery, and scarcity.

And the reason for this is that most of the time provisions are extremely expensive, and the rich who, as has been said, make it without difficulty, spend extravagantly and enjoy a very good life. And those who do not have much money or opportunities to earn, suffer a lot, and no matter how much they want to change their situation, they continue living in poverty because the jobs they can get pay so little that they do not cover their expenses. And the reason for this has been explained.

12.

In recreations and their opposites, people are extreme to various degrees, and this is true for eating, drinking, taking walks, and all other kinds of pleasures; and while they are enjoying one of these things it is always in the extreme and for a long time. But at other times they have a very hard life, as most days they do not come home for the night.

And the reason for this is quite obvious from what has been said. Since most people conduct affairs with the grandees at the court, they are so busy in the city that they do not have time for recreation and barely any even for their essential needs.

And when they or the grandees take a break and they are absolutely free, those who are not scholars and are not engaged in studying try to make up for not eating and drinking by having all other kinds of amusements and recreations.

13.

This leads to another two extremes with regard to the time when people drink wine. Sometimes they drink it in great quantities, and sometimes they do not have it with their meals at all.

And the reason for this is that when they are busy dealing with the grandees, they eat very little and do not drink wine, because these grandees do not want the people they talk with to drink wine or smell of it. And when they return home and are free, those who do not have other things to do drink wine in great quantities to make up for the time when they did not drink any and because other pleasures and entertainments enhance their taste for wine and the appetite.

14.

There are two more common extremes: during the day, no one eats at regular or convenient times. Some people eat a lot in the morning, and others have a lot late, almost at suppertime, both in summer and in winter.

And the reason for this is that the city is very big, and those who have to go to Galata because they trade and have warehouses or special jobs there eat very early in the morning in order not to waste the time needed for their affairs. They go to their shops after eating and are busy there till nighttime.

And those who conduct affairs with the grandees have to leave at dawn, and as they are very busy, they stay there most of the day.

So, when they return home and eat, it is already late.

15.

Merchandise of all kinds is, most of the time, in one of two extremes: either very expensive or very cheap.

And the reason for this is that it is a city of the court where, in addition to the courtiers and grandees who temporarily or permanently reside there, a great number of people of all sorts come to resolve their affairs. Yet not only aliens leave the city but, very often, at the Grand Signor's order, also those of the court. And the merchandise, [all or most of which comes in small quantities while the city is heavily populated, is very expensive, which happens because there is always an infinite number of people. But when all kinds of merchandise arrive from many different countries] and the city is partly empty, it becomes extremely cheap, because there is no one to buy it.[7]

The only kind of merchandise or craft produced in the city is expensive jewelry with many precious stones, and most rich merchants trade in it. And in jewelry, there are also two extremes: goldsmiths either get double price for it and even three or four times its price, or there is no one to buy it for half or even one third of the price.

And the reason for this is that such jewelry is meant only for the weddings and betrothals of princes or grandees, as well as the king's children and grandchildren or other women in his family. For this purpose and for such occasions the jewelry is made little by little. And when such events approach and the goldsmiths get special orders, the prices go through the roof, because, no matter how much jewelry is available at such moments, the king and his courtiers order more. And because they need jewelry so much and are able to pay whatever they are asked, the merchants sell it at a high price and make a lot of money.

But afterwards, when the goldsmiths do not get any commissions, even though they are willing to sell their jewelry at a very low price, no one wants it, because the grandees buy it only when it is necessary and do not bother getting it beforehand at a lower price for the time when they will need it.

And the merchants do not want to risk holding onto their jewelry, because what they will gain when there is a demand may not cover what they lose while waiting for that time, thus the latter is certain and the former uncertain.[8] And because of this, jewelry costs very little or nothing.

16.

This leads to two extremes concerning the merchants themselves, especially those trading in jewelry: some of them are extremely rich, and others are poor as can be.

And the reason for this is clear and obvious from what has been said. Since in order to make such expensive jewelry one needs many precious stones of all sizes, everyone makes it little by little using what one can get hold of, in the hope of receiving special orders in the future.

And because most of the time such orders do not come soon, there are few of them, and they are infrequent, and because often what is expected and promised does not happen and sometimes one of the parties dies—because of all this, those who can hold on to their jewelry and wait for a better time, get big profits and make up for their waiting, as later there is not enough jewelry, so they can ask any price for their merchandise, and they become extremely rich.

And those who cannot hold onto their jewelry, in order to survive are forced to do one of the following: either pawn it at exorbitant rates, which ruins them, or take out the stones and pearls and thus lose more than half of what they have paid; because, as they say, there is a difference between what one wants to get for his merchandise and what it is really worth. This is true for all merchandise, but with jewelry the difference is extremely large.[9] And as a result, in the end, these merchants find themselves deeply in debt and poor without any hope of recovery.

17.

In people's status or ranks, there are always two extremes: Some are held in high regard and greatly honored by everyone and are visited by those who consider themselves inferior or subordinate to them; and others are not esteemed at all, and no one ever remembers about them. The exception is the learned and competent people who are revered by everyone.

And the reason for this is obvious. In this city, people's worth is almost always measured not by their character but solely by their position, connections, and influence at the court. Except for the people always revered for their learning or pedigree, those who have the power to do good or wrong are honored depending on how much influence and power they have to elevate or destroy others. As for those who do not have such power, no one respects them despite their wealth, because everyone pretends to be important and prosperous and not needing others, except those who surpass them in influence and power.

As for the people who are in these extremes, none of them remains in the same status for a long time; they are in constant movement and are rapidly transferred from one extreme to the other, which is true for their positions and ranks as well as wealth and poverty.

And the reason for this is also quite obvious and evident from experience. Since all these favors are attained at the court by chance and without any natural causes, everything depends on the turn of the celestial wheel, which is never still and determines the order of these changes. In addition, there are natural causes. For instance, one's patron at the court may die and be replaced by another person, and those who come along with him are elevated while the others are debased and forgotten, as one can observe every day.

And the same is true for the merchants. Given what makes them rich (which was explained above), it is natural that slow trade or adverse wind, which cause prices to drop, is enough to ruin them, and they move to the extreme of hardship.

18.

With regard to friendships and enmities, people are always in one of two extremes: some are extremely good friends and others are bitter enemies full of cruel hatred and extreme loathing.

And the reason for this, in my view, is as follows. Because those who are usually at peace and on speaking terms, being mostly virtuous, do not stop talking to one another with great pleasure at times of leisure and recreation (as is the custom of this country) and perform all the duties of friendship—kindness, assistance, and conversation—which do not lack while they continue to communicate, because of this, while their friendship lasts, it is extremely good. And when they stop speaking to each other, which happens only for a weighty reason, former friends, full of cruel hatred, harm each other as much as they can, remembering the cause of their enmity with an evil intention of taking revenge.

These two extremes have a lot in common with the previously discussed ones: people easily move from one extreme to the other for the smallest reason, rapidly and sometimes unexpectedly, and despite being extremely loyal friends or extremely bitter enemies, are not steadfast or firm in either.

And the reason for this, I believe, is that most people do not need one another very much. Because friendships and enmities, as is natural, occur only between equals, friendships between grandees and other influential people in the city are not steadfast due to the lack of a weighty reason for them, since these people think they do not need one another, though they constantly assist one another. And, in the same way, the rich help the rich and the poor help the poor. And, since individuals who might need each other have no common ground, people cannot form strong unions or brotherhoods. And, for the same reason, they easily make friends in order not to show that they are offended or hold a grudge against others or dislike them.

19.

With regard to the Jewish religion and pious deeds, people are in two extremes. There are some, though very few, who are so extreme in evil and in hideous vices that they are like a contagious plague for the republic, and no one but God is safe from them. And there are many others, so extreme in virtue and goodness and pious deeds that they spend more of their wealth in the service of God than on their own needs.

And the reason the bad people are so bad is that they are neither educated nor virtuous, and they are either very rich or extremely poor, because, as has been said, most people are in one of these extremes.

And the poor who are not virtuous because they are unable to support themselves by work (as has been explained), invent ways of harming and insulting others as much as possible in order to extort money from them. And most of the time they are paid very well merely for giving up their wicked deeds and abandoning their vile conduct, and thus they make money by being quiet and not saying anything. And because these people are constantly thinking of evil schemes and plans of offending others, they have no time for pious deeds or virtuous conduct. And because by nature man is more inclined toward evil than toward good, once they have chosen this course and way of living, habit makes them even more vile and wicked.

And the vicious rich, as they have more power to harm others, are more dangerous, their offenses are more hurtful, and the damage they cause is more significant. And since no one dares to stop them, they persist in their evil doings pursuing their wicked plans without any obstacles or impediments, constantly augmenting the evil they cause.

And the reason good people, both rich and poor, are so extreme in their goodness is as follows. Those who are inclined toward the good—despite having many opportunities to do evil and thus making money without working (which all people by nature want to do)—must have a very important motivation whose foundation is great prudence, divine inspiration, or a natural inclination toward virtue. Hence, one must be extreme in goodness and have an extreme inclination toward virtue, which is how most of these people are.

20.

With regard to prayers and piety, the Jews are in two extremes: some never go to the synagogue to pray on the Sabbath or during the week, and others, who are the majority, do not miss a prayer on any day, morning, afternoon, or night. And some are so pious that they do not only never miss communal prayers but fast and say prayers every Monday and Thursday the year around, and every *Rosh Hodesh* eve they fast and spend the whole day, from morning till night, at the synagogue praying and reading the Scriptures with their *tefillin* and *talliths* on, like on Yom Kippur.

And the reason for this is that these people, as has been said, are in one of two extremes: either very busy or completely idle. And those who are engaged in affairs with the grandees in the mornings and afternoons cannot excuse themselves from them, as they find it impossible, and, as a result, they form a habit of skipping prayers, so that even when they can, they do not pray, because skipping prayers has become a habit for them. As for the good ones or those who do not have affairs with grandees in the mornings and afternoons, which is the time of our prayers, not having anything to do at home (as has been said), they would have to be very wicked to watch others go to the synagogue to pray and not join them without any excuse or reason.

And those who are so pious that they fast on the days mentioned above and spend every *Rosh Hodesh* eve as well as Yom Kippur at the synagogue, they are so good that, being kind and seeing the evil done by some wicked people in the republic, which they cannot ban or prohibit, they ask God to disregard their evil deeds and not to inflict the punishment they deserve on those who are good. And they ask for this with all their piety, as we all do on Yom Kippur, with determination and renewed will.

21.

As for the alms and the tsedaka [charity] usually collected in the city separately in each synagogue, some people are accustomed to giving large amounts at all times and in all places, and others never give anything anywhere.

And the reason for this is clear from what has been said about the extraordinary expenses people have in the city. Those who make a lot of money—and indeed it is very much, as has been said—give abundantly without zeal or pain. And those who do not make as much are ashamed to give little as they do not want to appear poor, but they do not want to struggle or limit their spending. Thus they find it better not to give anything, and, with this view, it quickly becomes a habit for them.

22.

The houses and lodgings of the inhabitants of this illustrious city fall into one of two extremes: the good houses are magnificent and absolutely perfect, and the others are low, unlivable, dark, smelly, stuffy, freezing in the winter and very hot in the summer.

And the reason for this is obvious: since it is a city of the court which has innumerable people and grandees, a tiny plot costs a fortune, and building on it is even more expensive, and only very rich and successful people can buy this land and build on it, and they build houses whose splendor corresponds to their power.

Since land is very limited, especially in the Jewish neighborhood, there is no space for courtyards, which are not made, and the best lodgings are built on the top floor so that they would be open to the north wind, which is salubrious. Because of this, ground-floor rooms are very dark, and there is no wind from anywhere, as there are buildings on all sides and no space between them. And because the service spaces are inside the houses and the sewage thrown down [from the top floor] goes to the bottom level inside, as there is no other place or empty space in the building, the bottom stories are very smelly. And because the city is very humid, in winter when the moisture freezes, it gets colder, and the closer to the ground the more humid it is. And in summer, since fresh air cannot enter from anywhere, the bottom story closed on all sides is extremely hot, and it gets so bad that it is unlivable.

23.

The coins circulating in this city, whether aspers, ducats, or copper coins, are in one of two extremes: either very good, new, shiny, and unadulterated, or very bad, counterfeit, and clipped.[10]

And the reason for this is as follows. In this city, coins circulate in great quantities, more than in any other part of the kingdom, especially the coins paid out at the court on the day of the Divan, and their amount is infinite. And all other coins—and there are a lot—are of low quality, rough, counterfeit, or clipped. Thus, only those coins that come from the Treasury are good, and, due to the great number of deals and transactions concluded in the city, they are used as soon as they are received, thus they never remain in anyone's hands for a long time and do not mix with other coins. Hence, the gold and silver coins can be only in one of two extremes.

As for copper coins, which are not distributed by the court, it is well known why they are in the two extremes. When new coins are minted, they equal one [denier] *tournois*, as is stipulated by the king's law and decree, and at that time only new coins are in circulation.[11] Similarly, when they devalue to two for one [denier] *tournois* or when they equal as little as before, that is three for one [denier] *tournois* everyone puts the new coins aside for another time and uses the old ones that were saved for such a time and that come from all parts of the kingdom. Hence, copper coins are only either new or very old.

24.

Those who come to this city to resolve their matters at the king's court or the houses of his courtiers and grandees get their affairs settled in one of two extreme ways: either through paying a lot of money or without paying anything at all. And those who spend moderately are unable to settle their affairs or conclude their matters.

And the reason for this is as follows. By conducting an affair with a grandee with the help of money, one attracts many intermediaries and negotiators both inside and outside the grandee's household, and all of them want to feast and be sweetened, and not even for speaking or

negotiating in one's favor, but merely for not speaking against him or harming him. And everyone wants to feast and to feed and those who can feed the grandee with whom they negotiate, do all they can in order to win a favor from him.

And those who cannot pay what is demanded do not get anything done, because one displeased person is enough to destroy what the others have arranged. And those who do not want to pay anything at all, despite putting their matters at risk, conclude them quickly and have everything resolved and settled without any delay or expense, as they defend their rights or prove their cause at the court or before a pasha, on the day of the Divan, without any intermediaries.

And most of the time, what one accomplishes or could accomplish with a lot of money is accomplished if one solicits his matter himself, without paying anyone, because, though the authorities hear very well what one tells them, they do not act unless they see that what is asked of them is reasonable. And if no one knows about one's matter because he does not talk to any intermediaries, he does not acquire enemies, who could harm him, and conducts his matter without any trouble. And the fear that the matter will fail or the desire to settle it quickly and in a certain way prompts one to act and negotiate with the help of money, which is what most people do, thinking that it is safer, whereas in reality it is more dangerous.

25.

Virtuous women, who are the majority, are so honest and reticent that they do not speak to any men no matter how close they are to the family and are not even seen by them. And those who are not virtuous—there are very few of them, and they belong to the low classes—are so dissolute that they speak to such men more than to their husbands.

And the reason for this is that the houses in Constantinople, as we have said, are very narrow, and there is not enough space to build patios or even verandas, which is why they expand more in height than in length or width. And since the women have no place to relax or chat with their neighbors, the virtuous and honorable ones, who are the majority, are forced to stay in their rooms completely secluded with their daughters or female slaves, doing handwork or other things. And because they are used to this and are not accustomed to doing washing, cleaning, or other such things which are done by the slaves or hired maids, they do not go out to the reception room while there are men around, even if they are close to the family.

And those women who are not very virtuous do not mind being dissolute, and since they have no other place to relax or chat but the windows and doorways that face the street, they talk and chat from there with men and women at the windows and doorways on the opposite side or on their own side and with those who pass by on the street. This habit, together with constant idleness without a minute of work, makes them so dissolute that they never leave the windows and doorways from where they speak and chat with everyone, both men and women.

And the women of low classes, when they get to this extreme, go to their husbands' shops to buy and sell, and what their husbands do any which way they do with great persistence and in an orderly way.

26.

With regard to the children of the inhabitants of Constantinople, there are two extreme [*sic*] extremes: some are still young and have eight or ten children and expect to have even more, and others are already old, do not have children and do not expect to have any.

And the reason for this is that as we have said, [the climate in] the city is very temperate, and the air is very thin and very good, and this place is exceedingly humid, and for this reason it is favorable for quick conception, which is why the inhabitants multiply in abundance, and usually the women conceive every year. Because most women are not used to raising children, they always have wet nurses who raise and nurse the children, and the women conceive again. And thus the people multiply in abundance with the help of the place and the temperate air, as well as rest and repose.

And because the air is thin and the earth is humid, the air easily corrupts. And because of these reasons and also because innumerable people come to the city from various places and bring infections, there are always plagues. And they are so cruel that when a plague enters a home, especially if there are young children, it does not go away until it takes—*has ve-shalom* [God forbid]—what it can get, leaving a person who had many children without any. And those whose homes it does not enter, because they are cautious and flee to faraway places, do not lose their children. But because of our sins, there are very few children as sooner or later the plague comes for everyone, and when people get old, they are childless and unable to have more children, and thus they die at once ending their lives and their family lines.

* * *

There are many more extremes which I will not relate here in order not to surpass the number of twenty-six, which stands for the name of our merciful God representing his essence, compassion, and infinite benevolence in which I hope to recover from the many travails, tribulations, and calamities that we have endured in this affair in the service of our glorious God and our republic, resisting our unfortunate fate and adverse destiny that, during this laborious journey, have been cruelly shooting at us their poisonous arrows.[12] In particular, because of our sins, we were deprived of the best and most precious members of our delegation, and six times we saw occasions and dispositions of planets favorable for the fulfillment of our goal when it could have been easily achieved. But every time, contrary to all human expectations, our plans were destroyed for one reason or another, which, in my view, came about through the intercession of the divine providence, as in such universal cases it cannot be anything else.

And we have to believe this in the hope that it is for the better, although at present we do not know this, because we ourselves were the cause of why these six times our goal was not achieved until this day, the end of the holiday of Sukkot of 5328 [1567], sometimes because of the negligence of petitioners in Salonica and sometimes because of our disagreement about the way of conducting our affair. And so we are here, in Constantinople, hoping that on the seventh time the perfect result will be accomplished, arranged by God's mercy and through his divine providence, which he will grant us as he did with the creation of the universe, when he did not bestow ultimate perfection on the things he had created until the seventh day when he ceased his work, which all the time while it was being performed was regarded imperfect. And when, having stopped the work, he reposed, all the things he had created have reached the ultimate perfection that can be received through the divine grace due to the supremacy of the seventh day when the Lord of the universe reposed and rested.

And thus he wanted, and ordered, and commanded in his Law [Gen 2: 2–3] that among the days the seventh day would be celebrated, sanctified, and distinguished from all other ones by its superiority. And he commanded that among the months the most distinguished would be the seventh month and in that month he saved our fathers and led them away from the labors and tribulations of Egypt, and he commanded that our main holiday commemorating our liberation [i.e., Passover] would be celebrated in the seventh month, which is Nisan.[13] And, according to our sages, our salvation and redemption are to come in this month.

And he wanted that among the years the seventh one would also be distinguished from all preceding years by its supremacy. For this reason, he commanded that in that year all debtors would be freed of their debts and their creditors could not demand them [Deut 15:1], because in that year—superior to the others by the virtue of being the seventh one—everyone would be liberated. And for this reason, the Jewish slaves, after serving six years, would be freed in the seventh year [Ex 21:2–6; Deut 15: 12–18].

And God wanted to demonstrate the supremacy of this number not only in inferior but also in superior things, and so he created seven planets and celestial bodies in seven skies whose influence and dictate were to regulate, rule, and govern the inferior world.

And conveying and representing this design, the cosmographers divided the inhabited part of the terrestrial sphere into seven climates.[14]

And mathematicians attribute to this perfect number of seven many properties, one of which, distinguishing it from all other numbers, is that by adding the first even number, which is two, to the second odd number, which is five, we obtain seven. And the same thing happens when we do the opposite, namely, add three, which is the first odd number (because one, in spite of being the foundation of all numbers, is not a number, as is clear from the definition of number which is understood to be a sum of several ones, so that three is the first odd number) to the second even number, we obtain seven. And this is not true of any other number, which points to its ultimate perfection and supremacy, as it can be obtained in different ways.

And it has another important property which points to its ultimate perfection: it is similar to the primary cause in that [it does not consist of other numbers], nor is it contained in any of them, which is not true of any other number.[15] This is so because, according to the mathematicians, there are nine numbers, and since, as is well-known, one is not a number, the first number is two, which, while not consisting of other numbers (as one is not a number), is contained in eight because two times four is eight. And five, while not consisting of other numbers, is contained in ten, because two times five is ten. And six consists of three twos or of two threes, and, as has been said, eight, nine, and ten consist of other numbers. And seven does not consist of any nor is it contained in the other numbers which points to its perfection, namely, of being self-sufficient and not containing parts of anything or being a part of anything, except for being contained in itself, which is certainly the ultimate degree of perfection for which it is greatly revered.

Hence, since this greatly honored number possesses ultimate perfection, I hope that with the help of the divine providence, during the seventh conjunction that we are awaiting, the labors and fatigues we have endured in this journey will come to an end. As God wanted us to repent in spirit and bear dangers to our lives and detriment to our persons and property, we are suffering even today, hoping that through the divine grace and mercy we will be liberated during this seventh conjunction, as God commanded that slaves would be freed from their captivity in the seventh year, as has been said. And all of us who have labored in this affair can certainly say that during all six of these conjunctions, until the seventh one, we have endured more than a year of fortunate captivity.

Notes

Translated by Olga Borovaya from the following edition: Moisés Almosnino, *Crónica de los reyes otomanos*, ed. Pilar Romeu Ferré (Barcelona: Tirocinio, 1998), 207–234.

1. "Respite," for lack of a more precise term, is my translation of *refrijeryo*, lit. "refreshment," "cooling off."

2. "Fervor" stands for *kemamyento de sangre,* lit. "burning of the blood."

3. Here, "climate" corresponds to *tyempo* in the original, i.e., weather, but Almosnino obviously means "climate." He uses the term "climate" to refer to parts of the inhabited world. (See n. 14.)

4. *Mar mayor* and *Mar Oseano*, respectively. *Mar mayor* means "ocean-accessible sea" as opposed to "inland sea" (*mar menor*), such as the Sea of Marmara. In the sixteenth century, *Mar Océano* was the Spanish term for the Atlantic.

5. "In the city" is opposed to Galata, now part of Istanbul.

6. In the original, this paragraph and the following one are convoluted and contain numerous pleonastic expressions. I had to abridge and partly paraphrase them.

7. A few lines are missing in the manuscript transcribed by Pilar Romeu. The passage in brackets is taken from Cansino's version quoted by Romeu. (*Crónica de los reyes otomanos*, 219.)

8. This is a paraphrase of Almosnino's confusing and ungrammatical sentence that can be understood only from a larger context.

9. This is a paraphrase of Almosnino's explanation that is convoluted and seems to lack logic. Apparently, the goldsmiths take out the stones in order to sell them and the gold separately (or just the gold), thus losing both on the stones and the original value of the broken items. However, they hardly expect to get the price of the original jewelry, which is why the saying quoted by Almosnino—*de kyeres a tyenes*—is irrelevant.

10. "Asper" is the European term for the Ottoman silver coin *akçe*, the official Ottoman currency.

Aside from their own gold coins (*sultanı*), the Ottomans widely used Venetian ducats, the two coins having the same weight.

11. *Livre tournois* was a French currency and a unit of account used in France in the Middle Ages and the early modern period. 1 livre was divisible into 20 sous, and 1 sou was divisible into 12 deniers. (Romeu erroneously vocalized it as *tornes*. It should be *turnus*. (*Crónica de los reyes otomanos*, 227.) I thank Francesca Trievellato for helping me resolve this problem.

Since at the time coins did not have any indication of their value, their official value was determined by royal edicts.

12. The numeric value of the Hebrew letters *yod heh waw heh* representing God's name is 26 (10+5+6+5).

13. Nisan, which used to be the first month of the Hebrew calendar, became the seventh month only in the first or second century CE (see "Calendars" in *The Anchor Bible Dictionary*, vol. 1, 814–820.)

14. Ancient and medieval scholars divided the inhabited area of the earth into seven climates that lay between parallels of latitude and are characterized by similar weather patterns and equal length of the longest day.

15. The clause in brackets is missing in the text, but appears (below) as part of the same phrase.

BIBLIOGRAPHY

Adler, Marcus Nathan. *The Itinerary of Benjamin of Tudela: Critical Text, Translation and Commentary.* New York, 1907.

Atçıl, Zahit. "Why Did Süleyman the Magnificent Execute His Son Şehzade Mustafa in 1553?" *The Journal of Ottoman Studies* 48 (2016): 67–104.

Akrish, Isaac. "Sefer kiryat arbain." In *Sephardi Lives: A Documentary History of the Ottoman Judeo-Spanish World and its Diaspora, 1700–1950*, edited by Julia P. Cohen and Sarah A. Stein, 124–125. Stanford, CA, 2014.

Ahmed, Shahab, and Nenad Filipovic. "The Sultan's Syllabus: A Curriculum for the Ottoman Imperial medreses Prescribed in a fermān of Qānūnī I Süleymān, Dated 973 (1565)." *Studia Islamica*, No. 98/99 (2004), 183–218.

Alcoba, Laura. "La Question du pouvoir au miroir ottoman." In *Littérature et exotisme, XVI–XVIIIè siècles*, edited by Dominique de Courcelles, 17–34. Paris, 1998.

Almosnino, Moisés. *Crónica de los reyes otomanos.* Edited by Pilar Romeu Ferré. Barcelona, 1998.

Almosnino, Moses. *Extremos y grandezas de Constantinopla, traducido por Iacob Cansino. . . .* Madrid, 1638.

———. *Regimiento de la Vida.* Edited by Samuel Mendes de Sola and associates. Amsterdam, 1729.

Almosnino, Moshe ben Baruk. *Regimiento de la vida. Tratado de los suenyos.* Edited by John M. Zemke. Tempe, 2004.

Alpert, Michael. "Dr. Angel Pulido and Philo-Sephardism in Spain." *Jewish Historical Studies* 40 (2005): 105–119.

"*Al-Zarqālī (or Azarquiel), Abū IIsḥāqibrāhīm Ibn Yaḥyā Al-Naqqāsh.*" *Complete Dictionary of Scientific Biography.* http://www.encyclopedia.com/doc/1G2-2830904769.html. Accessed July 25, 2012.

Amadís de Gaula. Constantinople, 1540.

Amador de los Ríos, José. *Estudios históricos, políticos y literarios.* Madrid, 1848.

———. *Historia social, politica, y religiosa de los judíos de España y Portugal.* Madrid, 1960.

Arbós, Cristina. "Los cancioneros castellanos del siglo XV como fuente para la historia de los judíos españoles." In *Jews and Conversos: Studies in Society and the Inquisition*, edited by Yosef Kaplan, 74–82. Jerusalem, 1985.

Aristotle. *Categories.*

———. *Metaphysics*

———. *Meteorology.*

———. *Nicomachean Ethics*

———. *On Generation and Corruption.*

———. *Politics.*

———. *Problems.*

Artunç, Cihan. "The Price of Legal Institutions: The *Beratlı* Merchants in the Eighteenth-Century Ottoman Empire." *The Journal of Economic History* 75, no. 3 (2015): 720–746.

Asá, Abraham. *Sefer Tsorche Tsibbur: Dinim kojidos de libros de konsuelos*. Constantinople, 1733.

Asher, A., trans. and ed. *The Itinerary of Rabbi Benjamin of Tudela*. Vol. I. London and Berlin, 1840.

Ashkenazi, Jonah. *Hakdamah del estanpador, in Tanach: Arbaa v'esrim*. Constantinople, 1739.

Attias, David. *La Güerta de oro*. Livorno, 1778.

Ávila Gallego, Daniel de. *Diálogo del Colorado*. Edited by Pilar Romeu Ferré. Barcelona, 2014.

Aviñón, Juan de. *Sevillana medicina*. Sevilla, 1885.

Barnai, Jacob. "Christian Messianism and the Portuguese Marranos: The Emergence of Sabbateanism in Smyrna." *Jewish History* 7, no. 2 (1993): 119–126.

———. "Organization and leadership in the Jewish community of Izmir in the seventeenth century." In *The Jews of the Ottoman Empire*, edited by Avigdor Levy, 275–286. Princeton, 1994.

Beinart, Haim. "The *Conversos* and Their Fate." In *Spain and the Jews*, edited by Elie Kedourie, 92–122. London, 1992.

Beit-Arié, M. "La caligrafía hebrea en España: desarrollo, ramificaciones y vicisitudes." In *Moreshet Sefarad: el legado de Sefarad*. Vol. 1, edited by Haim Beinart, 289–301. Jerusalem, 1992.

Bekius, Réné. "Polyglot Amsterdam Printing Presses 1620s–1720s: Armenian and Jewish Printers Compared." *Journal of Semitic Studies*, Supplement 24 (2008): 23–64.

Bellaiche Cohen, Annie. "Un Journal judéo-espagnol: *El Verdadero Progreso israelita* à Paris, en 1864." In *La Presse judéo-espagnole, support et vecteur de la modernité*, edited by Rosa Sánchez and Marie-Christine Varol Bornes, 37–51. Istanbul, 2013.

Belon du Mans, Pierre. *Les observations de plusieurs singularités et choses mémorables trouvées en Grèce, Asie, Judée, Egypte, Arabie et autres pays. . .* Paris, 1555.

Benaim, Annette. *Sixteenth-Century Judeo-Spanish Testimonies: An Edition of Eighty-Four Testimonies from the Sephardic Responsa in the Ottoman Empire.* Leiden, 2012.

Benbassa, Esther, and Aron Rodrigue. *Sephardi Jewry: A History of the Judeo-Spanish Community, 14th–20th Centuries.* Berkeley, 2000.

Ben-Menachem, Naphtali. "Writings by Rabbi Moses Almosnino." *Sinai* 19 (1946–47): 268–85. In Hebrew.

Ben-Naeh, Yaron, and Giacomo Saban. "Three German Travellers on Istanbul Jews." *Journal of Modern Jewish Studies* 12 (2013): 1, 35–51.

Bergdolt, Klaus. *Wellbeing: A Cultural History of Healthy Living.* Translated by Jane Dewhurst. Cambridge, UK, 2008.

Berlin, Charles. "A Sixteenth-Century Hebrew Chronicle of the Ottoman Empire: The *Seder Eliyahu Zuta* of Elijah Capsali and Its Message." In *Studies in Jewish Bibliography History and Literature in Honor of Edward Kiev*, edited by Charles Berlin. 21–44. New York, 1971.

Bnaya, Meir Zevi. *Moshe Almosnino of Saloniki: His Life and Work.* Tel Aviv, 1996. In Hebrew.

Bodian, Miriam. *Hebrews of the Portuguese Nation.* Bloomington, 1997.

Bora, Siren. "Formation of the Jewish Press in Izmir: The First Jewish Newspaper *Üstad.*" *Tarih ve Toplum* 127 (July 1994): 18–22. In Turkish.

Borovaya, Olga. *Modern Ladino Culture: Press, Belles Lettres, and Theater in the Late Ottoman Empire.* Bloomington, 2011.

———. "Shmuel Saadi Halevy/Sam Lévy Between Ladino and French: Reconstructing a Writer's Social Identity." In *Modern Jewish Literatures: Intersections and Boundaries*, edited by Sheila Jelen, Michael Kramer, and L. Scott Lerner, 83–103. Philadelphia, 2011.

Boruchoff, David A. "Historiography with License: Isabel, the Catholic Monarch and the Kingdom of God." In *Isabel la Católica, Queen of Castile: Critical Essays*, edited by David Boruchoff, 225–294. New York, 2003.

Boyar, Ebru, and Kate Fleet. *A Social History of Ottoman Istanbul.* Cambridge, UK, and New York, 2010.

Braude, Benjamin. "Foundation Myths of the *Millet* System." In *Christians and Jews in the Ottoman Empire.* Vol. 1, edited by Benjamin Braude and Bernard Lewis. 69–88. New York and London, 1982.

———. "International Competition and Domestic Cloth in the Ottoman Empire, 1500–1650." *Review of the Fernand Braudel Center* 2 (1979): 437–451.

Bravo, María Antonia del. "Angel Pulido y el sefardismo internacional." *Hispania Sacra* 92 (1993): 739–762.

Bregoli, Francesca. *Mediterranean Enlightenment, Livornese Jews, Tuscan Culture.* Stanford CA, 2014.

El Buletino mensual de la comunidad israelita de Rodes, November 1928.
Bunis, David M. *Guide to Reading and Writing Judezmo*. New York, 1975.
———. *The Historical Development of Judezmo Orthography: A Brief Sketch*. New York, 1974.
———. "Judeo-Spanish." In *Encyclopedia of Jews in the Islamic World*, edited by Norman Stillman. Leiden, 2010.
Busbecq, Ogier Ghiselin de. *The Turkish Letters*. Baton Rouge, 2005.
Camargo, Martin. *Ars dictaminis, Ars dictandi*. Turnhout, 1991.
Cantero Burgos, Francisco. "El Cancionero de Baena: judíos y conversos en él." *Sefarad* 26 (1967): 71–101.
Caplan, Meir Judah. ["A letter to the Editor."] *El Verdadero progreso israelita*, Sept. 30, 1864, 33–34.
Carlebach, Elisheva. *The Pursuit of Heresy*. New York, 1990.
Carmoly, Eliakim. *La Famille Almosnino*. Paris, 1850.
Carpenter, Dwayne E. "A *Converso* Best-Seller: *Celestina* and Her Foreign Offspring." In *Crisis and Creativity*, edited by Benjamin Gampel, 267–281. New York, 1997.
Carrión, Sem Tob de. "Proverbios morales." In *Diccionario filológico de literatura medieval española*, edited by C. Alvar and J. M. Lucía, 941–944. Madrid, 2009.
Casco Solís, Juan. "Topografías Médicas: Revisión Y Cronología." *Asclepio* 53, no. 1 (2001): 213–243.
Cassuto, Umberto. *Gli ebrei a Firenze nell'età del Rinascimento*. Florence, 1918.
Chartier, Roger. *Order of Books: Readers, Authors, and Libraries in Europe Between the Fourteenth and Eighteenth Centuries*. Translated by Lydia G. Cochrane. Stanford, CA, 1994.
Cicero. *On Friendship*.
Cohen, Dov. "Un bien conocido negociante i luchador comunal: Muevas notisias sobre Uziel (1816–1881), precursor de la prensa en djudeoespaniol." In *La Presse judéo-espagnole, support et vecteur de la modernité*, edited by Rosa Sánchez and Marie-Christine Varol Bornes, 231–252. Istanbul, 2013.
Cohen, Julia P. *Becoming Ottoman: Sephardi Jews and Imperial Citizenship in the Modern Era*. Oxford, 2014.
Cohen, Julia P., and Sarah A. Stein. "Sephardic Scholarly Worlds: Toward a Novel Geography of Modern Jewish History." *The Jewish Quarterly Review* 100, no. 3 (2010): 349–384.
Cohen, Marc. "Aristotle's Metaphysics." In *The Stanford Encyclopedia of Philosophy*, edited by Edward N. Zalta. Summer 2014 Edition. http://plato.stanford.edu/archives/sum2014/entries/aristotle-metaphysics/. Accessed September 9, 2014.
Copenhagen, Carol Anne. "Letters and Letter-Writing in Fifteenth Century Castile. A Study and Catalogue." PhD diss., University of California, Davis, 1984.

Costa Gomes, Rita. "Letters and Letter-Writing in Fifteenth Century Portugal." *Reading, Interpreting and Historicizing: Letters as Historical Sources. EUI Working Paper*, no. 2 (2004): 11–38.

Crews, Cynthia. *Extracts from the Me'am Lo'ez (Genesis) with a Translation and Glossary*. Leeds, 1960.

Dan, Joseph. *Jewish Mysticism and Jewish Ethics*. Seattle and London, 1977.

Dankoff, Robert. *An Ottoman Mentality: The World of Evliya Çelebi*. Leiden, 2004.

Danon, Abraham, "Abu Suad i rabi Moshe Almosnino." *El Tyempo*, April 17, 1902, 5–6.

———. "La Communauté juive de Salonique au XVIè siècle." *Revue des Études Juives* 40 (1900): 206–230; 41 (1900): 250–265.

Darling, Linda T. "Mirrors for Princes in Europe and the Middle East: A Case of Historiographical Incommensurability." In *East Meets West in the Middle Ages and Early Modern Times*, edited by Albrecht Classen, 223–242. Berlin and Boston, 2013.

Díaz-Mas, Paloma. *Sephardim: The Jews from Spain*. Chicago, 1992.

Die Allgemeine Zeitung des Judentums, July 23, 1842, 39–40.

The Digitized Ladino Library at the Sephardic Studies Project at Stanford University. http://ladino.stanford.edu.

Dogan, Mehmet Ali. "Evangelizing the Jews: Western Missionaries and their Encounters with the Sabbatean/Dönme Community in the Ottoman Empire." *International Journal of Turcologia* 9, no. 18 (2014): 65–82.

Dundar, Fuat. "Empire of Taxonomy: Ethnic and Religious Identities in the Ottoman Surveys and Census." *Middle Eastern Studies* 51, no. 1 (2015): 136–158.

["Editorial."] *El Jurnal isrealit*, December 27, 1860, 1.

Einbinder, Susan L. "Pen and Scissors: A Medieval Debate." *Hebrew Union College Annual* 65 (1994–1995): 261–276.

Elliot, Matthew. "Dress Codes in The Ottoman Empire: The Case of the Frank." In *Ottoman Customs: From Textile to Identity*, edited by Suraiya Faroqhi and Christoph K. Neuman, 103–123. Istanbul, 2004.

Emmanuel, Isaac S. *Histoire des Israélites de Salonique: Histoire sociale, économique et littéraire de la Ville Mère en Israël*. Paris, 1936.

Encyclopedia Judaica. 2nd ed., edited by Michael Berenbaum and Fred Skolnik. Detroit, 2007.

———. "Abraham Zacuto."

———. "Almosnino, Sephardi Family."

———. "Ashkenazi, Jonah ben Jacob."

———. "Ethical Literature."

———. "Istanbul. Hebrew Printing,"

———. "Ladino."

———. "Manasseh (Menasseh) ben Israel."

———. "Shabbetai Zevi."

The Encyclopedia of Jews in the Islamic World, edited by Norman Stillman. Leiden, 2010.

———. "Ashkenazi, Jonah ben Jacob."

———. "Assa, Abraham Ben Isaac."

———. "Culi (Hulli), Jacob ben Meir."

———. "Hatt-i Sherif of Gulhane (Tanzimat Fermani)."

———. "Judeo-Spanish."

———. "Salonica."

Evliya Çelebi Efendi. *Narrative of the Travels in Europe, Asia, and Africa.* London, 1968.

Fellous, Sonia. "Moise Arragel un traducteur juif au service des Chrétiens." In *Transmission et Passages en monde juif*, edited by Esther Benbassa, 119–136. Paris, 1997.

Ferguson, Charles A. "Diglossia." *Word* 15 (1959): 325–340.

Filippini, Jean-Pierre. *Il Porto di Livorno e la Toscana (1676–1814)*. Vol. 3. Naples, 1998.

Finkel, Caroline. *Osman's Dream: The History of the Ottoman Empire*, 1300–1923. London, 2005.

Fisher, Alan. "Süleyman and his Sons." In *Soliman le Magnifique et son temps*, edited by Gilles Veinstein, 117–126. Paris, 1992.

Fishman, Joshua. "Bilingualism and biculturalism as individual and as societal phenomena." In *Language and Ethnicity in Minority Sociolinguistic Perspective*, edited by Joshua Fishman, 181–201. Clevedon & Philadelphia, 1989.

Fleischer, Cornell H. *Bureaucrat and Intellectual in the Ottoman Empire*. Princeton, 1986.

———. "The Lawgiver as Messiah." In *Soliman le Magnifique et son temps*, edited by Gilles Veinstein, 150–178. Paris, 1992.

Fotić, Aleksandar. "Belgrade: A Muslim and Non-Muslim Cultural Centre (Sixteenth–Seventeenth Centuries)." In *Provincial Elites in the Ottoman Empire*, edited by Antonis Anastasopoulos, 51–75. Rethymno, 2005.

Frakes, Gerald C., ed. *Early Yiddish Texts: 1100–1750*. New York, 2004.

Franco, Moïse. *Essai sur l'histoire des Israélites de l'Empire Ottoman depuis les origines jusqu'à nos jours*. Paris, 1897.

———. "La littérature actuelle des Israélites d'Orient." *Le Journal de Salonique*, July 6, 1905, 2.

Frankel, Jonathan. *The Damascus Affair: Ritual Murder, Politics, and the Jews in 840*. Cambridge, 1997.

[Fresco, David.] "Los judyos de Turkia en el dyies i syshen siglo." *El Tyempo*, June 28, 1897, 4.

Fuchs, Barbara. "Don Quijote and the Forging of National History." *Modern Language Quarterly* 68, no. 3 (2007): 395–415.

Fudeman, Kirsten. *Vernacular Voices: Language and Identity in Medieval French Jewish Communities*. Philadelphia, 2010.

Galino Carillo, María Angeles. *Los Tratados sobre educacion de principes (siglos XVI y XVII)*. Madrid, 1948.

García Moreno, Aitor, ed. *Relatos del pueblo ladinán (Me'am Lo'ez de Éxodo I)*. Madrid, 2004.

Gaster, Moses. "The Hebrew Version of the Secretum Secretorum: A Medieval Treatise Ascribed to Aristotle." *Journal of the Royal Asiatic Society* (1907): 879–912.

"Gates of the East." *The Voice of Jacob*, Feb. 13, 1846, 80–81.

Gerlach, Stephan. *Aeltern Tage-Buch der von zween. . . .* Frankfurt, 1674.

Gilles, Pierre. *The Antiquities of Constantinople*. New York, 1988.

Ginio, Eyal. "Jews and European Subjects in Eighteenth-Century Salonica: The Ottoman Perspective." *Jewish History* 28, nos. 3–4 (2014): 289–312.

Göçek, Fatma Muge. *East Encounters West: France and the Ottoman Empire in the Eighteenth Century*. New York, 1987.

Goffman, Daniel. *Izmir and the Levantine World, 1550–1650*. Seattle and London, 1990.

———. "Izmir: From Village to Colonial Port City." In *The Ottoman City between East and West. Aleppo, Izmir, and Istanbul*, edited by Daniel Goffman, Edhem Eldem, and Bruce Masters, 79–134. New York, 1999.

———. "Jews in Early Modern Ottoman Commerce." In *Jews, Turks, Ottomans*, edited by Avigdor Levy. Syracuse, 2002.

Gonzalo Maeso, David, and Pascual Recuero, eds. *Me'am Lo'ez. El gran comentario bíblico sefard*. Vol. 0: *(Preliminar): Prolegommenos*. Madrid 1964.

———. *Me'am Lo'ez. El gran comentario bíblico sefard*. Vol. 1: *Beresit* [Genesis], Parte 1. Granada, 1969.

Goodblatt, Morris S. *Jewish Life in Turkey in the XVIth Century as Reflected in the Legal Writings of Samuel de Medina*. New York, 1952.

Graetz, Heinrich. *Geschichte der Juden von den ältesten Zeiten bis auf die Gegenwart*. Vol. IX. Leipzig, 1866.

Gruner, Oskar Cameron, trans. *The Canon of Medicine of Avicenna*. New York, 1973.

Gutwirth, Eleazar. "*Acutissima patria*: Locating Texts before and after the Expulsions." *Hispania Judaica* 8 (2011): 19–38.

———. "Dialogue and the City, circa 1400: Pero Ferruz and the Rabbis of Alcala." *Jewish History* 21 (2007): 43–67.

———. "Elementos étnicos e históricos en las relaciones judeo-conversas en Segovia." In *Jews and Conversos*, edited by Yosef Kaplan, 83–102. Jerusalem, 1985.

———. "Expulsion from Spain and Jewish Historiography." In *Jewish History, Essays in Honour of Chimen Abramsky*, edited by Ada Rapoport-Albert and Steven Zipperstein, 141–161. London, 1988.

———. "Hebrew Letters, Hispanic Mail: Communication Among Fourteenth-Century Aragon Jewry." In *Communication in the Jewish Diaspora in the Pre-Modern Period*, edited by S. Menache, 257–282. Leiden, 1996.

———. "*Hercules furens* and War: on Abravanel's Courtly Context." *Jewish History* 23 (2009): 293–312.

———. "Italy or Spain? The Theme of Jewish Eloquence in *Shevet Yehudah*." In *Daniel Carpi Jubilee Volume*, edited by Minna Rozen, D. Porat, and A. Shapira, 35–67. Tel Aviv, 1996.

———. "Jews and Courts: An Introduction." *Jewish History* 21, no. 1 (2007) 3: 11–13.

———. "A Judeo-Spanish Letter from the Genizah." In *Judeo-Romance Languages*, edited by I. Benabu and Joseph Sermoneta, 127–138. Jerusalem, 1985.

———. "A Medieval Manuscript of Gnomic Verse in Judeo-Spanish Aljamía." In *Circa 1492*, edited by Isaac Benabu, 98–108. Jerusalem, 1992.

———. "Medieval Romance Epistolarity: The Case of the Iberian Jews." *Neophilologus* 84, No. 2 (2000): 207–224.

———. "On the Hispanicity of Sephardic Jewry." *Revue des Études Juives* 145, no. 3–4 (1986): 347–357.

———. "Profayt Duran on Ahitofel: The Practice of Jewish History in Late Medieval Spain." *Jewish History* 4, no. 1 (1989): 59–74.

———. "Religión, historia y las Biblias romanceadas." *Revista Catalana de Teologia* 13 (1988): 115–134.

———. "Towards Expulsion: 1391–1492." In *Spain and the Jews: The Sephardi Experience, 1492 and After*, edited by Elie Kedourie, 51–73. London, 1992.

Gutwirth, Eleazar, and Miguel Angel Motis Dolader. "Twenty-Six Jewish Libraries from Fifteenth-Century Spain." *Library* 18, no. 1 (1996): 27–53.

Hacker, Joseph. "Authors, Readers, and Printers of Sixteenth-Century Hebrew Books in the Ottoman Empire." In *Perspectives on the Hebraic Book. The Myron M. Weinstein Memorial Lectures at the Library of Congress*, edited by Peggy K. Pearlstein, 17–64. Washington D.C., 2012.

———. "The Intellectual Activity of the Jews of the Ottoman Empire During the Sixteenth and Seventeenth Centuries." In *Jewish Thought in the Seventeenth Century*, edited by Isadore Twersky and Bernard Septimus, 95–135. Cambridge MA, 1987.

———. "Superbe et désespoir: L'existence sociale et spirituelle des Juifs ibériques dans l'Empire ottoman." *Revue historique* 578 (1991): 261–293.

———. "The Sürgün System and Jewish Society in the Ottoman Empire during the Fifteenth to the Seventeenth Centuries." In *Ottoman and Turkish Jewry: Community and Leadership*, edited by Aron Rodrigue, 1–66. Bloomington, 1992.

Hacker, Joseph, and Adam Shear. *Jewish Culture and Contexts: Hebrew Book in Early Modern Italy*. Philadelphia, 2011.

"Hakdamah del komponedor," *Shaarei mizrach*, Dec. 29, 1845, 1.

Hammer, Joseph. *Geschichte des Osmanischen Reiches*. Pest, 1827.

Harris, Tracy K. "What Language did the Jews Speak in Pre-Expulsion Spain?" In *Sephardic Identity: Essays on a Vanishing Jewish Culture*, edited by George K. Zucker, 99–111. Jefferson, NC, 2005.

Hassán, Iacob M. "La literatura sefardí culta: sus principales escritores, obras y géneros." In *Judíos. Sefardíes. Conversos*, edited by Angel Alcalá, 319–30. Valladolid, 1995.
Hattox, Ralph S. *Coffee and Coffeehouses: The Origins of a Social Beverage in the Medieval Near East*. Seattle and London, 1985.
Heller, Marvin J. *Printing the Talmud; A History of the Individual Treatises Printed from 1700 to 1750*. Leiden, 1999.
Hippocrates. *Airs, Waters, Places*.
———. *Aphorisms*.
Horowitz, Elliott. "Coffee, Coffeehouses, and the Nocturnal Rituals of Early Modern Jewry." *AJS Review* 14, no. 1 (Spring 1989): 17–46.
———. "The Early Eighteenth Century Confronts the Beard: Kabbalah and Jewish Self- Fashioning." *Jewish History* 8, no. 1–2 (1994): 95–115.
Howe Lybyer, Albert. *The Government of the Ottoman Empire in the Time of Suleiman the Magnificent*. Cambridge, MA, 1913.
ibn Verga, Selomoh. *La vara de Yehudah (Sefer sebet Yehudah)*. Barcelona, 1991.
Illescas, Gonzalo de. *Historia pontifical y católica*. Barcelona, 1606.
Imber, Colin. *Ebus-su'ud: The Islamic Legal Tradition*, Stanford, 1997.
Inalcik, Haul. "Istanbul: An Islamic City." *Journal of Islamic Studies* 1 (1990): 1–23.
Israel, Jonathan I. *European Jewry in the Age of Mercantilism, 1550–1750*, 2nd ed. Oxford, 1989.
Jarcho, Saul. "Galen's Six Non-Naturals: A Bibliographic Note and Translation." *Bull. Hist. Med.* 44, no. 4 (1970): 372–377.
Jerusalmi, Isaac. *From Ottoman Turkish to Ladino. The Case of Mehmet Sadik Rifat Pasha's Risale-i Ahlik to Judge Yehezkel Gabbay's Buen Dotrino*. Cincinnati, OH, 1990.
Jewish Encyclopedia, edited by Isidore Singer. New York, 1901–1906.
———. "Aaron Afia."
———. "Approbation."
———. "Gambling."
———. "Judaeo-Spanish."
———. "Judah ben Samuel Rosanes."
———. "Moses b. Baruch Almosnino."
———. "Profiat Duran."
———. "Turkey."
———. "Yakov Culi."
Kahana, Maoz. "The Allure of Forbidden Knowledge: The Temptation of Sabbatean Literature for Mainstream Rabbis in the Frankist Moment, 1756–1761." *Jewish Quarterly Review* 102, no. 4 (2012): 589–616.
Kamen, Henry. "The Expulsion: Purpose and Consequence." In *Spain and the Jews*, edited by Elie Kedourie, 74–91. London, 1992.
Kerkhof, Maxim, ed. "Un fragmento desconocido del compendio de dichos de sabios y philósofos, traducido del catalán al castellano por Jacob Çadique

de Uclés en 1402." 1999. http://parnaseo.uv.es/Lemir/textos/Kerkhof/Dichos.htm. Accessed April 13, 2013.

Kobbler, Franz. *A Treasury of Jewish Letters: Letters from the Famous and the Humble*. Philadelphia, 1953.

Klein, Elke. "The Widow's Portion: Law, Custom, and Marital Property Among Medieval Catalan Jews." *Viator* 31 (2000): 147–163.

Konortas, Paraskevas. "From *Ta'if e* to *Millet*: Ottoman Terms for the Ottoman Greek Orthodox Community." In *Ottoman Greeks in the Age of Nationalism: Politics, Economy, and Society in the Nineteenth Century*, edited by Dimitri Gondicas and Charles Issawi, 169–179. Princeton, NJ, 1999.

Lazar, Moshe, ed. *The Five Ladino Scrolls: Abraham Asá's Versions of the Hebrew and Aramaic Texts*. Culver City, 1992.

Lehmann, Matthias. *Emissaries from the Holy Land: The Sephardic Diaspora and the Practice of Pan-Judaism in the Eighteenth Century*. Stanford, CA, 2014.

———. *Ladino Rabbinic Literature and Ottoman Sephardic Culture*. Bloomington, 2005.

———. "A Livornese 'Port Jew' and the Sephardim of the Ottoman Empire." *Jewish Social Studies* 11, no. 2 (2005): 51–76.

Lehmann, Matthias, trans. "David Attias." In *The Jew in the Modern World: A Documentary History*, edited by Paul Mendes-Flohr and Jehuda Reinharz, 445–446. New York, 2010.

["A letter from Rafael Uziel."] *Les Archives Israélites*, May 27, 1847, 549–550.

Leviant, Curt, ed. and trans. *King Artus: A Hebrew Arthurian Romance of 1279*. New York, 1969.

Lévy, Sam. *Salonique à la fin du XIXè siècle: Mémoires*. Istanbul, 2000.

Lewis, Bernard. "A Letter from Little Menachem." In *Studies in Judaism and Islam, presented to Shelomoh Dov Goitein*, edited by Shelomo Morag et al., 181–183. Jerusalem, 1981.

———. *The Muslim Discovery of Europe*. New York, 1982.

"Licht und Schattenbilder aus der jüdischen Geschichte der Gegenwart: Die Juden in Rhodus." *Der Orient*, August 8, 1840, 245–248.

Lindberg, David C. *Roger Bacon and the Origins of Perspectiva in the Middle Ages*. Oxford, 1996.

Lleal, Coloma. *El judezmo. El dialecto sefardí y su historia*. Barcelona, 1992.

Loeb, Isidore. "Josef Haccohen et les Chroniqueurs Juifs." *Revue des Etudes Juives* 16 (1888): 28–56.

López de Mendoza, Iñigo, and Marqués de Santillana, *Proemio e carta al condestable de Portugal*, edited by Ángel Gómez-Moreno. Barcelona, 1990.

Lowry, Heath W. "When did the Sephardim arrive in Salonica? The Testimony of the Ottoman Tax-Registers, 1478–1613." In *The Jews of the Ottoman Empire*, edited by Avigdor Levi, 203–214. Princeton, 1994.

El Luzero de la pasensia, Nov. 21, 1885.

Lybyer, Albert Howe. *The Government of the Ottoman Empire in the Time of Suleiman the Magnificent*. Cambridge, MA, 1913.

Macedo, Helder. "A Sixteenth Century Portuguese Novel and the Jewish Press in Ferrara." *European Judaism* 33, no. 1 (2000): 53–58.

Maciejko, Pawel. *The Mixed Multitude: Jacob Frank and the Frankist Movement*. Philadelphia, 2009.

Maimonides, Moses. *Treatise on Asthma*. Translated by Fred Rosner. Philadelphia, 1994.

———. *Two Treatises on the Regimen of Health*. Translated by Ariel Bar-Sela, Hebbel E. Hoff, and Elias Paris. Philadelphia, 1964.

Mañero Lozano, David. "Historiografía novohispana y prosa de ficción del Siglo de Oro." *Criticón* 106 (2009): 79–97.

Mantran, Robert. "L'historiographie ottomane à l'époque de Soliman le Magnifique." In *Soliman le Magnifique et son temps*, edited by Gilles Veinstein, 25–32. Paris, 1992.

Manzalaoui, M.A. ed., *Secretum Secretorum. The Book of Good Governance and Guiding of the Body*. Oxford, 1977.

Marcus, Simon. "A-t-il existé en Espagne un dialecte judéo-espagnol?" *Sefarad* 22 (1962): 129–49.

Markova, Alla. "Un fragmento manuscrito de una novela de caballerías en judeoespañol." *Sefarad* 69, no. 1 (2009): 159–172.

———. "El Tratado del Astrolabio de Mosé Almosnino en un manuscrito de Leningrado." *Sefarad* 51, no. 2 (1991): 437–446.

———. "An Unknown Manuscript, on Astronomy by Moshe Almosnino." In *Hispano-Jewish Civilization after 1492*, edited by Michel Abitbol, Yom-Tov Assis, and Galit Hasan-Rokem, 41–54. Jerusalem, 1997.

Meir Estrugo, José. *El Retorno a Sefard: Cien años después de la inquisición*. Madrid, 1933.

Menavino, Giovanni Antonio. *Trattato de costumi et vita de Turchi*. Florence, 1548.

Mesthrie, R. "Koinés." In *Concise Encyclopedia of Sociolinguistics*. Amsterdam, 2001.

Mevorakh, Barukh. "The Influence of the Damascus Blood Libel on the Development of the Jewish Press in 1840–1846." *Zion* 23–24 (1958–1959): 46–65. In Hebrew.

Mexía, Pedro. *Silva de varia lección*. Edited by Antonio Castro Diaz. Madrid, 1989.

Meyuhas Ginio, Alisa. "Everyday Life in the Sephardic Community of Jerusalem According to the *Meam Loez* of Rabbi Jacob Kuli." *Studia Rosenthaliana* 35 (2001): 133–142.

"Miasma Theory." In *Encyclopedia of Public Health*, edited by Lester Breslow. New York, 2001.

Miller, Elaine R. "The Debate over Pre-Expulsion Judeo-Spanish: Status Quaestionis." In *Languages and Literatures of Sephardic and Oriental Jews: Proceedings of the Sixth International Congress for Research on the Sephardi and Oriental Jewish Heritage*, edited by David M. Bunis, 167–187. Jerusalem, 2009.

———. "Hebrew Verb Forms in the Valladolid Taqqanot of 1432." In *Proceedings of the Twelfth British Conference on Judeo-Spanish Studies*, edited by Hilary Pomeroy and Michael Alpert, 57–68. Leiden and Boston, 2004.

Minervini, Laura. "An *Aljamiado* Version of 'Orlando Furioso': A Judeo-Spanish Transcription of Jeronimo de Urrea's Translation." In *Hispano-Jewish Civilization After 1492*, edited by Michel Abitbol, Yom-Tov Assis Galit, and Hasan-Rokem, 191–201. Jerusalem, 1997.

———. "The Formation of the Judeo-Spanish Koiné: Dialect Convergence in the Sixteenth Century." In *The Proceedings of the Tenth Conference on Judeo-Spanish Studies*, edited by Annette Benaim, 41–53. London, 1999.

———. "'*Llevaron de acá nuestra lengua . . .*': Gli usi linguistici degli ebrei spagnoli in Italia." *Medioevo romanzo* 19, no. 1–2 (1994): 133–192.

Mintz-Manor, Limor. "The Jewish Discovery of America," *Jews & Journeys: Travel & the Performance of Jewish Identity.* An Online Exhibition from the Herbert D. Katz Center for Advanced Judaic Studies 2011–2012. Fellows at the University of Pennsylvania. http://www.library.upenn.edu/exhibits/cajs/fellows12/. Accessed June 5, 2012.

Molho, Isaac. "Un humaniste séfardi de Salonique: Moshe Barouh Almosnino (1518–1581)." *Otsar Yehude Sefarad* 7 (1964): 49–68.

Molho, Michael. "Dos obras maestras en ladino de Moisés Almosnino." In *Estudios y ensayos sobre tópicos judíos*, 95–102. Buenos Aires, 1948.

———. *Kontribusyon a la Istorya de Saloniko.* Salonica, 1932.

———. *Literatura sefardita de Oriente.* Madrid, 1960.

Montequio, Joseph ben Isaac Moses. "*Sefer Ketonet Yosef.*" In *Sephardi Lives: A Documentary History of the Ottoman Judeo-Spanish World and its Diaspora, 1700–1950*, edited by Julia P. Cohen and Sarah A. Stein. Stanford, CA, 2014.

Morreale de Castro, Margherita. "El superlativo en ísimo y la versión castellana del Cortesano." *Revista de Filología Española* 39, no. 1–4 (1955): 46–60, 46.

Naar, Devin. "Fashioning the 'Mother of Israel: The Ottoman Jewish Historical Narrative and the Image of Jewish Salonica." *Jewish History* 28 (2014): 337–372.

———. "Jewish Salonica and the Making of the 'Jerusalem of the Balkans,' 1890–1943." PhD diss., Stanford University, 2011.

Necipoğlu, Gülru. *The Age of Sinan, Architectural Culture in the Ottoman Empire.* London, 2005.

———. *Architecture, Ceremonial and Power, The Topkapı Palace in the Fifteenth and Sixteenth Centuries.* Cambridge MA, 1991.

———. "A Canon for the State, A Canon for the Arts: Conceptualizing the Classical Synthesis of Ottoman Arts and Architecture." In *Soliman le Magnifique et son temps*, edited by Gilles Veinstein, 195–216. Paris, 1992.

———. "The Süleymaniye Complex in Istanbul: An Interpretation." *Muqarnas* 3 (1986): 92–117.

Nehama, Joseph. *Histoire des Israélites de Salonique*. Salonica, 1935.

Nelson Novoa, James. "Consideraciones acerca de una versión aljamiada de los *Diálogos de amor* de León Hebreo." *Sefarad* 65 (2005): 103–126.

———. *Los* Diálogos de amor *de León Hebreo en el marco sociocultural Sefardí del Siglo XVI*. Lisbon, 2006.

———. "Ms. Parma Pal. 2666 as a Document of Sephardi Literary and Philosophical Expression in Fifteenth-Century Spain." *European Judaism* 43, no. 2 (2010): 20–36.

———. "The Peninsula Hither and Thither: Philosophical Texts in Vernacular Languages by Sephardic Jews before and after the Expulsion." *Hispania Judaica* 8 (2011): 149–166.

Nicolay, Nicolas de. *The Navigations, Peregrinations, and Voyages Made into Turkie*. London, 1585.

———. *Quatre premiers livres des navigations. . .* Lyon, 1568.

Offenberg, Adri K. "The Printing History of the Constantinople Hebrew Incunable of 1493: A Mediterranean Voyage of Discovery." *The British Library Journal* 22 (1996): 221–235.

Olival, Fernanda. "Rigor e interesses: os estatutos de limpeza de sangue em Portugal." *Cadernos de Estudos Sefarditas* 4 (2004): 151–182.

Olson, Glending. *Literature as Recreation in the Later Middle Ages*. Ithaca and London, 1982.

Ortola, Marie-Sol, ed. *Viaje de Turquía*. Madrid, 2000.

Pascual Recuero, Pascual. "Las 'crónicas otomanas' de Moisés Almosnino." *Miscelanea de estudios arabes y hebraicos* 33 (1984): 75–104.

Penny, Ralph. "Dialect Contact and Social Networks in Judeo-Spanish." *Romance Philology* 46, no. 2 (1992): 125–140.

Pulgar, Fernando del. *Letras*. Biblioteca Virtual Miguel Cervantes. Biblioteca Virtual Miguel

Cervantes. http://www.cervantesvirtual.com/obra/letras-o/. Accessed November 29, 2012.

Quintana, Aldina. "Aportación lingüística de los romances aragonés y portugués a la coiné judeoespañola." In *Languages and Literatures of Sephardic and Oriental Jews: Proceedings of the Sixth International Congress for Research on the Sephardi and Oriental Jews*, edited by David Bunis, 221–255. Jerusalem, 2009.

———. "From Linguistic Segregation Outside the Common Framework of Hispanic Languages to a de facto Standard." In *Studies in Modern Hebrew and Jewish Languages Presented to Ora (Rodrigue) Schwarzwald*, edited by Malka Muchnik and Tsvi Sadan, 697–714. Jerusalem, 2012.

———. *Geografía lingüística del Judeoespañol: Estudio sincrónico y diacrónico.* Bern, 2006.
———. "The Merger of the Hispanic Medieval Heritage with the Jewish Tradition in Judeo-Spanish Texts (I): Private Letters." *Hispania Judaica* 7 (2010): 317–333.
———. "Responsa Testimonies and Letters Written in the 16th Century Spanish Spoken by Sephardim." *Hispania Judaica* 5 (2007): 283–302.
———. "Sobre la transmisiôn y el formulismo en el Me'am Lo'ez de Yacob Juli." In *IJS Studies in Judaica 3: Proceedings of the Twelfth British Conference on Judeo-Spanish Studies, 24–26 June 2001*, edited by Hilary Pomeroy and Michael Alpert, 69–80. Leiden, 2004.
Ramberti, Benedetto. *Libri tre delle cose de Turchi*. Venice, 1539.
Ray, Jonathan. *After Expulsion: 1492 and the Making of Sephardic Jewry*. New York, 2013.
Richler, Benjamin. "Manuscripts of Avicenna's *Kanon* in Hebrew Translation: A Revised and Up-to-Date List." *Koroth* 8, no. 3–4 (1982): 145–168.
Rodrigue, Aron. "From *Millet* to Minority: Turkish Jewry in the 19th and 20th Centuries." In *Paths of Emancipation*, edited by Pierre Birnbaum and Ira Katznelson, 238–261. Princeton, 1995.
———. "Salonica in Jewish Historiography." *Jewish History* 28 (2014): 439–447.
Romero, Elena. *Creación literaria en lengua sefardí*. Madrid, 1992.
Romeu Ferré, Pilar, ed. *Fuente clara*. Barcelona, 2011.
Romeu Ferré, Pilar. "Diferencias y paralelismos entre la *Crónica de los Reyes Otomanos* de rabí Mosé ben Baruh Almosnino y los *Extremos y Grandezas de Constantinopla* de Iacob Cansino." *Proceedings of the 3rd International Congress of Misgav Yerushalayim* (Jerusalem, 1994): 189–200.
———. "Ejemplificar con el ejemplo: mesalim *y* ma'asiyot en el *Regimiento de la vida* de Moises Almosnino." *Orientalis* 17–18 (1999–2000): 315–322.
———. "Turquismos en la *Crónica de los reyes otomanos* de Mosé ben Baruh Almosnino." *Miscelanea de estudios arabes y hebraicos* 37–38 (1988–1989): 91–100.
Romeu, Pilar and Iacob M. Hassán, "Apuntes sobre la lengua de la *Crónica de los reyes otomanos* de Moisés Almosnino según la edición del manuscrito aljamiado del siglo XVI." *Actas del II Congreso Internacional de Historia de la Lengua Española* II (Madrid, 1992): 161–169.
Roth, Cecil. *The House of Nasi: Doña Gracia of the House of Nasi*. Skokie IL, 2001.
———. *The House of Nasi: The Duke of Naxos*. Philadelphia, 1947.
———. "The Marrano typography in England." In *Studies in Books and Booklore: Essays in Jewish Bibliography*, edited by Cecil Roth, 1–11. Westmead, 1972.
———. "The Role of Spanish in the Marrano Diaspora." In *Studies in Books and Booklore: Essays in Jewish*, edited by Cecil Roth, 111–120. Westmead, 1972.

———. "The Spanish Press in Smyrna." In *Studies in Books and Booklore: Essays in Jewish Bibliography*, edited by Cecil Roth, 23–26. Westmead, 1972.

Rozen, Minna. "Contest and Rivalry in Mediterranean Maritime Commerce in the First Half of the 18th Century: The Jews of Salonika and the European Presence." *Revue des Études Juives* 147 (1988): 309–352.

———. *Facing the Sea: The Jews of Salonika in the Ottoman Era (1430–1912)*. Afula, 2011.

———. *A History of the Jewish Community in Istanbul: The Formative Years, 1453–1566*. Leiden, 2002.

———. "Individual and Community in the Jewish Society of the Ottoman Empire: Salonika in the Sixteenth Century." In *The Jews of the Ottoman Empire*, edited by Avigdor Levy, 215–274. Princeton, 1994.

———. "The People." In *The Cambridge History of Turkey. Volume 3: The Later Ottoman Empire, 1603–1839*, edited by Surayia Faroqhi, 255–271. Cambridge, 2006.

———. "Public Space and Private Space Among the Jews of Istanbul in the Sixteenth and Seventeenth Centuries." *Turcica* 30 (1998): 331–346.

———. "Strangers in a Strange Land: The Extraterritorial Status of Jews in Italy and the Ottoman Empire in the 16th to the 18th Centuries." In *Ottoman and Turkish Jewry: Community and Leadership*, edited by Aron Rodrigue, 123–166. Bloomington, 1992.

Rycault, Paul. *The Present State of the Ottoman Empire*. New York, 1971.

Şahin, Kaya. "Imperialism, Bureaucratic Consciousness, and the Historian's Craft." In *Writing History at the Ottoman Court*, edited by H. Erdem Çipa and Eniine Fetvaci, 39–57. Bloomington, 2013.

Sánchez de Uribe, Tomás Antonio. *Colección de poesías castellanas anteriores al siglo XV*. Vol. I. Madrid, 1779.

Sanjian, Avedis K., and Andreas Tietze, ed. *Eremya Chelebi Komurjian's Armeno-Turkish Poem 'The Jewish Bride.'* Wiesbaden, 1981.

Saperstein, Marc. "Moses Almosnino: Sermon on *Eleh Fequde*." In M. Saperstein, *Jewish Preaching, 1200–1800: An Anthology*, 217–239. New Haven and London, 1989.

Saraiva, Antonio Jose. *The Marrano Factory. The Portuguese Inquisition and Its New Christians, 1536–1765*. Leiden, Boston, and Köln, 2001.

Schaub, Jean-Frédéric. *Les juifs du roi d'Espagne. Oran, 1507–1669*. Paris, 1999.

Scholem, Gershom. *Sabbatai Sevi: The Mystical Messiah*. Princeton, 1973.

Schwartz, Seth. "Language, Power and Identity in Ancient Palestine." *Past and Present* 148 (1995): 3–47.

Schwarzwald, Ora (Rodrigue), ed. *Sidur para Mujeres en Ladino: Salonica, Siglo XVI*. Jerusalem, 2012.

———. "Ladino Instructions in *Meza de el alma* and in *Seder Nashin* from Thessaloniki in the Sixteenth century." In *Around the Point: Studies in*

Jewish Literature and Culture, edited by Hillel Weiss, Roman Katsman, and Ber Kotlerman, 121–134. Cambridge, 2014.

———. "Ladino Literature." In *Cambridge Dictionary of Judaism and Jewish Culture*, edited by Judith Baskin. Cambridge, 2011.

———. "Linguistic Features of a Sixteenth-Century Women's Ladino Prayer Book: The Language Used for Instructions and Prayers." In *Selected Papers from the Fifteenth Conference on Judeo-Spanish Studies*, edited by Hilary Pomeroy, Chris J. Pountain, and Elena Romero, 247–260. London, 2012.

———. "The Relationship between Ladino Liturgical Texts and Spanish Bibles." In *The Hebrew Bible in Fifteenth-Century Spain: Exegesis, Literature, Philosophy and the Arts*, edited by Jonathan Decter and Arturo Prats, 223–243. Leiden and Boston, 2012.

———. "Le style du *Me'am Lo'ez*: une tradition linguistique." *Yod (nouvelle série)* 11/12 (2006–2007): 77–112.

———. "Two Sixteenth-Century Ladino Prayer Books for Women." *European Judaism* 43, no. 2 (2010): 35–49, 40.

[Segura, Pinchas de.] "A Sermon Delivered at the Great Synagogue of Smyrna on the Arrival of Sir Moses and Lady Montefiore in that City." Izmir, 1840. In Hebrew.

Sephiha, Haim-Vidal. *Le ladino, judéo-espagnol calque*. Paris, 1973.

Silay, Kemal. "Ahmedi's History of the Ottoman Dynasty." *Journal of Turkish Studies* 16 (1992): 129–200.

Şişman, Cengiz. *The Burden of Silence: Sabbatai Sevi and the Evolution of the Ottoman Dönmes*. Oxford, 2015.

"Textos clasicos españoles ladinizados." http://btjerusalem.com/aspamiac.htm. Accessed May 18, 2013.

Terzioğlu, Derin. "The Imperial Circumcision Festival of 1582: An Interpretation." *Muqarnas* 1 (1995): 84–100.

The Times, January 6, 1840, 4, col. D.

Tirosh-Samuelson, Hava. "Jewish Philosophy on the Eve of Modernity." In *History of Jewish Philosophy*, edited by Daniel H. Frank and Oliver Leaman, 499–563. London, 1997.

———. "Review of Meir Zevi Bnaya, *Moshe Almosnino of Salonika: His Life and Work*." *Jewish Quarterly Review* 89 (1998): 250–252.

———. "The Ultimate End of Human Life in Post-Expulsion Philosophical Literature." In *Crisis and Continuity in the Sephardic World: 1391–1648*, edited by Benjamin R. Gampel, 223–254. New York, 1997.

Trachtenberg, Joshua. *Jewish Magic and Superstition: A Study in Folk Religion*. New York, 1939.

Trivellato, Francesca. *The Familiarity of Strangers: The Sephardic Diaspora, Livorno, and Cross Cultural Trade in the Early Modern Period*. New Haven & London, 2008.

Trudgill, Peter. *Dialects in Contact*. Oxford, 1986.

———. "Migration, New Dialect Formation and Sociolinguistic Refunctionalisation: Reallocation as an outcome of dialect contact." *Transactions of the Philological Society* 97, no. 2 (1999): 245–256.

Tsur, Yaron. "Dating the Demise of the Western Sephardi Jewish Diaspora." In *Jewish Culture and Society in North Africa*, edited by Emily Gottreich and Daniel Schroeder, 93–107. Bloomington, 2011.

"Turkey: Progress." *The Voice of Jacob*, July 31, 1846, 180.

Uyar, Mesut and Edward Erickson, *A Military History of the Ottomans: from Osman to Atatürk*. Santa Barbara, 2009.

Valensi, Lucette. *Birth of the Despot: Venice and the Sublime Porte*. Ithaca and London, 1993.

Valle, Carlos del. "El manuscrito hebreo del *Tratado del astrolabio* de R. Mosé Almosnino." *Sefarad* 51, no. 2 (1991): 455–457.

Varlik, Nükhet. *Plague and Empire in the Early Modern Mediterranean World: The Ottoman Experience, 1347–1600*. Cambridge, 2015.

Várvaro, Alberto and Laura Minervini. "Orígenes del judeoespañol (II)." *Revista de Historia de la Lengua Española* 3 (2008): 149–195.

The Voice of Jacob, July 8, 1842, 142.

Wacks, David. *Double Diaspora in Sephardic Literature*. Bloomington, 2015.

———. "Toward a History of Hispano-Hebrew Literature in its Romance Context." *eHumanista* 14 (2010): 178–209.

———. "Vernacular anxiety and the Semitic imaginary: Shem Tov Isaac ibn Ardutiel de Carrion and his critics." *Journal of Medieval Iberian Studies* 4, no. 2 (2012): 167–184.

Wainman, A. W. "An Analysis of the Judeo-Spanish Glossary in *El resimiento de la vida* by M. Almosnino (Salonica, 1564)." *Actes du premier Congrès international des études balkaniques et sud-est européennes*, no. 6 (Sofia, 1972): 175–179.

Wasserstein, Abraham, ed. *Galen's Commentary on the Hippocratic Treatise Airs, Waters, Places in the Hebrew Translation of Solomon ha-Me'ati*. Jerusalem, 1982.

Watson, William J. "Ibrahim Muteferrika and Turkish Incunabula." *Journal of the American Oriental Society* 88, no. 3 (1968): 435–441.

Wear, Andrew. "The Spleen in Renaissance Anatomy." *Medical History* 21 (1977): 43–63.

Yaari, Abraham. *Hebrew Printing at Constantinople*. Jerusalem, 1967. In Hebrew.

———. "Hebrew Printing in Izmir." *Aresheth* 1 (1958): 97–222. In Hebrew.

Yérasimos, Stéphane. "La communauté juive d'Istanbul à la fin du XVIè siècle." *Turcica* 27 (1995): 101–130.

———. "Dwellings in Sixteenth Century Istanbul." In *The Illuminated Table, the Prosperous House, Food and Shelter in Ottoman Material Culture*, edited by Suraiya Faroqhi and Christoph Neumann, 275–300. Istanbul and Würzburg, Germany, 2003.

Yerushalmi, Yosef Hayim. "The Re-education of Marranos in the Seventeenth Century." *The Third Annual Rabbi Louis Feinberg Memorial Lecture in Judaic Studies*. Cincinnati, 1980.

———. "Servants of Kings and Not Servants of Servants: Some Aspects of the Political History of the Jews," *Tenenbaum Family Lecture Series in Judaic Studies*. Delivered at Emory University, Atlanta, GA, on February 8, 2005.

———. *Zakhor: Jewish History and Jewish Memory*. Seattle, 1998.

Zamora Vicente, Alonso. "Judeo-español." In *Dialectología española*, 2d ed., edited by A. Zamora Vicente, 349–377. Madrid, 1989.

Zemke, John M. *Critical Approaches to the "Proverbios morales" of Shem Tov de Carrion: An Annotated Bibliography*. Newark, 1997.

Zonta, Mauro. "Influence of Arabic and Islamic Philosophy on Judaic Thought." In The Stanford Encyclopedia of Philosophy. Spring 2011 Edition, edited by Edward N. Zalta. http://plato.stanford.edu/archives/spr2011/entries/arabic-islamic-judaic/. Accessed December 1, 2015.

Zwiep, Irene E. *Mother of Reason and Revelation: A Short History of Medieval Jewish Linguistic Thought*. Amsterdam, 1997.

INDEX

OLGA BOROVAYA was born in Russia, where she received an M.A. in Romance literatures and a Ph.D. in cultural studies. Since 1998, she has been doing research and teaching at Stanford, Johns Hopkins, and other American universities. Borovaya is the author of *Modernization of a Culture* (Moscow, 2005) and *Modern Ladino Culture: Press, Belles Lettres, and Theater in the Late Ottoman Empire* (IUP, 2011).

www.ingramcontent.com/pod-product-compliance
Lightning Source LLC
LaVergne TN
LVHW010352080826
844660LV00004B/253

* 9 7 8 0 2 5 3 0 2 5 5 2 4 *